Reviewery

Reviewery

Christopher Ricks

H A N D S E L   B O O K S
an imprint of
Other Press • New York

Book design by Terry Berkowitz; set in Adobe Garamond by Alpha Graphics of Pittsfield, NH.

Production Editor: Robert D. Hack

10 9 8 7 6 5 4 3 2 1

Library of Congress Cataloging-in-Publication Data

Ricks, Christopher B.
    Reviewery / Christopher Ricks.
        p. cm.
    Includes index.
    ISBN 1-59051-019-4
    1. English literature—20th century—History and criticism. 2. American literature—20th century—History and criticism. 3. Literature—History and criticism—Theory, etc. 4. Arts, Modern—20th century. 5. Books—Reviews. I. Title.

PR473 .R49 2002
820.9'0091—dc21

2002024389

4

Contents

Publisher's Note

Lives

Robert Bernard Martin
Gerard Manley Hopkins: A Very Private Life   3

Leon Edel, editor
Henry James: Letters Vol. III, 1883–1895   11

Leon Edel, editor
Henry James: Letters Vol. IV, 1895–1916   15

Paul Delany
The Neo-Pagans: Rupert Brooke and the Ordeal of Youth   18

Richard Ellmann
James Joyce   22

Leon Edel
Bloomsbury: A House of Lions   34

Miranda Seymour
Ottoline Morrell: Life on the Grand Scale   40

David Pryce-Jones, editor
Cyril Connolly: Journal and Memoir   48
Joseph Hone, editor
*J. B. Yeats: Letters to His Son W. B. Yeats
and Others, 1869–1922*   48

Peter Ackroyd
T. S. Eliot   59

Christopher Sykes
Evelyn Waugh   69

Brendan Behan
The Scarperer and *Hold Your Hour and Have Another*   73

Norman Mailer
The Executioner's Song   79

Arguments

Erving Goffman
Forms of Talk   93

Jennifer Platt
Realities of Social Research: An Empirical Study of British Sociologists   102

Stanley Milgram
Obedience to Authority   113

Norman Podhoretz
Making It   124

George Steiner
In Bluebeard's Castle   130

Critics

John Crowe Ransom
Selected Essays, edited by Thomas Daniel Young and John Hindle   141

F. R. Leavis
The Living Principle: 'English' as a Discipline of Thought   147

W. K. Wimsatt
Day of the Leopards   155

William Empson
Using Biography   159

Jean-Paul Sartre
Saint Genet   168

Leslie Fiedler
What Was Literature? Class Culture and Mass Society   174

Donald Davie
Trying to Explain   182

Stanley Fish
Is There a Text in This Class?   192

Philip Larkin
Required Writing: Miscellaneous Pieces 1955–1982   201

Novelists and Poets

Ernest Hemingway
Islands in the Stream   213

Ivy Compton-Burnett
The Last and the First   220

Christina Stead
The Man Who Loved Children   229

Brian Moore
The Emperor of Ice-Cream   234

Brian Moore
The Mangan Inheritance   240

Kingsley Amis
One Fat Englishman   250

V. S. Naipaul
The Enigma of Arrival: A Novel in Five Sections   256

Ian McEwan
The Comfort of Strangers   266

Donald Davie
Ezra Pound: Poet as Sculptor   276

Donald Davie
Czeslaw Milosz and the Insufficiency of Lyric   281

Seamus Heaney
Death of a Naturalist   286

Seamus Heaney
Door into the Dark   290

Seamus Heaney
Field Work   293

Other Arts

Marshall McLuhan
Understanding Media   303

Richard Whelan
Robert Capa: A Biography   311

Contents

Samuel Beckett
The Theatrical Notebooks of Samuel Beckett: The Shorter Plays,
edited by S. E. Gontarski   315

Philip Norman
Shout! The True Story of the Beatles   329

John Sparrow
*Visible Words: A Study of Inscriptions in and as Books
and Works of Art*   333

Saul Steinberg
The Discovery of America   338

Stanley Kubrick
A Clockwork Orange   348

Francis Ford Coppola
The Conversation   359

Frederick Wiseman
Blind. Deaf. Adjustment and Work. Multi-handicapped.   366

Index   379

Publisher's Note

Except for the period they cover, the fifty reviews and review-essays in this book represent the range of Christopher Ricks' interests over the last four decades. At first it seemed to me appropriate to call the book, say, *Modern Instances*, for the reader who runs a finger through the "Contents" in the hope of finding there Ricks on Chaucer, Coleridge, Dickens, Donne, Dryden, Hazlitt, Housman, Johnson, Keats, Middleton, Milton, Pope, Shelley, Sterne, Swift, Tennyson, or two dozen others to whom Ricks as reviewer has devoted himself once or, as in several cases, half a dozen times, will be disappointed. This book is a modern collection. Hopkins is the only pre-twentieth-century figure in it, but then Hopkins, not just because Bridges' first edition of the poems appeared in 1918, has often been felt to belong more truly to the twentieth century.

We wish to thank the editors of the magazines, journals, and newspapers in which these reviews were first published. Originally the reviews had titles, but as most of these originated in editorial offices, we have dropped them. Some American and British differences in spelling have been standardized, generally in the American way.

In arriving at the final shape of this book, Christopher Ricks had the help of three friends—David Ferry, Marcia Karp, and Lisa Rodensky—of whose kindness and keenness he has asked me to express his appreciation here.

Harry Thomas

Lives

Robert Bernard Martin
Gerard Manley Hopkins: A Very Private Life

T he virtues of Robert Bernard Martin's new life of Hopkins are such as to make it not only a good life of a great poet but the best we are likely to have until such time as the world becomes profoundly moved again by those religious controversies that so moved Hopkins. Martin, as in his previous biographies (Kingsley, Tennyson, FitzGerald), does his homework, spade-work, and leg-work; every reader of *Gerard Manley Hopkins: A Very Private Life*, even the best informed, will at least have to admit to having learned from it many a new substantial fact about Hopkins and his setting; and since there is no substitute for a biographer's assiduous fair-minded clarity, this is a book to be thanked.

Hopkins's life can have no surprises now, though it had plenty then. Gifted, craving, stubborn, idiosyncratic, and brave in the face of his parents' dismayed resistance, he made his way to the Church of Rome and (*a fortiori?*) to the Society of Jesus. No less bravely, and with no grand preceder here who could be to him in poetry what the tranquilly obdurate Newman had been in religious conversion, Hopkins made his even lonelier way to the heights and depths of his own art. "Slaughter of the innocents": with this laconic journal entry in 1868 he recorded the burning of his early poems, a sacrifice demanded of him (he exacer-

The New Criterion (September 1991)

batedly believed) by his religious vocation. But the tentative encouragement of his superior upon a later tragic occasion in 1875 released him and his writing—released him *from* and *to*. And thanks to his friend Robert Bridges, who tended (though he also doctored) the manuscripts, the world has since 1918 known the studded studied work of the most original poet of the Victorian age.

Hopkins's two central choices of life were of such a scale, and of so entire a commitment, as to protect him and his story against all pettiness. It is one of the odd but natural accomplishments of Martin's biography that it restores to Hopkins's world the petty things, even the pettifogging ones—the frictions, misunderstandings, squalors, and squabbles—so that there can be felt the sheer plod, and the sheer fret, of so much that went with and came to Hopkins. Balliol competitiveness; the frequency of his enforced moves within the Order; the shabby-genteel institutions, all come down in the world, which housed his life; the number of examination scripts which he had to mark; the unsanitary conditions in Dublin where he enjoyed, or rather didn't, his professorship of Greek: these diverse and daily encroachments gradually coalesce until they are precipitated as Martin's most striking report: that for Hopkins to die as he did when he was nearly forty-five was for him to hit almost exactly the grim "average" for the Society of Jesus: "In 1868 a survey in the Jesuit private journal, *Letters and Notices*, indicated that the life expectancy of a man becoming a novice at twenty-one was twenty-three more years rather than the forty years of males of the same age in the general population."

As is now usual even in a biography devoted to movements of mind, we are regularly made privy to such movements of body as Hopkins's diarrhea and his operation for hemorrhoids (performed "by Mr. Gay and Mr. Prance"). And as is now *de rigueur*, sex is not left in peace or unpeace: the new habit is to front us with Hopkins's spilt "old habits," encoded or inscribed by him as "O.H." (where Clough, in *his* diaries, had satisfied himself with an asterisk). But there can be no blanket objection to these layings-bare, and Martin, though he is not always persuasive (is that really what Hopkins's agonized ship-wrecked nun means when she cries, "O Christ, Christ, come quickly"?), is not prurient. Hopkins's decision to be circumcised in adulthood is described, pondered, and left in the decent obscurity of its learned footnote (as to whether it was a medical necessity or a psychological need). On the central question of Hopkins's homosexuality, the biographer is circumspect, though occasionally the transitions leave something to be desired. "We have plenty of other evidence to show that Hopkins's most intense physical attraction was to men. The tight Anglo-Catholic circles in which he moved in Oxford were in part substitutes for family life." Or: "Hopkins was certainly moved deeply by his sexual feeling for other men, but there is no proof, or even responsible suggestion, that he ever had sexual relations with anyone else." Well, you could hardly have sexual relations other than with someone else, and there does creep in a less-than-responsible suggestion of anyone-else-than-men.

There is little reason to doubt that Hopkins's instincts were homosexual (there are several journal entries about being tempted by choirboys or by loitering men); there is much reason to doubt that he ever consummated his desires; but there is no reason to doubt that in any case the siege of contraries by which the life of the senses engages the life of the spirit is one which would, whatever Hopkins's predilections of sexuality, have moved, stirred, fascinated, and torn him.

If the whole sexual matter now seems (and not just to the emancipated) to have been overwrought and overfraught in Hopkins's day, it is as well to remember that his day was not of his making. Martin dryly reminds us of that equivocal bath-toiletry issued to the novices: "modesty powder" to render the water opaque. And something must be acknowledged as happening to masochism once it is institutionalized as mortification. I for myself wish that Hopkins had not wished for his hair-shirt, for his sore chain, for his scourge, and for his "custody of the eyes" (the penance of looking nowhere but at the ground); but all of these self-inflictions were not self-inflictions to him, and they are his business—or are his understanding of what it was for him to be about his Father's business. The stakes being what they were for him, he would have gone singing to the stake.

Which brings even a grateful reader of this biography to a clutch of reservations. At no point do you feel that the biographer would go to the stake—or, more damagingly and perhaps less unfairly, that he much feels what it was for Hopkins to be willing to do so, or for others to be willing to go to the stake for Hopkins, for him, his faith, or his art.

Partly this is a matter of the very qualities of style which make Martin so amenable and so accessible a writer: his equability, equanimity, equity. These virtues can, and sometimes do, slide into their adjacent vice: blandness. Then the texture of the writing loosens: far, far too often something is "surely" so (meaning that no one can be sure of it but); and there is the reiterated evasive "almost," often with a robust but eviscerated sequel ("almost instinctively," "almost hallucinatory"), and often doubled up ("almost as if," "seems almost to"). A biographer may need to choose, too, between three such different ways of putting things as: "he might be described as having a retroactive umbilical cord," "Liverpool was to lay a great hairy paw in the middle of that romantic illusion," and "in that remark is encapsulated all the openness . . ."

But these are local demurrals, and there are two broader ones. First, you would not divine from the tone of this book, as against its concessive announcements, how very extreme, bizarre, rebarbative even, Hopkins is as a poet, or feel from this amiable encompassing of his art that there could ever really have been any justified incomprehension of, or principled hostility to, his whole policy and proceedings. It is not that Martin should have included more literary criticism of his own—his talents lie mostly elsewhere, though he does give, for instance, an enlightening account of why Hopkins affects the dangling participle. But any full account of Hopkins's life in relation to his art needs to realize, to make real to us, the facts of—and the implications of—that critical tradition of resistance to Hopkins which has brought into unusual concurrence such superb poet-critics as A. E. Housman, T. S. Eliot, Yvor

Winters, and Donald Davie, all insisting on the sheer price that Hopkins paid for the solitude of his powers and the intransigence of his innovations. Davie may be judged to be impatient in his moral and political scoldings of Hopkins's muscle-bound monstrosity, but some such impatience has been felt by many independent (in both senses) readers of Hopkins. The name of Housman is not to be found in this life of Hopkins, and yet it is Housman's sense of things (like his art) which constitutes one unignorable, albeit not unanswerable, critique of Hopkins. (Housman, or earlier, Christina Rossetti, of whom Hopkins once said: "The simple beauty of her work cannot be matched.")

Housman acknowledged receipt of the poems in a cant-free letter to Bridges in 1918:

> I value the book as your gift, and also for some good condensed lines and an engaging attitude of mind which now and again shines through. But the faults which you fairly and judicially set forth thrust themselves more upon my notice; and also another. Sprung Rhythm, as he calls it in his sober and sensitive preface, is just as easy to write as other forms of verse; and many a humble scribbler of words for music-hall songs has written it well. But he does not: he does not make it audible; he puts light syllables in the stress and heavy syllables in the slack, and has to be helped out with typographical signs explaining that things are to be understood as being what in fact they are not. Also the English language is a thing I respect very much, and I resent even the violence Keats did to it; and here is a lesser than Keats doing much more. Moreover his early poems are the promise of something better, if less original; and originality is not nearly so good as goodness, even when it is good. His manner strikes me as deliberately adopted to compensate by strangeness for the lack of pure merit, like the manner which Carlyle took up after he was thirty.

There is something too easy about such current acceptance of Hopkins as supposes that Housman here says nothing which deserves the compliment of rational opposition. Anthony Burgess was not merely being flippant about "The Windhover" when in his novel *The Doctor Is Sick* his hero peeringly blinks his eyes at the magazines in the seedy shop-window:

There was the one Charlie had brought him: *Brute Beauty*. And there were others he had never seen before: *Valour; Act; Oh!* He rubbed his eyes, which were troubling him with an odd impairment of vision. Were those really *Air, Pride, Plume, Here*?

Hopkins warned a friend against "doing what I once thought I could do, *adopt an enlightened Christianity*." Insofar as a biographer of Hopkins is necessarily a critic of the poetry, he may need to be warned against adopting an enlightened Hopkinsianity.

The radical question about this honorably unradical biography is that of its engagement with Hopkins's unenlightened Christianity, his beliefs, his sensibility, his allegiances, even his violences and superstitions. And here Martin falls short, or at any rate stops short. I don't know whether Martin has religious beliefs; I do know that I don't. I don't know whether there would have been imaginative ways in which Martin could have made good his enlightened pluralistic good-nature in the face of Hopkins's passion and partisanship; I do know that for me the book dithers and hedges.

> Looking back at the events from 1866 from a century and a quarter later, we can easily see that more than religion was at the heart of the conflict between Hopkins and his family, and that it was as much concerned with independence and revolt, with the age-old struggle between father and son, even with the choice between blood father and spiritual father, as with the choice of a particular Church. Because the true conflict was never stated, the overt terms in which the contest was conducted were far more bitter than the immediate situation warranted.

But the pressure within "more than religion" (as if "independence and revolt" were not themselves viewable under a religious aspect), and then the hardening of this to equipollence ("*as much* concerned with . . ."), and then the further intensifying of it to "*the true* conflict" (leaving the religious commitment as in some way false): these impel, not what Martin wishes to claim (alternative descriptions of the same phenomena), but a slighting of the religious in favor of the psychological.

Martin's dealings here are not altogether straight: "we are *forced* to conclude that his unconscious drives *may have been* as powerful . . ." (my italics again). The insistence that Hopkins had leapt "an enormous barrier, one as much concerned with growth and maturation as with religion," not only is insufficiently respectful of Hopkins's sense of the matter, and not only sets "growth and maturation" against "religion" (where a believer would duly urge that it is only a true religious decision which can bring about growth and maturation), but it also gives a misleading sense of what Martin actually enforces. *As much* is not what he most believes. You can hear his secularizing psychologizing bent (I share it, but that doesn't lessen the problem it raises for him as a biographer of so entirely religious a figure) in such phrasing as this: "what strikes a modern reader is how often his spiritual inclinations fitted his psychological needs," where "inclinations" is not justly poised against "needs."

Martin says the liberal thing:

> Hopkins's perceptions of his motivations are frequently startling, combining as they do an initial attribution to religious reasons, then a subsequent shrewd awareness that they also spring out of the predispositions of his own personality. The two views of the matter are not in conflict, simply phenomena discussed in differing vocabulary but with similar patterns.

Shrewd, eh? *Simply*, eh? But what is bound to precipitate "conflict" is any allocation of priority, of what is pre-, to the one and not the other. The effect is persistently of unsettling this equable *also* (a matter merely of "differing vocabulary") with an implacably psychologizing predisposition. "As he did so often, he was claiming religious sanctions for necessities imposed upon him by his own personality, but his confusion of the two was far from being hypocritical, since it was completely unconscious." This is itself an imposition.

So in the end the biography achieves neither an ecumenical accommodation nor a skeptical reservation, but a tacit favoritism. Hopkins, who was very harsh, might retort upon his friendly biographer what he wrote angrily to his friend Bridges, on religious and doctrinal dedication:

> It is long since such things had any significance for you. But what is strange and unpleasant is that you sometimes speak as if they had in reality none for me.

Leon Edel, editor
Henry James: Letters Vol. III, 1883–1885

H enry James thought that perhaps the greatest of letter writers was
Thomas Carlyle, but he admitted that if you then thought of "the
other most distinguished masters of expression," you were struck by
their "general *pleasantness.*" And the letters of James himself, the most distinguished Master? They are a great pleasure, and they have a pleasantness which is both general and particular. General, as when he decides
that English children are England's glory:

> I think they are the most completely satisfactory thing the country pro-
> duces. The people are but the children magnified (not altered, not modi-
> fied), and it is the children who are just of the right size. The elders strike
> one so often as too big for what they are.

Particular, as when James is affectionately amused by the Grand Old
Man who was not too big for what he was: Gladstone disliking an
unParliamentary expression, deploring "the vulgarity of the son of a
Tory Duke having talked about 'pooh-poohing' something or other in
the House of Commons."

James pooh-poohed nothing. He was unenviously grateful to anyone who could turn a true phrase, and so he loved the old ambassador

from the USA, James Russell Lowell, who asked to be forgiven for a memory which was rapidly becoming "one of its own reminiscences." James had a fascinated respect for those whose reminiscences spanned the century, and though he smiled at the completeness with which the aged actress Fanny Kemble enacted herself, he did not laugh at her: "she moves in a mass, and if she does so little as to button her glove it is the whole of her 'personality' that does it."

Sometimes James flattered his friends, but he did not flatter himself. If the Master was going twice a week to a fencing-master, he knew that this was not because he had any hope of cutting a figure but because he wanted to cut his figure: it was "to help me to combat not the possible enemies of the salon or the street, but a dreadful aggressor within myself: the symptoms of a portentous corpulence."

Even when his prose is plump, it has its genial warmth—though you do start to fear for fundamental English when simply to sit becomes the rounded thought that "my sedentary part shall press the dear old fireside chair." This is not the language of a fireside-chat, but it can have its high comedy, as in the shortest missive in this book, the legendary telegram with which James set himself in train: "Will alight precipitately at 5.38 from the deliberate 1.50." He could be heavy-handed, but more often he was light-hearted and even-handed. When an American friend was wondering whether to spend the winter in London, James drew up two lists, AGAINST ("Darkness") and FOR ("Good fires"). AGAINST ends with "Presence of H. James etc.", and FOR ends with "Presence of H. James."

The presence of H. James can be felt in all its variety and strength in the dozen years of this third volume of the letters. The years are darkened by many deaths. James has to acknowledge that in the midst of life, in the middle years, we are in death. "It is astonishing how one's wayside is strewn with *ends* after one has reached middle life!"

It is true that the particular person whom James then believed to be "sinking to his end," George Meredith, lived for another 21 years. But mostly James was not imagining death. His brother Wilky, his sister Alice, his nephew Herman, and his aunt Kate; his revered old acquaintances, like Fanny Kemble and Mrs Procter, and his loved young friends, like Wolcott Balestier; his loving rival, Robert Louis Stevenson; and the woman who loved James more than he loved her but whom he greatly cared for, Constance Fenimore Woolson: these deaths toll through the letters, and take their toll. Yet James listens for dear life. "The house is full of people—Mr and Mrs Gladstone among others. So life goes on even when death, close beside one, punches black holes in it."

James's life, for all its comforts (travel, friendship, being lionized), had other black holes. The balance of a year's royalties from Macmillan for 7 or 8 books amounted—if that is the word—to £2.17.6. These were the years of his hate-affair with the theatre. He wrote one of his best novels, *The Tragic Muse*, with its superb portrait of an actress. Yet his attempt to be a playwright ended in fiasco and boos. "But you can't make a sow's ear out of a silk purse." It was the more painful because James had thought that plays would put money in his purse.

Yet through all this, he is his resilient brilliant self. His love of life and of language can triumph over almost anything. He can make an exquisite case for remaining unmarried: "Poor boy—and poor woman! I wouldn't be a mother! That's one of the reasons I have never married—because if I had I should have been." He can fear that he may be writing "that deadliest of all things, a scenery-letter," having already made it the liveliest, as he does from Ireland: "The very waves have a brogue as they break." He can rotate an unthinking phrase so that it catches the light of thought, murmuring to Stevenson: "You never think of sending me your books—that is, I hope you don't, because you don't do it."

Occasionally his wording suggests more than it might wish: the difficulty of finding the right actor for his play becomes "the difficulty of putting one's hand on a young man who can *touch* an important little part of a boy of twenty." (*His* italics.) Usually he is wonderfully alert to the unintended or half-intended. He sent someone "a writhed smile of friendship." "I leave my absurd accidental 'writhed' there—for wreathed—because it is so comical—it will make you laugh! The anguish of effort isn't in my smile." Lovely, the move from "smile" to "make you laugh." Through all the troubles and turmoil, these brave letters show James writhed in smiles.

Leon Edel, editor
Henry James: Letters Vol. IV, 1895–1916

Henry James in old age was princely, not lordly. He was generous. This might take the simplest form, as when he asks a publisher to send £100 as an advance to a friend "without his knowing it comes from me". Then there is the generosity of his advice: urging someone, with good reasons, to stand firm against a blackmailer, or beseeching Edith Wharton not to act or conclude but to bide in the extremity of her marriage-misery. In these letters of his last 20 years, James succeeded in something without which no good advice will hold good: in so proffering it as to make people actually want to take it.

Generous with his time, his energy, his company and his money, he was nowhere more magnificently munificent than with his letters themselves. For he had to push his pen untiringly in order to make a living and to make his life worth living. These are the years (1895–1916) of great stories like *The Turn of the Screw*; of great novels like *The Ambassadors*; of his supreme study of a nation and a culture, *The American Scene* (James was rueful about Thomas Hardy's having snitched the title *The Return of the Native*); of the revision, at once titanic and tiny, of his fiction for the New York Edition, along with prefaces which were newly wise about his old instincts; and of his autobiography. Plus miscellaneous writings on this, that, and the every other. So that for James to have been willing, of

Sunday Times (6 May 1984)

all things, to *write* to his friends enshrines the paradox by which we ought to be especially grateful for the letters of a professional writer.

Dr Johnson (we learn from Mrs Thrale)

> was always unwilling to touch pen and ink without being paid for it; would I believe make rather a hard bargain than an easy one, and once observed to Mr Thrale [who was a brewer] that a man never gave that away freely he was used to sell, or delighted in doing that gratis which he was wont to be paid for: "Would you not rather," added he, "make any man a present of money than of porter?"

"I am an abandonedly bad writer of letters," insisted James, a good writer of them, and then he went on to say something which makes him even handsomer: "I throw myself simply on my confirmed (in old age) hatred of the unremunerated pen—from which one would think I have a remunerated one!"

James remonstrated when Charles Eliot Norton regretted the publication of a famous man's letters: "The best letters seem to me the most delightful of all written things—and those that are not the best the most negligible". Those of James are a delight. Brimming with revelations about his own writings and with courteous penetrations into those of friends and contemporaries, they yet have world enough and time for new anecdotes and old ghosts, for comic tones and tragic notes. Friends and siblings support him, there in his indomitable bachelorhood, and so does his new home at Rye with its plans for an ancient garden ("I have reacted against quick trees").

He did not forfeit his integrity, and it is monstrous that his great phrase "beyond the mere twaddle of graciousness" ("as conscious as I am myself of all that, in these questions of art and truth and sincerity, is beyond the mere twaddle of graciousness") has so often been lopped of its "beyond" and then turned upon James himself. He did love courtesy, but he loved truth more, and his letters to writers like Edith Wharton, H. G. Wells and Mrs Humphry Ward, like those to the young sculptor whom he loved, are superb not because of any graciousness but because of the steely comic grace with which they press their good-natured strictures.

In James's hands, the imagination is a continual victory over negation. He turns to positive advantage things which loom negatively. When he visits the USA, he finds fascinating the very fact that it has "NO fascination"—and he can explain how this can be. He sees love itself as an imagining which can convert gall to manna: "For you yourself, dear Grace, are a presence so terrifically arranged as an absence." He revels in the madness which led the Vanderbilts to build their great palace of Biltmore in the wilderness of North Carolina: "so gigantic and elaborate a monument to all that *isn't* socially possible there". When the "oldest city in America" has hardly any signs of its age he sees that this "has perhaps almost the pathos the signs themselves would have if there *were* any".

A friend is seen to have a positive gift: "that exquisite art in him of not bringing it off to which his treasure of experience and intelligence, of accomplishment, talent, ambition, charm, everything, so inimitably contributes". And a doctor leaves James positively, happily, stumped: "He at any rate finds so little the matter with me that it's rather difficult to say what he does find".

These negations are often exquisitely comic, but they can modulate into pathos and tragedy. Pathos, when James joins in the hope that his racked brother Robertson may at last be calm: "Heaven grant he be truly a spent volcano". Tragedy, when he unflinchingly praises the deliberated suicide of a ravaged old friend: "I am wholly *with* him in it, and no vulgar shock nor unintelligent regret diminishes to me for a moment the big, decent decorum of it".

With this fourth volume, Leon Edel completes his edition of the letters. It is wonderful to have them. (And would have been even more so to have a complete edition.) Not that the text is entirely to be trusted, and Prof. Edel has a way of foisting in a word here and there in square brackets when it isn't necessary. The annotation is skimpy and inconsistent, and some dark force must have been at work when, for of all places a *James* letter, there is converted to *Sir Fitzgerald Stephen* the book by Leslie Stephen about his brother, *Sir James Fitzjames Stephen*. But this is a dear book. Thanks to James, and therefore thanks to Edel.

Paul Delany
*The Neo-Pagans: Rupert Brooke and
the Ordeal of Youth*

Rupert Brooke was a natural beauty, but he did not have a beautiful nature. Not until now, though, has it been revealed just how ugly was his love life (his lust life, mostly), or just how brutal was his daily language when he was not putting on his performance of being very much the open-hearted, open-necked young poet. His Georgian poetry or poesy was calculatingly on its best behavior. Its cadences came from Brooke's weekending world of social flatteries and of tinkling talk, and the poems themselves are like charming weekend guests at a country house, genially pointless acquaintances never to ripen—as the poems of Thomas Hardy do—into lifelong friends or unique lovers. Slender and affable, Brooke's poetic talent set itself easily to be liked. This earned him much prompt warm applause and some subsequent coolness.

He was born a hundred years ago into privilege and gratification. Death in 1915—he died in the Great War but not exactly of the war— suddenly extinguished the talent while lighting the reverential flame. The guardians of Rupert Brooke's tomb proved to be eminent men who duly lived very long, and they permitted no one to besmirch the name and fame of the dead young hero. One witness in particular was stifled:

Boston Globe (2 August 1987)

Brooke himself. "This is the sort of letter that doesn't look well in a Biography," he admitted, truthfully and prophetically. Sure enough, his custodian-biographers obliged by suppressing all such self-exposures. The old school tie (Brooke had been idolized at Rugby School and then at King's College, Cambridge) was drawn tight about his embalmed neck, with a touch of the noose. And sanctification set in.

But along has come, fortunately, this trans-Atlantic bounder Paul Delany. He has a nose for corruption, and his dispelling the odor of sanctity comes as a welcome breath of fetid air. *The Neo-Pagans: Rupert Brooke and the Ordeal of Youth* is less about ordeal than about ordure. What a set it was that pivoted upon and pirouetted around Rupert Brooke.

The Neo-Pagans (Virginia Woolf gave them the dubbing) were a mutual admiration society of bright young things. They therefore got on both very well and very badly with that other mutual admiration society, Bloomsbury. Very well, because the merger of the two societies, who knew how to manage these things, would have happily expanded the field for mutual admiration. Very badly, because Bloomsbury was, after all, a competing society. Bloomsbury won, because it was a great deal more talented and had not only greater gifts but more stamina for nastiness. The Neo-Pagans fell back into bickering and back-biting. It is not (Delany shows) that the Great War destroyed them, but that they relished the thought of the war because it provided an external warrant for their state of self-destruction.

Many of them were wounded in love, but more—to adopt Bob Dylan—were wounded in hatred. If you have read all of Iris Murdoch's novels and crave another one, read *The Neo-Pagans*. For this is the Iris Murdoch world (she has taken one of her titles from a Brooke poem), a world of preposterous amatory permutations and of lists of lusts. A. yearns for B., who torturedly fancies C., who is perversely drawn to A., who . . . and so *ad infinitum*. Or *ad nauseam*. Brooke himself flitted and flirted, descending upon sister after sister before diversifying.

He was fascinatedly repelled by sex, homosexual and heterosexual, and the whole story is a living proof of Freud's grim account of "the

19

most prevalent form of degradation in erotic life": the hideous itchy fissure between love and desire.

Women became dirty for Brooke if they wanted him back, in both the senses of to want someone back; but spurning was then more than he could bear. After a couple of hundred pages of these groupings and gropings and gripings, the reader longs for the company of unclassy D. H. Lawrence, that piercing comprehender of the Brooke myth. These self-styled great lovers, these sex-chasers, would have been happier if they had simply given sex up. But gilded youth declined to be gelded.

Brooke came on as a Greek God. The gods, who don't like to see Englishmen purporting to be gods, bided their time, and then struck. The old line about Brooke was "Whom the gods love, die young". Delany in effect stresses the other maxim, "Whom the gods wish to destroy, they first drive mad". Brooke did indeed suffer a violently mad phase.

Here, thanks to Delany's sharp eyes and strong stomach, is the real Brooke at last. Clinically repellent in his homosexual adventure. Horridly torrid in his madness, his misogyny and his anti-Semitism. Laxly awash with self-pity. The very blossom of young manhood in an epoch of supreme national and cultural aplomb, Brooke's Light Blue Cambridge blood was yet infected by petulance, rancor and snobbery. He even managed to condescend to Thomas Hardy, of whom one corpuscle is worth more than Brooke's whole corpus. The fine flower of a civilization? Lilies that fester smell far worse than weeds.

Oh, he took in Henry James, who was very susceptible to beautiful young men. He did not take in the young T. S. Eliot, who was saddened by this willed illusion of so perceptive a man as Henry James, and by James' failing to detect the essential vulgarity and cheapness of Dear Rupert.

But then Eliot was rightly scornful of the cult of youth by which the Neo-Pagans affected to live, their determination to sport in nature and never never to grow up, their Peter Pantheism.

Brooke was a much smaller poet than some who survived the war (Robert Graves, Siegfried Sassoon), and much smaller than many who died in it: Wilfred Owen, with his rhymes of hell; Isaac Rosenberg, with his great grotesquerie; and Edward Thomas, an acquaintance of Brooke but the friend of Frost and the heir of Hardy. But Brooke made the better myth than any of the others, this crucial early victim with the perfect profile. He was an absurdly casual casualty of the war, mowed down not by a machine-gun but by a mosquito.

> If I should die, think only this of me:
> That there's some corner of a foreign field
> That is forever England.

Now that Delany has shown what else we must think of Brooke, perhaps his ghost can be left to rest in a peace that in his well-grounded self-disgust he never enjoyed.

Richard Ellmann
James Joyce

"Is this the great James Joyce?" asked Sylvia Beach admiringly. It was a difficult question for him to answer. "Yes" would have been ungraciously immodest. "No," ungraciously churlish. "Don't know," ungraciously winsome. "James Joyce," he agreed, extending his hand and his imagination.

Ask the same question of Richard Ellmann's superb biography, *James Joyce*, and the answer will be differently and doubly a reward. Is this the great James Joyce? Yes, for nothing could more powerfully proclaim Joyce's greatness (nothing except of course his books) than such an exact and humane evocation of all that Joyce triumphed over: in others, bigotry, snobbery, and incompetence; in himself, loneliness, ill-health, and family tragedy. Then there is too the deftly modest answer. "Is this the great James Joyce?" "James Joyce." For this biography does not pretend that Joyce was always the great James Joyce. His vengefulness, his infantilism, and his extravagance, both financial and psychic, they are all here, themselves witnessing to Joyce's enduring belief that the ordinary really is extraordinary, and vice versa. Nothing is extenuated by Ellmann, or set down in malice—though the malicious are rightly allowed their say.

Grand Street (Spring 1983)

So the book is entitled to what would sound like the same question: Is this the great *James Joyce*? Yes. James Joyce.

Twenty-three years after Ellmann first did honor to Joyce and to himself, he has undertaken a thorough revising, correcting, and augmenting of his book. The new material engages every aspect of Joyce's life and interests (literary, amatory, political, domestic), and it fascinatingly and freshly corroborates not only Ellmann's sense of Joyce but the literary world's sense of Ellmann: as a masterly biographer, of exemplary industry and fair-mindedness, and also as the man who did most to establish that a great feat of twentieth-century literary scholarship could take as its subject a twentieth-century figure. Today it is obvious enough; in 1959 it was either not obvious or not acknowledged.

Those of us who have learnt from Ellmann virtually all that we know of Joyce's life are not required to be anything more than grateful. A reviewer will feel some slight obligation to the higher ingratitude, to remind men that even the best of books is not perfect. Randall Jarrell defined a novel as "a prose narrative of some length that has something wrong with it." In which spirit, the following cavils are offered. First, that since the human voice cannot unequivocally say *"Finnegans Wake"* (it might be saying "Finnegan's Wake," the source ballad), it is not quite right to say that Eugene Jolas, once he had at last seen that the hitherto-unrevealed title must be *Finnegans Wake*, "threw the words in the air." For it is only if those words are thrown on the page that they can exactly be put. Second, that this revised edition has added, on page 657, an anecdote about Joyce's exclaiming in the street, "I am free! I am free!" which is simply a variant wording of the one that survives, on page 557, from the first edition: "No, I'm free, *free*." Third, that a newly added note can be hasty. Joyce says in a letter that even the most notable Frenchman "couldn't produce that because the Kingdom of God cometh not with observation"; there was no note to this in 1959, but now there is one that says: "Joyce was quoting Emerson's essay on 'Nature': 'This kingdom of man over nature which shall not come with observation . . .'" But this is very roundabout and not worth the carriage, given Luke 17:20: "The kingdom of God cometh not with observation." Fourth, that it would have been worth newly footnoting the famous and delicious story about Joyce's dictating a bit of *Finnegans Wake* to Beckett:

> In the middle of one such session there was a knock at the door which Beckett didn't hear. Joyce said, 'Come in,' and Beckett wrote it down. Afterwards he read back what he had written and Joyce said, 'What's that "Come in"?' 'Yes, you said that,' said Beckett. Joyce thought for a moment, then said, 'Let it stand.'

For the Joyceans have argued that the phrase "Come in" does not appear in *Finnegans Wake* in the imperative, and have proposed "What is that?" as an alternative candidate.

Fifth, and last of these nigglings, there is the fact that although the illustrations have been quadrupled (from thirty to one hundred and seventeen), their quality in reproduction has been quartered (not Ellmann's fault, but still), as sometimes their size has been. For instance, the amazing desolating photograph of the Joyce family in 1924 (Joyce, Nora, and the grown-up children George and Lucia, each in a different world or at least on different planes of this one) used to be a full page of clarity and is now a quarter page of fog. A much-less-good photograph of Joyce, Pound, Ford Madox Ford, and John Quinn, blurred and oblique, has been allowed to banish the superb one of them all, each erect in his sharp-edged quiddity. (New XXXV versus Old XV.) Anyway, such cavils are the best/worst that this reviewer can do by way of narrowing his eyes.

Others will find this wide-eyed. Hugh Kenner, in a wittily elaborated interrogation, has recently argued that Ellmann often falls victim to the Irish Fact, "definable as anything they tell you in Ireland, where you get told a great deal" (*Times Literary Supplement*, December 17, 1982). Crisply grudging, Kenner would make a grand inquisitor:

> One's natural question, turning through Ellmann Mark II, is what Joyce's biographer has learned in a quarter-century. The answer reduces to this, that his files have grown ampler.

A different question, though not an unnatural one, would ask what has happened to the world in the quarter century since Ellmann first wrote this biography; or ask what has happened that is particularly germane to Joyce, to his life's work, and to his life. More years have elapsed between these two editions than had elapsed between Joyce's death and the original edition. "What Joyce's biographer has learned in a quarter-century" is a pinched and clenched formulation in comparison. In any case, Ellmann isn't the sort of biographer who allows his own experiences much to color those which he is recreating. Nothing about Joyce's expatriation, for instance, is in any way affected, in the revised edition, by Ellmann's having himself become in effect an expatriate between 1959 and now. More pertinently, the landscape of our hopes is different not just from Joyce's but from what it was a quarter of a century ago.

In the great world, the biggest thing that has happened between 1959 and now is that the great world nearly ceased to permit of any further happenings at all. The destruction of life on the planet, which was flatly likely as Soviet ships moved towards Cuba in 1962, might perhaps be thought to bear strongly upon all writers, as writers, or upon none. But Joyce's hopes were such as to give a particular force to any such prospect. A very great many of his hopes have indeed become harder to sustain since 1959. The continuing challenge of Joyce for many of us is the way in which his achievement and his allegiances urge us to trust certain hopes, high and low; and the counter challenge which our time puts to Joyce is to ask what remains of his hopes once his credulities have been winnowed away.

The continuance of the human race on the globe mattered more to Joyce than, for instance, to T. S. Eliot, since Joyce was—for all his crotchets and superstitions—a humanist. The immortality of which Joyce so often spoke was not the Christian afterlife to which Eliot aspired; it was of the earth, earthy, even if it depended on such airy people as professors. Of the scheme of *Finnegans Wake*, Joyce said: "If I gave it all up immediately, I'd lose my immortality. I've put in so many enigmas and puzzles that it will keep the professors busy for centuries arguing over what I meant, and that's the only way of insuring one's immortality."

The outbreak of the Second World War meant, to Joyce's exasperation and sadness, that even the name of Joyce wasn't enough to get people to read *Finnegans Wake*, which had just been published in 1939. What then would Joyce have thought about the threatened outbreak of that Third World War which will leave no world and no readers at all? Again, the linearity of a human history which would end with humanity's self-destruction is, to put it mildly, inimical to Vico and those recurring cycles of history which were such a stay for Joyce's mind.

> Joyce did not share Vico's interest in these as literal chronological divisions of 'eternal ideal history,' but as psychological ones . . . 'I would not pay overmuch attention to these theories, beyond using them for all they are worth, but they have gradually forced themselves on me through circumstances of my own life.'

But Joyce's "cyclological" interest requires that there be at least some reality to Viconian cyclic recurrence, just as Vico's cycles are now being endlessly recycled in all the post-apocalyptic visions of the future which see things starting up again, from the body and blood of Charlton Heston in *The Omega Man*, and the beached Statue of Liberty in *Planet of the Apes*, through to the upbeat ending of Robert Frost's bloodcurdling wishfulness in "A-Wishing Well" in 1959, a wishfulness which would have been difficult to sustain a few years later:

> I am assured at any rate
> Man's practically inexterminate.
> Someday I must go into that.
> There's always been an Ararat
> Where someone someone else begat
> To start the world all over at.

It is not only that, in our age of global peril, Joyce's hopes look more merely hopeful than they used to, but that a newly revised biography of

Joyce can strongly, albeit tacitly, bring home all these changes of span, these changes of danger, changes in consciousness, and the accompanying changes in the face which we turn upon all the great writers of the past, as we seek to divine the ways in which we can still trust their hopes as against those in which we cannot.

Yet it would be absurdly grandiose to try to relate a quarter century of the world's history to Joyce's life, much though he would have liked the thought. It is more prudent to take two particular focuses: Ireland, and the other great Irish expatriate, Samuel Beckett.

Joyce lived for twenty-two years in an Ireland that was under British tyranny. He did not, since he then became an expatriate (Trieste, Zurich, Paris), live in the subsequent Irelands, but he lived through them: the Ireland of the Easter Rising of 1916; the Ireland of the Free State and of civil war with the Irish Republican Army; the later Ireland of the usual. When Ellmann wrote of Joyce and Ireland in 1959, he was writing during a lull; the battles seemed old unhappy far-off things. It was not that Ellmann wrote with complacency; it should not even be said that he "could be forgiven" for writing as if in Ireland most things had become forgiven. But they had not. Since 1959, the Irish question has shown itself as what it always was. There are terrorism and counterterrorism in Northern Ireland, and gunrunning and mouthing and the impotent proscribing of the I.R.A. in the Republic of Ireland. Some believe that Northern Ireland is under British tyranny; others believe that there is a terrorist effort to impose upon Northern Ireland an Irish tyranny. Audible from a great distance are the Irishmen in the U.S.A., who have less of a claim—historical and other—to reside in North America than have the British to reside in Northern Ireland, and who (while demanding "Brits Go Home") have no intention themselves of going home and leaving North America to such few of its aborigines as have been suffered to live. The one certainty is that it is all a nightmare.

Everything about Ireland in Ellmann's *Joyce* therefore makes very different reading today from that which it made in 1959. Ellmann's equanimity is sane and may well be salutary, but it would certainly have been very difficult for him now to have called it newly into being. For even when we discount all those things about Joyce's relation to his "native dunghill" which are burlesque or jest or fantasy or pique, or even what could charitably be described as a love-hate relationship, the fact remains that Joyce repeatedly gives voice to exactly those radical criticisms of his country which continue to make so many of its neighbors in Northern Ireland determined not to put themselves under its yoke. The real sovereign of Ireland is the Pope, says Joyce in 1907; and the Reverend Ian Paisley could not ask for more and would simply ask whether anything has changed. "I quite see, of course, that the Church is still, as it was in the time of Adrian IV, the enemy of Ireland: but, I think, her time is almost up." That was in 1906. Later (and now added by Ellmann), Joyce described Irish priests as "barbarians armed with crucifixes." Both sides in Northern Ireland are now armed with crucifixes and more.

Of course Joyce would often flash out against what was indeed British oppression, turning upon his brother Stanislaus with the questions: "What the devil are your politics? Do you not think Ireland has a right to govern itself and is capable of doing so?" But it is not clear that either his life or his work can do anything at all to help with the horror that is now Ireland—anything at all except the keeping alive of an eternal unsoldierly flame of comic hope and happiness such as sometimes seems the thing without which all would be lost and sometimes seems wishfully unthinking. Interviewer: "Do you think Irish self-government a good thing?" Joyce: "I don't think anything about it." Ellmann's revised edition adds a very important note which would have felt quite different, much more equable, in 1959, but which was perfectly timed for publication in 1982 since Joyce in 1932 spoke of fifty years:

> Joyce declined to attend as guest of honor a St. Patrick's Day party in 1932 for fear that the presence of the Irish Ambassador, Count O'Kelly, would imply his endorsement of the new state. 'I do not mind "larking" with Dulanty in London but I care nothing about politics,' he wrote. 'Ire-

land, with Ulster in, will probably be a separate republic in ten or fifty years and I do not suppose anyone in England will really care two hoots whether it is or not. They are doing many things much more efficiently, I am told, than was possible under the old régime but any semblance of liberty they had when under England seems to have gone—and goodness knows that was not much.'

Well, you now have a republic, but you won't even now have "Ireland, with Ulster in" except either by massive bloodshed or by the gradual persuading of the majority in Northern Ireland that the political fact which Joyce announced in 1932—that "any semblance of liberty they had when under England seems to have gone"—has itself gone, for good.

Joyce was pacific almost to the point of pacifism, and he made this a central tenet in his admiration of Ulysses, "the only man in Hellas who is against the war." He thoroughly approved of the economic boycott ("especially," adds Ellmann drily, "since it was of Irish manufacture"); "fighting England with the knife and fork" was "the highest form of political warfare I have heard of." The lowest forms have recently asserted or reasserted themselves. "Joyce waged literature like a battle," says Ellmann of Joyce's punitive immortalizing of his enemies. But battles were not for him. The other great comic novelist of his day, Italo Svevo, described his young teacher in one of his assignments, "Mr. James Joyce described by his faithful pupil Ettore Schmitz"; and the description ends with superb acuteness: "Surely he cannot fight and does not want to. He is going through life hoping not to meet bad men. I wish him heartily not to meet them." Joyce's hoping not to meet bad men helped to keep him out of Ireland for the last half of his life, for twenty-nine out of his fifty-eight years. It could hardly be said that the chances of meeting them there have lessened, though in 1959 it probably looked otherwise.

The line between hope, to be emulated and to be fired by, and credulity, to be resisted, is always demanding our attention when Joyce is in the vicinity of violence and war. "It's no use," Bloom unforgettably and touchingly says. "Force, hatred, history, all that. That's not life for men and women, insult and hatred." You can say that again; must say it again, unfortunately, as you contemplate what "force, hatred, history" and "insult and hatred" are continuing to wreak upon Ireland. Joyce was entirely unpugnacious when Wyndham Lewis said that the Irish were pugnacious; instead he murmured, "Of course, I know very little about them. . . . That's not been my experience—a very gentle race." The moral victory there is Joyce's, but that is not the same as supposing that he was right. On other occasions, his trust in humor leads him to folly—but these are the occasions of life, not of art, even when it is his art that he is glorifying. "Now they're bombing Spain. Isn't it better to make a great joke instead, as I have done?" Yes, of course, but it is not better to put it like that, any more than it was acutely funny of Joyce to speak of the Second World War, even in its earliest stages, as *un drôle de guerre.*

"What is the use of this war?" Joyce demanded of Beckett, who thought (Ellmann reports) that it had a use and a reason. Beckett was right, and not only because by 1945 his courage had won him that undroll thing the Croix de Guerre. And just as the recrudescence of age-old violence in Ireland is the most important political fact that needs to be taken into consideration in estimating the difference between the world of Ellmann's first edition and that of his revised edition, so it is Samuel Beckett who is the most important literary fact. By 1959 Beckett had written much of his greatest work, but this is not the same as saying that in 1959 his greatness was evident or acknowledged. Since 1959 there have died both of Joyce's great sponsors and coevals in modernism: Ezra Pound and T. S. Eliot. Their deaths have made it all the more clear that their great enterprises have had only one true successor.

It was Eliot who said: "What happens when a new work of art is created is something that happens simultaneously to all the works of art which preceded it. The existing monuments form an ideal order among themselves, which is modified by the introduction of the new (the really new) work of art among them." Those to whom Beckett is the really new, and is the great writer of our age, will not be basing this belief on his having gained the Nobel Prize in 1969 (anyway Joyce should have

gained it too), but on the indeflectible courage, the incomparable imagination, and the vitality of language with which he has entered the depths
of death and life. All great writing is a critique of previous greatness;
profoundly respectful, certainly, in Beckett's relations to Joyce, but necessarily entailing some revaluation. Beckett, who wrote one of the
earliest and one of the very best appreciations of *Finnegans Wake* (*Work
in Progress*, as it then was), has nevertheless since created in his own art
an achievement which cannot but expose as tragically wasteful the linguistic and literary theories that hurried Joyce from life and that en-
slaved him to his preposterous and bankrupting pet, *Finnegans Wake*.
Ulysses was in no doubt that you should fear the gifts of such Greeks as
he; the author of *Ulysses* came to forget that the one gift more ruinous
than a wooden horse is a white elephant.

Many of the most interesting changes now made by Ellmann gain
their compound interest from their telling us not only more about Joyce
but more about Beckett. So there is a new footnote to Joyce's remarks
about the Roman Catholic Church as "built upon a pun": "As Samuel
Beckett writes in *Murphy*, 'In the beginning was the pun.'" The new
note is as much a tribute to Beckett as an illumination of Joyce, and the
more so in that Ellmann could have quoted *Murphy* (1938) in 1959 if
he'd wanted to. Again, a sentence about Joyce which used to run: ". . .
and he asked a friend to do some research for him in the possible permutations of an object," now runs: ". . . and he would ask Beckett . . ."
Perhaps Beckett hadn't then wanted to be named; perhaps Ellmann
hadn't then thought that the particular name mattered; but what is clear
is that in 1982 the great masters of "the possible permutations" within
literature must include Beckett as well as Joyce.

"A new love affair, a dream notebook, previously unknown letters,
a limerick about Samuel Beckett—these and much more have been
newly incorporated": the blurb gives this salience to Beckett because
everything about Beckett, and not only about Joyce, is now seen to
matter. The limerick itself, as Ellmann admits, is "bad," but Ellmann is
right to value it, and to value the new Beckett-based corrections and
additions. An exchange that has become famous now goes:

> Joyce: "How could the idealist Hume write a history?"
> Beckett: "A history of representation" [formerly "representations"]

A characteristically moving and muted addition is this sentence: "There came a day, however, when he stopped calling his young friend 'Mr. Beckett,' and called him simply 'Beckett,' a concession which, being almost without precedent during Joyce's residence in Paris, gratified its recipient immensely."

"I think he has talent," Joyce wrote of Beckett ("a compliment in which he rarely indulged," remarks Ellmann). Beckett the man would in all sincerity detest the idea of his work as in any way in competition with Joyce's, and no doubt he would the more repudiate the idea that if there had to be such an undesirable competition it could ever be adjudged in his, Beckett's, favor. But Beckett's art, not least in its latest and loveliest manifestations as *Company* (1980) and *Ill Seen Ill Said* (1981), cannot help raising the profoundest doubts as to Joyce's final phase of desperate esperanto. The love and loyalty that Joyce drew from Beckett are a tribute to both of them; such love is to be believed in, but its statements are not necessarily to be believed. Ellmann may have sensed this when he chose what is a disconcerting place at which to append a very recent (1981) communication from Beckett about Joyce. The text itself continues to say:

> Samuel Beckett spoke to Joyce of the Nazis' persecution of the Jews, but Joyce pointed out there had been similar persecutions before.

At which point, there is a new note:

> In later life Beckett thought this ability to contemplate with telescopic eye Joyce's most impressive characteristic, and quoted four lines from Pope's *Essay on Man* to illustrate:
> Who sees with equal eye, as God of all,
> A hero perish, or a sparrow fall,
> Atoms of systems into ruin hurled,
> And now a bubble burst, and now a world.

But Beckett's own greatness—achieved, like Joyce's, in art—constitutes some criticism of such a "characteristic," however truly "impressive" it may be.

Joyce thought he was against the heroic. He believed that he was sure "that the whole structure of heroism is, and always was, a damned lie." "I dislike to hear of any stray heroics on the prowl for me." But he was a heroic writer, not least as making the world reconsider what it is to be heroic, whether within a book (like Bloom) or in writing one (like Joyce). Ellmann's biography is genuinely that smaller but invaluable thing that we call a heroic undertaking. It is Beckett—and this is not to be found in Ellmann, since though Beckett penned it in 1980 he did so for the celebration in 1982 of the anniversary of Joyce's birth—who has recently created the shapeliest memorial to Joyce, the greatest single sentence about him, one which bows down and goes deep:

> I welcome this occasion to bow once again, before I go, deep down, before his heroic work, heroic being.

Leon Edel
Bloomsbury: A House of Lions

I n Bloomsbury there are nine characters in search of an author. This Pirandello pirouette was turned by Leon Edel 15 or 20 years ago. Since then, the ratio has reversed to nine authors in search of any one Bloomsbury character, especially for such important dramatis personae as Professor Edel's: the economist John Maynard Keynes, the man of letters Leonard Woolf, the novelist Virginia Woolf, the biographer Lytton Strachey, the artists Vanessa Bell and Duncan Grant, the artist-critic Roger Fry, the art critic Clive Bell and the literary critic Desmond MacCarthy.

So *Bloomsbury: A House of Lions* has to admit that every one of these big cats will soon have exhausted its nine lives. But Professor Edel's book is deftly different. Artful and craftful, he weaves his way and their ways. "The warp and woof of their experience" is fashioned into a very professional piece of tailoring. Probably for Professor Edel the highest compliment that could be paid to his telling of their youthful lives—he leaves them when they enter on reminiscent middle age—would be to say that they themselves would unquestionably have complimented him highly. So be it. Yet too high a price is paid for this high compliment. For it is earned by his tacitly agreeing to do

New York Times Book Review (1 July 1979)

little else than compliment them. Because they spent so much of their energies complimenting one another, they scarcely seem to stand in need of such attentions.

Virginia Woolf thrilled thus to herself and to her friends: "Gordon Square is like nothing so much as the lions house at the Zoo. One goes from cage to cage. All the animals are dangerous, rather suspicious of each other, and full of fascination and mystery." It is perfect Bloomsbury awe, because the fascination and mystery of which it speaks are deliciously its own. The whole point of forming such a group while vociferously denying that you form a group is that this combination makes possible a good deal of cunning self-admiration. To the indirect self-congratulation at one's magnanimity (how magnificent of me to announce how magnificent they are) is added a direct self-congratulation (how magnificent that they are we).

Do lions purr so persistently? When the Bloomsbury lions gather, is the collective noun a pride of lions, or is it vanity? Are these the lords of creation, or the hostess's dream: literary lions?

"What is a lion?" asked Thackeray. "A lion is a man or woman one must have at one's parties." Professor Edel is throwing a party to celebrate these celebrities. The occasion is vivacious, and you will feel flattered to be there. But the trouble with feeling flattered is that you are then part of a creepy network of flattery. One of Bloomsbury's mentors finds himself touchingly described as "of the onanistic persuasion." Here Bloomsbury did not need much persuasion. It was one of their very few sincere forms of self-abuse.

As the first page reminds us, they were big on personal relations. But they were even bigger on public relations, and the one sort of book that they least need now is that which carries on their good work. The best possible light is here put on everything that they ever did, and the objection to the best possible light is that it is very different from illumination. Their biographer's equanimity is equal to any Bloomsbury preposterousness, provided that it emanates from their self-sylishness. A crucial chapter, as witnessed by its title "Houses of Lions," prostrates itself before Vanessa Bell, alias the Virgin Mary:

"It seemed to her a part of the fitness of things that a baby, a daughter, was born at 2 A.M. on Christmas Day, the first Christmas of the peace. In the Charleston of that Yuletide it was as if some Sussex Nativity Play were being enacted. There were assorted attendants and at least one Wise Man, Maynard Keynes . . . In the distance, as she lay in one of the upstairs front bedrooms of Charleston Farms, she could hear the farmhands going about their morning chores singing Christmas carols. It was a peaceful birth in a still world."

Better, certainly, than a still birth in a peaceful world. But isn't the whole vignette in ignoble taste? The metallic homosexual Keynes as one of the Magi? Not all Professor Edel's frankincense, myrrh and gold can disguise the central tawdriness. But then for Professor Edel, Duncan Grant, the child's father, and Clive Bell, the mother's husband, are the "two fathers"—God and Joseph, presumably.

The endless permutations of their sexual escapades grind grimly on. Lytton Strachey praises his young love Duncan Grant to Keynes, unaware that Keynes has already snatched him. Roger Fry complains to Clive Bell that Bell's wife, Vanessa (she of the Sussex Nativity Play), is now thick with Duncan Grant instead of him, Roger. The coarsely candid Dora Carrington fondles Strachey as her "buggerwug." The refined Virginia Woolf excites herself by slumming it: "Sex permeated our conversation. The word bugger was never far from our lips." The words that were never far from my lips were those that were wrung from Matthew Arnold when he contemplated the talented and destructive sordor of the Shelley circle: "What a set!"

The earliest example in the dictionary under Bloomsbury—"A school of writers and esthetes living in or associated with Bloomsbury, that flourished in the early 20th century"—is from Keynes in 1914: "She is asking no one but a few of my 'Bloomsbury set'!" They wished to be thought of as a set when it suited them and not when it didn't. Having profited from group publicity and group groping, they found it prudent to insist on their independence of one another because it would otherwise be less than authoritatively disinterested for them to laud one another.

Their biographer knows all this, and isn't so wanton as to conceal it, but he always manages to dress it up. Leonard Woolf: "We were *never* a group!" Virginia Woolf: "The Bloomsbury group is largely a creation of journalists." (On which Professor Edel: "She is being, one feels, ingenuous." I don't feel so; I feel that she is being disingenuous.) Clive Bell: "Neither a chapel nor a clique but merely a collection of individuals." But it is clearly shown, from their own statements, that these denials are false. And? "Now in the aftertime these accusations and denials are almost irrelevant, for we find Virginia's letters and diaries sown with allusions to 'Bloomsbury.'" Yet what Professor Edel has shown is that the denials are untruths, not that they are irrelevant. They seem to me centrally relevant to what Bloomsbury was up to: the maximizing not of its responsible talents—which were substantial—but of its talent for irresponsibility.

They created a corporate limited-liability self-importance. "We are the mysterious priests of a new and amazing civilization," intoned Strachey. Roger Fry could congratulate Vanessa Bell—"You have genius in your life as well as in your art, and both are rare things, so you can feel pretty well pleased with yourself"—while sounding not exactly displeased with himself ("Kept me your devoted friend"). Virginia Woolf returned such compliments, except that returned is not quite the word: "I continue to think him the plume in our cap." As in some Steinberg cartoon, each of them was a plume in another one's cap. Virginia Woolf is quoted in the book's penultimate and climactic page: "Where they seem to me to triumph is in having worked out a view of life which was not by any means corrupt or sinister or merely intellectual; rather ascetic and austere indeed; which still holds, and keeps them dining together, and staying together, after twenty years; and no amount of quarreling, or success, or failure, has altered this. Now I do think that this is rather creditable."

I should find it creditable if it were said of someone by someone who did not mean *we* when saying *they*.

Professor Edel is very adept at all the tricks that Bloomsbury itself practiced. There is the unremitting and unjust disparagement of the

Victorians. There is the pretense that the only alternatives to the Bloomsbury creed were abject or half-witted; so Strachey's flibberti-gibbetry is provided with this as its defining contrast: "History is an art, not a compilation written by journeymen." So much for Carlyle. "Un-remitting toil. That was the secret they learned at Cambridge; it became the secret of Bloomsbury." But it was a very open secret, and whom are they being defined against? Lazy Meredith? Ah, but they had "solid work habits." Unlike their adversary D. H. Lawrence?

Then there is their claim, voiced by Virginia Woolf, that "if people, with no special start except what their wits give them, can so dominate, there must be some reason in it"—as if to be the daughters of Sir Leslie Stephen were not to enjoy a special start. There is the laying flat of the surrounding intellectual and cultural landscape so that Bloomsbury may tower. You'd never guess from this book that there were some not-ungifted writers who, when they were not the adversaries of Bloomsbury, were unmistakably a serious and principled alternative to it and to its sense of things, especially to its sense of its own high superiority. Novelists like Thomas Hardy, Joseph Conrad and Rudyard Kipling, and critics like A. C. Bradley.

A similar tactic is the repeated allusion to the attacks on Bloomsbury, mentioned only in order to be summarily dismissed. Were they snobs? This (profitless, apparently) question is raised on the first page; and the answer is: only in the eyes of foolish egalitarians. But here Professor Edel throws away the largest single advantage that he enjoys as an American writing about these English people: that of penetrating another culture's very important system of snobbery and its relation to art. The one thing that he shouldn't have done was to brush aside the question of their snobbery; just as it may be too easy for an English reader to be stung into fury and injustice by it, so it is too easy for a foreigner to find another country's snobbery somehow quaint or peripheral. If you're not under it, you won't smart under it. Professor Edel misses his challenging opportunity. No challenges are permitted. "Not all would be silent, of course; and a miner's son named Lawrence would characterize our personages as resembling beetles and spiders." "Our personages" has just the right wrong drawl.

If all fails, there is bluff. A Bloomsbury attendant noted that they "produce the most brilliant and fantastic conversation that one can hear anywhere in England." Unable to produce any for our delighted admiration, Professor Edel avers that "brilliant and fantastic conversation" has a way of not getting itself recorded; he admits that the accounts of their parties "sound like intellectual parties anywhere"; and so he insists that "we must take it on trust that they were remarkable." But why should we? Especially as it is not true that great conversation goes unrecorded. William Allingham's diary shows us the conversational powers of mind of Browning, Carlyle, Tennyson. Byron's conversation still lives, "his very self and voice." And wasn't there an 18th-century biography that had some success in recording brilliant and fantastic conversation?

For Lytton Strachey, "We are as remarkable as the Johnson set." It did hideous damage to most of them that they countenanced such hollow self-aggrandizement. For where was there any one of them who had a tenth of Johnson's humanity, learning, wisdom and staunchness? Was MacCarthy a critic as remarkable as Johnson? Was the biographer Strachey the equal of Boswell, or was he as a historian the equal of Gibbon? Was the painter Grant the equal of Joshua Reynolds? Was Leonard Woolf the political equal of Edmund Burke? It is only Keynes who is not outclassed in any such comparison, for the economist of the Johnson set—Adam Smith—might have reckoned Keynes a man of economic consequence.

Miranda Seymour
Ottoline Morrell: Life on the Grand Scale

O ttoline. Even better, *Lady* Ottoline. All together, now: Lady Ottoline Morrell. And there is conjured up the great hostess of yesteryear. Over six feet and flame-haired as well, in all her lofty extravagance, with her famous interior decorating and her notorious exterior decoratedness. Her preposterous hats, her peacocks. "After all, there's only one Ottoline." By 1928, when D. H. Lawrence wrote this in a letter to her, he was trying to cheer her up in her raddled years, urging her to let bygones be. Lawrence didn't mean much more than that the grand social figure was somehow unique—while he held "after all" in reserve, in case they were to quarrel again about his having created from her the inflammable Lady Hermione Roddice of *Women in Love.*

She was christened Ottoline Violet Anne Cavendish Bentinck, back in the summer of 1873, and a silver-spoon mouthful it was. As for "Morrell," it was a Tory family of solicitors into which Lady Ottoline married, in 1902, and to which she brought lustre, being so liberal with her favors as hostess and mistress. The name rhymes, we are told, with Durrell, stressed on the first syllable. Lytton Strachey ponderously dubbed her Lady Omega Muddle.

The New Yorker (9 August 1993)

She is immediately "Ottoline" in Miranda Seymour's generous and disconcerting biography, *Ottoline Morrell: Life on the Grand Scale*. Only three lines into the introduction we meet her, without a proper introduction. This unmisgiving "Ottoline" is an impertinent portent: it sides. For this is a biography with a mission: to protest against the leechlike behavior of Lady Ottoline's false friends—the spite that travestied an honorably passionate woman as a grotesque figure of fun. The biographer's indignation, together with her affection for the strangely touching figure, lends the story pace and verve. Seldom does Seymour's laudable praise dwindle into a P.R. job for O.M.

What was it, exactly, that Ottoline did? Well, good works, all her life. These were pious at first, like hymn groups and Bible classes. In her late twenties, there was a scheme for urban women's libraries, and attempts to find work for unemployed women. But it was after 1915, when she and her husband, Philip, settled into their country house at Garsington, near Oxford, that, conscientiously, she provided a haven for conscientious objectors during the Great War. And, flamboyantly, she hit her social stride. Addicted to winning friends and influencing people, she hostessed. She was a matron of the arts.

Neither she nor her husband inherited a great deal of money, but they did not do at all badly; she had the money and the taste to create the Italianate gardens of Garsington, and fashioned her home as a venue, all color and culture and chatter. When, in the late twenties, lacerated by ingratitude and chafed by money worries (not by any such poverty as many have to reckon with), she and Philip sold Garsington and moved to the modesty of Gower Street, in London, it was a kind of dying. For Lady Ottoline, the final dying (a medical botch) came in April, 1938.

The stage army of high culture had trooped through her halls. The jamboree starts to feel like a Saul Steinberg march-past. Here come the Poets, among them Siegfried Sassoon, back from the trenches, alongside T. S. Eliot, buttoned-up, desperate to be invalided out of the war between the sexes. And the Painters: Augustus John, all bluff, beaming bohemianism; Henry Lamb, insinuatingly devious in person as in his art, a brilliantly malicious portraitist; Dorothy Brett, whose portrait of Lady Ottoline gave great offense. ("I have not made a prostitute of you," Brett maintained. "I swear I haven't.") Best of the lot, both humanly and on canvas, are the two painters whose work is still a tonic: Duncan Grant, refinedly genuine, and Walter Sickert, who always saw the real thing. And here come the Critics: Roger Fry, who was artily exquisite in wincing, and Clive Bell, the author of *Civilization* as he knew it, who went in for whinnying. Bringing up the rear, the Men of Letters and the Women of Letters: Logan Pearsall Smith and Vernon Lee, Axel Munthe and Virginia Woolf, who mimed friendship to Lady Ottoline's face, and sniffily mimicked her behind her back. Amid all the hubbub stands Lady Ottoline, breasting the babble. (She was not above babble herself. Even in the maladroit, she showed flair: "What a dear Wittgenstein is—I *love* him!" Or in insisting that Gilbert Murray's "Wind, wind of the deep sea" is "the only line in English to express the passionate soul of the Greeks.")

This is a cast of thousands, with bit parts and bitch parts for both sexes—but those who really count are few. First, there is her husband, a decent dull dog, a Member of Parliament, not only Liberal but liberal. He was always loyal, if seldom faithful, a figure to make the most continent consort of our day seem colorfully ostentatious. (I mean, of course, Denis Thatcher.) Second, there is their daughter, Julian, so little the recipient of Lady Ottoline's attentions, so important in that very omission, even in her protests a waif.

But in the end it is less her family or her friends, or even her treacherous "friends," who animate her story than it is her lovers. The body of the book gives them body, rather as God—in whom she unremittingly, though relaxedly, believed—had given Lady Ottoline body. In 1917, Virginia Woolf wrote to her sister Vanessa:

> I was so much overcome by her beauty that I really felt as if I'd suddenly got into the sea, and heard the mermaids fluting on their rocks. How it was done I can't think; but she had red-gold hair in masses, cheeks as soft as cushions with a lovely deep crimson on the crest of them, and a body

shaped more after my notion of a mermaid's than I've ever seen . . . swelling, but smooth.

Mermaids are sexually precarious, and it seems that Lady Ottoline did not much like sex, though it was not for want of trying. The roll of Lady Ottoline's lovers is impressive, most of them thrilling to the blueness of her blood. "Were it not for imagination, sir," rumbled Dr. Johnson, "a man would be as happy in the arms of a chambermaid as of a duchess." Lady Ottoline was not even a duchess, only the half-sister of a duke—but in due course she opened her arms.

She opened them to Bertrand Russell, a fellow aristocrat, all pyorrhea and satyriasis and ripe prose. Russell, whom she found physically unattractive, is at his most spiritually unattractive when he combines high-minded concern with low insistence, as he did in 1914, when he wrote to reassure Lady Ottoline about its not mattering that he was now sleeping with Helen Dudley:

> I do not want you to think that this will make the very *smallest* difference in my feeling towards you, beyond removing the irritation of unsatisfied instinct. I suppose it must give you some pain, but I hope not very much if I can make you believe it is all right and that she is not the usual type of American.

But Lady Ottoline had her own means of removing the irritation of unsatisfied instinct. She gave herself to Henry Lamb, wheedler and diddler, and to Roger Fry, "an untrustworthy dog," she came to feel, "who softly pads up to one and licks one's hand, but who will nearly always turn and bite." Finally, endearingly, there enters Lionel Gomme, a young man from the village who in 1920 did some work in the gardens at Garsington. He was young enough to be her son (to be *her* son, Julian's twin, who had died in infancy), and he was Lawrencianly working-class enough to become Lady Ottoline's Lover—a relief from culture and from intellect, and a good sort. Suddenly, two years later, he lay in her arms in the stable yard, dead of a huge hemorrhage.

And then there surfaces the snag. For here I am, well on, and I have not yet uttered the word that the literary world seems to need a daily shot of: Bloomsbury. The snag is not only Lady Ottoline's but her biographer's. For it is a genuine but grievous source of strength to Miranda Seymour's book that it shares the predicament of its grande dame: it can live neither with nor without Bloomsbury. Seymour's Mission Rehabilitation is powered by two rocketing arguments about Bloomsbury's Lady Ottoline. First, that she was very effectively, and lastingly, caricatured and slighted by Bloomsbury. Second, that Bloomsbury doesn't much matter to her story anyway. The two claims are pitched at once:

> The main responsibility for Ottoline's spectacularly bad press lies with the Bloomsbury Group. Its members did not, as this biography will show, play a large part in her life, but it is the Bloomsbury annals which have effectively controlled our image of her since her death in 1938.

In practice, however, Seymour is no more able to cast off the spell of Bloomsbury than was Lady Ottoline. If Bloomsbury did not play a large part in her life, why is this biography billed as it is? "Miranda Seymour restores Ottoline Morrell's leading role in the Bloomsbury circle." The book is even summed up as "an unveiled look at Bloomsbury." I know, I know, a reviewer makes life too easy for himself or herself by making play with blurbs. But this time the contradiction is real. Although Seymour maintains that "Ottoline's connection with Bloomsbury would barely fill a chapter," pretty well every chapter of her book is filled with Bloomsbury talk. The realities are these. First, that Bloomsbury still entirely controls the terms within which Lady Ottoline is to be considered. Second, that, for reasons understandable but grim, Lady Ottoline wanted it that way—and so does Seymour's publisher, for when this book sells, as it should, it will be not because it understands a memorable woman, spirited and perverse, but because it teems with Bloomsbury tit-for-tattle. Ours is a literary world that is no less in collusion with Bloomsbury (even while teasing itself with protestations

of disapproval) than it was back then. Our world vibrates to Bloomsbury's. It is not just a matter of some uniquely English phenomenon or
of some particular historical moment. The delectations of Bloomsbury
are endemically snobbish, as Lady Ottoline herself knew and said, and
they are quite as much so in the United States now as they were in England then and are now. And the essence of snobbery is treachery. For
although the Bloomsbury set was much more treacherous about Lady
Ottoline than she was about them, she remained in thrall to them.
Sometimes she even picked up their habits. She touched pitch. It is a
serious objection to Seymour's disposition that no more than Lady
Ottoline does she see anything betraying about such an admission as
this:

> Lytton's malice was always enjoyable when someone else was the target;
> it amused Ottoline to hear Fry dismissed as "a most shifty and wormy
> character," of Clive Bell "strutting around in dreadful style" as the great
> art expert . . . and of Lamb as an unscrupulous brute.

But aren't these people supposed to be *friends*? They lived on carrion comfort, the whole pack of them, and Lady Ottoline never sufficiently managed to protect her central decency against the unremitting
indecency of backbiting. A sympathetic biographer can, and should,
protect Lady Ottoline against them, but should not, and in the end
cannot, protect Lady Ottoline against herself. She craved their company
even while distrusting it. And, pathetically, no matter how treacherously
venomous they were, Lady Ottoline came back for more.

Logan Pearsall Smith had said to her, in 1911, "You have the gift of
life, and it is a temptation to your friends to become vampires." Soon,
because of her affair with Russell (who was married to Pearsall Smith's
sister), he was her undying enemy. Vampirishly, Virginia Woolf urged
Lady Ottoline to write her memoirs: "Pick us all to pieces. Throw us to
the dogs." But Woolf picked Lady Ottoline to pieces and threw her to
the dogs: "as garish as a strumpet" and "like a foundered cab horse."
Woolf wrote to her sister in 1926:

> You will be delighted to hear that Ottoline and Philip are behaving scandalously . . . it is said that Garsington presents a scene of unparalleled horror. Needless to say, I am going to stay there.

Needless to say? Because there would be so many opportunities for saying needlessly cruel things behind people's backs. Talk, talk, talk, and never a good word said—so all such society seemed to Lawrence. Woolf (and she was not the only two-faced one) was proud of how she doubly dealt with what "is called being intimate with Ottoline; I succumb: I lie; I flatter; I accept flattery; I stretch and sleek, and all the time she is watchful and vengeful and mendacious and unhappy and ready to break every rib in my body if it were worth her while."

I doubt whether Lady Ottoline wanted to break every rib in Virginia Woolf's body. I *don't* doubt that Lady Ottoline never sufficiently wanted to break with Virginia Woolf, or with the crew as a whole. They were too horribly entertaining and too entertainingly horrible. But then neither can Seymour break with them. She deplores them, but she, too, implores their company.

For my part, by the time Lady Ottoline, her jaw hideously destroyed by cancer, is being set down by Woolf—in what Seymour assures us is a "jocular" phrase—as tied up "in a nose-bag like an old horse," I felt I needed the bath that visitors to Garsington sanctimoniously said they wanted after the hospitality they had received.

A sad, bad business. Miranda Seymour cannot but be mired in the sadness, and, of course, it is businesslike of her to behave as if she could escape the contradiction that she, like Lady Ottoline, embraces. Lazily incurious, for all their gossip, those of Bloomsbury roused themselves enough to inflict upon Lady Ottoline a diversity of suffering. Oh, only petty fabrications, snickerings, predatory taking of advantage, duplicity— nothing worse. Without them, though, there is no story. But without her there would not have been the fine story that is *Women in Love*.

Lawrence thrilled to a painting by Mark Gertler, *The Merry-Go-Round*, vividly praised by Seymour, which evokes at once the huge tragedy of the Great War and the petty tragedy of the social whirl. The true merry-go-round was less merry than miserable. But then that, too, is an old story. In the words of Alexander Pope:

> As Hags hold Sabbaths, less for joy than spite,
> So these their merry, miserable Night;
> Still round and round the Ghosts of Beauty glide,
> And haunt the places where their Honour died.

David Pryce-Jones, editor
Cyril Connolly: Journal and Memoir

Joseph Hone, editor
J. B. Yeats: Letters to His Son W. B. Yeats and Others, 1869-1922

U nlike the publication in 1975 of the touching acute letters of Cyril
    Connolly to Noel Blakiston, the publication of Connolly's Jour-
nal (1928–1937) does not serve him, except right. He found D. H.
Lawrence insufficiently magnanimous ('Notice how carefully Lawrence
refuses to recognise virtue in anyone but himself'), and his sponsor
David Pryce-Jones now finds F. R. Leavis much the same, so it may be
legitimate to cite the famous excoriation of Bloomsbury that was voiced
by Lawrence and amplified by Leavis: 'they talked endlessly, but endlessly—and never, never a good thing said. They are cased each in a hard
little shell of his own and out of this they talk words. There is never for
one second any outgoing of feeling and no reverence, not a crumb or
grain of reverence: I cannot stand it.' The reason why 'never a good
thing said' was such a good thing to say is that it aligns speaking well

with speaking well of others. In that world, a very special thrill attached to speaking ill of one's friends.

Mr Pryce-Jones could reasonably retort that Connolly's allegiances were by no means with Bloomsbury but with that distinct district Chelsea. Certainly there is evidence of the malicious rage which, for instance, Virginia Woolf vented upon, for instance, Cyril Connolly. 'There we spent one night, unfortunately with baboon Conolly [*sic*] and his gollywog slug wife Jean to bring in the roar of the Chelsea omnibus.' 'We spent a night with the Bowens, where, to our horror, we found the Connollys—a less appetising pair I have never seen out of the Zoo, and the apes are considerably preferable to Cyril. She has the face of a golliwog and they brought the reek of Chelsea with them.' One knows what Pryce-Jones means when he then murmurs about 'the fine sensibility of feeling and expression for which Virginia Woolf is celebrated'. But the trouble is that his own sarcasm (not irony) has some of the flat brutality of the Bloomsbury world.

Woolf's remarks about the Connollys' appearance are indeed detestable, and don't even have the flat-tongued straight face with which an Oxford friend of Connolly, gazing upon the most porcine of all Connolly photographs, once murmured: 'It's a pity he's not as nice as he looks.' In that mode of feline understatement, nothing can overtake the words of Kenneth Clark (who was all eyes), that 'Cyril was not conventionally handsome.' The crayon sketch of Connolly on the jacket, by Augustus John, is no oil painting. But what might make us reluctant to spring to Connolly's defence is that he said the same sort of thing about others, while characteristically mingling it with self-disgust: 'Back in London met Princess Bibesco and did not care for her much, her egoism is as tiresome and her appearance about as unprepossessing as my own.' Evelyn Waugh being 'our valued friend', 'it amused me to hear Peter laughing at Evelyn's "provincial little Arnold Bennett *arriviste* appearance".'

If Chelsea (and Oxford) might be at odds with Bloomsbury (and Cambridge) for territorial competitive reasons, the two were at one when it came to making bad blood. 'Never tell lies,' the young Connolly had adjured himself, except 'to damage the character of a friend'. He lived down to this, and so did they all. The hero of his novel *The Rock Pool* recalled the boredom of college life and 'the quiet afternoons spent running up bills in shops, which formed his only exercise', but Connolly was even more exercised in running down people.

In theory and even in practice, there was to be the solidarity of sodality and sodomy, but no front ever remained undivided. The Memoir and the Journal alike witness to the febrile frailty of the friendships. A typical progress is to begin by delighting in, say, Harold Nicolson for not being an owl ('Sexually, I represent a buffer state,' said the old buffer-bugger), and to end with dark mutterings: 'Most unpleasant memory of last six months was drink with Nicolson in Café Royal. He must have been trying to humiliate me. Is enemy and shall be considered so.'

Connolly has his regrets: 'How stale, fatigued, third rate, is the vocabulary of defamation.' But they don't move him to try something larger than defamation, he simply tries to enlarge its vocabulary. So the next page has this: 'Pretentious lunch with Lady Bonham Carter— Madame de Margerie like a nightmare, hotted-up Lady Colefax.' Then this: 'a three-cornered conversation with Elizabeth [Bowen] on the awfulness of women writers and the nastiness of her friend Mrs Woolf'. 'There is something wrong with a world in which one meets Mrs Lowinsky and Roger Hinks and Mrs Royde-Smith. They smell of middlebrow.'

The Journal will record sayings without comment and with delectation; to be worthy of record, an exchange should crushingly compact several reputations into the smallest space. 'Logan [Pearsall Smith] said of Hardy's second wife that she had tried first to get off with George Moore —or so he said. "George Moore would have said that of the Virgin Mary," said B.B. [Berenson], "if he'd ever heard of her."' But is it witty or humorous to predicate that George Moore hadn't heard of the Virgin Mary?

Like self-love, ill will is a busy prompter but not much of an actor, and even less of a producer. Hence the fact that so many of Connolly's jokes here are not forceful but forced. 'How to be popular. By being funny,' he had noted as a schoolboy. But the ill-intentioned ill-directed animus makes for a curiously impotent anger. Mr Tossoff of the Daily Squirt, the lovely Diana Brassiere, the Hon Halytosis and Lady Badbreath: can this be the famous parodist and wit? 'Will you leave a message—Lady Arse A.R.S.E. Arse is very sorry she is unable.' Humbert Wolfe himself managed better jokes than 'the Bumboat of Wolfe'. The baffled ineffectuality of these thrusts has to do with Connolly's own implication. The Bumboat business was a bit near the bone.

Again it is not that Connolly should be unloved for having as a young man been so 'buggeristical' (Woolf's word for Connolly's patron Logan Pearsall Smith), but that there is something unlovable about the malice with which he later speaks of 'the pirate gang of London buggers' once he himself was no longer jolly rogered. No doubt they were malicious about him, but two cases of 'it ill becomes' don't make something becoming. Connolly found a disproportionate relish in setting down things like this: 'They fulminate about the subtenants, "Eddie Gathorne-Hardy, Brian Howard and Mr Banting—worthless, no talent, homosexual sewer rats".' There is even something chilling about the fact that the last words of the last entry in the Journal should be 'The Homintern'.

Connolly busied himself with, even traded on, his having self-knowledge, especially as to his cynicism and selfishness. He recognised some truth all right, and sometimes humbly. But as Stevie Smith says, in her tiny flint of a poem 'Recognition not Enough':

> Sin recognised—but that—may keep us humble,
> But oh, it keeps us nasty.

Mr Pryce-Jones scorns the *Scrutiny* insistence that Connolly exemplified the corrupt penetration of literature by the social world. Yet his own editing makes it seem that if this accusation is not true, this is largely because literature takes second place to the really important thing, the social world. The annotations are very informative, and they know their priorities. It is judged necessary to say that 'Peter Rose Pulham was a photographer and artist in vogue, briefly attracted to

Nancy Stallybrass,' and to square the right social brackets: '1936 Food Tour. Harry [Sir Henry d'Avigdor-Goldsmid], Betty [Fletcher-Mossop]'. It is judged unnecessary to give the source for (just after these 'sewer rats'):

> Misunderstood.
> The now retired
> profession of the calamus.

As someone who knows, I think we should be told.

But more important than whether Mr Pryce-Jones truly weighs these things is whether he truly acknowledges the things that are to be weighed. At the very end of the book he offers two or three spirited pages of Connolly pastiche. The excuses and reasons put into Connolly's mouth ring very true as Connolly sentiments, but that is not the same as saying that they speak the truth. Connolly's shade is not just being co-operated with, it is being colluded with, when he is given such whingeings as these: 'Critics and professors can write their books with mumbo-jumbo titles like *The Romantic Image* and *The Great Tradition*, they are paid by the taxpayer to sit in a library, but they are forgotten the day they retire. I had to keep myself safe from them. I had nothing but my talent—they had colleges, cliques, pensions, the party line.' Well, Connolly was a busy journalist, and he certainly might have got one of those two titles slightly wrong like that: but would he really have had the face to claim that F. R. Leavis was forgotten the day he retired? Or to say of Leavis and such that whereas he, Connolly, had nothing but his talent, they had colleges? Connolly had Eton College. He had Balliol College. He had not only his talent but much privilege and many patrons because of his colleges. What he did not have was the right to be unremittingly aggrieved.

'More and more' the author of *The Rock Pool* felt 'that cultivated people are shrimps in a rock pool, from whom I can learn nothing.' The vexation of being fascinated with people from whom one can learn nothing exacted its toll. The rueful comedy of Connolly's best book,

Enemies of Promise, did constitute an insurance policy protecting Connolly against all contingencies including acts of God: but outside comedy, he was allured by the portentous and the pretentious, since they offered some hope of concealing from him the implications of his seeing cultivated people as shrimps while not being interested in any other kind of person. The bored dislike and distaste in the Journal suggest Elizabethan and Jacobean plays, which have been said by Rupert Brooke and C.S. Lewis to be about beetles.

'It is always easier to obey *if you dare not disobey.* German women are to their lords like so many black beetles': John Butler Yeats (father of the poet and of the painter Jack B. Yeats) was aware that people had a propensity to see others as beetles, but he thought it bad for them and for their art, and he deprecated the propensity when he found it in his son William Butler Yeats: 'I wish Willie had Jack's tender gracious manner, and did not sometimes treat me as if I was a black beetle.' To judge by these entrancing, life-enhancing letters, John Butler Yeats never treated anybody as a black beetle. The contrast with Connolly and that world could not be more marked. Where Connolly and his circle wanted to make bad blood, J. B. Yeats wanted people to be of good heart. Where Connolly, a young man in a hurry, has little time except for dispatching others, the tones of J. B. Yeats (who spoke of himself as an old man in a hurry) are essentially those of gratitude and dignity, and they bring home that far from being the alternative to humour and wit, gratitude and dignity are the conditions for the best of both.

When Ezra Pound edited the first excerpts from J. B. Yeats's letters, in 1917, he acknowledged the difficulties of the enterprise: 'In making a selection from them my great fear is not that I shall leave out something, for I must leave out a great deal, but that I shall lose the personality of the author; that by snatching at salient thoughts I shall seem to show him as hurried, or even sententious. The making of sages is dangerous, and even the humane and delightful Confucius has been spoken of in my hearing as a dealer in platitudes, which he was not. If Mr Yeats senior is shown in these pages as a preacher, and the vigour of his thought might at times warrant this loathsome suspicion, the fault is in reality mine, for in the letters themselves there is only the air of leisure.' Full of sly jokes and deep turns, the letters can make even the simplest acknowledgment a delight to contemplate. J. B. Yeats reassures John Quinn, in accents such as cannot once be heard in Connolly's Journal: 'In your last letter you slipped in a sentence which I meant to answer but did not. It was to let you know if I wanted anything, for which I give you thanks and say I do not want anything.' The reciprocation is perfect, and entire gratitude meets secure self-possession. This man of 79, after a lifetime of intelligent effort as a painter, and with success and fame and money continually eluding him, out there in New York in 1918, happy and unembittered and often saddened, never incites any condescension and never rejects any solicitude. With reassuring equanimity he returns Quinn's words ('for which I give you thanks and say I do not want anything') but not marked 'Return to Sender.' It makes a change from 'I want! I want!'

The Oxford-Chelsea axis was so knowing as to have forgotten what wisdom felt like. So a representative reflection by Connolly, there on the first page of the Journal, may sound as if the world-weary wisdom of a thousand years were in it but doesn't actually stand a moment's contemplation. Of love: 'we, the introverts, never realise that it takes two to make a love affair, just as at cards we never realise that our partners may have anything in their hand.' The words are neither believed nor to be believed; only the exacerbatedly sophisticated would fabricate such implausible naivety, such doleful impercipience. Contrast this blasé factitiousness about love with the humorous penetration with which J. B. Yeats comprehends hatred:

> To keep his faith alive, Carlyle was obliged all his long life to be incessantly scolding and prophesying and speaking to the people. Coventry Patmore was a companionable man, and consequently a poor believer in the dogmas he so intolerantly professed. Always did he write in the heat of hatred, the most companionable of all the passions. The man who hates is the furthest from being a solitary and is a man dependent on

having about him the people he hates whether in actual presence or in his mind's eye. In my own life, I knew a well educated and rather pretty woman, who was the most hospitable soul alive. Why thus hospitable? Because she was burning to meet people whom she might contradict in incessant wrangle; we were given a Circean welcome.

J. B. Yeats had the reputation of being the best conversationalist in London, in Dublin, and then in New York. And ever a good thing said. Good will, as usual, proves to be much less sentimental than ill will, while being endlessly resourceful in transubstantiating gall to manna. When J. B. Yeats consoles his son the poet for a bad notice (by John Davidson), the consolation is a true one (is not, in Frank Kermode's great phrase, 'too consolatory to console') because it is so unexpected in the turn it takes: 'I laughed very much and without any bitterness over the offending criticism and assuming Davidson to be the author liked him all the better. It is a good sign when a man does not know how to wound.' The last sentiment would have been anathema to Chelsea and Bloomsbury. But J. B. Yeats was a free spirit, and he knew just what prison-house it was that most closed upon the writer and the Irishman: 'The Irish took to hatred when they deserted the statesman Isaac Butt for the politician Parnell. Hatred is a prison where people can only rave and foam at the mouth and tear their blankets and attack the keepers and yell obscenities, finally to be quelled and put in punishment cells. The many fine movements in history which have so ended!' (20 September 1915). The tragedy of it all is not fully felt until that last sentence.

Such an Irishman in New York (he was there for the last 14 years of his life), provided that he has magnanimity, is perfectly placed to limn the eternal national triangle, and J. B. Yeats can move with effortless imaginative cogency from an individual psychology, via the social and class and moneyed realities, to the traits of nations:

Thanks to Quinn I did a portrait of a Miss Coates whom you met in Paris. She has that kind of cleverness which draws all its ideas from the outside, not from within. The effect is that after a time you become exhausted and depleted, since she cannot replenish you. This is a little obscure, but she was a good subject to paint, only being an American woman she would not let me have my way. However on this matter Quinn and I hold opposite opinions as he backed her up and ruined the portrait. In America liberty is not understood, either for artists or any one else. They are so mad for justice that liberty comes second best. If we had liberty who'd bother about justice. England is the only country where they understand liberty, and there consequently no one cares about justice.

One is more than usually grateful for this when one remembers Connolly, with his American wife, ogling the thought of her money, and his condescensions to her country: 'money must logically become the only criterion in a country where the rich have no natural piety, the poor no feudal ideas and where the army, navy, church and politics are all unfit for gentlemen.'

J. B. Yeats's level dismay at the kind of cleverness which exhausts and depletes and cannot replenish you: this, too, has its applicability to Connolly's strivings. But another of Yeats's formulations brings out why Connolly the regular reviewer was simply so much better at the job to be done than you would ever guess from the embittered memoirist. J. B. Yeats wrote about the *New Republic* in 1915: 'I think all American magazine writing far too frightfully clever. It is as if a man had by mistake hired an acrobat for a footman, so that when he asked for a glass of water it was handed to him by a man standing on his head.' Connolly had all the acrobatic cleverness but as a newspaper reviewer he wisely curbed it and he never stood on his head—not least because he knew that then the money would fall out of his pockets.

These letters of J. B. Yeats have something good to say of and about almost everything. 'I could have nerves if I liked. I know better.' His words can sketch others with a glinting insouciance, as in this (which I prefer to the George Moore who hadn't heard of the Virgin Mary): 'Meanwhile, the sky began to blacken and we all felt anxious while Moore, in his peculiar manner, kept softly gesticulating his despair.' He can observe himself and all observers, as when thinking about Isadora

Duncan on stage: 'Several people said: Is it not like watching a kitten playing for itself? We watched her as if we were each of us hidden in an ambush.' He can turn a sentence which is itself 'as real as the toothache and as terrible and impressive as the judgment day'. In his vitality, he is aware of the innumerable unexpected forms which vitality may honourably take: 'Dowden's mind moved very slowly, in fact was apparently without any of the impulses of progress and change—full of vitality in his way, which was that of a lichen clinging to its rock.'

Greatest of all, J. B. Yeats can bring you near to tears (not at all the same as the 'capacity for nervous weeping' which he diagnosed in Swinburne), and this at the suffering of a complete stranger. As when he writes to his son the poet about an Irish girl whom he spoke to in a park in New York:

> I then noticed that she held a baby in her arms, and that when I glanced toward it *she tried to conceal it from me with her hand*. It was asleep, but wasted and scrofulous and very sick, its arms and legs so thin that the hands and feet looked large; in its wasted neck there were lumps. I could not resist questioning her and found that she had had two other children who died in infancy and that her father and mother in Ireland were dead and that she did not expect to go there again, and that her husband was a healthy man, etc etc. She spoke with resignation as if to the will of God, or Fate—I did not know which. She spoke of the child's sickness as being due to teething, as if she wished to think it temporary. As a contrast all around were swarms of healthy children, obstreperous and noisy. She looked at them as if she did not see them . . . I would have given worlds to have painted a careful study of her and her sick infant and carried it away with me to keep my sorrow alive. *Here we have art as portraiture*, a kind of art great in its way; there is also the conflict of feelings—the ghastly repulsive sickness of the infant, the real charm of the mother's face and form, her mother pride all abashed, her hopelessness, and yet her effort to be hopeful that it was only teething. This hopefulness, in itself a conscious lie, said perhaps out of a social instinct to ease the situation as she talked to me, and then her manifest love as she looked down at the child asleep, *blissfully sleeping*.

Nothing in the poetry of the man who received this letter is to me as profoundly moving as that. John Butler Yeats may have been the greatest of all the greatly gifted family.

So it is lovely to have these letters reissued. And then one must grumble. For the first edition in 1944 was 'produced in complete conformity with the authorised economy standards', but it did have 17 illustrations plus a frontispiece. This reissue is produced in complete conformity with the unauthorised economy standards; though subsidised by the Arts Council, it offers no evidence of artistic powers in J. B. Yeats except for a self-portrait on the jacket. Indeed, this edition fakes a new page 21 to replace the old one which listed the illustrations, and nowhere does it say anything at all about its having taken the liberty of expunging them. Again, though the memoir by Joseph Hone is extremely good, and has done better than wear well (it has weathered well), there is now something needlessly frustrating about all the excisions and truncations; forty years on, these letters could and should have been re-edited. The selection had its perversities and misjudgments even then, as if to distance itself from Ezra Pound's selection of 1917, which had many great things not chosen here, as had Lennox Robinson's *Further Letters* (1920). In 1972 William Murphy published an excellent edition of *Letters from Bedford Park* (1890–1901), 65 letters which show all the man's wisdom, including the loving stringency which he bent upon his son the poet: 'Willie has been out of sorts lately. He overworks himself, or rather over fatigues himself, seeing people and talking to people on various paradoxical subjects in which he believes or persuades himself he is interested.'

J. B. Yeats is a great-hearted understander of life, and so is ill-served by a mere reprinting, docked of its pictures. He ought to be backed. 'Himself was a horse he never backed: but he loved praise, because he thought it meant liking.' I like the man who could say this about his friend Frederick York Powell. As of Powell, it should be said of J. B. Yeats, 'his health was contagious'—was, and is.

Peter Ackroyd
T. S. Eliot

Peter Ackroyd has written a benign life of T. S. Eliot. Given the malignity visited on Eliot, this is a good deal. Fair-minded, broad-minded and assiduous, here is a thoroughly decent book. It has none of the sleazy sanctimony of Robert Sencourt's biography, or the vanity of T. S. Matthews'. That it is a feat to be without spite is coincidentally manifested by the appearance of Geoffrey Grigson's *Recollections*. Grigson's jacket proffers, as a representative gnome: 'I never heard T. S. Eliot laugh.' Back in the book this stands on its lordly own in a section of 'Items'. Some have never heard Geoffrey Grigson do anything but sneer. His *Recollections* are happy to rebuke everybody for sneering, especially at Eliot: 'Eliot in those Thirties was still a name to earn a sneer'; Auden's work 'allowed for sneering much as Eliot's *The Waste Land* only eight years before had allowed for the inimical sneering, which still had not died away'. Perhaps Grigson never heard Eliot laugh because Grigson's company was inimical to laughter. Elsewhere Grigson likes to offer himself as better acquainted with Eliot than are those who wrongly suppose him a glum man. How gracefully the names are floated: 'Braque might be there, or Jean Hélion, from Paris, or Eliot gayer than his reputation, actually singing "Frankie and Johnny".'

Frankie and Johnny, or Tom and Viv? He was her man, but he done her wrong? The marketers of Ackroyd's book have done both him and Eliot wrong in sensationalising it. The new *Vanity Fair*, which unlike the old one is not a magazine for which a T. S. Eliot would write; announced its excerpts as 'The First Mrs E., No Mermaid She'. Ackroyd is entirely without such fishy vulgarity. Plainly it is the Tom and Viv bits which we are all likely to home in on; what can be said is that Ackroyd treats these painful and touchy matters of marital misery with dignity and delicacy. He shows for how long the marriage was not as black as the lugubrious relishers liked to paint it (both Bertrand Russell and Virginia Woolf were impure witnesses for the prosecution), and he shows too that there was often a sportive collusion, easily misconstrued, between Eliot and his first wife. The happiness of Eliot's second marriage necessarily looms less large. Partly this is because loom isn't what happiness does. Literary biography these days (Lowell, Berryman) is bad news that stays news. Anyway, for reasons of honourable privacy, we are not to know much about how it was that Eliot and his second wife, Valerie Eliot, made each other so touchingly happy. Hereabouts there is little news, and for the biographer no news is bad news. Ackroyd, a good man, does not repine at this. He simply devotes to these last eight years of Eliot's life only 15 pages: 'Happy at Last'.

The lines of Eliot's life are well known, and Ackroyd does not effect, or seek to effect, any radical re-limning of them. His strength is local detail, patience, circumstantiality, respect. He denies that there lurks any secret which would unlock an enigmatic Eliot, though he argues that Eliot compacts even more paradoxes than the rest of us. He eschews psychobiographical plunges, and this makes the book at once more satisfactory to the hungry and less satisfying to the greedy. But who are we, to seek, as if in some duel with Eliot, satisfaction? Ackroyd does not bring himself to quote Eliot's styptic comments on a biography in 1927: 'The chief interest of this early biography of Spinoza by a mediocrity who knew him, but who could hardly have appreciated him, is that it shows that Spinoza had already become at his death a symbolical figure, without being in any way a myth.' (Ackroyd need not wince: he is not a mediocrity except in the sense that we all are, in comparison with such a genius as Eliot.) One of the sadnesses of Eliot's story is that at his death, nearly forty years after he wrote these words, he had indeed become a symbolical figure but had not managed to stave off becoming a myth. There is a poignancy of premonition in these words of 1927, the year in which Eliot became a Christian and an Englishman. You can hear it in the unenvious longing for composure in this man who was by no means merely discomposed but who did shudder at such a possibility: 'Here and there is an anecdote, but all anecdotes of Spinoza are essentially the same, in that they all illustrate the same attitude of that composed mind.' Ackroyd shows, as in a different way did Ronald Bush in *T. S. Eliot: A Study in Character and Style*, that there is integrity even in Eliot's disintegrative impulses, yearning for the stable repetition of 'the same . . . the same'. More simply heartening, Ackroyd's book is a witness, oddly for a biography, to Eliot's having achieved what he so admired in Spinoza: 'He was a man of the greatest reticence, but with nothing to conceal; a man of intensely "private life", but wholly transparent.'

Ackroyd's telling of the facts deserves nothing but praise, and a good many of the facts are new. His interpretation of Eliot's nature, though, deserves to be contended with, since it is properly contentious. In one continuingly important respect it distorts Eliot, though it does so with Eliot's complicity, Eliot sometimes choosing—for reasons of modesty and pride and prudence—to present himself as being other than his doings. For Eliot is to Ackroyd a person of lifelong caution and even timorousness, whereas to me he is rather a person of diverse principled temerity. Being J. Alfred Prufrock would actually ask more courage than is usually supposed; writing 'The Love Song of J. Alfred Prufrock' was an act of great courage. Ackroyd will say of Eliot in 1920 that his pride and self-preservation 'did lead Eliot to a most extraordinary caution in both private and public affairs'. Ackroyd speaks of Eliot as 'a timid man'; he quotes with concurrence Virginia Woolf's wishing in 1923 that Eliot had more 'spunk' in him, and refers to 'his tentativeness and indecision'. And this vein, of insisting on Eliot's thin-bloodedness, runs right through to the end of Eliot's life, where it is said of his efforts on behalf of the incarcerated Pound that 'in this case at least his native caution was justified,' and where it is equably reported that Pound and Wyndham Lewis 'hoped that the Nobel Prize would free him of that cautiousness which had smoothed his ascent.'

Now it would be wrong to imply that Ackroyd nowhere speaks of Eliot's resolve or willpower, but the prevailing impression is of the essential Eliot as quintessentially cautious. But this misreading, as it seems to me, can be plausible only if you positively disattend to what the man did. Caution was what Eliot sufficiently possessed to be able—with a discreet air, of course—to throw it to the winds. What after all are the great choices of life that a man might make? He might choose to leave his native land, and to take another nationality. He might choose to leave the secure prospects of a profession to which he had been trained, and to launch himself not even upon a boat but upon a raft. He might choose to marry a strange woman whom he suddenly and unexpectedly loved, against the manifest and unrelenting wishes of his family. He might later choose, against all his own hopes and his own sense of marriage as a sacrament and against his family's codes, to admit that he had no choice but to leave this wife, despite his anguish at her anguished madness and despite his knowing how exposed to malignancy this decision would leave him. He might choose to become a Christian, a faith not held by his family (Unitarians were not, for Eliot, Christians) or by his most urgent admirers or by many of his truest friends. He might choose, again despite all the prurient gossip which it might excite, to marry at the age of 68 a woman 38 years his younger, a woman who had been his secretary. He might choose to write scarcely a poem for the last twenty years of his life. He might choose to embark upon a career as a popular playwright, when thought by most of his intimates to be old enough to know better. And, over and far above all this, he might, throughout a lifetime of his wrung poetry, choose always the braver thing, choose always to be profoundly inaugurative and never to repeat not only others but himself. If Pound and Wyndham Lewis thought that the publication of *Four Quartets* demonstrated a poet's 'cautiousness' they should have thought again.

The point is not whether all of Eliot's choices of life were wise, but whether they were deeply decisive. His life seems to me an awe-inspiring succession of great decisions. Ackroyd necessarily speaks of particular decisions, often humanely, but the atmosphere of his book tacitly disparages them. When he says that 'Eliot's life was governed by such choices,' I want to say: no, Eliot's life was the government of such choices. Since Eliot was not a buffoon or a pair of ragged claws, he indubitably had to steel himself. But the trouble with speaking, as Ackroyd does, of 'his native caution' is that this then becomes central or ruling, whereas for every ounce of native caution Eliot had at least an ounce of native boldness. Ottoline Morrell's gibe at Eliot—'the undertaker'—misfires, given that he truly undertook great things.

If this is so, Ackroyd underrates how sheerly unusual was Eliot's course of life. Eliot may speak of his pusillanimity, but it may be pusillanimously self-gratifying of us to concur. Yet at the same time Ackroyd does the opposite: he finds Eliot more unusual, in my judgment, than is warranted by Ackroyd's own adducings. Ackroyd repeatedly finds 'odd' or 'peculiar' or 'curious' or 'extraordinary' actions or reactions in Eliot which are not patently any such thing. To say this, is to agree restively with Donald Davie, who has praised Ackroyd's book for demonstrating Eliot's essential commonplaceness. To Davie, though, this makes the book valuable as the exposure of something lamentable, whereas others of us may judge it to be—both in Eliot's life and in his art—a testimony to Eliot's commonalty.

Ackroyd regularly registers with an air of mild surprise things in Eliot which are quite properly ordinary. It should not be cause for even one raised eyebrow that when Eliot's friends sought to inflict charity on him in order to release him from working in Lloyds Bank, Eliot 'seemed shy and awkward, covered with embarrassment when money was mentioned'. The episode is indeed worth recounting, but for a different reason: that Eliot was an honourable and decent and in this happy respect an ordinary man, and that honourable, decent ordinary men are embarrassed by such charity, not least when they simply don't want it. A newspaper then printed a lying account of Eliot's having pocketed the charity money while nevertheless staying on at the bank, and it referred to Eliot's 'nervous breakdown'. Ackroyd says: 'not only was his nervous collapse trumpeted to the public—which for such a proud and reticent man was an intolerable intrusion—but he also believed his position in the bank to be jeopardised by this account of his supposed double-dealing.' True, but the sympathy isn't perfectly judged: Eliot was indeed 'a proud and reticent man', but even if he hadn't been, this would still have been 'an intolerable intrusion'. Ackroyd's manner too much invites us to consider Eliot a special case in ways which minister to the condescensions of unneeded kindliness.

Again, there is Bertrand Russell's going to bed with Vivien Eliot. Since Russell may have been as much a liar as he was a lecher, the facts are uncertain, and it is uncertain whether Eliot knew anything. Ackroyd says: 'It was a situation with which he was not yet used to dealing, and no doubt, given his own reticent and defensive temperament, he would have found it peculiarly difficult to respond in an active or decisive manner.' But 'peculiarly' is too slippery there: it is peculiarly difficult even for the very unpeculiar to deal with such situations. There are, and were, very few husbands simply and equably 'used to dealing' with such a situation, and a man would not have at all to be of a reticent and defensive temperament to find it peculiarly difficult to respond in an active or decisive manner. Naturally one knows what Ackroyd means, and he is well-intentioned, but the cumulative effect of these ways of putting it is to alienate Eliot from the central and ordinary human responses, as who should say: 'For *Eliot* this was no joke.' Vivien Eliot made lacerating scenes at parties and suchlike. Ackroyd's solicitude for Eliot here seems to me punctilious and, though not misplaced, misvoiced: 'For a man who was peculiarly attentive to manners and to the formal courtesies of "society", the behaviour of a deranged wife would inevitably lead to anxiety and a sense of shame not far from panic.' Well, yes, but again a man wouldn't have to be *peculiarly* attentive to manners to find that the behaviour in public of a deranged wife would lead to anxiety. Exactly the wrong sort of specialness is being attributed to Eliot by this way of couching it. Davie's attribution of commonplaceness would be nearer the mark, though without the perversity of simply scorning the commonplace.

The other question about Ackroyd's very capable and capacious book may be as much a question for the Eliot estate as for Ackroyd. As everyone knows, this is not an official or authorised biography. Eliot wished there not to be one. True, everyone suspects that in the end Mrs Eliot will prefer there to be an unwished substantiated biography instead of unwished unsubstantiated ones. When the play *Tom and Viv* was exciting passions, the correspondence columns were full of the clang of claims against and by the Eliot estate. All this has now resurfaced—cries of censorship, of obstruction, and so on. One is reluctant to add to the nagging, and clearly Mrs Eliot has more important things to do in her viduity than endlessly to set the record straight. The snag is that it really isn't clear from Ackroyd's biography exactly what the constraints now are. His acknowledgements pages end with an anti-acknowledgement: 'I am forbidden by the Eliot estate to quote from Eliot's published work, except for purposes of fair comment in a critical context, or to quote from Eliot's unpublished work or correspondence.' But unfortunately neither part of this is quite clear, and this matters because there are a great many occasions when, in simple fairness, one wants to know whether Ackroyd is paraphrasing because he is forbidden to quote. He is not a first-rate paraphraser, and when he is dealing with things in the public realm (where a reader or a reviewer can test the matter), he is inclined to be, not inaccurate exactly, but approximate. Thus Eliot did not 'define' wit as 'the recognition, "implicit in the expression of every experience, of other kinds of experience which are possible"'. Eliot said of wit, 'It involves, probably, a recognition . . .', which is not the same as a definition. No doubt, though, Ackroyd is largely to be trusted. But when he hobbles, is it because his legs are tied?

Forbidden 'to quote from Eliot's published work, except for purposes of fair comment in a critical context': did this book have to accept a retrenchment such as was inflicted on Ronald Bush's book? The proof-copy of Bush had many more lines of Eliot's poetry than survived; he and the publishers were made to quote less, not from unpublished or uncollected or private materials, but from the poems themselves.

In 1917 Eliot wrote with prophetic exactness about Turgenev, expatriate in Paris: 'A position which for a smaller man may be merely a compromise, or a means of disappearance, was for Turgenev (who knew how to maintain the role of foreigner with integrity) a source of authority, in addressing either Russian or European; authority but also isolation.' Eliot published this but did not collect it. Did Ackroyd choose, mistakenly, to paraphrase it rather than to quote it? 'In the same period he had written of Turgenev's exile in Paris that the Russian knew how to make use of his transplantation—how, by maintaining his role as a foreigner, he could acquire authority.' This, not surprisingly, is immeasurably weaker and less precise than Eliot's words: it loses all the wit and penetration of the parenthesis—'(who knew how to maintain the role of foreigner with integrity)'—a parenthesis itself exiled and authoritative and stamped with integrity whereas most parentheses are compromises or means of disappearance. If Ackroyd chose only to paraphrase, I think he chose wrongly, a false economy. All these choices have their relevance to Eliot's life of choices.

Added to which, there is the ambiguity of 'forbidden to quote from Eliot's unpublished work or correspondence'. For it is not entirely clear whether 'unpublished' governs 'correspondence' too. From Eliot's unpublished work or from his correspondence? From Eliot's unpublished work or from his unpublished correspondence? If this biographer had any choice in the matter, it would be culpable (or rather the culpability would be his, since there exists a culpability in any case) that the book at some places constitutes a regression. Ackroyd has worked well and hard, and it is painful that the state of explicit and exact knowledge of Eliot is in some ways *less* advanced here than in, say, the collection which Allen Tate edited and which Ackroyd draws on, *T. S. Eliot: The*

Man and His Work (1967). For the contributors to that volume, among them Stephen Spender, Herbert Read and Bonamy Dobrée, were all allowed to quote from Eliot's correspondence. Compare Ackroyd with what Ackroyd was presumably not allowed to publish although it had previously been published (this being what I mean by regression):

> To what territory or tradition he did belong is another question, and one which he himself found it difficult to resolve: in a letter to Herbert Read he described how he could not consider himself to be a Northerner in the United States because of his Missouri origins, and how because of his Northern ancestry he could not claim to be a Southerner. He did not believe himself to be an American at all.

> 'Some day I want to write an essay about the point of view of an American who wasn't an American, because he was born in the South and went to school in New England as a small boy with a nigger drawl, but who wasn't a southerner in the South because his people were northerners in a border state and looked down on all southerners and Virginians, and who so was never anything anywhere and who therefore felt himself to be more a Frenchman than an American and more an Englishman than a Frenchman and yet felt that the USA up to a hundred years ago was a family extension. It is almost too difficult even for H.J. who for that matter wasn't an American at all, in that sense.'

The letter, made public nearly twenty years ago, is so much more illuminating and exact than Ackroyd's approximation. It isn't just that the words 'an American at all' were said by Eliot of Henry James, not of himself, but that the letter has comedy, pathos, resilience, and—because of the rueful third-person and the movement of it all (no pause after 'and who so was never anything anywhere')—an entire absence of self-pity. Ackroyd catches none of that, and it is very bad (differently bad) if this is because they pinioned his arms.

John Ruskin wrote to Charles Eliot Norton: 'So, I know perfectly well that you would work for five years, to write a nice life of me; but I don't care about having my life written, and I know that no one *can* write a nice life of me, for my life has not been nice, and can never be satisfactory.' Eliot, who has his affinities with Ruskin, might have said much the same. Still, Ackroyd *has* written a nice life of Eliot. If this is more a matter of valuable niceness than of invaluable nicety, he could probably retort that because of the Eliot estate no one (yet?) *can* write a nice life of Eliot.

Christopher Sykes
Evelyn Waugh

C hristopher Sykes's life of *Evelyn Waugh* is a triumph of will and good
nature. Among the things it had to triumph over were Waugh's
ill will and ill nature, the routine disgruntlement and sour grapeshot
which he deployed to protect himself against the recognition that at
heart and at soul he was not disgruntled but anguished.

Mr Sykes, whose good books include *Four Studies in Loyalty* and
Troubled Loyalty, here had his work cut out for him: Waugh taxes his
loyalty, but fortunately Mr Sykes can afford it.

Waugh was a man whose own personal loyalties were violent and
capricious. His biographer has been, in all senses, a good friend, and the
affectionate dignity of this book is a matter of its revealing to us, without
exculpation or inculpation, not only Waugh's intolerable vulgarity,
as when he replied to a straightforward ungushing compliment about
Brideshead Revisited with this brutal witlessness: "I thought it was good
myself, but now I know that a vulgar, common American woman like
yourself admires it, I am not so sure"—not only this brutality, but, also
Waugh's simple generosity, candour and selflessness.

In 1928 the young Waugh introduced his first substantial book, a
study of Rossetti, by scathingly reminding the world that, like life, a
written life is subject to fashion:

Sunday Times (11 September 1975)

> No doubt the old-fashioned biography will return, and, with the years, we shall once more learn to assist with our fathers' decorum at the lying-in-state of our great men. . . . Meanwhile we must keep our tongue in our cheek, must we not, for fear it should loll out and reveal the idiot? We have discovered a jollier way of honouring our dead. The corpse has become the marionette.

Mr Sykes has resisted the temptations both of the too-old-fashioned biography, with its mendacious lying-in-state, and of the flippant cutting-down-to-size of gifted men whose size so clearly dwarfs the cutter.

Mr Sykes tells the story with lucidity and concern: the schoolteaching, the loss of religious faith, the journalism, the traveling, the disastrous one-year marriage, the entry into the Roman Catholic Church, the always manly and intermittently farcical war career, the secure second marriage, the aping of the squirearchy, and the monkeying about with the BBC (all employees of which, however grand, Waugh referred to as "the electricians"). All these make a various, touching and bitterly funny study in troubled loyalty. And though Mr Sykes does not set up as a critic, he gets down his well-inside-informed judgments, not just about the winged penetrating achievements, from *Decline and Fall* to *Unconditional Surrender*, but also about the many unachieved books to which Waugh nearly devoted himself, but then decided were not worth his candle: a history of the papacy, and another of the Jesuits; a life of Swift; *In the Steps of Caesar*, *Noah, or The Future of Intoxication*; and—a work about past sobrieties, not future intoxications—*Bloody Mary*.

Yet it is a central honesty and a final limitation—the honourable limitation that comes of being honest—that this book does not answer the question which it cannot but raise: What was the matter with Waugh? For clearly there was something hideously wrong with a man who suffered as Waugh did through his persecution-mania, his self-hatred, and his "fits of devastating gloom" (the devastation not being only his); his lifelong deadly drinking; his grim insomnia, against which his drugs proved powerless except insofar as they precipitated his death in his early sixties; his violent irascibility and bullying; his madness which became the disturbing serenity of *The Ordeal of Gilbert Pinfold*.

All these feed his wild swings and contradictions. Some of his shudderings and judderings are religious, the loss of faith, the finding of a rather different one, and the late fears, apparently, that he might lose it again.

And there is his sexual *volte-fesse*, with his early bouts of homosexuality succeeded by his bitter punitiveness, as when he rebuked Mr Sykes for his essay on Robert Byron: "You said nothing about his perpetual buggery." Or the marital twistings, with his insouciant first marriage, his haggard divorce, and—after his second marriage—his sharp unkindness to people who were divorced. There are social contradictions, too, with his miming of the country squire—or his scorn of those who did not deserve to be officers though it is clear that he was quite unfitted to be one (by temperament not by class).

Waugh disliked the assumption of a TV interviewer that "anyone sufficiently eminent to be interviewed by him must have something to hide." I don't think he had anything to hide, but he did have something hidden. God (perhaps) knows what it was. Mr Sykes doesn't. Waugh didn't. Lady Diana Cooper asked him what was making him so seriously unhappy:

> Nothing at all [he said]. "I have been assigned to a very interesting mission with Randolph who is an old friend. My private life is one of the greatest felicity: I have a wife and children whom I love deeply. My professional life is at the moment all that I could wish. I have just finished a book with which I am very pleased, and think is the best I have written. I can say that I have every cause for happiness."

And the cause, then, of his unhappiness? No cause, no cause. "I have vast reasons for gratitude but am seldom conscious of them."

Hilaire Belloc's laconic words after meeting Waugh were: "He is possessed." And when Waugh went mad, he pleaded with the priest to exorcise the devils that were tormenting him. Later, "I get crustier." But is was a hellish volcanic crustiness. Rebuked for unChristian behaviour, Waugh replied: "You have no idea how much nastier I would be if I was not a Catholic. Without supernatural aid I would hardly be a human being."

His best appalling jokes ask for no more mercy than he did. As when he replied to the televised question about capital punishment, "But supposing, Mr Waugh, that you were ordered to carry out the hanging yourself, what would you say then?":

> I would say that there was something very odd about Home Office administration, if novelists were called on to perform an operation which I believe requires training and considerable technical skill.

Or when, in hospital after an operation for piles, he replied to Mr Sykes's kindly remark that it must be good to be relieved of the pain, with this fair exchange:

> "No," he said, "the operation was not necessary, but might conceivably have become so later on."
> "Not necessary? Then why did you have it done?"
> "Perfectionism."

Brendan Behan
The Scarperer and *Hold Your Hour and Have Another*

The name Behan is said to mean bee-keeper, but the good thing about Brendan Behan was that he didn't keep them in his bonnet. Not that it would have been surprising if he had turned into a crank—after all, he was involved in a fatiguing series of balancing-acts, and it would have been easy to totter. An Irishman all right, but stingingly critical of blarney and Irishness, and using them in his books only to ridicule them or to outwit his persecutors. A *New Statesman* reader, but half-afraid of and half-contemptuous of intellectuals. A Roman Catholic, but scornful of the Church for its loving support of all the wrong political causes—and moreover a man who took the line, still dangerously bizarre in Ireland, of being as much against anti-Protestant vindictiveness as against anti-Catholic ditto. A leftist with a long memory but no rancor, who ringingly announced that his ambition was to be a rich Red. A card-carrying, indeed bomb-carrying, member of the Irish Republican Army, who spent the best years of his life (in more senses than just the schooldays one) behind bars, but who was later to find himself sentenced to death by the I.R.A. for removing his toes from the party line. (Fortunately the sentence was passed in his absence, so

New York Review of Books (30 July 1964)

he was able to send a courteous note suggesting that it be executed in the same manner.) Such self-warring loyalties and likings would be enough to drive a man to drink. Not, apparently, that Behan needed much driving.

It would be good if one could think of his passionate boozing as nothing more than a plain man's delight in good fellowship. But it does look more obsessive than that, and Behan's death in March of this year has, as everyone has pointed out, a great deal in common with Dylan Thomas's. With both, there was a willed thoroughness about seeming hard-drinkingly normal that itself ended up not normal. With both, there was the fatal fact that the modern publicity industry prefers its celebrities drunk. The appeal now is from Philip sober to Philip drunk. There was no intrinsic reason why Behan's famous insobriety in 1956 alongside Malcolm Muggeridge on B.B.C. television, or later under Ed Murrow, should ever have done him any harm. In fact it must have, and just because it was in a worldly sense the making of him. Drinking became, perilously, part of making money rather than spending it, and Behan, like Thomas, now had a reputation to keep down. Again like Thomas, there is one's nagging feeling that he drank because he didn't really want to write, was perhaps dismayed at how quickly he had run through what he had to say, and so was trying to stave off a sense of bankruptcy. The force of these pressures on Behan and the force with which his witty courage withstood them can both be seen in that extraordinary face, so photogenic and so exuberantly ugly, with the rubbery dimpled gentleness of a baby and yet the strength of "a hillocky bull in the swelter of summer."

Any reader of *Borstal Boy* or of *Brendan Behan's Island* will feel that with the death of Behan we lost a very unusual man, notable for a fairmindedness and a generous humanity that never became theoretical or tepid. How unusual he was as a writer is another matter. *Borstal Boy* is sure to last because of its sufficiently unusual warmth, knowledge, and detail—far from being flamboyant or outrageous, it is by and large a work of considerable quiet dignity. Behan doesn't rant during "God Save the King" or even remain seated—he slips out with a warm tact as if going to the lavatory: "I did not want to insult my friends and I did not want to stand for 'God Save the King'." But both *The Quare Fellow* and *The Hostage* will be seen as having been overrated—understandably overrated, because of the dreary poverty of contemporary drama, a poverty which leads to an excessive gratitude for any work of sense, observation, or humanity. Behan's plays are not inferior to, say, John Osborne's; that is, they make a real and pleasant change from the usual vapidities, but if the same material, informed with the same degree of understanding, had been presented in the form of a novel, critics would hardly have been prostrate with admiration. That a play turns out to be not execrable now elicits a natural but dangerous warmth. In the case of Behan, the point matters, because so much of the tone, the stuff, and the sympathy of the plays is indeed to be found, often verbatim, in his other writing.

He was born in 1923 in Dublin, the son of a house-painter. He was apprenticed to the trade himself, and his respect for such skills comes out in some oddly touching episodes in *Borstal Boy*. At the age of sixteen he was arrested in Liverpool for possessing I.R.A. explosives:

> My name is Brendan Behan. I came over here to fight for the Irish Workers' and Small Farmers' Republic, for a full and free life, for my countrymen, North and South, and for the removal of the baneful influence of British Imperialism from Irish affairs. God save Ireland.

Too young for the heavy sentence he would otherwise have received, he was given three years in Borstal. (He was eventually to spend eight years locked up.) He had written and published pieces in verse and prose since he was twelve, in various Republican and Left-wing magazines, and in Borstal he won an essay competition. But it was not until the 1950s that there was a real breakthrough. He was liked as a writer by the Dublin intelligentsia—according to him, because he had hardly published anything. But the intelligentsia was not too keen on some pieces of pornography which he had written, in English, for French magazines. Short of money, he wrote a serial about Dublin's underworld, *The Scarperer*, which ran for thirty days in the *Irish Times*. He took the precaution of using a pseudonym ("Emmet Street"), and he drew on his prison experiences. The result, now republished, is lightweight but enjoyable. Behan was still feeling his way towards his own characteristic form, but the story (of a man who is helped to "scarper" from prison only to find that he is to be murdered) has a genuine suspense. But what mattered to Behan was that the *Irish Times* believed in his abilities, even to the extent of sending him ninety pounds to live on while he completed the story.

Then from 1954 to 1956 he wrote weekly articles for the *Irish Press*, some of which have now been collected as *Hold Your Hour and Have Another*. A somewhat ingratiating use of charm, an uneasiness about looking like a highbrow, and a feeble use of malapropisms—these are real faults, and such a book does Behan no service. But then whose weekly pieces would be worth reprinting? And even here there is evidence of Behan's extraordinary gifts as an anecdotalist. The thing about the anecdote is that it so totally doesn't need any gifts of characterization; Behan seems to have been as completely without such gifts as a writer could possibly be, and yet he was saved by anecdotes. The British officer loftily murmuring "I see they have cripples in their army"—to be met by the Irish retort "We have, but no conscripts." Or, "at one of the street battles in Cathal Brugha Street that helped to pass the depression for the people," Paddins shouting "You have the best of men in your jails, and I dare you to take me now"—only to be softly undone by the public speaker: "I am not," he said, "a collector of curios." Or the old lady who does nothing but embroider notices which say "Beware!" This is Behan's world, and he sees it with an unsentimental sanity and optimism. As an anecdotalist he may have embroidered, but not at any rate "Beware!"

What is worrying about *Hold Your Hour*, though, is that it already shows that for all his energy and width of sympathy he was dangerously short of material. Mainly this was because of his dilemma as a no-nonsense ordinary man who happened also to be rather a reader. *Borstal Boy* shows that Dickens, Hardy, Dostoievsky, and of course *The*

Ragged Trousered Philanthropists all meant a lot to Behan, and the book even had the courage to offer an epigraph from Virginia Woolf. But the *Irish Press* was afraid of Virginia Woolf—or perhaps Behan was afraid it might be. So he tended to neglect, as sources of inspiration or information, much that past literature makes available. History, yes—Behan like all Irishmen knew a lot of history and deployed it brilliantly. As he said in *Borstal Boy*, "I was never short of an answer, historically informed and obscene." But literature he seems to have found a bit suspect, going along with snobbery and effeminacy. So despite the strength of history and of his pub-talking oral traditions, Behan found himself cut off from an important and reinvigorating source of creativity. Clearly he knew about this; one of his sketches about "Brending Behing" ends: "'Sad case,' said Crippen, looking at me with commiseration. 'Only went to school half the time, when they were teaching the writing—can't read.'" Behan coped with the problem with dignity but also with some embarrassment. And sometimes he fell back on an amiable but unconvincing pretense, as when he praised Sean O'Casey: "All I can say is that O'Casey's like champagne, one's wedding night, or the Aurora Borealis or whatever you call them—all them lights." See that tell-tale shift from *one's* to *you*; Behan, blunt man, doth protest too much. Likewise when he beautifully quotes Keats as at last the Borstal boys reach the sea, only to retreat from a feared sentimentality with "By Jasus, this equals any fughing Darien." In fact Behan's dedication to the drama is related to this dilemma—it offered the appearance of a way out, since of all the literary forms it is the one which can apparently go furthest in dispensing with literature.

It was his macabre comedy of prison life, *The Quare Fellow*, which in 1956 made Behan. He had written it as a radio-script, *The Twisting of Another Rope*; then it became a one-act play, and finally three acts. *The Hostage* was commissioned by Gael Linn, the organization for reviving the Irish language. It took Behan a fortnight. Applauded in Irish, it was disliked in English; Behan's friend Alan Simpson has suggested that the worthy Irish patrons didn't understand the obscenities when in their "native language." Possibly too the pitying humor with which Behan now regarded the I.R.A.'s religiosity seemed renegade. But in England both the plays, with their music-hall mixture of comedy and tragedy, song and dance, were the successes that Behan deserved and needed. 1958 was a good year for him; not only *The Hostage* but also *Borstal Boy* (banned in the Republic of Ireland and in Australia). But since then the stream was running dry. There was a radio play, *The Big House*, set in the early Twenties, which was adapted for the stage in 1963. (It is printed in *Brendan Behan's Island*, a delightfully reminiscential scrapbook that shows Behan at his best.) But *The Big House* is like second-rate Dylan Thomas, "Under Milk and Water Wood." There were a couple of radio sketches; there was the jazz revue, *Impulse*, with Behan as compère, which petered out in Toronto in 1961; there were two new plays which came to nothing and were at last shelved, *Richard's Cork Leg* and *Checkmate*. But something was going badly wrong. To look back now over Behan's work is to see how terribly repetitive he was. Three times he used the anecdote about Queen Victoria giving five pounds to the Battersea Dogs' Home at the same time as to the Irish famine fund, so as not to seem to be encouraging rebels. The jokes, the songs, the historical incidents—all return word for word again and again and again. Not because they are obsessions, but because Behan was short of material.

> "Where the hell were you in nineteen-sixteen when the real fighting was going on?" "I wasn't born yet." "You're full of excuses."

A good old joke, and worth using once. But only once. There could be a very long list indeed of these verbatim repetitions. There is nothing immoral about them, but they make very sad reading because, in its sheer mass of detail, such a list would be clear proof that Behan's undeniable vigor was not correspondingly matched by fertility of imagination. As a writer he was unlikely to have had much more to give the world. Which is not to deny that as a man he still had a shrewd compassion.

Norman Mailer
The Executioner's Song

G ary Gilmore robbed the unresisting service-station attendant, told
him to lie down, and then shot him in the head. Twice, fast. The
next day, Gilmore robbed the unresisting motel-manager, told him to
lie down, and then shot him in the head. Once only, because the gun
jammed, and so the man died slowly. Convicted, Gilmore chose to die
as quickly as the law would allow, and chose to be shot. He had at this
time spent 18 of his 35 years locked up, and he wanted no more of it,
knowing that whatever lifetime he might gain could be only a death-
watch. He waived his right of appeal, and flung himself on the justice
of the courts. That shook them. But in the end, in January 1977, after
every stay of execution had been prised off by the combined efforts of
Gilmore and his prosecutors, Gilmore's bad life came to a good end.
He was then brave. He was dignified. Generous, too, giving his eyes to
someone young who needed them, and giving his pituitary gland to the
sick child of his cousin Brenda, the woman who, though she still loved
him and had been the one to get him released on parole only nine
months earlier, had since turned him in and had given her undeviating
testimony. Gilmore was generous, and humorous with it. 'Well, Moody,
I'm going to leave you my hair. You need it worse than I do.' Thy need,
or necessity or whatever, is greater than mine.

London Review of Books (16 March 1980)

Norman Mailer's book about Gilmore is a work of genius in its range, depth and restraint. It has speed, which Gilmore had, and patience, which he had not. It has lucidity, even when dealing with legal entanglements. It has forbearance, even when witnessing brutalities and insensitivities. Its justice is larger than indignation, and its responsible equanimity is at one with its equity. Nothing is extenuated, and nothing set down in malice. For this murderer we need words which acknowledge an undying recalcitrance, words like those which Dr Johnson needed for Othello: 'yet we cannot but pity him.'

There are a hundred or more people to whom justice and mercy must be done if they are to be done to Gilmore—from Gilmore's beloved Nicole (19 years old, with three broken marriages, two low-profile children, and now this very high-profile ex-convict who, for these few months, loved her madly and sanely), through Gilmore's family, out to the cell-mates, the warders, the lawyers and judges, and finally the journalists, bookmakers and entrepreneurs of what became a mass-media undertaking. The only person missing is Mailer. True, Mailer hadn't been on the scene, and it is a posthumous Gilmore whom he, and not only we, must meet. But this is a fact of the matter, not the whole truth of it. Mailer here has better things to do with his self than to attend to it or upon it.

You could call the book a feat of self-abnegation if the word 'feat' didn't suggest a bravura. Gilmore, who had no self-control once he had decided to throw a switch inside his head and to vent the pent, but who had gigantic self-control once the imminent death was not that of another but of himself, is here complemented by an artist who most unexpectedly shows in this sane and magnanimous book a high form of self-control: a control over the extent to which, and the ways in which, self is present at all even to be controlled exactly. The author of *Advertisements for Myself* is here advertising nothing, least of all himself.

How does Mailer effect this? He does not himself have a voice in the book, which is divided in two, 'Western Voices' and 'Eastern Voices'. But the book's amplitude allows there to be little of him which goes unvoiced. So Nicole's deranged sister April is not a mouthpiece or surrogate for Mailer, but her spooky ways of thinking, and of not think-ing, are strings which vibrate in sympathy with his strings without his ever having to touch hers. Likewise with the different concurrence between Mailer and the psychiatrist Woods, on Gilmore and high risk: 'Gilmore had been keeping in touch with something indispensable to be in touch with.' It is a question of Mailer's being in touch with all these people who are not he, and not of his doling himself out through the book.

Pre-eminently it is the monstrous, amiable, ruthless and disconcert-ingly candid Lawrence Schiller who stands in or weighs in for Mailer in the second half of the book—Schiller, 'something of a carrion bird' (before Gilmore, he had been the mass-mediator for Jack Ruby on his deathbed, and for Susan Atkins in the Manson trial), detested by those whom he outdoes ('Schiller is a scavenger, a snake'), and yet having the kindly effrontery to introduce himself to Nicole with 'I'm the big bad wolf, Larry Schiller.' Schiller mediates between Gilmore and Mailer. The book is copyright Norman Mailer, Lawrence Schiller and the New Ingot Company Inc. But Mailer is big enough to incorporate even Schiller, whose wheelings around, like his dealings, do have a burly power. Sometimes he was 'ready to cry in his sleep that he was a writer without hands,' so it is good that he fell into Mailer's hands. The crea-tor of the film *The American Dreamer* meets his match in the man who now redeems *An American Dream*.

There may have been much of Mailer in Gilmore, too, the religious, superstitious, existentialist Gilmore. But it is part of the simple sanity of the book that such things are now subjected to an intimate vigilance. 'Whether the life is criminal or not,' Mailer once notoriously said, 'the decision is to encourage the psychopath in oneself.' *The Executioner's Song* is something wiser: it contemplates the life and death of a crimi-nal, and seeks to encourage the steady contemplation of the psychopath in him and in oneself, but not only of that.

Diana Trilling, in an essay which paid Mailer the compliment of fear as well as of admiration, was rightly horrified by what Mailer said in 1961 about a brutal murder. What he said was this:

> Let's use our imaginations. It means that one human being has deter-
> mined to extinguish the life of another human being. It means that two
> people are engaging in a dialogue with eternity. Now if the brute does it
> and at the last moment likes the man he is extinguishing then perhaps
> the victim did not die in vain. If there is an eternity with souls in that
> eternity, if one is able to be born again, the victim may get his reward.

Let's use our imaginations again. *The Executioner's Song* thinks again,
and feels anew. American dreams are now pushed back to where they
belong, and what is contemplated by daylight is an American tragedy.

For the unlikeness between Mailer and Gilmore is as unignorable as
any likeness. Sparring, Gilmore said: 'I don't lead, I'm a counterpuncher.'
Mailer knows that as a writer he's a counterpuncher, but it's the fact that
he is not assimilating himself to Gilmore which allows him not to be a
tub-thumper.

Mailer is here the element, which is very different from his being in
his element. He is the medium, not the message. Better still, there is no
message. Probably nobody but Mailer could have written this book, in
that there may be no other writer of such synthesising power who so
knows the massiveness both of the world's facts and of the self's fantasies. Yet the book, though it marshals a great many of Mailer's enduring concerns, has a powerful sense of having written itself. It makes
compelling reading partly because it was written not from Mailer's com-
pulsions but with its own impulsion.

Mrs Trilling turned upon Mailer T. S. Eliot's praise of Henry James
as having a mind so fine that no idea could violate it: 'Of Mailer we can
say that his novelist's mind is peculiarly violable by idea, even by ideology.' But the greatness of *The Executioner's Song* is, surprisingly, in
Mailer's having manifested a mind, not so fine exactly, but so strong,
that no idea can violate it, even ideas about the hideous violation done
by Gilmore and to him. 'His mastery over, his baffling escape from,
Ideas,' Eliot had mused.

Spurred by the obvious affinities between Mailer and Lawrence, we
might call up another moment in Eliot's criticism, when, four years after

those words on James and ideas, Eliot spoke in 1922 of Lawrence and theories:

> He has never yet, I think, quite surrendered himself to his work. He still theorises at times when he should merely see. His theory has not yet reached the point at which it is no longer a theory, he still requires (at the end of *Aaron's Rod*) the mouthpiece for a harangue. But there is one scene in this book—a dialogue between an Italian and several Englishmen—in which one feels that the whole is governed by a creator who is purely creator, with the terrifying disinterestedness of the creator. And for that we can forgive Mr Lawrence his subsequent lapse into a theory of human relationships.

Mailer has surrendered himself to this work, and is content to see. His disinterestedness is in his being so little afraid of what may unjustly be said of his disinterested justice.

This book promulgates no ideas or theories, though it contains a great many, as well as intelligent speculations, all voiced or thought by others. Mailer sustains in his daytime world what Empson praised in Spenser's dream-world—the artist pouring quite different allegiances into his even work 'with an air, not of ignoring their differences, but of holding all their systems of values floating as if at a distance, so as not to interfere with one another, in the prolonged and diffused energies of his mind'. The issues are here only as they issue from other minds, for instance the unmuddy mind of Gilmore (his heart is another matter):

> But what do I do now? I don't know. Hang myself?
>
> I've thought about that for years, I may do that. Hope that the state executes me? That's more acceptable and easier than suicide. But they haven't executed anybody here since 1963 (just about the last year for legal executions anywhere). What do I do, rot in prison? Growing old and bitter and eventually work this around in my mind to where it reads that I'm the one who's getting fucked around, that I'm just an innocent victim of society's bullshit? What do I do? Spend a life in prison searching

for the God I've wanted to know for such a long time? Resume my painting? Write poetry? Play handball? Eat my heart out for the wondrous love you gave me that I threw away Monday nite because I was so spoiled and couldn't immediately have a white pickup truck I wanted? What do I do?

The Executioner's Song has a respect for ideas, and yet ideas are not to the book's own purpose. It is Gilmore and the others who are entitled to purposeful ideas, as when Gilmore addresses the Pardons Board: 'He did not rise to this occasion like a great ham actor, but chose to be oblivious to it. Merely there to express his idea. Gilmore spoke in the absolute confidence of the idea, spoke in the same quiet tone he might have employed if talking to only one man.' The book's own level tones are therefore different from those of dedicated professionals, those of the psychiatrist or lawyer no less unshockable than Mailer but differently so. Unlike the gratuitousness of Gilmore's murders, the book has the freedom of art. It does not seek to make anything happen: it seeks to show what happened, and it finds. It does not despair of knowing why, but it knows that it doesn't know.

Every imaginable explanation of Gilmore and his conduct is given the right to be heard. The book is long and large, not only because its magnanimity asks room for the large hearts of many others; and not only because there were a great many participants; but also because there are so many possibilities for the understanding of it all. Should we see Gilmore as nursing a kid's low threshold for frustration, so that he just had to have that newly-painted truck instead of his dud car? Two deaths, at about $125 each, towards the $400 which was due? Or Gilmore as a lover, maddened by the break with Nicole who had said she was through with him and was now nowhere to be found? 'I killed Jenkins and Bushnell because I did not want to kill Nicole.' Or Gilmore as a callous killer from way back, boasting of a killing done in jail? Cold steel. Questioner: 'How would you describe your personality?' Gilmore: 'Slightly less than bland.' Or Gilmore as somewhere afraid of himself as a would-be child-molester? Or as hating Mormons (his victims were

Mormons, not that this is unusual in Utah) because of how the Mormon Church had treated his mother? Or Gilmore as the devil, or as evil? 'I am one of those people that probably shouldn't exist.' Or Gilmore as the victim of evil medication? 'They shot me with that foul drug Prolixin and made a zombie out of me for four months.' Or Gilmore as the victim of society at large, or of its not having allowed him to be at large? 'He was in prison so long, he didn't know how to work for a living or pay a bill.' Or Gilmore as the victim of his young life, with a criminal father who had too many aliases, and with a mother who . . . ? Yet Gilmore turns the tables upon the questioner who sits so sly. 'What do you think of your mother and her role in your early life?'

> I love my mother. She's a beautiful strong woman. Has always been consistent in her love for me. My mother and I have always had a good relationship. Besides being mother and son we're also friends. She's a good mother of pioneer Mormon stock. A good woman. What do you think of your mother?

Why? 'That night I knew I had to open a valve.' A danger valve, for others and for Gilmore. Everybody asked why. 'I don't know,' he mostly replied. When the question was pitched less high, he could send up the whole idea of such whys and wherefores. 'Why did you take things without paying for them—beer—guns?' 'Didn't always have time to stand in those long checkout counter lines.'

But the real question stays. 'Is there any cause in nature that makes these hard hearts?' Or out of nature? And what of these hearts which can throw a switch in the head, from tender to hard? With Regan and Goneril, there are reasons enough why our nearest may not at all be our dearest. Nobody has managed not to hurt each and every member of the family. But then it is not any lack of reasons which makes the mystery, it is the chasm between the piled reasons and the snatched act. For Gilmore's murderousness we have more reasons than we know what to do with. He remains eternally distant, this man who could set down in answer to the question, 'Did Jensen resist and did Jensen show fear?':

Jenkins did not resist.

He did not show undue fear.

I was struck by his friendly, smiling, kind face.

Respect is the heart of the book. Those who wouldn't respect Gilmore's wishes (which were not a death wish—till the end he was serious about ways of escaping from the prison) didn't respect what was worthy of respect in him. 'The only thing I ask is just respect my own thoughts about death.' When they said he was mad or suicidal or publicity-seeking or up to some ploy, they lacked respect for more than just Gilmore. Mailer isn't sentimental, for he flinches from nothing about Gilmore which is contemptible. But from the beginning, Mailer respects that which should be respected, very various too, in all of those whose lives touched Gilmore's life and death, including those whom he killed. Gilmore's cousin Brenda, the first person we meet in the book, is a triumphant evocation of a person who triumphs over everything. But then the whole book is astonishingly free from scorn or condescension; even the preposterous Dennis Boaz (writer, lawyer, hippy, changer of his own mind but of no one else's) is acknowledged for his intrepidity and for the directness of his speech on behalf of Gilmore's wishes.

A great many intelligent and sensitive things are said about respect in the course of the book, none of them by Mailer, since he is not there to speak, but all getting his due as well as their own. A small example would be the presentation (not treatment) of Gilmore's parole-officer, Mont Court, where the contrast would be with the cheap collusion between the plot and the audience in the treatment of the parole-officer in the Dustin Hoffman film about a murderous recidivist, *Straight Time*. But a more incriminating example, just because of its hateful influence on Gilmore himself, would be the film of *One Flew over the Cuckoo's Nest*. Gilmore loved the film; he said that he'd watched them film it, and that he'd even been sent over to that very same mental-institution. He had seen the film before; then he took Brenda to it and behaved throughout with odious aggression; and then, after killing the gas-station attendant, he took half-crazy April to it: 'This is one movie

I want to see again.' Skilled, unscrupulous, the film ministered to all that was worst in Gilmore (and not only in him). In the perverted intelligence with which the film infects the audience with its systematic injustice, in its assurance that nobody except its favourites has either a character or a belief which could possibly be respected, it is the perfect and deplorable contrast to Mailer's admirable and discriminating respect. Such is Mailer's justified confidence here that he can even allow us to acknowledge that Gilmore was alert about pseudo-respect:

> When a girl finally decided to let you fuck her she'd always put on this act like she was being taken advantage of and 9 times outa 10 the girl would say 'Well, will you still respect me?' Some goof-ball shit like that. Well the cat was always so hot and ready to go by then that he was ready to promise anything, even respect. That always seemed so silly, but it was just the way the game was played. I had a chick ask me that once, a real pretty little blond girl, everybody really was hot for her ass and I had her alone one nite in her house. We was both about 15 and necking pretty heavy both getting worked up and I was in and I knew it and then she came up with that cornball line: 'Gary, if I let you do it would you still respect me?' Well, I blew it, I started laffing and I told her: 'Respect you? For what? I just wanta fuck and so do you, what the fuck am I sposed to respect you for? You just won a first place trophy in the Indianapolis 500 or something?' Well, like I said I blew that one.

'Don't I have the right to die?' Whether the life is criminal or not, this is a question for our time. Whose life is it anyway? Much of the power of the story of Gary Gilmore comes from some cruel parallels between judicial justice and what passes for medical mercy. Gilmore is a contemporary of Karen Quinlan and of many others whom modern medicine deprives of a dignified death. The ironical words of Clough have been turned to a different irony and to a decent injunction:

> Thou shalt not kill; but needst not strive
> Officiously to keep alive.

Officials of the American Civil Liberties Union strove officiously to keep Gilmore alive. 'Rather than live in this hole, I'd choose to be dead.' He knew what his co-operative enemies ought to have meant when they said of the death penalty: 'that's too good for him.'

'You sentenced me to die. Unless it's a joke or something, I want to go ahead and do it.' Going ahead meant that the jokes could be on them. As when, the courts continuing to lurch into concurring with Gilmore, and the ACLU still wishing to save Gilmore from himself and to save others on Death Row from the likely consequences of Gilmore's execution, Gilmore asks: 'What else can they do? Go to the United Nations?' None of the prosecuting jokes is as good as those which Gilmore makes in defence of his right to die, or as good as those which are simply a way of seeing the bizarre circumstances themselves. After Gilmore's first suicide attempt, a newspaper cartoon showed him in a hospital bed: 'The nurse was saying, "Mr Gilmore, wake up. It's time for your shot." At the foot of the hospital bed was a five-man firing squad.' But this is less sharp than the mere radio report: 'Dr L. Grant Christensen said Gilmore can leave the hospital and return to Death Row if he continues to improve.'

Gilmore's humour and wit were real, but they could be really brutal.

> '"It was like in a movie," I say to them, "and I couldn't stop the movie."'
>
> 'Is that how it came down?' asked Gibbs.
>
> 'Shit, no,' said Gilmore. 'I walked in on Benny Bushnell and I said to that fat son of a bitch, "Your money, son, *and* your life."'

> 'Hell,' said Gilmore, 'the morning after I killed Jensen, I called up the gas station and asked them if they had any job openings.'

Yet you can understand his reaching for whatever dark humour he can find through which to contemplate the eclipse of his own life, and he goes straight on from those brutalities to a self-inflicted one:

'What's your last best request when they're hanging you?' he asked, and answered, 'Use a rubber rope.' Pretending to be bouncing on the end, he put his face in a scowl, and said, 'Guess I'll be hanging around for a while.'

He sent an invitation to his execution:

BANG!   BANG!
A real live Shoot'em up!
Mrs Bessie Gilmore of Milwaukie, Ore cordially invites you to the execution of her son: Gary Mark Gilmore, 36
Place: Utah State Prison. Draper, Utah
Time: Sunrise
EARPLUGS AND BULLETS WILL BE FURNISHED

It has to be admitted that the 'real live' is dauntless. They couldn't stop Gilmore, who gazed at all the money-making and dilated on it:

Oh, hey, man, I got something that'll make a mint. Get aholda John Cameron Swazey right now, and get a Timex wristwatch here. And have John Cameron Swazey out there after I fall over, he can be wearing a stethoscope, he can put it on my heart and say, 'Well, that stopped,' and then he can put the stethoscope on the Timex and say, 'she's still running, folks.'

Nothing, not even his worst witticism, is as bad as the armchair esprit of those who never find it necessary to have what Gilmore, in a repeated pun, called the courage of their convictions ('Don't the people of Utah have the courage of their convictions? You sentence a man to die—me—and when I accept this most extreme punishment with grace and dignity, you, the people of Utah want to back down and argue with me about it. You're silly').

'If you had a choice, would your execution be on television?'

No.
Too macabre.

Would you like *your* death televised?
At the same time, I really don't give a shit.

This is a human voice which comes from someone who had done many inhuman things, and as a voice it is preferable to this:

SEE SELVES ON 'VIDEO'
          THEN TWO DIE IN CHAIR
Chicago, April 21, 1950–(AP)–Two condemned murderers saw themselves on television last night and a few hours later died in the electric chair . . . The doomed men . . . were filmed in death row yesterday afternoon. The film was then put on a 7 p.m. newsreel show and viewed by the men on a set loaned them by the warden.

And is preferable to this, the prompt commenting voice of Marshall McLuhan: 'This situation is a major feat of modern news technique. Hot spot news with a vengeance.' Mailer's book is hot spot news that stays news, and it is without any vengeance.

Arguments

Erving Goffman
Forms of Talk

U nruffled, the announcer said, "She'll be performing selections from the Bach Well-tempered Caviar." Erving Goffman's *Forms of Talk*, his tenth book since he published *The Presentation of Self in Everyday Life* in 1959, is characteristically well-tempered in its understanding of virtually every kind of ruffle and unruffle. The essays collected in it ought to prove as pleasurable to the general public as to Goffman's fellow sociologists. The chapter which marvels acutely at the announcer's equanimity is on "Radio Talk." Its subtitle is "A Study of the Ways of Our Errors." Goffman's largeness of spirit is evident not only in the happy phrase itself but in the wide application of its "our": he doesn't just mean radio announcers, since he discusses all the ways in which their face-saving maneuvers (despite the fact that we cannot see their faces, saved or unsaved, any more than we can see the countenance which an announcer wants to keep himself in) are much the same as those of everyday, face-to-face talk.

Again, "our errors" has the sense to mean not just the likes of us but the likes of sociologists. As is frequent in Goffman's work, one of his humane impulses is a principled dissatisfaction with his profession, not merely in his judging that some of his colleagues don't do well enough by delicacy and by interrelationship, but in his knowing that they and

New York Review of Books (16 July 1981)

he couldn't ever do well *enough*. Just as some of the greatest art is alive to the limits even of the greatest art, so Goffman, in a manner very unusual in his neck of the sacred woods, incorporates the best form of self-criticism. Only a cynic would mistake it for cynicism.

One of the errors of our ways (we being the nonsociologists) is an unprincipled dissatisfaction with sociology. George Watson has justly observed that "it is an over-notorious fact that sociology is in practice ill-written, perhaps because sociological works which are not ill-written are commonly thought of as something else." So one could rejoice too much at the fact that Goffman—who writes like an angel, especially about the fact that we all often talk like poor Poll—is the Benjamin Franklin Professor of Anthropology at the University of Pennsylvania. The publisher's praise of *Forms of Talk* says truly that it is the variety of different situations analyzed in Goffman's work "that has made it so necessary for students of interaction in many disciplines."

Yet to apply Goffman within literary criticism, as I found when publishing *Keats and Embarrassment,* is to meet the reflex hostility of the dwarfish critic. It is only in a very torrid world that Goffman could stand accused of creating, as one such critic put it, "a chilling fiction of social life which turns us all into inauthentic actors." Goffman's are notes away from the supremacy of fiction, which is the reason why they so acknowledge fiction's diverse ubiquity.

Moreover, Goffman's beliefs are so respectful of others' that one fine complement to his book would be a very different one, Paul Goodman's best, *Speaking and Language.* A delight in Goffman's microscopic powers can be perfectly at one, also, with a delight in the attention paid to talk by one of the great macroscopes: Thomas Carlyle, who created what must be the most telling description of a genius in a desperate state of talk.

> I have heard Coleridge talk, with eager musical energy, two stricken hours, his face radiant and moist, and communicate no meaning whatsoever to any individual of his hearers—certain of whom, I for one, still kept

eagerly listening in hope; the most had long before given up, and formed (if the room were large enough) secondary humming groups of their own. . . .

Jonathan Swift, sociolinguist extraordinary, whose *Polite Conversation* would be well worth Goffman's illuminating candle, pointed out that it wasn't enough just to know what to say:

> The true Management of every Feature, and almost of every Limb, is equally necessary; without which an infinite Number of Absurdities will inevitably ensue: For Instance, there is hardly a polite Sentence in the following Dialogues which doth not absolutely require some peculiar graceful Motion in the Eyes, or Nose, or Mouth, or Forehead, or Chin, or suitable Toss of the Head, with certain Offices assigned to each Hand; and in Ladies, the whole Exercise of the Fan, fitted to the Energy of every word they deliver; by no means omitting the various Turns and Cadence of the Voice, the Twistings, and Movements, and different Postures of the Body, the several Kinds and Gradations of Laughter, which the Ladies must daily practise by the Looking-Glass, and consult upon them with their Waiting-Maids.

Goffman himself is untiringly perspicacious about the various turns and cadence of the voice and the several kinds and gradations of laughter. One of the latest Wittgenstein bootleg publications, *Culture and Value*, includes an observation of which the humorous acumen is exactly in the spirit of Goffman's starting points: "In a conversation: One person throws a ball; the other does not know: whether he is supposed to throw it back, or throw it to a third person, or leave it on the ground, or pick it up and put it in his pocket, etc."

The nonsociologist, all the same, is bound to feel what everybody always feels about the main contentions which issue from somebody else's discipline: that it is odd that certain things need to be said. So when the publishers praise Goffman for "his insistence that talk be placed in an interactional framework and studied as part of the total physical, social, cultural, and verbal environment in which it occurs," the nonsociologist will wonder that the insistence was called for. Goffman is very good at showing not just that the simple formulae, notions, and models won't do, but exactly why they won't do; yet an outsider must feel something of a stranger when meeting a sentence like this:

> I am arguing here that what in some sense is part of the subject matter of linguistics can require the examination of our relation to social situations at large, not merely our relation to conversations.

Tiens! Yet it is just such forms of talk as these about which Goffman himself is penetratingly imaginative. "Coordinated task activity—not conversation—is what lots of words are part of," he says (rather as Paul Goodman had an affectionate page about working together wordlessly on a car until it finally starts: "At *this* point, of consummation, they are almost sure to say something, if only 'Oof!'"). Goffman adds: "And these are not unimportant words; it takes a linguist to overlook them."

It takes a sociolinguist of humor and imagination (intimately related) to notice the things which Goffman so eloquently and unstuffily calls into play, his practice being the validation of his complaint that in much sociolinguistics "the essential *fancifulness* of talk is missed." His pleasure in fancifulness depends upon a keen feeling for social reality, just as Leigh Hunt praised a moment in Keats as "a fancy founded, as all beautiful fancies are, on a strong sense of what really exists or occurs."

The first essay in *Forms of Talk*, "Replies and Responses," is wonderfully resourceful about the implications of the resourcefulness within such an exchange as this at an airport, when a man neither silently puts down his bag en route to the ticket counter nor explicitly asks the woman sitting there to watch the bag for him. Instead:

> He: [Laconically, almost *sotto voce*, as if already lodged in conversation with the recipient]: "Don't let them steal it."
>
> She: [Immediately utters an appreciative conspiratorial chuckle as speaker continues on his way.]

The second essay, "Response Cries" (my favorite, for the range of its comedy and surprise), listens to ways in which, unexpectedly, it is permissible in our society to talk to yourself. Taking time to ponder such things as the proprieties of picking up money in the street, Goffman listens to what we say, for instance, when we trip over something. His taxonomy of response-cries not only brings home how foolish it is to use the word taxonomy pejoratively, as if a taxonomy weren't a thrilling thing, but it also rises above even a taxonomy in its bizarrerie of relationships. There is the transition display (*Brr!*, *Ahh!*, *Phew!*); the spill cry (*Oops!*, *Whoops!*, *Oopsadaisy!*); the threat startle (*Eek!*, *Yipe!*); revulsion sounds (*Eeuw!*—and one might throw in *Yuk!*); the strain grunt (Goodman's *Oof!*); the pain cry (*Oww!*, *Ouch!*); the sexual moan (no notation forthcoming); floor cues (*Good God!*, from someone reading the paper, inciting an inquiry which it can't quite bring itself to ask for); and audible glee (*Oooooo!*, *Wheee!*). On all these, Goffman notices relations between the things he notices, and though serious, is never in deadly earnest.

The next essay, on "Footing," is about the changes in alignment or position taken within an uttered sequence, the cadenced laminations. The argument would be very apt, for instance, to Frost's important principle of "the sound of sense" ("Ask yourself how these sentences would sound without the words in which they are embodied"), since it seems from Frost's instances as if what he calls "the posture proper to the sentence" is actively the changes in footing or in posture; as with Frost's example:

> *One—two—three—go!*
> *No good! Come back—come back.*
> *Haslam go down there and make those kids get out off the track.*

Goffman's fourth essay is a lecture on "The Lecture"; and his fifth is "Radio Talk." The former has many jokes, none cheap, at Goffman's own expense (though any lecturer would fit and foot the bill); the latter avails itself of Kermit Schafer's anthologies of hilarious radio bloopers or clangers.

97

What, though, does a nonsociologist—in my case, a literary critic—learn from all this? The delight he may feel as a general reader would be more than enough, but it is something different from the claim that "students of interaction in many disciplines" can profit greatly from Goffman. So let me seize upon one thing which, first of all, is central to *Forms of Talk*, being indeed the preoccupation that holds the five essays together, and, secondly, is a central preoccupation of literary criticism today: self-reflection.

The grace of self-reflection, by which some part of art's attention is well turned upon itself, upon its own proceedings, has rightly been valued highly by much recent criticism, especially as a power for wit and humor, and as a reminder, in its admission of its own art, that "the truest poetry is the most feigning." The principle of self-reflection has proved to be of deep, wide, and delicate application, from the proper respect in which the art of Saul Steinberg is now held, to the profound rotation effected by Walter Jackson Bate's comprehension of the burden of the past and the English poet. But the principle, like all others, has always been tempted to escalate its claims, to make itself the one thing necessary, as if art's own nature were the only thing with which art were ever occupied. Then a proper self-attention becomes solipsism and self-regard, and poems are held to have no other subject than their own poemness.

Few things are more important in literary criticism just now than to protect the newly restored insights into the worth of disciplined self-reflection against its foes: those who have never had the imagination to see how much self-reflection could honorably effect, and those who have never had the imagination to see how little it can honorably effect unless it be continually braced—as by the thrust of an opposing arch—against an equal respect for all the ways in which the reflection of something other than self (other than art itself) is indispensable.

When the back-up women, early in Bob Dylan's song "New Pony," ask eerily "How much longer?" and then repeatedly ask it, without its apparently having any direct connection with the drama in the song, there is a crucial sense in which the question is a question about the song itself. A great many of Dylan's best songs (it is part of their comedy, rueful or ravaging) are, in part, about how and when they are ever going to manage to end. "How much longer?" But it would demean the song to make it sound as if the question within the song were only, or even mainly, about the song itself. A friend of mine has shown me how various—some sad, some funny—are the tacit applications of "How much longer?" to the amatory goings-on which are the song's impulse and substance. "New Pony": but "How much longer?"

In a similar way, it does, I believe, need to be noticed that one of the feats of Dylan's rhyming is its self-reflection, as when he rhymes on the word "rhyme" ("Crickets talking back and forth in rhyme," against "time," for instance, an exquisite stridulation), or as when he sings:

> The highway is for gamblers, better use your sense.
> Take what you have gathered from coincidence.

One of the things which you should gather from this is that the rhyme, like any rhyme, is a gamble, a coincidence of sound and sense, igniting a new sense through its new sound-chime. Yet it would sell Dylan short if one were to make this the only or the ruling sense of the lines, the thing not to be missed. Self-reflection is a good partner, but it is not good enough to be any art's master.

Forms of Talk (which, not incidentally, has many good asides about singing) is everywhere apt to this double duty toward self-reflection, this double defense. It repeatedly illuminates reflective moves in talk, and it has recourse throughout to the inescapable prefix, in references to self-reference, self-correction, self-responding, self-talk (a whole essay), self-congratulation, self-management, self-disassociation, self-reporting, self-direction, self-monitoring, self-concern, self-centering, self-orientation, self-consciousness, self-communication, and even self-abuse.

But it is not just that Goffman is so variously acute about the ways in which talkers refer to themselves; he is endlessly fertile about the vistas of regression and about the ways in which an utterance (not just the utterer) may be in part self-referring. After all, his witticism "the ways of our errors" depends upon our momentarily blinking at what might itself be an error. So here is Goffman lecturing on "The Lecture"; and writing, often in brackets, on such things as "the parenthesizing parenthesis"; on how we manage to talk about the management of talk itself; on the ways in which a remedial utterance (an apology, say) may itself then become something that needs to be remedied; on the way in which the introducer of a lecturer is himself introduced; or on the regressions that threaten the central principles of the social world, so that tact can itself become tact-lessness, or consideration inconsiderate. (*National Lampoon*'s greatest creation is the lethally decorous Politenessman.)

Who but Goffman could so do right by *Oopsadaisy*?

> When a parent plucks up a toddler and rapidly shifts it from one point to another or "playfully" swings or tosses it in the air, the prime mover may utter an *Oopsadaisy!*, stretched out to cover the child's period of ground-lessness, counteracting its feeling of being out of control, and at the same time instructing the child in the terminology and role of spill cries.

"At the same time": Goffman does not elevate self-reflection into what is really at stake, but he does give it such a part as it plays.

"Every conversation, it seems, can raise itself by its own bootstraps." So Goffman is drawn not just to frames, but to frames of frames.

Let me take what I have gathered from coincidence, and point out that he who is here so good on the way in which a lecturer uses text-parenthetical remarks (momentaneous qualifications or additions) so as to become "a broker of his own statements" and "his own go-between," or on the way in which an announcer serves as "his own straight man"— he, Erving Goffman, is here his own general editor. Or rather, he is one of his two general editors, which constitutes a proper arch. Like the announcer, he values, and not just as maneuver, "a dual voice, commenting on one's own production even while producing it." This, without reducing the utterance to solipsism or infinitely pointless regress. For even while Goffman tacitly corroborates the plausibility and the value of literature's being to some degree self-reflective or self-referential by his showing how much of daily talk is valuably so, he also explicitly honors the necessity for maintaining the relation between the substantive and the self-referential or self-reflective. He is severe only in his warnings, which are in part self-warnings:

> I am not trying to wriggle out of my contract with you by using my situation at the podium to talk about something ready to hand, my situation at the podium. To do so would be to occupy a status for purposes other than fulfilling it. Of that sort of puerile opportunism we have had quite enough, whether from classroom practitioners of group dynamics, the left wing of ethnomethodology, or the John Cage school of performance rip-offs.

Goffman fears for "the vulnerability of the line between the process of referring and the subject matter that is referred to." The vulnerable line is our lifeline.

> If, because of what I refer to, you attend the process through which I make references, then something is jeopardized that is structurally crucial in speech events: the partition between the inside and outside of words, between the realm of being sustained through the meaning of a discourse and the mechanics of discoursing. This partition, this membrane, this boundary, is the tickler; what happens to it largely determines the pleasure and displeasure that will be had in the occasion.

The wisdom and madness, as well as the pleasure and displeasure. For we may change the first ideal in the Victorian trinity from self-reverence to self-reference, only if we more than maintain the other two: self-reference, self-knowledge, self-control.

And, of course, there would be much to say, thanks to Goffman, about Goffman's unremitting propensity to begin sentences, and even paragraphs, with "And, of course."

Jennifer Platt
Realities of Social Research: An Empirical Study
of British Sociologists

I t was more than a joke when T. S. Eliot said, thirty-three years ago, "Already we need another science, the science of the Behaviour of Sociologists". Now that the sociology of sociology is afoot, there will be no end of beckoning vistas: even to review such a book as Jennifer Platt's *Realities of Social Research* is to engage, if that is the word, in the sociology of the sociology of sociology. Our echoes roll from soul to soul, and grow for ever and for ever; or, little fleas have meta-fleas upon their backs to bug them.

"A detailed empirical investigation of the nature of the process of doing social research, its causes and its consequences": since Mrs Platt decided to divorce such doing from all consideration of what was done— all consideration of the value, interest, insight, or human consequence of the actual research projects—this investigation is, in its evocation of any life of the mind, altogether abstract, the triumph of meta over mind. Yet it is not humanly abstract; for although the social contingencies, those of the world of sociology and of the great world, are at no point to be seen bearing upon any activities of mind, they certainly are felt to bear upon, bear down upon the suffering sociologists. Bent upon 121 such individ-

Times Literary Supplement (20 February 1976)

uals who were bent upon fifty-five projects, Mrs Platt, with corrugated concern, appraises the pressures of research grants and timetables; of university organization (and "university-based invisible colleges", whatever they may be); of non-university settings; of team organization; of research careers and career structure; of private lives upon the projects, and of the projects upon private lives. Mrs Platt believes that the story is mostly a grim one; so do I, but for different reasons.

T. S. Eliot explained himself:

> Already we need another science, the science of the Behaviour of Sociologists. I mean that the moment the sociologist ceases to confine himself to description within his own terms, and to offering dispassionate predictions of the results of two or more alternative procedures, the moment he betrays any emotional interest in what has happened or in what will happen, elements too personal to be part of the "science" come into play: they appear to us, when we disagree, as *prejudice*, and when we agree, as *wisdom*.

Not, of course, that Mrs Platt is unaware of the problems raised by the personal; she is careful to footnote some things as subjectivities, and she offers professional grounds for defining success, in triplicate, as completing the research, completing it on time, and getting it published, thereby not concerning herself at all with the actual worth or substance of the sociological processes which are here processed. Her judgment is that the point of any other procedure could only have been "to judge the intellectual success of the works, in order to relate this to the manner in which they had been done, and to devise an acceptable criterion of success that represented more than personal judgment would be a task of enormous difficulty". ("More than personal judgment" would, within a different conception of the nature of judgment and of the personal, be thought to mean "less than personal judgment".) And again, Mrs Platt is aware that prejudice or bias is a crucial matter for sociology. But being aware, and even conscientious, is not the same as being vigilant, and *Realities of Social Research* strikes me as fraught with biases, some incidental and some at the heart of its enterprise.

To start with smallish things: though there may be some benefits to be gained from confident quantification, and sociology must by its nature make the most of them, what but an inapposite professional bias could retail without irony such quantification as this?

> One well-known methods textbook has an appendix on "Estimating the Time and Personnel Needed for a Study", which says: "It appears to be an almost universal rule that every operation takes longer than one would anticipate if everything went smoothly", and goes on to suggest as a rule of thumb that 50% or more should be added to initial estimates to allow for contingencies. (B. Selltiz et al., *Research Methods in Social Relations*, Revised One-Volume Edition, Methuen, 1971, p. 503, Appendix A.)

It is a short step (two pages) from this to conceiving of information as a grand total of tiny tottings: "One project managed to collect 250 items of information on each of 15,000 cases!" Perhaps it was a Joycean subconscious which created the footnote which refers to a book called *The Summetrical Family*.

Then there is the case of the gander's sauce. Mrs Platt, though judicious about it, is alert to the possibility of "sex discrimination", which gathers ground later as "sexist discrimination". But is she alert to the implication of speaking as she does about the preservation of anonymity by name-changing? "On several occasions I had to decide not to change a male to a female because, had I done so, the behaviour reported might have been construed as typically feminine, and therefore explicable by the sex of the person." The implication is that there is no such thing as the construing of behaviour as typically masculine; and what could be more casually sexist than to assume that one sex continually finds itself typed and the other never does?

Again, the whole question of anonymity shows the sociologist as willing to extend to herself (or himself) a charity or consideration which is denied to those to whom she is cool. By various complicated stratagems and withholdings, Mrs Platt conceals the identity of her subjects; she gives good grounds for doing so (for instance, "that immediate colleagues might be able to identify each other, and thus learn things that they would not have said to each others' faces") but these are exactly the grounds which would be given by—but not received from—those subjects of her sociologists' researches whom she finds too touchy about confidentiality and anonymity. The animus which underlies a remark like "there was great anxiety that no individual or organization should be identifiable in the report" becomes open in a sentence like this:

> This means that pre-censorship has to be exercised to avert possible objections, even if the research procedure might seem quite innocuous to any professionally competent person; consequently certain questions are not asked, exceptional emphasis is laid on the preservation of confidentiality and anonymity, and so on.

But why should we accept, without any description whatsoever of the substantive nature of such researches, that what is for Mrs Platt the right way for her to proceed (total anonymity for all who wish it) is somehow "exceptional" and unjustified when the wishes of the sociologized happen to be at odds with those of the sociologists?

A similar indiscriminate discrimination is at work when it is a matter of the receiving end of the word "objective". Like her fellow sociologists, Mrs Platt is at ease with the word when it issues from sociological lips. "We did this report quite objectively", says a sociologist in protest against his work's having been subverted; and Mrs Platt has no qualms about the word when it is hers ("an objective lack of career opportunities"). But if a client or a sponsor uses the word, it is at once suspect, and indeed is liable to find itself disdainfully held up between antiseptic quotation-marks. "It is striking how often it was reported that when there was an objection to the content of a research report it took the form of a demand for greater 'objectivity'". "The pressures for 'objectivity' normally seem to imply simply leaving out all the sociology and publishing nothing but a list of facts." The point is not that the word never masquerades for rhetorical purposes, but whether non-sociologists have a monopoly of the masquerading. Without our being given any specific details, why should we agree to think ill of those impugned? I am objective; they are "objective", or—even worse—"they wished to appear objective". And as to facts, can Mrs Platt really believe that the nature of integrity is such that all it needs for its maintenance is the right standard policy? "One established unit had a standard policy on this that enabled it to maintain its integrity." Any objection from a sponsor on the lines of "You can't publish that" was met with this: "our standard phrase is 'is it in any way erroneous in fact? If so, would you please specify'." But one does not have to be sentimental about sponsorship and censorship to be aware that there are a great many misrepresentations and distortions, legitimately to be protested against, which could not possibly crystallize out as "erroneous in fact". After all, Mrs Platt would presumably not feel that a reviewer of her book could be sure of having maintained his integrity provided he made no errors of fact. But once again the assumption is that the only threats to sociologists' integrity come from outside; what might often be a reasonable procedure (though not reasonably "a standard policy"), in the face of improper pressures from sponsors, will constitute the opposite of a resistance to the improper pressures from within. All such pressures should be pondered at the same sitting. Sociologists are not exempt from the fate of human beings: to have a duty, not only not to be at the mercy of other men's opinions, but also not to be at the mercy of their own. A questionnaire could do worse than begin with the question "Quis custodiet ipsos custodes?"

Anyone who supposes that in the intellectual warfare of sociology there are only Four Columns might like to study Mrs Platt's rather serene account of how Denis and his senior were at odds. "Denis was of left-wing views, and the research findings seemed to run counter to left-wing beliefs." Seemed? If they had only seemed, Denis would not have found them incredible. But then this particular *party pris* is now so familiar as to be tedious and not worth attending to, apparently.

> "It will surprise nobody that all the political views mentioned were left wing; the reasons for this have been discussed by various writers and will not be pursued here."

What will, however, surprise some people is that sociologists are so surprisedly indignant at any principled distrust of sociology. Mrs Platt levels her level tones:

> Two headmasters objected to sociometric tests on semi-ethical grounds. In one case it was proposed to do them on the children, and the objection was that
>
>> " . . . I was a bloody fascist, they were spending all this time teaching the children the Christian virtues of love thy neighbour, etc";
>
> in the other case it was proposed to do them on the teachers and the head turned it down because he said he knew the staff would object,
>
>> "because it involved one member of the staff rating another, because there were questions not just about liking but about things like who would you go to for advice and therefore it would be treated as a breach of professional ethics".
>
> (My impression is that school-teachers in general are peculiarly sensitive subjects of social research; the reasons might repay investigation.)

This seems to me a succession of ways of being blank. We are by mere say-so to believe, first, that the objection did not amount to the ethical. Secondly, to believe that the objection to these (altogether unspecified) "sociometric tests" on the children could reasonably be paraphrased, or paraphrased without demur, as "I was a bloody fascist . . .". Thirdly, to believe that the point about "professional ethics" (the tests again being in no way described to us) can legitimately usher in the lethal mildness of that parenthesis. Perhaps schoolteachers are "peculiarly sensitive" in this matter (I hope so), but any such "investigation" is not likely to be of their reasons or principles, judging from the quoted outburst from the sociologist who found himself resisted; no, an investigation will be likely to seek only such "reasons" as "repay investigation" in the only coin current for the sociologist: sociopathology.

The *Realities of Social Research* are grim ones. For no pondering of this book should let itself forget the first impression made by the innumerable quoted interviews: an impression of a world empty of intellectual passion and filled with shrill aggrieved brutality. That sociologists should speak as sociologists write was to be expected, though even so one might have flinched from offering as parody some of the things said here.

> "The first year post-graduate being exposed to book-learning and the library aspect."

> "It had a good effect on teaching, a good effect on my syllabus creativity."

> "These sort of career considerations mitigate against proper team research because if your lords and masters say 'you've got to collect your own data' it's going to make chaps cagey about sharing ideas in the team situation."

> "In career terms it made my career. . . . The book had got me into the publications racket straight away. From the moment it was published I was never short of invitations to publish."

> "I got some sort of social work kick out of interviewing them, because I used to interview them, some of them, in very open-ended cathartic interviews."

Pride's purge?

Yet threatening as these burly cynicisms and rapacities are, they are less lastingly dispiriting than is the central fact about the book: that it is an unwearying litany of vengeful grievance and aggrievedness. Not since Satan's day has there been so obdurate a sense of injured merit. The word grievance comes again and again and again; and so do disillusion, complaint, resentment, disappointment, dissatisfaction, conflict, and (the professional jargon hugged in self-pity) alienation. Grievance is the droning note, whether it be aimed at fund-givers, at seniors or at juniors, at those who try to work alongside sociologists and at those who don't, at those who sponsor research and at those who don't. But let grievance speak for itself.

> "That is the major reason why none of this damn stuff has yet seen the light of day. . . . I cannot do it in term, it is absolutely unthinkable,

we have the worst staff/student ratio in the faculty, we're teaching like buggeree and all these other commitments. . . ."

"She was so bloody seldom there."

"And at the same time be expected to do one hundred percent teaching."

"If I wanted to do a paper on the research no-one was interested, but if they did a paper on explanation and we said something about somebody it had to go towards the whole philosophical thing."

"The point was that after that the key bastard of [the group] would then talk to me."

"My role had been totally usurped. Karen, Liz and Mary would always go to him if they disagreed, and the case was put in such a way that I sounded unreasonable."

"I'm extremely alienated; I just want to do research I like rather than what I'm paid to do."

"My consciousness was not raised. I think they treated me very badly . . . because I was a woman."

"[The director] got quite a lot of teaching and I didn't get any, though I'd done quite a lot in India and then I wasn't treated as suitable for teaching."

"In fact it was blackmail: he was my supervisor and if I didn't do the book, he could block it."

"If you phoned Vic at ten past five you couldn't get him; his commitment to the project was reflected in temporal restrictions on when he would work."

Only occasionally is such grinding grievance lightened by something that really does seem, even for a sociologist, a bit on the eager-for-grievance side: "On top of that he had to do observation in the evening, sometimes involving heavy drinking".

Yet why should one be surprised that the sociology of sociology lays bare so much grievance? For sociology itself is always in danger of becoming mere grievance-mongering. Such is the central unrecognized import of this bleakly important book. You can trace it in the earliest shaping of the enterprise itself, as when Mrs Platt's letter-statement to her respondents finds it necessary to say, with exclamatory protestation,

"This does not mean, however, that I am not interested in model projects in which everything went by the book!". It is there in the sociologist's conception of what is interesting and of what a fellow sociologist's interests are likely to be:

> There probably is some bias towards projects regarded as "interesting", especially in the sense of having suffered mishaps of various kinds, because other people tended to define my interests in this way and hence tell me about the existence of such projects more than others.

The eliciting, or provoking, of a sense of grievance is clear in the questions which open-ended closed-minded interviews thrive on: "Did anyone feel that this was a grievance that they couldn't get a higher degree out of it?" "Did you find that you couldn't have any private life?" "Did the research give you any domestic problems?" So that it becomes a natural part of such a study that it should itself then feel faintly aggrieved when anybody suspected it of grievance garnering:

> Sometimes on this sort of project there were undertones of hostility in the interview, because I seemed to be suggesting that there must have been conflicts and disasters where there had been none. I did not want to do this, yet nor did I want to make it too easy to paper over the cracks if there had been any.

For it is the glissade which is the professional hazard. The blurb may speak of "the constraints to which research projects are subject" and of "factors which will affect" research; the first page may speak of "social contingencies"; but the conduct of such an inquiry more and more comes to think of, and speak of, such pressures as inherently malign, or inherently more likely to be malign than benign. So constraints become, not ever the valued resistance which alone can make possible true freedom or true creativity, but always a hindrance, an infringement, a curtailment. As in the notion (chimerical in quite a different sense from that intended) of "a hypothetical ideal world in which the course of research is influenced only by the perceived intellectual demands of the topic, and there are no external constraints".

The realities of social research are what such social researchers conceive the realities of society to be: that society can only deform, and that the most important thing about a human being is his being a victim. It is not surprising, then, that the sociology of sociology embodies, though it does not diagnose, an addiction to victimization and to grudges. If injustice did not exist, it would be necessary to invent it. "His colleagues perceived him as having been sacked by the steering committee, and were not pleased with this; his own account of the matter was that he had freely chosen to leave to take up a place on an MA course!" Yet how characteristic that the sociologist feels impelled to continue: "At any rate, he left, and another research assistant had to be found to replace him." At any rate?

In the end Mrs Platt does show a mild alarm. "This book as a whole, and this chapter in particular, may seem to lay too much emphasis on the things that can go wrong in research." But sociology, unless in the service of a rare magnanimity of mind (Erving Goffman has it) such as would suppose neither that sociology alone is incapable of being a victimizing force nor that society is capable of being nothing but a victimizing force, will always be tempted to lay too much emphasis on the things that can go wrong. "In the current state of the field it is legitimate and appropriate to pay more attention to the things that go wrong than to the things that go right." But the sociologist will be likely to confront in that spirit not just his field but the field full of folk. "This unhappy atmosphere of negative learning" is not just something about British sociology in the 1960s, as the closing pages wistfully trust. Human nature and professional proclivity gratify each other; of her respondents' responding, Mrs Platt suggests that "Motives not peculiar to social scientists, such as pleasure in talking about oneself, the wish not to appear to have anything to hide, and the gratification of recounting one's grievances, no doubt also contributed". Not peculiar to social scientists, no, but there is for the sociologist a peculiar professional thrust in the gratification of recounting, and counting, and counting on, one's own and others' grievances. The enduringly painful thought is that, here as in so much else, sociology is in impoverishing collusion with the ideology which it supposes itself to be resisting. T. S. Eliot mixed wisdom and prejudice more profoundly:

> In the Puritan morality that I remember, it was tacitly assumed that if one was thrifty, enterprising, intelligent, practical and prudent in not violating social conventions, one ought to have a happy and "successful" life. Failure was due to some weakness or perversity peculiar to the individual; but the decent man need have no nightmares. It is now rather more common to assume that all individual misery is the fault of "society"; and is remediable by alterations from without. Fundamentally, the two philosophies, however different they may appear in operation, are the same. It seems to me that all of us, so far as we attach ourselves to created objects and surrender our wills to temporal ends, are eaten by the same worm.

Stanley Milgram
Obedience to Authority

'Persons Needed for a Study of Memory', said the advertisement in the local paper. And then (you may remember) the volunteers for Professor Stanley Milgram's experiment at Yale University found themselves being told to give electric shocks of increasing intensity to a man—strapped in an electric chair—whenever he made a mistake in pairing words. (But the 'victim' was an actor, and the experiment was at work, not on the shockee, but on the shocker.) To his dismay as a human being and to his gusto as a psychologist, Professor Milgram found that a hideously high proportion of the subjects would indeed do just as they were told; would give what they believed—after themselves being given a 'sample' but genuine shock—to be increasingly painful shocks; would ignore the implications of the markings on the shock generator (including Danger: Severe Shock); would even ignore the victim's shrieks, his plea to be let out and released from the experiment, and even his agonised cries reminding them that he had—in their hearing—agreed to take part only if he would be free to quit. And (last twist) he had said he had a heart condition. Yet despite all this, very few of the subjects could bring themselves to disobey the authority in the laboratory.

The experiment and the book, *Obedience to Authority*, are fascinating, and Professor Milgram understands the rigours of his game. Did it

the new review (September 1974)

make a difference that it was all being done in a handsome laboratory at Yale? Well, try a primitive laboratory there, and then try an office-suite downtown with no letter-head other than the concocted 'Research Associates of Bridgeport', a private firm conducting research for industry. Did it make a difference if the subject was a man or a woman? (The victim was always a man. Squeamish, Milgram?) Or how near the victim was, and how much of his pain could be seen and heard? And so on. Milgram's methodology is not only cogent but—in its grisly way—imaginative. His findings are dismaying. But so are his seekings.

> God said to Abraham 'Kill me a son'
> Abe said 'Man, you must be putting me on . . .'

'The dilemma inherent in obedience to authority is ancient, as old as the story of Abraham.' But *Obedience to Authority* refuses to acknowledge the dilemma inherent in its own obedience to authority, in this case the authority of experimental psychology as a discipline, an ethos, and an ideology.

To anyone who is not an experimental psychologist, there is something morally equivocal—and often unequivocally immoral—about a discipline built upon systematic deception. Like most of the famous experiments (Milgram mentions Asch's in 1951, where the answers of five accomplices coerce the sixth person, the 'naive subject', into saying that one line matches another when it manifestly doesn't), Milgram's exploits a multiplicity of deceptions; not just the basic set-up or frame-up, of simulated shocks and screams, but the rigged drawing of lots, faked 'phone-calls and absences, and the deception-within-deception of the genuine 'sample shock' (it was genuine, and so wasn't a sample). I shall read two works which Milgram cites: Herbert Kelman's 'Human Use on Human Subjects: The Problem of Deception in Social Psychological Experiments', and Jay Katz's *Experimentation with Human Beings*; but if Milgram's notion of ethics is anything to go by, I fear that all that would be made clear would be that psychologists are very *aware of the problem.* They are unlikely to act upon their awareness, since by now it is too late: their methods and modes are what they are. Milgram's Appendix on 'Problems of Ethics in Research' shows that an anxious professional awareness is perfectly compatible with a deep obliviousness to what the fuss is all about.

Then again, to an outsider it must seem that experimental psychology is unique not just because of its fishiness and duplicity but because it is digging a pit and its heirs will fall into the midst of it. For where, in a few years' time, will they find the needed supply of 'naive subjects'? Already naive subjects are not easy to come by. Milgram couldn't use the usual Yalees: 'The possibility that students from Yale would have heard of it from fellow students who had already participated in it seemed too great a risk.' Search-parties, search-committees, Naive-Subject Gatherers? Volunteers for such experiments must be sympathetic to such experimentation and so are likely to know at least something about the ways of psychologists—yet they mustn't know enough to have reached the wise stage of not believing a word that their experimenter says. There is something eerie about a discipline which so resolutely damages the possibilities for its own successors. Naive subjects go down, not like nine-pins to be set up again, but like virgin forests, and the discipline will reap its dust-bowl.

Milgram's Appendix on 'Problems of Ethics in Research' acknowledges that 'for some critics, the chief horror of the experiment was not that the subjects obeyed but that the experiment was carried out at all'. But his replies to Diana Baumrind and to Dannie Abse, reprinted there, are a great deal less cogent than the experimentation had been.

What about the welfare of the subjects, and what they went through? Milgram first deals with this by playing down their suffering and strain all the while they believed the whole thing was real, the shocks, the screams, the tug within themselves. The Appendix speaks mildly of 'stress': 'But momentary excitement is not the same as harm. As the experiment progressed there was no indication of injurious effects in the subjects.' No, but nor is harm the same as indignity or suffering;

the subjects could have suffered a great deal (and did, I think) without this meaning that they were perceptibly harmed. The blandness of the Appendix's way of putting things is at odds with the book itself, while the line about 'no injurious effects' is grimly akin to the chilling reassurance peddled by the experimenter to the subjects about the victim: 'Although the shocks can be extremely painful, they cause no permanent tissue damage'. Do the words 'momentary excitement' convey what is conveyed by the book's own words?

> Subjects were frequently in an agitated state . . .
>
> [As soon as the giving of shocks ended, many] heaved sighs of relief, mopped their brows, rubbed their fingers over their eyes, or nervously fumbled cigarettes. Some shook their heads, apparently in regret . . .
>
> There were in some subjects striking reactions of emotional strain . . .
>
> Normal subjects do not tremble and sweat unless they are implicated in a deep and genuinely felt predicament . . .
>
> [The subject] witnessed a harrowing scene in which the aggressive coparticipant single-mindedly pursued his plan of increasing the shock step by step . . .
>
> One can sense their intense inner struggle . . .
>
> Trembling, anxious laughter . . .
>
> The cries of pain issuing from the learner strongly affected many participants, whose reaction to them is immediate, visceral, and spontaneous.

Yet momentary excitement, Milgram says—and Milgram is an honourable man—'is not the same as harm'. And is what an ordinary person feels the same as 'momentary excitement', when he is doing as he is told and giving electric shocks with this scenario?

The Learner's Schedule of Protests

75 volts	Ugh!
90 volts	Ugh!
105 volts	Ugh! (*louder*)
120 volts	Ugh! Hey, *this* really hurts.
135 volts	Ugh!!

150 volts   Ugh!!! Experimenter! That's all. Get me out of here. I told you I had heart trouble. My heart's starting to bother me now. Get me out of here, please. My heart's starting to bother me. I refuse to go on. Let me out.

165 volts   Ugh! Let me out! (*shouting*)

180 volts   Ugh! I can't stand the pain. Let me out of here! (*shouting*)

195 volts   Ugh! Let me out of here. Let me out of here. My heart's bothering me. Let me out of here! You have no right to keep me here! Let me out! Let me out of here! Let me out! Let me out of here! My heart's bothering me. Let me out! Let me out!

210 volts   Ugh!! Experimenter! *Get* me out of here. I've had enough. I won't be in the experiment any more.

225 volts   Ugh!

240 volts   Ugh!

255 volts   Ugh! Get me *out* of here.

270 volts   (*Agonized scream.*) Let me out of here. Let me out of here. Let me out of here. Let me out. Do you hear? Let me out of here.

285 volts   (*Agonized scream.*)

300 volts   (*Agonized scream.*) I absolutely refuse to answer any more. Get me out of here. You can't hold me here. Get me out. Get me out of here.

315 volts   (*Intensely agonized scream.*) *I told you I refuse to answer.* I'm no longer part of this experiment.

330 volts   (*Intense and prolonged agonized scream.*) Let me out of here. Let me out of here. My heart's bothering me. Let me out, I tell you. (*Hysterically*) Let me out of here. Let me out of here. You have no right to hold me here. Let me out! Let me out! Let me out! Let me out of here! Let me out! Let me out!

Momentary excitement while *inflicting* that? The subjects say otherwise. 'I'm shaking, I'm shaking.' 'I was going through hell.' But the subjects' suffering is observed by the experimenter with a greater imperturbability than the victim's suffering is observed by the subjects. No wonder Milgram wants to diminish this into momentary excitement:

SUBJECT (*spontaneously*): Surely you've considered the ethics of this thing. (extremely agitated): Here he doesn't want to go on, and you think that the experiment is more important? Have you examined him? Do you know what his physical state is? Say this man had a weak heart (quivering voice).

EXPERIMENTER: We know the machine, sir.

SUBJECT: But you don't know the man you're experimenting on . . . That's very risky (gulping and tremulous). What about the fear that man had? It's impossible for you to determine what effect that has on him . . . the fear that he himself is generating.

Milgram's first self-exculpation, then—to speak in mild words of what his subjects went through—won't wash. Another is this:

An impartial medical examiner, experienced in out-patient treatment, interviewed 40 experimental subjects. The examining psychiatrist focused on those subjects he felt would be most likely to have suffered consequences from participation. His aim was to identify possibly injurious effects resulting from the experiment. He concluded that, although extreme stress had been experienced by several subjects, 'none was found by this interviewer to show signs of having been harmed by his experience . . . No evidence was found of any traumatic reactions.'

But even if one had complete trust in this impartial psychiatrist (who impartially chose him as impartial?) one could still say that what is at issue is not simply a matter of injurious or traumatic *effects*, not simply a matter of whether they *suffered consequences*, but of whether they suffered.

But Milgram is confident that he can clinch that one. As far as he is concerned, the only test of whether the experiment was justified is whether or not the subjects subsequently thought so.

84% of the subjects stated they were glad to have been in the experiment; 15% indicated neutral feelings; and 1.3% indicated negative feelings. These procedures [misinformation and illusion] are justified for one reason only: they are, in the end, accepted and endorsed by those who are exposed to them.

The central moral justification for allowing a procedure of the sort used in my experiment is that it is judged acceptable by those who have taken part in it. The participant, rather than the external critic, must be the ultimate source of judgment.

But though such a later judgment by the subjects is obviously relevant to judging the ethics of the whole thing, it cannot—without a terrible dereliction of responsibility—be allowed to constitute the sole criterion. Milgram proffers a blustering analogy:

Imagine an experiment in which a person's little finger was routinely snipped off in the course of a laboratory hour. Not only is such an experiment reprehensible, but within hours the study would be brought to a halt as outraged participants pressed their complaints on the university administration, and legal measures were invoked to restrain the experimenter. When a person has been abused, he knows it.

But perhaps he doesn't; finger-snipping would be a very different kind of painful indignity from that which the subjects suffered. The indignities of Milgram's experiment are much more like those which rigged TV quizzes and interrogations inflict upon their willing subjects. But Milgram's are the more harrowing and the more deceit-ridden.

Yet at this point the weakness of Milgram's reply is truly illuminating. Suddenly the conditions which had hitherto been so appallingly coercive—the conditions of laboratory authority, and of 'the mystique of science of which the experiment is a part'—have evaporated. Milgram, who has previously been acutely sensitive to these pressures and infringements of individual liberty of mind, suddenly and conveniently forgets that there are any such things. Why isn't it the case that the subjects who had earlier so placatingly gone along with the authority of science when it told them to give electric shocks are now—with equal and adaptive facility—going placatingly along with the authority of science when it wants them to approve of this truth-seeking scientific experiment of which they had been the unwitting subjects? It can hardly be pretended that during and after the 'debriefing' the subjects were in any doubt as to whether the authority of science would now like them to like the experiment which had been lavished on them. It would make sense to make the subjects the judges of the ethics of the experiment only if they could be credited with unintimidated independence of mind and with imperviousness to the mystique of science. But what the whole book shows is that these very people found this mystique and authority irresistible, and why should they suddenly be credited with the power to resist, just because the faked part of the experiment is over? Indeed, Milgram is caught in a fatal contradiction here, since he claims that a crucial piece of evidence against any suggestion that the experiment might have harmed them is their undamaged resumption of their old ways:

> What they [conversations after 'debriefing'] showed most was how readily the experience is assimilated to the normal frame of things.
> The same mechanisms that allow the subject to perform the act, to obey rather than to defy the experimenter, transcend the moment of performance and continue to justify his behavior for him. The same viewpoint the subject takes while performing the actions is the viewpoint from which he later sees his behavior, that is, the perspective of 'carrying out the task assigned by the person in authority.'

Yet Milgram's self-defence entails attributing to these people an unprecedented ability to 'defy the experimenter', since—now, after debriefing—the experimenter is necessarily asking for their approval of what was done to them. Once what is chillingly called the dehoax has taken place, what form is now taken by the notion of 'carrying out the task assigned by the person in authority'? Patently, justifying the experiment as a contribution to science and as humanly decent. The subject kowtows to the professor no less now than he had done before. (The very wording suggests the therapeutic victories which are epistolarily announced in newspaper advertisements: 'With sincere thanks for your contribution to my life . . .'.) 'When the experiment was explained to subjects they responded to it positively, and most felt it was an hour well spent.' Well, they would, wouldn't they. 'The worst the obedient subject says of himself is that he must learn to resist authority more effectively in the future.' But the snag is precisely that the subject is saying this to an authority who wants him to say it; the saying of it therefore manifests no resistance to the immediately potent authority, since this is an authority (as has by then been made clear to him) which wants him to resist authority. Milgram is obliged to exempt his own ideology, ethos and auspices from pressure-putting; but when he both exults in the subjects' concurrence with him about the experiment *and* praises their newly won powers of resistance to the likes of him, he is forgetting the truth which he himself presses in the case of My Lai: 'The respondents to Kelman's question did not reside completely outside the authority system they were asked to comment upon but had already been influenced by it.' Those words are apt to Milgram's dehoaxed subjects, one of whom mouthed the metallic cliché: 'If this experiment serves to jar people out of complacency, it will have served its end'. But the terrifying complacency of experimental psychology? Does that get jarred?

What the subjects were put through in the real experiment, the meta-experiment, though it was less painful (but painful enough) than what the 'victim' was put through in the fake experiment, was more ignominious and demeaning. Like his subjects, Milgram is 'caught up in what seemed a mad situation . . . and in the interest of science one goes through with it'. Like the zealous subject: 'I'm one for science.' Isn't he, no less than his subjects, subjected to this dangerous responsibility-freezing authority-system?

> The psychological laboratory has a strong claim to legitimacy and evokes trust and confidence in those who come to perform there.
> The idea of science and its acceptance as a legitimate social enterprise provide the overarching ideological justification for the experiment.

Throughout *Obedience to Authority*, Milgram is naked to the same institutionally indurating pressures which he looses upon his subjects. Again and again, his words invite *tu quoque*, with Milgram stationed in relation to his subjects exactly as he stations the subjects in relation to the 'victim'.

> The real focus of the experiment is the teacher.
> Even the forces mustered in a psychology experiment will go a long way toward removing the individual from moral controls.
> The victim's suffering possesses an abstract, remote quality for the subject. 'It's funny how you really begin to forget that there's a guy out there, even though you can hear him. For a long time I just concentrated on pressing the switches and reading the words.'
> Conscience . . . is per force diminished at the point of entering a hierarchical structure.
> Ideological justification . . . permits the person to see his behavior as serving a desirable end.
> This investigation deals with . . . those who willingly comply because society gives them a role and they are motivated to live up to its requirements. The actions are almost always justified in terms of a set of constructive purposes, and come to be seen as noble in the light of some high ideological goal. In the experiment, science is served by the act of shocking the victim against his will.

That goes for the subject-victim too, and a pun on *shocking* is the nub.

Hoax, agonised screams, dehoax. A critic of Milgram had feared that 'participants will be alienated from psychological experiments'; the fact is grimmer: it hooked them. 'Many indicated a desire to be in further experimental research.' (This is known as meta-credulity.) 'A few days after his participation he wrote a long, careful letter to the staff, asking if he could work with us.'

So that for me the horror of the findings is not only where Milgram finds it (yes, it is there), but in the vision of man which such experimental psychology embodies, its sense of what is or is not a human way to treat human beings. And not just human beings. Perhaps the brutalising drive of it all is clearest in this glacially imperturbable footnote:

> Recently, I have learned that other experimenters (Sheridan and King, 1972) have replicated the obedience experiments but with this difference:

in place of a human victim, they used a genuine victim, a puppy, who actually received the electric shock and who yelped, howled, and ran when he was shocked. Men and women were used as subjects, and the authors found that the women were more compliant than the men. Indeed, they write: 'Without exception, female subjects complied with instructions to shock the puppy all the way to the end of the scale.' See also Kilham and Mann, 1972.

See also William Blake (1757–1827):

Each outcry of the hunted Hare
A fibre from the Brain does tear.

Norman Podhoretz
Making It

D isappointing, *Making It*. Norman Podhoretz celebrates himself in a puff-by-puff account of how he, a New York intellectual, slowly came to realise that power and money were not only enjoyable but good for the soul. The disappointment is that the American reviews had made it all sound unprecedentedly loathsome and egomaniacal, whereas *Making It* is nothing as interesting as that. A clumsy vanity doesn't come to much of a break-through, and Mr Podhoretz may even seem a bit flat to compatriots of Dr Rowse.

Before he was 30, Mr Podhoretz had become editor of the American Jewish monthly, *Commentary*. Founded in 1945, it had been a good journal for 15 years before Mr Podhoretz took over. Judging from his own anthology, *The Commentary Reader*, he didn't much improve it but he hasn't let it run down either. Able to call on Hannah Arendt and George Lichtheim, on Saul Bellow and Lionel Trilling, on Philip Rahv and Dwight Macdonald, *Commentary* represents something important and valuable in American life. But not anything as unique as Mr Podhoretz makes out—after all, there are few journals in America which have been unable to call on those names.

Still, Mr Podhoretz's point isn't so much that he and *Commentary* have both been successes, but that he needed first to be weaned from a

The Listener (29 August 1968)

pernicious and prevailing 'gospel of anti-success' which a liberal education in general and Columbia in particular had drugged him with. For
D. H. Lawrence, sex had become corrupted into the 'dirty little secret'
of pornography. For Mr Podhoretz, success has taken over as the dirty
little secret of American life (he even outdoes Lawrence in reiterating
the phrase). Envy and snobbery, an unjustified hauteur towards the
world of business, have created a furtive guilt about success. The corrupt ones are those who make out that power and the most expensive
steaks in the world might be bad for you.

Not only a success story, then, but the story of an education. Unfortunately the Education of Norman Podhoretz is not quite that of a
Henry Adams. He has soon travelled all over his own mind and heart,
and then neither his descriptions nor his arguments carry conviction.

What does he need to establish? That his success is remarkable, for a
start. But does a somebody (as he calls himself) write quite so humourless
a Diary of a Somebody? Mr Podhoretz has written interesting essays and
reviews, and he once assembled them as a piece of book-making-it. And
he edits a worth-while magazine. Big wheel, big deal. But no Englishman
would need to feel culturally disadvantaged because he had neither heard
of Mr Podhoretz nor was much aware of *Commentary*—and there are
even intelligent Americans for whom it all doesn't do much more than
ring a faint bell. From Mr Podhoretz's airs, anybody would think that we
were being told about the making it of the President.

Next he would have needed to establish that he genuinely possesses
those literary abilities and standards, that Columbia and Downing education. Otherwise his story would merely become another of those about
a man finding that he'd never really been anything but a power-and-
money man. He makes much of the concern for 'standards' which he
learned as a pupil of Dr Leavis. It would be interesting to know what Dr
Leavis thinks of a critic concerned for standards who can summarise the
stylistic ambitions of Saul Bellow *vis-à-vis* Henry James as: 'Saul Bellow
to Henry James: Up yours, buddy.' Or who can discuss his own literary
reputation with an irony which does not hold off Wall Street but win-
somely embraces it: 'After much active trading my stock had registered

an impressive gain.' (And so through 16 lines.) Dr Leavis is not the only one of Mr Podhoretz's heroes who might have preferred to figure as one of his villains: Mr Podhoretz's gratitude for Dr Leavis's 'indoctrination sessions, thinly disguised as tea parties' is of a piece with his gratitude to Dr Leavis for being a critic to whom critical error 'was a sin as cardinal as adultery, as foul as idolatry'. *Make Me an Offer*, wrote Wolf Mankowitz, another pupil of Dr Leavis's. Mr Mankowitz has as much success to point to as Mr Podhoretz, and at least he does not speak of 'standards'.

And then Mr Podhoretz would have needed to establish that his book was—as he claims—candid, frank. It is not. It reports private conversations, but in all the important ways it is uncourageous. Take the CIA. Now here really was a chance for Mr Podhoretz to show that he occasionally attended to conversations of which he was not the subject. Naturally, he feels obliged to mention the CIA, since otherwise we might doubt his inwardness. Irving Kristol is leaving *Commentary* for *Encounter*. Where does that leave 'the family' (this being Mr Podhoretz's salt-and-water name for the whole *Partisan Review/Commentary* crowd)? 'Very few members of the family who participated in the activities of the Congress for Cultural Freedom knew for certain, if at all, that it was being covertly supported by the CIA.' That 'if at all' hastily steps back from even the most general of tittle-tattle. Mr Podhoretz congratulates himself on having 'total recall', but in some areas the recall seems partial.

Nor are the private disclosures any more candid. The supposedly fearless part of the book is the account of how a previous editor of *Commentary* was a sadist and moreover didn't estimate Mr Podhoretz at his true worth. Not only is this editor a figment, made out of merging together two editors (and claiming that they somehow always acted as one man), but he is an unnamed figment. 'The Boss' stalks malignly through the pages, and Mr Podhoretz will be believed by those who on principle believe him. Mr Podhoretz names anybody who praises him, but he reduces those who criticise him to the unnamed and the uncheckable. 'A critic' once said something disparaging, and 'a well-known English critic' wrote a review of him which was insufficiently torrid. Not to worry, since people with—in both senses—names were rallying round. Far from the fearless rapture which it congratulates itself on, *Making It* is old-fashionedly committed to no names, no pack-drill. In the same spirit, Mr Podhoretz's failures are always abstract while his successes are always specific.

He says that his book is 'a frank, Mailer-like bid for literary distinction, fame and money all in one package'. But Mailer, whatever his faults, has astonishing creative powers, and Mr Podhoretz is a book reviewer. Mailer can look back on *The Naked and the Dead*; when Mr Podhoretz looks back, he comes up with: 'And this was how I became the first and possibly the only young literary man ever to be invited to write both for *Partisan Review* and the *New Yorker* in the course of a single week.' Mr Podhoretz, who thinks he knows the English, will not be surprised to hear them murmur 'My, my,' or 'Surprise, surprise.'

Mr Podhoretz's self-protective irony is odd, because he remarks in his preface that the trouble with America is that nobody will talk about success 'except in tones of irony'. His own ironies continually exaggerate both his own reaction and ours so that we will give him the benefit of a quizzical doubt. So money becomes The Big Money and even 'the call of Mammon'. Shocked people vent 'horrendous pieties'. 'My first brief safari into the wilds of New York literary society' may culminate in drunken retching, 'but my cup of regurgitable bourbon had not really run over.' The mature Podhoretz (who alludes at one point to *Great Expectations*) is looking back on the young Podhoretz with a wise and wrinkled smile—that young Podhoretz who actually believed in 'the "tragic sense of life" which, in common with all students of literature barely out of their diapers, I was certain I shared with Shakespeare'. Mr Podhoretz is not, as he imagines, a rogue elephant, but a roguish one. There is his penchant for inconsequential and unsolemn literary allusions, which are meant to be at once his literary credentials and his manly ribbing: 'to Downing I came, burning, burning.' St Augustine? T. S. Eliot? Don't be such a young prig, says our genial host, and smilingly recalls the time when the *New Yorker* dropped him: 'I had wild imaginings of people fleeing from me who sometime had me sought.'

And the larger concerns? That intellectual America has been in the grip of a cult of failure is merely asserted. (It certainly isn't what New York literary life, for example, looks like from over here.) Nor does Mr Podhoretz think at all about his claim that there is something peculiarly American about the two contradictory attitudes towards ambition or success. 'The two warring American attitudes toward the pursuit of success' seem the universal and unsurprising reflection of the fact that it won't do to despise the energies of ambition and it also won't do to forget the unscrupulousness of ambition. 'Those ancient American enemies, commerce and culture', are indeed ancient and are not especially American. Anyway Mr Podhoretz can't quite bring himself to make the full Panglossian claim, so he stops short at a question: 'Was it perhaps even possible that success had become a roughly accurate measure of intrinsic quality in the post-middlebrow world of American culture?' Hubert Humphrey would welcome such literary politics of joy.

I for one don't believe that the 'gospel of anti-success' yet has as many adherents as the other gospel of unscrupulous careerism. Nor do I believe that Mr Podhoretz—for all his talk of guilt and self-pity—has effected anything as self-searching as 'confessions' here. He has settled for something very different: owning up. Such a mixture of false manliness with vague self-accusation is pleading to be let off, slily aware that *qui s'accuse, s'excuse*. Nor do I believe that Mr Podhoretz was ever the utterly naive victim of otherworldliness which his scenario demands. Few people would seem to have been gifted with such an eye to the Main Street chance.

As to his literary success, many will be willing to accept his own extended comparison with Miss Susan Sontag, the 'unmistakable authority' of whose writings bears comparison, it seems, with his own work ('those early pieces of mine unquestionably had authority'). Anybody who wants an unfaked and shrewd analysis of 'the gospel of anti-success' ought to forget about *Making It* and instead remember Thom Gunn's 'Lines for a Book':

I think of all the toughs through history
And thank heaven they lived, continually.
I praise the overdogs from Alexander
To those who would not play with Stephen Spender.
Their pride exalted some, some overthrew,
But was not vanity at last . . .

George Steiner
In Bluebeard's Castle

These essays of George Steiner about modern culture and modern
barbarism were the T. S. Eliot Memorial Lectures, and their subtitle, "Some Notes Towards the Redefinition of Culture," alludes to
Eliot's *Notes towards the Definition of Culture* (1948). Or, in Mr. Steiner's
conscious prose, is "intended in memoration of Eliot's *Notes*." So I was
reminded of, and should like to memorate, some things that Eliot said
about I. A. Richards in 1927, which Steiner had no need to mention
but which are apt to his book. (It was to Richards and Mrs. Richards
that Steiner recently dedicated *Extraterritorial*.)

Eliot said of I. A. Richards that "there is a certain discrepancy between the size of his problems and the size of his solutions." That there is
"something almost comic about the way in which Mr. Richards can ask
an unanswerable question . . . and answer it with a ventriloquial voice
from a psychology laboratory situated in Cambridge." That Richards was
desperately hopeful:

> Poetry "is capable of saving us," he says; it is like saying that the wall-
> paper will save us when the walls have crumbled. It is a revised version of
> *Literature and Dogma.*

The New York Review of Books (18 November 1971)

Not long after 1927, the walls crumbled. Mr. Steiner's book, which is yet another revised version of Matthew Arnold's *Literature and Dogma*, seems to wish to show that liberal humanists were gullible not just in thinking that the wallpaper would save us but also in not realizing that the wallpaper itself was explosively mined; for in Steiner's view, culture, or liberal optimism about culture, is not only no protection against barbarism but even encourages it. Yet just as the bishop who wrote *Honest to God* did not think it necessary to cease drawing his stipend, so Mr. Steiner shows no sign of wishing to dissociate himself other than notionally from that world of liberal culture—of lectures, universities, indeed university presses—which he claims to be by its very nature not only no bulwark against barbarism but an active encourager of it. I do not myself find much (and Mr. Steiner might find less) in Eliot's metaphor of wallpaper and walls, but such a metaphor does suggest that the one thing more absurd than trusting that the wallpaper will hold up the walls is the suspicion that the wallpaper knocked them down.

Steiner's book includes four lectures. "The Great Ennui" claims that "certain specific origins of the inhuman, of the crises of our own time that compel a redefinition of culture, are to be found in the long peace of the nineteenth century." (Mr. Steiner is fond of "certain specific," because it is not very specific.) The argument is that the French Revolution produced deep changes in the quality of hope, and that the subsequent disillusionment ("What was a gifted man to do after Napoleon?" asks Mr. Steiner, and does not stay for an answer) left "a reservoir of unused, turbulent energies" and so created a "nostalgia for disaster."

"A Season in Hell" claims that the death camps were the outcome of "the blackmail of perfection" which the Jews three times visited upon Western life: the intolerable idealisms of, first, monotheism; then Christian adjuration; then messianic socialism. "When it turned on the Jew, Christianity and European civilization turned on the incarnation—albeit an incarnation often wayward and unaware—of its own best hopes." And this "hatred which reality feels towards failed utopia" was not hindered by humanistic traditions, since there are "in humanistic culture express solicitations of authoritarian rule and cruelty." (Those words are part of a question, but like most of Mr. Steiner's the question is rhetorical.) Moreover, by abolishing the Christian hell, humanism encouraged the hellish; Mr. Steiner summons "It may be" at this point, but that is to secure his certainty, not to admit our doubt:

> We know of the neutral emptiness of the skies and of the terrors it has brought. But it may be that the loss of Hell is the more severe dislocation. It may be that the mutation of Hell into metaphor left a formidable gap in the coordinates of location, of psychological recognition in the Western mind. The absence of the familiar damned opened a vortex which the modern totalitarian state filled.

The presence of the familiar damned did not stanch the Inquisition, but liberal flagellants have all along suspected that somehow it was all their fault. Why couldn't they have left hell well alone?

"In a Post-Culture" claims that traditional culture is irreparably damaged because nobody any longer wishes to create objects or ideas that will outlast their time; and "Tomorrow"—rather in the manner of a sermon's last-minute reassurances—suggests that things are perhaps not so bad after all since music and science proffer new cultures.

> Personally, I feel most drawn to the *gaia scienza*, to the conviction, irrational, even tactless as it may be, that it is enormously interesting to be alive at this cruel, late stage in Western affairs.

In a book about enormities, "enormously" is shallowly heartening and deeply disheartening; "cruel" dwindles into a mere word.

Words? But what about the intellectual reach? Ah, but a man's reach should exceed his grasp less excessively than this. A man should be capable of thinking that there may be subjects on which he is not capable of thinking. Otherwise, however much he speaks of the mysterious and the appalling, the final effect will be of an effrontery of blitheness. Mr. Steiner does not tire of insisting that these days "language is close-woven with lies" (things being comfortably melodramatized for us by an avert-

ing of the eyes from the painful ancientness of this justified suspicion);
but his own accents are too totally unintimidated. The more necessarily
complicated are the arguments about this century's barbarism, the more
there is needed an essential simplicity of language, a constant sense of
those perils of rhetoric about which Mr. Steiner can forever rhetoricize.

Set side by side two ways of speaking. Mr. Steiner's:

> In our current barbarism an extinct theology is at work, a body of tran-
> scendent reference whose slow, incomplete death has produced surrogate,
> parodistic forms. The epilogue to belief, the passage of religious belief
> into hollow convention, seems to be a more dangerous process than the
> *philosophes* anticipated. The structures of decay are toxic. Needing Hell,
> we have learned how to build and run it on earth. A few miles from
> Goethe's Weimar or on the isles of Greece. No skill holds greater men-
> ace. Because we have it and are using it on ourselves, we are now in a *post-
> culture*. In locating Hell above ground, we have passed out of the major
> order and symmetries of Western civilization.

Goethe's thought (in translation): "From Homer and Polygnotus I
every day learn more clearly that in our life here above ground we have,
properly speaking, to enact Hell." I don't know whether Mr. Steiner was
at all remembering this thought of Goethe's; I do know that Goethe
evinces a dignity, an unreflecting indifference to all ostentation, such as
earns the right to the insistent authority of "properly speaking." I know
too that when Matthew Arnold realized that what he next needed to say
was precisely what Goethe had said, he was able to incorporate Goethe's
self-respect and dignity as his own—was able to do more than merely
quote Goethe, or enlist Goethe, or arrange for Goethe to put in a brief
appearance as a guest star. There is admittedly a sense in which those
words of Steiner have a more personal ring than Goethe's, but it is a
sense in which the personal is the less truly individual.

For what Mr. Steiner has is not a style but styles, factitiously personal and at odds with each other, as the title *In Bluebeard's Castle* is
irreconcilably at odds with the subtitle, "Some Notes Towards the
Redefinition of Culture." You can't seek to outdo T. S. Eliot in shrewd

133

fastidiousness while refusing to renounce the Fiedleresque *frisson*. At some points, the style is that of furrowed scrupulosity:

> At best, therefore, I can offer conjectures as to what may be synapses worth watching.

> This instability of essential terrain and the psychological evasions which it entails, characterize much of our current posture.

At other points, the style is that of plumped resonance, aspiring to poetry and as usual mistaking it for the poetic:

> The past drove rats' teeth into the gray pulp of the present; it exasperated, it sowed wild dreams.

Or it is poetic, and with the clumsiness of the poetic:

> Because the realness of his inward lies at his back, the man of words, the singer, will turn back, to the place of necessary beloved shadows.

There is more genuine creativity in two misprints which the sardonic compositor from Yale University Press thought up as criticisms of Steiner's prose: Mr. Steiner has not succumbed to worldly comfort, but he should heed the compositor's suggestion that he give up "wordly comfort," and he should heed too the warning that what he offers us is not an intellectual threshold but a flailing embrace, a "threshhold of complication."

But it isn't just a matter of style. There is the old problem of what it would mean for us to assent to, or dissent from, propositions so ample and fluid that we can't even imagine what would count as evidence for or against them. As when it is claimed that "until the French Revolution . . . history had been, very largely, the privilege and terror of the few. . . . It is the events of 1789 to 1815 that interpenetrate common, private existence with the perception of historical processes." How large is very largely? And the events in England in the seventeenth century?

No doubt a reason would be equally offered for disposing of the Civil War, but such a reason would be all too easy to offer since no stringencies are envisageable.

"It is not difficult to see in what ways an intensification and widening of the erotic could be a counterpart to the dynamics of revolution and European conquest." Sorry, but there are those of us who do find it difficult to see and who would need to be told a lot more about what those words mean and about what phenomena, what erotic changes, it is claimed are manifest, before we could even start to speculate other than luxuriously about the relationship (counterpart?) between the erotic and the dynamics of revolution.

A similar fundamental doubt—is the matter when put in this way accessible to argument at all?—comes up with Mr. Steiner's insistence that the Jews' responsibility for monotheism is responsible for their suffering: "The holocaust is a reflex, the more complete for being long-inhibited, of natural sensory consciousness, of instinctual polytheistic and animist needs." Mr. Steiner says that monotheism "tore up the human psyche by its most ancient roots. The break has never really knit." But what disturbs me is the very undisturbingness of this, the frightening ease with which such a speculation—just because it is so weightless a speculation—can now find itself casually at home, reassured and reassuring, in political polemic. As when Atallah Mansour (*NYR*, October 7, 1971) can accord it the parenthetical calm of an incontrovertible fact: "The Western world, Christian and Muslim alike, has been grateful to the Jews or has hated them (consciously or unconsciously) because they introduced monotheism."

In Bluebeard's Castle persistently wobbles between an inquiry into history and an inquiry into myth. It vacillates in order to suit its own argumentative convenience. "It is against their remembrance of that great [pre-1914] summer, and our own symbolic knowledge of it, that we test the present cold": as prestidigitation this is fine, with "remembrance" and "symbolic knowledge" eliding all the difficulties. Instead of insisting upon the crux—the relationship between historical truth and potent myths—it makes things too easy for itself by an artificial dissociation. "It is not these propositions in themselves I want to consider, but only the degree of exasperation, of estrangement between society and the shaping forces of spirit which they betray." Either "only" there is chimerical, or "society" is. "It may be that our framework of apocalypse, even where it is low-keyed and ironic, is dangerously inflationary." Yes—and?

But it matters, and matters to Mr. Steiner's own arguments, whether such apocalypticism is true to the facts or not. One page later, we are told not to worry—that is, to blankly worry: "Whether or not such intimations of utter menace are justified is not the issue. They permeate our sensibility." But the reason why it is not the issue is simply that Mr. Steiner does not intend to think about it, his sensibility being permeated by an attitude to historical truth which is so grandly concessive as to concede nothing in particular.

Christians have long claimed that the Enlightenment has long had everything its own way (as the rich claim that they have been taxed out of existence), has altogether triumphed, has secularized everything, and has at last been revealed to be bankrupt. But Christians rightly repudiate the idea that Christianity ever had its own way and was shown not to work; they and their apologists would be at least prudent to extend the same admission to the Enlightenment. Mr. Steiner wistfully wants a religion but not Christianity; this position, to which T. S. Eliot would not have been kind, radiates hell-bent good intentions of just the kind for which the Enlightenment is unjustly pilloried.

Myself, I believe that the Enlightenment enlightened. I believe too (and the point is distinguishable but not distinct) that Mr. Steiner has yielded to the religiosity which T. S. Eliot detested in G. K. Chesterton, and that Mr. Steiner should recall the words with which Eliot deprecated that irresponsible proliferator: "Mr. Chesterton's brain swarms with ideas; I see no evidence that it thinks." I believe, finally, that anybody who really wants to conceive of the possible relationships between traditional culture, the Christian religion, and the death camps—anybody, that is, who realizes that it will be only an unusually creative intelligence that will here be able both to notice and to speak—should defer the reading of *In Bluebeard's Castle* and should instead engage with Geoffrey Hill's "Ovid in the Third Reich":

> *non peccat, quaecumque potest pecasse negare,*
> *solaque famosam culpa professa facit.*
> (*Amores*, III, xiv)

> I love my work and my children. God
> Is distant, difficult. Things happen.
> Too near the ancient troughs of blood
> Innocence is no earthly weapon.

> I have learned one thing: not to look down
> So much upon the damned. They, in their sphere,
> Harmonize strangely with the divine
> Love. I, in mine, celebrate the love-choir.

Critics

John Crowe Ransom
Selected Essays, edited by Thomas Daniel Young and John Hindle

As a poet and as a critic, John Crowe Ransom had his shrewd suspicions. So it may be fitting to approach this new selection of his essays (two dozen of them, amounting to 350 pages) with some crinkling of the eyes. Are these people hijacking Ransom? Yes. And no. Yes, because this is a determined bid to capture him for literary theory; the selection, which is decisively angled, and which is preemptively slanted by the introduction's pressures, is out to present Ransom as a theorist, and as the forefather of today's theory-boomers. (On occasions, it sounds as if Ransom is their John the Baptist; on others, as if the successors are belated necessary Paul et al.) Due is to be given, and dues are to be paid, to the revolutionary cause of international literary theory.

But no, it isn't hijacking, because Ransom goes quietly. Or some part of him does. He did write a lot of literary theory, and he actually used the word "theory" a lot, so that he doesn't have to be told condescendingly (as have been William Empson and F. R. Leavis) that theory, though he didn't say so, was what he was trying to say. There are those of us who, because of our own allegiances, have always seen Ransom primarily as a critic remarkable not for theory, but for principles and for practice: principles as less abstract, less concatenated, and less comprehensively proud than theory; and practice, as in sympathy with the New Criticism at least to the extent of agreeing that no criticism is long worth much that does not arise from and return to the very words. For us, it is salutary and even salty to be reminded of how substantial, coherent, and open to revision was Ransom's lifelong dedication to theory. Our concession might then wring from the other side an admission that a great deal of Ransom's best and characteristic criticism does go unrepresented here: all such as is more specific than speculative (the essays, for instance, on Edna St. Vincent Millay and on T. S. Eliot's "Gerontion"). We might all come together in agreeing that the best essays in this book are those which are themselves concretely universal: those which quote imaginatively and contemplate precisely as well as spinning sagely, such as the essays which engage with Hardy, Wordsworth, and *Julius Caesar*.

Yet the salience given here to Ransom's theorizing, which is meant to enforce his claims upon today's attention, has the unintended opposite effect of making him seem markedly antiquated. This is quite distinct from the notoriously delicious antiquities of his comic style, at once arch quivering and archer's quiverful. Nor is it a matter of his employing any dated terminology of theory (theory always lusting for new terms), since in this, as in all else, he is continent. Nor is it that Ransom the theorist is a charming horseless carriage, now overtaken by the pacesetting typesetting jet set. No, Ransom's theorizing feels antiquated because of the nemesis which attends upon theory's needing to bend itself upon some particular disputed nub. So thorough does theory set out to be, so complete within its own terms, that it can only ever achieve this by the most pointed of exclusions. To give such thoroughgoing attention is necessarily to withdraw attention from all else except as ramification. It is this which then brings about what comes to look like the fickleness of theory. Battle rages about a chosen territory of dispute. If a particular theoretical allegiance triumphs, then the issue is dead. If no allegiance triumphs, then both sides tacitly agree to leave the issue for dead. Honor is satisfied, face is saved, and they live to fight another day. But another day means another battlefield. And, looking backward with a wise affright, later generations wonder how it ever was that this particular field, that eminence, such a barren rock, was thought worth sacrificing a life or a lifetime for. "Yet I cannot but wonder," says Ransom, sweetly marveling, "if the critics of the future may not find a quaintness in this feuding."

It is nearly a hundred years since Ransom was born (1888), and it is fifty since his central essays. Central to them, as to the work of his contemporary I. A. Richards, is the distinction between poetry and science. But it is to be doubted whether there are now any potent literary theorists for whom the distinction between poetry and science is of any great moment. Ransom spent most of his life (as Richards did) upon something which no longer is acknowledged to be a nub, or even a gist or a pith. The efforts of recent theory have been to get accepted either as axiomatic or as proven (very different these, of course, and there is some sleazy vacillation as to which is really claimed) exactly some samenesses which Ransom took to be fascinating differences.

Science is not now believed to be the one thing which Ransom's arguments need it to be; prose is not equated with science or with certain extremities of technical discourse; the sciences are taken to be no less implicated in fictions than is poetry, and implicated too in tropes and figures of speech. "Any systematic usage which does not hold good for prose is a poetic device": perhaps, but Ransom is not able convincingly to isolate even one such usage. "The rational or 'tidy' universe that is supposed by the scientists": this was probably calumny then (1941), and would certainly be so now.

What were once the planks of Ransom's platform now feel like planks to walk. "A good many authorities have now assured us that science is simply the strict intellectual technique by which we pursue any of our practical objectives." But the authorities of 1929 are not those of 1984. The dozen pages of quotations which I jotted down about the poetry/science differentia teem with assertions which would at the very least need to be toughly argued for. Assertions about prose, about the language of literature as against the daily language, about science, metaphors, and (grim, this) about objectivity and subjectivity.

143

The point, at first, is not whether Ransom is right to stake his all on clarifying the poetry/science differentia, but whether a Ransom offered as a theorist of *this* can possibly be the Ransom for our day. There is a zombie pathos about a Ransom animated so. You may have the deepest doubts about what the regnant theorists have now agreed upon as the nub (intertextuality, say, or the sign) and yet still think that probably they are right to be signally indifferent to the science/poetry differentia that obsessed Ransom and Richards.

Not that Ransom seems to me to argue it out well anyway. For someone as refined and scrupulous and canny as his poems show him to be, he is sadly, humanly, susceptible to his own rhetoric, such a rhetoric as will make his arguments come true because all that might impede them will have been eliminated in advance. So "science" can glide into "hard science" or "applied science"; and "discourse" into "scientific discourse"; and "prose" into "discursive prose" or into "a perfectly logical prose" or "correct and formal prose"; and "rather than" can be used as if it is not obliged to choose whether or not it means "and not"; and it can all be gracefully ducked in the end with the aid of something called "prose-poetry." Or the terms can be coercively quadrated, pinned and penned as if foursquare: "Sooner or later we shall have to make an adaptation to the world which is submissive and religious, as well as an adaptation which is egotistical and scientific." "Irony is the rarest of the states of mind, because it is the most inclusive; the whole mind has been active in arriving at it, both creation and criticism, both poetry and science." Or this: "Science with its propositions, art with its tropes."

Granted, there is some truth, at certain historical moments, in these alignments; indeed one might have been willing to ask of all these formulations "What truth is there in them?" were it not that Ransom's whole enterprise is dedicated to not permitting that form of moderate question, but rather runs all the time upon the horn of the other sharper question: "Is this true?" In which case the answer has to be, since you ask, no. "The products of machines may be used, but scarcely enjoyed, since they do not have much aesthetic character." And books, beautiful books of character, poetical works, are they not the products of machines?

Ransom's victory over the machine is empty, because it is achieved only by argumentative machination. "What is the intention of poetry anyway, that it should not covet a perfect logical clarity as prose does, but clutter its discourse incessantly with figures?" But first, what is this prose which is supposed to covet a perfect logical clarity?

Ransom speaks of the "act of despair to which critics resort who cannot find for the discourse of poetry any precise differentia to remove it from the category of science." Yet it is not despair but a wise passiveness which is to be heard in T. S. Eliot when he acknowledges: "Criticism, of course, never does find out what poetry is, in the sense of arriving at an adequate definition; but I do not know of what use such a definition would be if it were found." And in any case, Ransom's own prose and his glissades in argument are themselves desperate. "For many years I had seen—as what serious observer has not—that a poem as a discourse differentiated itself from prose by its particularity." But Ransom is not being truly serious when he brings it about that he can observe this by the tautological stroke of simply refusing to deem prose any prose which does have such particularity. "A poem differentiates itself for us, very quickly and convincingly, from a prose discourse." Tautology, like hey presto, is very quick and very unconvincing. "The world of art is the actual world which does not bear restriction": this is slippery enough (*of* in "the world of art" being asked to hold the whole argument on its slender shoulders), yet Ransom has recourse to a further slipperiness: "Or at least defies the restrictiveness of science." *Or at least*: with one bound the argument is free. But free, too, from responsibilities which it should honor.

Ransom is to be honored for not being able to bring himself to muster a convincing argument given so poor a brief, rather as Milton, honest beyond the call of duty and of prudence, is to be honored for having failed to make sensical the War in Heaven. Ransom wrote out of a sense of a terrible war between science and the arts (the arts being perilously identified by him with poetry). The great threat to peace, to civilization, to cultivation, to conservatism indeed, was science, "the scientific way of life," "the tyranny of science," "the monopoly of the scientific spirit over the mind," "a society in which science claims to be paramount," "scientific bondage." Yet Ransom was, like the rest of us, in bonds (a gentleman in bonds, he was); and therefore he betrays an insufficient or partial sense of what bondage is, and of what his conservatism may legitimately claim. "The darkey is one of the bonds that make a South out of all the Southern regions" (1934). You can say that again, and with a different inflection. The answer to science, or rather to scientism, proves to be "natural piety"—Wordsworth's words constitute the recurrent faith of these essays, and they furnish the poignant ending to "Classical and Romantic": "The experience is vain and aimless for practical purposes. But it answers to a deep need within us. It exercises that impulse of natural piety which requires of us that our life should be in loving rapport with environment." This is beautiful, not least because of the implicit acknowledgment of how hard even such an aspiration is: the word "rapport," in its foreignness, can never be perfectly, easily, in loving rapport with its environment.

These essays are the work of a most intelligent, resourceful, and dedicated man who yet had a thousand times more conscience, comedy, and quiddity than their enterprise allows them to manifest. Whether Ransom set it up or not, his own critical discourse does bear out his claim that poetry is ("or at least" can be, on occasion) a far better thing. For his own hospitable magnanimous poetry is not in the bondage of a travestying literary-history such as here makes the literature of the seventeenth century and of the Romantics the only English literature which is to be truly respected. His poetry was not at the mercy of his own notions. Of Milton's propensity to preach, Ransom says: "He knew of this tendency in himself and opposed it." In his poems Ransom pitted himself against that least straw of men, himself.

F. R. Leavis
The Living Principle: 'English' as a Discipline of Thought

T he first quarter of *The Living Principle* is on 'Thought, Language and Objectivity', eager to establish the crucial claims: for language as the incarnation of human creativity and of creativity's relation to community and to continuity; for literature as a supreme discovery-invention of a supreme kind of thinking; and for literary study as a discipline of thought different from, and so necessarily in its way a critique of, though not an enemy of, philosophy. The second quarter of the book, 'Judgment and Analysis', enforces these beliefs with detailed comparison and analysis, incorporating with revisions and additions Leavis's excellent essays of twenty and thirty years ago on thought and emotional quality, imagery and movement, and reality and sincerity. The creative and critical fact here is Shakespeare, since it is he who makes, and finds, the most of the English language, and whose language is the greatest of debts—owed to Shakespeare, but owed too by Shakespeare to all those who have left no name behind them but have a memorial: the English language. And the last half of the book is on *Four Quartets*, on the paradoxical contradiction between how Eliot urges and what he urges, between Eliot's own creativity of apprehension, with its necessary grati-

Essays in Criticism (October 1976)

tude to human collaborative creativity as that is evidenced in a language which is itself grateful to time as the element of its life, and the beliefs enunciated by Eliot: that human life is null, abject, and without creativity; that time is nothing but death-dealing illusion; and that human beings are condemned to hopeless self-enclosure.

The vital interdependence of all the concerns which make up Leavis's book is succinctly manifest, and it amounts to a saddened deploring of the disjunction in Eliot which denies such vital interdependence:

> The point to be made in relation to the key that turns in the door and turns once only is that to recognize with full implicit belief, as should surely be natural above all to a major poet, the fact of human creativity is to know that the nightmare of hopeless self-enclosure *is* a nightmare, and, if irresistible and lasting, an insanity. Everyone, whether articulate about it in explicit recognition or not, is familiar with the relevant basic truth as it is manifested in the livingness of the language he participates in. Eliot himself, contemplating a poem that he recognizes as an achieved creation, must—like any poet or critic or cultivated person—assume that minds (which are also sentiences) can meet in it. But Eliot, even in his major work, and most significantly there, is not consistent; there is essential self-contradiction which the prepotent implicit intention entails disguising— in the first place from the poet himself.

What Eliot is compelled to say, with that language of genius which is also a genius about the nature of language, is for Leavis a denial of the very truths about language which *Four Quartets* embodies.

In 1922, Eliot wrote: 'The good academic mind is as rare in England as the good revolutionary mind; there is an originality about the good academic mind as essential to it as another originality is to the creative mind'. Leavis's originality is easy to impugn crassly, because it is not crassly or divorcingly novel; it is exactly of the kind which Leavis rightly attributed to Eliot himself ('to learn as Mr. Eliot learnt in general from Laforgue is to be original to the point of genius'; 'he was not a mere individual in isolation: he had a more important kind of originality'). The first thing, other than book-reviews, which Leavis published was in 1929, and it was 'T. S. Eliot—A Reply to the Condescending'. Leavis's first book, *New Bearings in English Poetry* (1932), had Eliot at the heart of it; it was Eliot's achievement which freed modern poetry from an inert dependence (the opposite of continuity's interdependence) upon Victorian poeticality, and which re-established the crucial continuity of English poetry, especially in its relation to the wit and the human completeness of the best seventeenth-century poetry. Leavis's preface, repudiating the wrong kind of claim to being 'original', speaks of the book as 'largely an acknowledgement, vicarious as well as personal, of indebtedness to a certain critic and poet'. In a published letter in the same year (his first such letter had been both to and about Eliot as editor of the *Criterion*), Leavis said that he had always imagined his critical approach to derive from Eliot as much as from anyone.

Yet the 'Yes, but—' which even Eliot precipitated from Leavis was already clear, not only in some pregnant withholdings in *New Bearings*, but in Leavis's next book, one that is very often forgotten, *For Continuity* (1933). This collection of early essays from *Scrutiny* is alive with respect for Eliot as a major poet and critic ('the distinction of his intelligence . . . he really does something with his words'), but it is also already alive to something—or rather, two related things—about Eliot which it cannot respect because it believes them to be evidence of Eliot's not fully respecting his own creative courage and convictions. First, Eliot's acquiescence in the social values of the literary world which are inimical to true values (what is Eliot doing belonging to the Royal Society of Literature?); and second, Eliot's hostility to D. H. Lawrence. For it is of course Lawrence who is, in Leavis's phrase, 'The Necessary Opposite' to Eliot; it was Lawrence about whom Leavis wrote his first substantial critical essay (*D. H. Lawrence*, Minority Pamphlet No. 6, 1930; reprinted in *For Continuity*); it is Lawrence whose genius provides for Leavis the essential critique of Eliot's different and more self-damaging genius; it is Lawrence whose art as a novelist furnished Leavis's study of continuity in the English novel, *The Great Tradition* (1948), with its tacit culmination, issuing seven years later in *D. H. Lawrence, Novelist* (1955), with its clenched appendix on 'Mr Eliot and Lawrence';

and so it is not surprising that Leavis's newest reappraisal of Eliot has been succeeded at once by his newest reappraisal of Lawrence: *Thought, Words and Creativity*, which has just been published in August 1976.

The Living Principle, by virtue of being explicit about both philosophy and religion in a way which Leavis had hitherto been chary of (fearing, as he explained in his famous exchange with René Wellek about 'Literature and Philosophy' in 1937, that any general statement of his 'philosophy' would be weak and distracting in comparison with the edged specificities of literary criticism), is the first of Leavis's books substantially to fulfil the promise which *Education and the University* made thirty years ago: a recognition of the positive implications of advancing (as against the justified warnings about foolish ways of uttering) the claim that a study of literature must lead one 'to consider the relation of humane culture to religion, and the place of religion in civilization'.

What is strongly new—a fresh start and yet a continuity—about *The Living Principle* is its delivering such positive acumen on poetry's not being philosophy and not being religion (and yet its not not being, either). Eliot, as the great religious poet of an age of which the religious plight partly consists in there not being the possibility of certain kinds of religious affirmation, is the perfect focus for the one relation; and for the other, likewise, in that he is perhaps of all our poets the one who had the most professional philosophical training; the one of whom (*à propos* of *Burnt Norton*) Leavis has penetratingly said that 'it seems to me to be the equivalent in poetry of a philosophical work—to do by strictly poetical means the business of an epistemological and metaphysical inquiry'; and yet is the poet who found himself impelled to say: 'I believe that for a poet to be a philosopher he would have to be virtually two men; I cannot think of any example of this thorough schizophrenia, nor can I see anything to be gained by it: the work is better performed inside two skulls than one'.

Yet the poignancy of that asseveration, Leavis might say (though he doesn't cite it), comes from there being a different form of schizophrenia within Eliot's profoundly philosophical poetry: that it announces a philosophy of negation such as its creativity contradicts, or that while being made possible only by a continuity (the language's) which itself furthers continuity, its burden is that there are no continuities in this life. 'Eliot gets no comfort from continuities—there are for him none that matter'. Yet continuity, tradition, time, development, pattern are the concepts and the terms of *Four Quartets*, and this gives a remarkable compactness to Leavis's criticism. Where his recent forays—*Lectures in America* (1969), *English Literature in Our Time and the University* (1969), and *Nor Shall My Sword* (1972)—have mostly been, or have mostly included, *either* high polemical argument about the breach in continuity which has been caused by destructive philosophies (Cartesian and Benthamite) *or* literary focusings, so that the effect has sometimes been of shrapnel, *The Living Principle* is a marriage of true matters of mind.

It has, too, something new in the line of the old 'Yes, but—'. The formula was one which often aroused unease, not (the usual objection) because Leavis is too dogmatic to permit of one's getting a 'but' in edgeways—your real dogmatism would never be caught giving such hostages to fortune as Leavis's declarative clarity insists on; no, the difficulty about Leavis's 'Yes, but—' has often been that the *yes* seemed to be in the tiniest of print and the *but* in the largest. So that although Milton's genius, or Shelley's, or even (during the moments in which Leavis was most bitterly critical of Eliot) Eliot's might explicitly be acknowledged, the effect was of holding more strongly, or even with more relish, to the *but*, the qualification or reservation or repudiation. The *but* seemed to make most of the running; or rather, since the *but* was often a matter of obdurate resistance, it was all rather like that great Steinberg drawing in which there careers down a hill a little chariot-perambulator spelling YES, with a stiff little man balanced on its prow of S, down towards the huge and inescapable monoliths which spell a shattering BUT.

The satisfactions of *The Living Principle* are more generous. For one thing, it conveys the lasting largeness of its gratitude to Eliot, not only for the triumphs of his genius but also for the way in which even what seem to Leavis to be defeats for Eliot can nevertheless be something to be grateful for, since they compel the most searching interrogation of—

more, discovery of—one's own beliefs. For another thing, the book is based too on a variation: 'No, but—', since *Four Quartets* moves Leavis to an explicit and reiterated *no*, as when he rejects Eliot's rejection of daily human reality, a *no* which nevertheless is ripe with many a *but* of heartfelt admiration and awe. 'My own tribute to Eliot's genius must be a profoundly convinced "No"'. 'One's indebtedness to the authors to whom one is most indebted is commonly in some measure a matter of their compelling one to a convinced "but"'.

And what tribute, by way of a convinced *no* or a convinced *but*, is then the right tribute to Leavis? My own resistance to his sense of Eliot would begin at two places where he seems to be self-hurried and there-fore unsatisfying or uncogent. The first is a matter of his argument at a crucial point: the Dantesque section of *Little Gidding*. Leavis wonder-fully elicits the distinction of the famous passage, and yet his praise of it is importantly evasive. Eliot has been imprisoned in a frustrating self-contradiction. 'Yet in this magnificent passage he comes near to escap-ing'. What exactly is it, in such a case, to come near to escaping? And that it may be Leavis who is coming near to escaping from his own stringencies becomes clear when two paragraphs later 'near to escaping' has unobtrusively become something crucially different: 'what Eliot achieves . . . is a momentary escape from the prison'. 'A liberating flash', a 'genuine and liberating impersonality'. Is Eliot liberated or not? 'Near to', 'momentary', 'flash', all seem to me differently to elide the crux, and Leavis falls back on the mere but ambiguous assertion that 'It is too late for Eliot to tell himself that, for all the paradoxes of his profound self-contradiction, he has always been committed to creativity'. Too late to be effected, or too late to be effective? Why is it too late? What critical principles govern what may well be a necessary critical idea, that of being too late? And why is it for Leavis to say, *tout court*, what moment of self-knowledge is too late? Between the stirrup and the ground, Eliot may have at last taken mercy on himself. But at this point, since Leavis does not then proceed to look with weighty patience upon the two ensuing sections which at once conclude this last poem of *Four Quar-tets*, the imprisonment seems to be Leavis's, ruled for a moment by the ruling idea which has mostly elicited the truth of the poem but which at this vital point is insufficient or at any rate insufficiently argued for.

The other place at which there arises a representative difficulty concerns, not argument, but description. Leavis has always seemed to me to be more patient in formulating principles than in substantiating descriptions. It is as if he abandons too quickly the hope that we might modify our reports—I take the word from his betraying sentence: 'we shall hardly get further here by argument: we are faced by a conflict of reports', as if argument could never move a man to reconsider or refine his report. The unconvincing moments in *The Living Principle* are descriptively brusque. So, although Leavis has not recently given us any different description either of Eliot's essential career or of the nature of heroism, he sees apparently no difficulty about saying now, altogether summarily: 'Eliot himself was in no danger of being a tragic hero of that kind, or a hero at all'. But seven years ago Leavis spoke of the 'heroic integrity of his poetic career': 'I see Eliot's creative career as a sustained, heroic and indefatigably resourceful quest. . . . The heroism is that of genius. . . . What I am intent on is justifying my attribution to Eliot of a heroic quality in the exercise of his genius'. The point is not that Leavis is not permitted to change his mind; nor is it that one could not imagine (though one might be sceptical about) the spinning of an argument which would claim that, despite Eliot's showing heroism in his career, he was for some reason in no danger of being 'a hero at all'. (But where then would the heroism come from?) The point is simply that a mere say-so, a nugatory descriptive aside, is being asked to do work quite beyond its powers. I was reminded of the occasion when Eliot, in 1938, rebuked someone for sneering at Leavis:

> I have had my own disagreements with Mr. Leavis; and Mr. Leavis, at one time or another, has expressed disapproval of nearly everybody; but it is impossible not to respect the work that he has done with *Scrutiny*, and his rather lonely battle for literacy. To dismiss a man who has done such work, with the words, 'Mr. Leavis, who can be trusted to come in on a good thing'—a knowing wink to the reader—is to make a sneer do the work of a demonstration.

But when all is said and done (and Leavis, astonishingly, has not yet had all his say), we have great good fortune in having a critic who earns Ben Jonson's 'To the Learned Critic':

> May others fear, fly, and traduce thy name,
> As guilty men do magistrates: glad I,
> That wish my poems a legitimate fame,
> Charge them, for crown, to thy sole censure hie.
> And but a sprig of bays, given by thee,
> Shall outlive garlands stol'n from the chaste tree.

W. K. Wimsatt
Day of the Leopards

W. K. Wimsatt, who died last December at the age of 68, was more than a scholar-critic of distinctive and distinguished power, he was an institution. In an age which has more and more come to distrust institutions, he wielded his genially stringent mind to urge upon literature and criticism the fact that much of their own value is like that of a living institution: a balance of past and present, of freedom and service, of theory and practice, of the concrete and the universal, of independence and interdependence.

Wimsatt's own principles were of such a kind, strong arches thrusting against each other and rippling up with a tension that was not destructive but bracing. His personal character, it seems, was just such an interlocking of humor and melancholy, of grumpiness and charm, of size and delicacy—and so was his professional self: Christian and classical, disputatious and courteous, principled and supple, erudite and homespun. The literature which he loved most, and about which he was best placed to show the world many things that were both new and true, was therefore the richly antithetical art of Alexander Pope and Samuel Johnson. And the institution which he loved most, and which he so strongly supported for so much of his life, was one which—in its hey-

New York Times Book Review (13 June 1976)

day and his—notably embodied such a dynamic life of checks and balances: Yale University, and in particular its English department.

Wimsatt was one of the best reasons why the English department at Yale was, for a good time, the best in the world. He was one of the best reasons because he was happy to incarnate one—a large one, but only one—of its imaginative possibilities. He had his own views, of course, and his own powerful personality, but it was characteristic that the passionate scruple of his arguing left no room for cults or cliques, and left so much room for other perspectives, other voices. He was extremely against extremism. His latest collection of essays, sadly his last, is *Day of the Leopards*. It is rich with his judicious and animating tensions.

The book is a tissue of truths. It may find its antithetical wisdom in a critic like Coleridge, with his conviction that poetry is a balance or reconciliation of opposite or discordant qualities. Or in a poet like Christopher Smart, with his "antiphonal logbook," *Jubilate Agno*. Or in a period, as when 18th-century poetry reconciles its new self-respect with paying its old respects in "Imitation as Freedom." Or in a historical coinciding, as when Crabbe publishes his traditional but antitraditional poem *The Village* in the same year as Blake's *Poetical Sketches*.

The critic who says here that "it may be necessary for the expositor himself to drive both sides of an interpretive difference" is driving, not driven. So that when elsewhere he says—about the valuable but seductive notion of "play" with which *homo ludens* has lately toyed so much—"I myself must confess to a double inclination, to take the concept of play very broadly, yet to stop short of making it a transcendental," we ought to relish the fact that this understatement isn't a confession at all, but a proper pride. For Wimsatt was a worthy heir of Coleridge, who "enjoyed the kind of classical sanity that compelled him to reject both solutions," and Wimsatt can truly, far more than Coleridge, be said to have enjoyed his sanity. For Wimsatt was never reduced to paralysis by the knowledge that for every principle there is another compensating principle, any more than any sane man is paralyzed by his knowledge that "Look before you leap" has its necessary counterpart "He who hesitates is lost."

The preface says, with dry humor, "I find no embarrassment in having taken both sides of the debate," and it alerts us to Blake's wisdom: "Without contraries is no progression." The first section is indeed called "Contraries," and it is worth remembering that Wimsatt entitled his last collection of essays, 11 years ago, *Hateful Contraries*. Given his increasing explicit suspicion of the language of violence, of all critical paratrooping, it is right to see "Contraries" as a de-escalation from "Hateful Contraries." For the preface issues its warning: "Disparity, irony, tension have their own poetic rights. And in this complex of rights lies all too ready an invitation to division, disruption, destruction."

The trouble with most warnings is that they are self-righteous, dull, humorless and mildly deranged. But over the years Wimsatt had perfected his talents as a warner. His most notable early essays, in *The Verbal Icon* (1954), were warnings against critical morasses: judging a poem by invoking its author's intentions, or by saying how you feel when you read it. And *Day of the Leopards* keeps up the good warning work. The title piece is a brief and bitter attack on the critical vocabulary of revolutionary extremism, the more telling because all of Wimsatt's courtesy cannot disguise the fact that he is deeply pained by its being *Yale* which has started to talk like this. There follow some other witty cogent warnings, with Wimsatt displaying his particular forte: his ability to argue very strictly on behalf of "loose" and limber concepts or principles.

So an essay on "genesis" returns to Wimsatt's famous piece of 30 years ago, on "the intentional fallacy," and warns us against thinking that the original warning has somehow been exploded or disconfirmed. Then an essay on Laokoön warns us against any easy assimilation of one art to another, of the kind which has become so handy and so useless. And an essay on Northrop Frye deploys all its attentive politeness to warn us against Northrop Frye. This first section, like the third section ("Poetry as Poems"), shows that Wimsatt's hand and mind had lost none of their cunning. If I were to resist the idea that he is among "our great critical theorists," that would be because he seems to me—despite his own protestations—to be committed to something better than critical theory: critical principles.

At any rate, these two sections have a clear continuity with his early argumentative explorations in *The Verbal Icon* and *Hateful Contraries*, together with the book where Wimsatt was in tensional union with Cleanth Brooks, *Literary Criticism: A Short History* (1957). But it would be wrong to give the impression that most of *Day of the Leopards* consists of warnings, positive—in both senses—though these are. For the heart of the book is its section of "Eighteenth-Century Essays." Here Wimsatt once more finds some searching things to say about Dr. Johnson, on whom he wrote *The Prose Style of Samuel Johnson* in 1941 and *Philosophic Words* in 1948; and likewise about Pope, to whom he had paid his acutely scholarly tribute in 1965, *The Portraits of Pope*, and about whom, a generation ago, he wrote one of his best critical essays, "One Relation of Rhyme to Reason." For Wimsatt was not only—and it is rare—genuinely interested in both rhyme and reason, he was very good at eliciting a relation between them. He was even better in his modest insistence that what he was showing us was not all the imaginable relations but one of them. The closing pages of this book pay to I. A. Richards a tribute (flanked with warnings) that was not self-directed but is self-deserved:

> The critical thinking of Richards has always cut close to the quick of poetic interest. It has been exciting. It has generated a world of ideas favorable to a general excitement with criticism. And for that reason I see it as a better kind of critical thinking than most of the now emergent vogues:—the boundless expansions of the school of 'consciousness,' the self-justifying apparatuses of transformational grammar, the neutralisms of historical hermeneutics, the despairs of the trope of 'silence,' the 'aleatory' assemblage of *textes* from newspaper, dictionary, or telephone directory, the celebrations of the 'death of literature,' the various other attempts to play midwife to the 'post-modern imagination.'

William Empson
Using Biography

O f books darkened by being posthumous, this one of Empson's, *Using Biography*, is among the most illuminatingly vital. Every page is alive with his incomparable mind, his great heart, and his unique accents. Profoundly comic and yet incandescent with convictions, *Using Biography* is so rammed with life that it shall gather strength of life with being. Inevitably his death, nine months ago when two years short of eighty, casts its shadow over all of a book which has as its poignant first words: 'I am reaching an age when I had better collect the essays which I hope to preserve.' There is the small accidental shock upon now meeting such innocent words as 'She wanted to have no more bother,' given that Empson came drily to relish as his own epitaph 'No more bother.' There is the resilience—down-to-earth, though—which acknowledges the arbitrariness of things, among them dying: 'As so often, some bug happened to intrude.' There is the gruffly laconic parenthetical annotation which now in retrospect has become half-elegiac, when he remembers seeing a clockwork-bird à la Byzantium:

> When I was small (born 1906) I was sometimes taken to visit a venerable great-aunt, and after tea she would bring out exquisitely preserved toys of

London Review of Books (7 February 1985)

an antiquity rivalling her own. Chief among them was the bird of Yeats in its great cage, wound up to sing by a massive key; a darkish green tree, as I remember, occupied most of the cage, and a quite small shimmering bird, whose beak would open and shut while the musical box in the basement was playing, perched carelessly upon a branch at one side. The whole affair glittered, but I cannot claim to have seen the Golden Bough; it was prettier than a gilt tree would have been; and of course the bird was not plumb on top of it, like Satan in Paradise. I remember being struck to hear my mother say, by way of praising the great age of the toy, that she remembered being shown it herself when she was a child after such a tea; and she and Yeats were born in the same year, 1865.

Empson may have given up writing poems forty or so years ago, but such prose is at least as well written as good poetry. And so is the touching vision of how it may have been that Andrew Marvell succumbed to the ague or the medication; this whole last paragraph of the hundred-page section on Marvell is instinct with a sense of what it is to make an end, whether or not betimes, whether or not Marvell was robbed even of discovering that 'Death's to him a strange surprise':

Marvell was a stocky fighting type, though a deskworker of course, and had been threatened with trouble on the tour to Russia for hitting out; but he genuinely wanted peace, and would prefer to walk away from a duel if the rules permitted. I suggest that he walked out from an evening party at a house in Hull, and used his eminence to walk out through a gate of the city, and walked for what remained of the night, indifferent to the fatal marshes; and returned at dawn to take the first coach back to London. As the coach jolted slowly on, and he got more and more feverish, he would reflect on how thoroughly tricky his situation had become, on every side. When he at last got home, irritated all over, and his doctor suggested a risky medicine, as the 'tertiary' returned, warning him that it would cause a long deep sleep, he accepted that eagerly. Nobody expected to die from the familiar ague, tiresome though it was; that was no problem. But from a real deep sleep he would expect to wake up, as often before, suddenly seeing a way out, knowing what to do.

This is great prose in its chastened apprehensions and its hush. 'To walk away', 'walked out', 'to walk out', 'walked for'; this has its incipient feverishness, as the closing 'real deep sleep', for all its touching hopefulness, has something of the strange depth of the poem 'Let it go' ('It is this deep blankness is the real thing strange') and of the craving for the deepest sleep in 'Aubade' ('I slept, and blank as that I would yet lie'). Empson would be vexed at the thought that such poignancies in his posthumous collection might now be taken as premonitions. But admonitions are another matter. 'Ignorance of Death' he knew about, and valued: but he was not ignorant of dying, and was as wise about it as about living.

One aspect of his genius is caught in his being so photogenic; phases of the quizzing phiz shine from his books' covers. Don't miss the photo (1948–9) newly added as a frontispiece to the *Collected Poems*, and its comic note: 'The other man is Charles Coffin, a patient and understanding listener, as the picture shows. We would be discussing a 17th-century poet; I do not think I ever discussed my own poetry like that.'

Using Biography is devoted to six authors: Marvell, Dryden, Fielding, Yeats, Eliot and Joyce. The central essays had been printed before, but are here revised and supplemented. Three related principles unify the book, all argued for and all good-naturedly shocked at the pretty pass to which things have come. First, that the knowledge of what a writer had in mind may be of unique use in understanding the art. Second, that therefore 'the intentional fallacy' is itself a fallacy and moreover beckons critics, not into the ascetic desert of disattending to intentions, but into the oily swamp of imputing wrong intentions. Third, that in our time the most prevalent mis-imputation of an intention has been Christian.

All six authors are seen in relation to Christianity, though not solely so. The possibilities other than Christianity are then an important part of the rescue-work. Marvell lived in an age when 'natural magic' and fairies were respectable, and when Christianity did not have a monopoly of the supernatural. Dryden lived in an age when deism not only was respectable but had unanswerably indicted the moral disreputability of Christianity's 'rigid satisfaction' in the crucifixion. Fielding was a better Christian than Christ, and moreover imagined, in the person of Tom Jones, another such who is yet very different from himself. Yeats was immune to Christian virulence, thanks to his trusting in reincarnation rather than in the Incarnation. Joyce has been subjected to posthumous conversion back to the religion he repudiated; Empson sketches the drives at work: 'and when you understand all that, you may just be able to understand how they manage to present James Joyce as a man devoted to the God who was satisfied by the crucifixion.' Whereupon he at once vaults into a new paragraph which yet keeps the previous one alive: 'The concordat was reached over his dead body.' It is one of his most searching jokes: 'The concordat [over His dead body] was reached over his dead body.' Yet even here Empson's magnanimity extends itself, for of this bad state of affairs in literary studies he says: 'As so often, the deformity is the result of severe pressure between forces in themselves good.'

And T. S. Eliot? He is not exactly accorded any rescue, since it is from him that we need to be rescued, in this matter. ('This is one of the scars left by the reactionary movement of T. S. Eliot.') Yet Empson's combative dismay can manifest itself in a compassionate joke, since he does at least apprehend the many things about Eliot's father that so racked the son: 'What the Unitarians had chiefly revolted against, though they seem to have lost their battle by being too tactful about it, was the nightmare belief that the Father was given a unique "satisfaction" by the Crucifixion of his Son. It was to this that Eliot returned, with glum eagerness; whether or not with some confusion between his own father and the Heavenly one.'

Using Biography, then, is unified by an educative mission and an anticrusade. But the argumentative unification of the book does in the end matter less than its unity of spirit. It has the supreme integrative virtue, magnanimity. Empson, granted, was exquisitely unsentimental as a writer and as a man (too full of courage to be sentimental), but this, far from marring his magnanimity, is what makes it something. He is incorruptibly implacable in the face of sadism, and he knows its various faces: in the Blessed and 'their eternal ringside view of the torments of Hell', in the rawness of Joyce's *Exiles*, in the squalor imagined by Fielding in Blifil, and even—where he is deeply grieved to find it—in Marvell, in the death by fire of the sailor-martyr in 'Last Instructions to a Painter'. Empson quotes two dozen lines and then speaks with the direct personal commitment that, prior to the current scientism and theoreticity, used to be thought germane to the understanding of literature: 'I find this disgusting, and all too likely to well up from the worst perversion, that of Gilles de Rais, the craving to gloat over the torturing of a tender innocent. Mrs Duncan-Jones was quite right, in her Academy lecture, to point out the strangeness of it, but (I think) not nearly censorious enough.'

Empson's magnanimity reserves the right to be censorious, and indeed there would be no claim to magnanimity if the right were waived. But magnanimous is what he is. This may be a matter of a u-turn of a phrase. He repents of a phrase well turned against Dryden's Hind: 'I said that Dryden was showing his famous clumsiness here, as he presumably expected reverence for "this simpering herbivore"; but my sarcasm was stupid, almost like Leavis.' For sarcasm is inferior to irony, which must be more magnanimous because, as Empson himself put the principle, an irony to be worth anything must be true to some degree in both senses. Even if he also or mostly means disparage or reservation, when Empson praises someone he means it. Even Kenner. The first of the Joyce essays makes no secret of its anger or its reckoning, but the praise part is pained irony, not self-pleasing sarcasm: 'But no one else has presented it in such a lively, resourceful and energetic manner, so the best name one can find for it is the Kenner Smear.' The second Joyce essay opens with a sentence which is exactly weighed and timed: 'It is wonderful how Professor Kenner can keep on about *Ulysses*, always interesting and relevant and hardly repeating himself at all.' This precipitates not Ooh but Ah.

Empson's own magnanimity is his element; the magnanimity of others is often his subject, and he can tease the matter out for us beautifully. Of a moment in Marvell: 'This style is what Dryden has been so rightly praised for; the opponent is totally ridiculed, but he is put in the distance, as another strange and pathetic example of the fates of men.' 'Fielding shows a Proust-like delicacy in regularly marking a reservation about Allworthy without ever letting us laugh at him.' 'Joyce can make a character ridiculous without any loss of sympathy for him, and a modern critic finds this hard to imagine, because he has been taught to be a brass-faced scold; though surely it was familiar to the public of Dickens.' Such examples have different implications and nuances, but they all witness not only to the authors' generosity but to the author's.

Again it is crucial to that continuity of life and work to which Empson trusts and ministers that these same ways of speaking should be as perfectly applicable to creators as to their creations. Empson at once acknowledges and dissociates himself from the craving to scold, as in the movement of the sentence which begins: 'Joyce was a self-important man, as he needed to be, and he . . .' Beautiful, the flickering surprise, along the way, of that light rebuke to the propensity to rebuke. The people who make books are not treated differently from those within the books. Empson loves Fielding for not liking sarcasm and its sniggers. Mrs Waters, her breasts exposed, declines Tom Jones's generosity. And is Fielding's sentence generous? 'Jones offered her his coat; but, I know not for what reason, she absolutely refused the most earnest solicitation to accept it.' Empson's unfolding of this creates a community of spirit in which the generosity of both of the characters, and of the novelist, is perfectly at one with that of the critic and, it is to be hoped, of the reader: 'When Fielding says he doesn't know the reason he always means it is too complicated to explain. Walking with her life-saver Jones she liked to appear pathetic, and she wanted to show off her breasts, but also she really could not bear to let him take his coat off, not on such a cold night.' Far from being sentimental, Empson's 'but also' (and by extension, Fielding's also) is what saves the interpretation from the prevalent sentimentality of cynicism. And the authenticity of Empson's response is audible in the comic propriety of his syntax and cadence: 'but also she really could not bear to let him take his coat off, not on such a cold night.' You can hear her sigh—to adopt a dramatisation which Empson loves to call in evidence. Of Mrs Palmer's deposition that she was legally Mrs Marvell: 'Tupper appears to think that she sounds like a cheat here, but I think she sounds very plain and true, as well as astonished and indignant. I can hear her panting.' Of Marvell's 'A Dialogue between the Two Horses': 'Woolchurch is wonderfully like a horse; you can hear him squeal.'

Just as a philosopher needs not only to mount a right argument but to explain how unstupid people have mounted wrong ones, so Empson is cogent not only at exposing but at explaining error. 'One must realise, as he is the villain in this story, that he too thought his actions were fully justified.' 'The reason why Mrs Waters gets misunderstood here is that here as always she is unusually generous minded.' 'The delusion about incest is the kind of mistake which is always likely if you interpret in selfish terms the remarks of a very unselfish character.' This power to rise from the tact of an instance to the touchstone of a principle is happily endemic in Empson. There is no contradiction, only magnanimity, in his being able both to exult in the achievement of *The Waste Land* and to insist that there remains a very important point of principle: 'The poem is inherently a mystery; I would never have believed that the Symbolist programme could be made to work at all, if it had not scored a few resounding triumphs, such as this.' This is an admission comparable in its dignity to Dr Johnson's return upon himself in the matter of *Paradise Lost* and blank verse: 'I cannot prevail on myself to wish that Milton had been a rhymer.' Empson does not prevail on himself. His glancingly intelligent gloss on intelligence came when he praised Copernicus for being more intelligent, '(less at the mercy of his own notions)', than people had noticed. Yet Empson, like Johnson, does hold to his own notions, since simply to cede them would be to be at the mercy of other men's. So two pages after declining to scold *The Waste Land*, he can observe that one nub of the Symbolist difficulty is that what validates scolding becomes unclear:

> Anyway, a touch of the craving to scold may be observed in the poem
> here, with its assumption that the poet is nobler and purer than anything

he contemplates. The French writers who invented Symbolism seem never to have thought of turning it to the uses of a cats' tea-party; but then, if Eliot was imitating Dickens, he was bound to scold, and Dickens would have shown no mercy to a Hapsburg courtier. The difference is that Dickens had a plot, which allowed him to show adequate reasons for his scolding; it is true that the plot is often perfunctory—no admirer of *Oliver Twist* would try to detail the itinerary of the villain; but to scold without even a residual plot, as a Symbolist, is bound to feel self-regarding. Even so, it felt a good deal more human than Mallarmé or Valéry.

Even the Christian religion is not denied Empson's magnanimity when for once in some aspect it deserves it. He really does honour Fielding's Gospel goodness, and it is an irony not a sarcasm when he praises the Church of England for having kept Christianity at bay. *Using Biography* is less a matter of abusing Christianity than of disabusing people of it. Repeatedly the effort of his historical imagination is to make you less quick to condemn: 'There was also a simple line of argument, which probably decided the last action of Charles II: that the cats said all prots would go to Hell, but the prots (or some Anglicans at least) admitted that some cats would not. It was therefore safer to become a cat at the end. This is not cynical; in moods when such people really did believe in God, they accepted the ample evidence that he was like a capricious earthly king.' This has unexpected reserves of pity and respect—unexpected, that is, in anyone other than Empson. The ones whom he does not respect are the latter-day saints, the sanctimonious distorters and narrowers of the great writers. Again and again his complaint against modern interpretations is that the art which they then praise would not deserve praise. 'It would ring very false if he only meant . . .'; 'But it makes the poem complacent and footling . . .'; 'There would be no point in the nastiness invented by Wittreich'; 'What it reveals is that all these critics have been libelling Yeats, not on purpose but because they cannot grasp the spiritual points at which he differed from Mr Chadband'; or, 'a degree of mean-mindedness positively incapacitating for a literary critic'. Empson shows in these essays, as ever, a degree of magnanimity positively capacitating for a literary critic. Of course he is immeasurably more capacious than the rest of us. Those of us who revere him and delight in him, then and now, are not the ones who need to be told how far short we fall of his genius and goodness. He has a touching parenthesis: '(As for myself here, I agree with Fielding and wish I was as good.)'

Jean-Paul Sartre
Saint Genet

Dame Edith Sitwell has spoken out: 'I do not wish to spend the rest of my life with my nose nailed to other people's lavatories.' So she will not be riveted to *Saint Genet*. For Jean Genet, 'Saint' may seem an exaggeration, precipitated simply by St Genest, patron of actors. But Sartre opens his secret black and midnight hagiography: 'When Genet plunges into his long excremental description of anal intercourse, he irresistibly brings to mind Marie Alacoque gathering up the dejecta of sick persons with her tongue.' Or, to adapt the attendant's words, it may be dejecta to you, but it's Genet's bread and butter. Sartre is very shocked by people who aren't shocked:

> I know people who can read the coarsest passages without turning a hair: 'Those two gentlemen sleep together? And then they eat their excrement? And after that, one goes off to denounce the other? As if that mattered! It's *so* well written.'

On the other hand, to be shocked is, it seems, almost as bad—it may align you with the bourgeois. Genet's obsession (and Sartre is very convincing on this) has been to write books which defeat and despise his readers, books which are sure to be mishandled because there is no clean

New Statesman (10 January 1964)

way of handling them. But then it is only a coprophage like Genet who can manage to have his cake and eat it.

As an attack on Genet, Sartre's monstrous book (published in France in 1952) would be notably convincing. We are told that Genet's work is fake, sham, insincere; that he doesn't give a damn about the pain of others, that he refuses to understand what goes on in people's hearts, that he is concerned only with satisfying his cruelty, that he lost faith but not religiosity. 'Genet gives us *nothing*: when we shut the book, we shall know no more than we did before about prison or ruffians or the human heart.' 'He has spoken at length about a sinister and iniquitous world and yet has managed to say nothing about it.' An odd way of praising. Similarly (and with equal descriptive truth), Genet is shown to offer us nothing more than a mirror-image of 'simple-minded theological morality', with all its ignorance and limitations; far from challenging a brutish bourgeois morality and its rights of property, he affirms them. Nor—in his analysis at least—is Sartre sentimental about Genet's saintliness: he shows very clearly that 'the sophisms of Genet' are 'merely a kind of rhetoric', 'a few faked states of soul, a few operations performed on language.' Sartre, in fact—and it makes his book even odder—sees quite as clearly as Orwell why saints are morally repulsive. 'Saintliness,' he says, 'with its sophisms, rhetoric, and morose delectation repels me. It has only one use at the present time: to enable dishonest men to reason unsoundly.'

Why on earth is all this not an indictment of Genet? Sartre's answer, for all the inordinate sophistication of its working-out, is really the traditional sentimentality so dear to literary historians: roughly, 'judging a work of literature means deciding what a writer's intentions were, and then seeing if he has carried them out.' Genet *means* to produce the fake, the sham; he does so; therefore he is a good writer. He means to repel, to disgust, to be indicted; he 'succeeds'; therefore etc. Most of the time Sartre's arguments are so cloudy that it is hard to see that they conceal this old favourite, but occasionally she looms up. 'One thought that the verse *meant* nothing; the fact is, it *meant to say nothing*.' 'He wills the impossible in order to be sure of being unable to achieve it.' So how, asks Sartre with more skill than sense, can you rebuke him for failure?

Still, even if one admits that Genet enjoys philosophical tricksiness, his real teaser remains what Tynan called the riddle of the sphincter. To praise him in terms of 'reflective scissiparity' is not much more interesting than praising him as a reflective scissi. It is better to concede, as Sartre does at one point, that Genet's obsessional confusions 'move me as does a cry of pain'—provided it is not assumed that a cry of pain is enough to create literature.

The merits of *Saint Genet* as philosophy must be left to philosophers. To a non-philosopher, a statement such as 'By Evil one therefore means both the Being of Nonbeing and the Nonbeing of Being' is likely to recall Swinburne's 'The Higher Pantheism in a Nutshell': 'Fiddle, we know, is diddle: and diddle, we take it, is dee.' Genet came along when Sartre wished to speak about 'freedom'; if Genet had not existed, it would have been necessary to invent him. Sartre's aim is 'to indicate the limits of psychoanalytical interpretation and Marxist explanation and to demonstrate that freedom alone can account for a person in his totality.' But without going philosophically into 'freedom', a reader can still feel that Sartre's aim gets nowhere near success; his analyses of Genet in terms of psychology and Marxism are so outstandingly feeble, so astonishingly weaker than one would have expected, that it almost seems he has deliberately (but silently) muffed them in order to show up 'psychology' and 'Marxism' in the interests of 'freedom'. At any rate, before you could 'indicate the limits' of such insights, you would have to do them justice. Example of psychological explanation of Genet's homosexuality, offered by Sartre as true: 'Having been caught stealing *from behind*, his back opens when he steals; it is with his back that he awaits human gazes and catastrophe.' But it would take more than the dogged italicising of *from behind* to make such a guess compelling. In fact his arguments are crowded with italics jostling and jockeying for position; in transcribing Sartre, one is tempted to de-emphasise it all into roman type, to sigh laconically '[my romans]', much as P. B. Medawar did when he was panning for sense in that other muddy French stream, the prose of Teilhard de Chardin.

Sartre's psychologising about women is even cruder—he simply asks a mandarin. Has not Simone de Beauvoir said that there is no such thing as feminine society, and that 'woman is an object to the other and to herself before being a subject'? *Ipsa dixit*. His opponents (who are presented throughout, with a dangerously two-edged rhetoric, as honest, decent, just, sensible, honourable) get theirs. But what then of the 'Marxist explanation'? It hardly has a look in, apart from an excursus on conspicuous consumption (genuinely very interesting, but not much to do with Genet), and a fine moment when Sartre wistfully contemplates the might-have been, concluding that all might yet have been well for the infant Genet, 'had his foster father worked in a nationalised branch of industry'. Elsewhere the 'Marxist' hypotheses are of such simplicity that they look like straw men devised by RC apologists. On man and woman: 'The very way in which he makes love reflects his economic situation and his pride in earning a living.' Can be taken as a symbol of? Or actually derives from? Is it true then that matriarchies eschew this position? Obviously this is a bright idea, and Sartre is not the sort of writer who believes in substantiating bright ideas. On the other hand, every position in the *Kama Sutra* could be happily allegorised into male economic exploitation. If the man were to be on his back, then there he is propt on beds of amaranth and moly while the poor woman toils and moils. Sartre is a hard man to satisfy.

It is not just that he simplifies (e.g. 'sociologists and psychiatrists' see crime 'as the result of a determinism'), but that he is utterly arbitrary. So of course is Genet—it is one thing to see a guitar as an erotic symbol ('round, low-slung rump'), it is quite another to insist that it symbolises the *masculine* rump. What a critic of Genet needs is a conscience about arbitrariness, but Sartre is blissful. He can say that Genet needs the hatefulness of French society 'as Prometheus needs his vulture', as if the myth insisted on such a thing. He makes a great deal of a moment when one of Genet's characters, Pierrot, finds a maggot in his mouth. Genet says:

> He found himself caught between fainting with nausea and dominating his situation by willing it. He willed it. He made his tongue and palate artfully and patiently feel the loathsome contact.

Yes, existentialist freedom. (And fellatio, of course. Sartre uses 'of course' like the patiently reassuring master of an idiot-school.) But why not spit out the maggot? Sartre's philosophising depends on the assurance that 'Pierrot cannot prevent the maggot's being in his mouth, but . . .' And why not? In this unwillingness to tell us what prevented Pierrot, we are really not far from a kind of cant, and Sartre is led to some of the least helpful and most abusable of today's paradoxes. It would be nice to hear, for a change, from 'victims' on the subject of that famous 'bond between executioner and victim'. And similarly with loathing as 'closer to love than indifference', or hate as a kind of love. As long as Sartre is speaking only of Genet or of himself (i.e. most of the time), such dubious moralising remains merely dubious. When he steps out to speak of Jews or of Negroes, it looks too much like a twisting of other people's different suffering into a preconceived and personal philosophising. Genet undoubtedly needs the simple-minded bourgeois morality on which he battens (like a cancer, in Sartre's image); but this is not at all the same as saying that 'he loves French society as the Negroes love America, with a love that is full of hatred and, at the same time, desperate.' Genet, as antichrist, positively wants to be despised and rejected of Frenchmen; the Negro, if he loves America, does so in spite of its contempt for him, and he wants to change America. To suggest anything else is not only fatuous but also heartless.

Most of the time, though, Sartre is more humourless than heartless. Fortunately his translator has preserved, and occasionally even bettered, his delightful unconcern about double-entendre. Genet, who has admitted that it only needs a mention of any kind of 'page' for him to have a 'luminous idea', must surely have relished Sartre's description of him as a man who 'hastens towards the moment when he will write "The End" at the bottom of the last page.' To say that 'At bottom, he would have liked to associate with magistrates'; to speak of 'proof *a posteriori*', of 'the Thief's *ars poetica*', of Genet's dildo as a 'pile-driver'—all this at any rate does something to jollify a book which by and large it is a pleasure to quit. Farewell, rewards and fairies. The rewards of *Saint Genet* (the most chaotic and preposterous book ever written by a very intelligent man?) are not proportionate to its length. As for the fairies, they are in use as girlish homosexuals, so that the translator at one point has to append a lugubrious warning: when Sartre says 'the subordinate fairies enjoyed limited powers', 'the word "fairies" is to be taken here in its literal sense.'

An Englishman has to speak tentatively about Genet—thanks to our jelly-bellied gag-waggers who won't let us read his more important books. To me it seems that in his plays Genet pays a bankrupting price for having no interest in other people. As an explorer of utterly generalised fantasies, he chooses to climb into very thin air. So that I get a sharper sense of the truths of fantasy from almost any scene of *The Alchemist* than from the whole studied rootless assemblage of *The Balcony*. It may be (though I doubt it) that convincing claims for Genet's greatness can be made. That they are not made by Sartre is agreed by Joseph McMahon, whose study of the canon, *The Imagination of Jean Genet*, is less involuted and more informative. But his praising words are less weighty than his demurs. Time soon knocks the edges off 'shocking' literature. The old ordure changeth, yielding place to new. So when Sartre tells us that Genet's prison (in *Notre Dame des Fleurs*) is a 'well of loneliness', it is hard not to wonder how long it will be before it is just a *Well of Loneliness*.

Leslie Fiedler
What Was Literature? Class Culture and Mass Society

T
hree pages into *What Was Literature?*, Leslie Fiedler packs within
parentheses a punch at "troubled elitists turning typically to
French." But if such people betray themselves by using a term like *jeu
d'esprit* (Fiedler's example), where does this leave their accuser? Fiedler,
whose style feels free to exercise *force majeur* and *droit du seigneur*, who
introduces us to an *arriviste*, a *poète maudit*, and more than one *enfant
terrible*; who points the finger at *demi-vierges*; who urges, and re-urges,
Épatez la bourgeoisie, and who looks down upon *haute cuisine* and
haute couture and *la vie bohème*; who is *plus royaliste que le roi*; and who
opens a *débat*, with *cinéastes* and the *auteur*—is there not something self-
contradictory about this author's hauteur?

   Hypocrite lecteur?, a reader might wonder, or *hypocrite auteur*, if it
weren't that he'd thereby be betraying that he is a troubled elitist turning typically to French. But again Fiedler—who is by turns a troubled
elitist, an untroubled elitist, and a troubled non-elitist, but never never
quite what he yearns to be: an untroubled non-elitist—is ahead of the
game even here. "I am, I must confess, still enough of a vestigial elitist
to be ashamed of my vulnerability (and yours, *hypocrite lecteur*) to so

New Republic (20 December 1982)

gross an appeal." It is a perfect Fiedler turn, not least in being a case of what he would call, and would scorn others for calling, *reculer pour mieux sauter*. For the very next sentence is this: "Nonetheless, I suspect that what chastens pride (rather than feeds it, like the ability to respond to refined sensibility or hermetic allusions) cannot be all bad." Pretty cool, to allude not only to Baudelaire but to T. S. Eliot's allusion to Baudelaire, and then at once to disdain those who go in for such allusions. "I was not Matthew Arnold nor was meant to be, but only a culture-climbing Jewish boy": the allusive largesse is princely.

But throughout the book this is what Fiedler, a brilliantly irresponsible polemicist, is up to. Just when you might accuse him of something (too many French phrases or literary allusions), you are to register that it is he who ups and reviles those who use French phrases or literary allusions. He is endlessly fertile, and weavingly repetitive, in all those self-admonishments that function as self-exculpations. "I must confess" is one of them. There are so many of these mock-confessions as to amount to Fiedler's self-absolution. So when he says that he finds something "hard to confess," one wants to rib him. Nobody finds it easier— or more handy—to confess than does old Fiedler. The word is at the heart of what is, for me, the ugliest moment in a book that urges us not to worry about sado-masochism so long as it has "mythopoeic power":

> Finally, however, she [Scarlett O'Hara] *likes* it (as perhaps only a female writer would dare to confess, though there are echoes of D. H. Lawrence in the passage), likes being mastered by the dark power of the male, likes being raped.

Fiedler's dark power is verbal cunning; it was there in the feint of "still enough of a vestigial elitist . . . ," and "vestigial elitism" puts in a further couple of appearances in the confessional, as does its accomplice "vestigial scorn." These are all designed to clear Fiedler of any suspicions of sanctimony.

The matter as well as the manner of this book is riven with contradictions, but in some ways it may be more important, or prior, to detect the manner's sleights and their plan to let Fiedler get away with having both his non-elitist cake and his elitist "let them eat cake." There is the combination of general fierceness with particular prudence; we hear repeatedly about the evil folly of "certain contemporary American critics" (as of "certain high-minded colleagues," "certain insecure fictionists," "certain old-line Anglophile professors," "certain aging professors," "certain cryptanalytical critics," and "certain moralistic enemies"), but who exactly they are remains discreetly uncertain. The rhetoric is all of brave defiance, the tactic is all of giving no hostages. Very few names are named, and nobody whose position arguingly opposes Fiedler's is ever engaged at any length or unshadowily. Here too Fiedler's audacity is thrillingly disreputable. Reminiscing, he despises one of his "fellow panelists, an indurated Francophile elitist of the old school," for believing that he, Fiedler, had sold out: "Like Alex Haley, she probably would have specified, had she deigned to recognize his humble existence." But this very woman, who is being condemned for not having the courage or the grace to specify, and for not deigning to recognize someone's existence, is herself being left unspecified and unnamed by Fiedler, who will not deign to recognize *her* existence. It is very easy, and very cheap, this unnaming anecdotal blackguarding and bluster.

But then when Fiedler is specific, he is often specifically misleading. Since he is no fool, one had better be alert to the ends this serves. Take what sounds like an innocent preamble: "From biographical sources. . . ."

> From biographical sources, I learn that Eliot admired the music-hall singer Marie Lloyd, and that he kept an autographed picture of Groucho Marx on his office wall. But all this smacks to me of "camp" and condescension, suggesting that he only liked pop culture when it "knew its place" (like the Irish, the Jews or other lesser breeds), not when it competed with its betters, like Shakespeare—and Eliot.

Now it is indeed from biographical sources that Fiedler learns about the Groucho Marx photograph, but it is not—or it should not be—from biographical sources that he learns that Eliot admired Marie Lloyd. For Eliot made public his thoughts and feelings about Marie Lloyd, reasoningly and exactly; and it is not to be believed that Fiedler has failed to read the *Selected Essays* of T. S. Eliot. Why then does Fiedler insinuate that it is "from biographical sources" that he learns of Eliot's admiration for Marie Lloyd? First, because it is then the easier to accuse Eliot of condescension and "camp," since it makes it sound as if this admiration were reserved for some separate place of archness (knowing its place) in Eliot's life, cut off from that which he was in earnest about; and anyway the accusation is the more easily made if there can be no question of our checking it—it being biographical only—against Eliot's actual published words, his actual tone. Second, the implication that all we have to go on in the matter is some unspecified biographical source allows Fiedler to avert our eyes from Eliot's having here mounted a radical argument on exactly the subject of Fiedler's book: Class Culture and Mass Society. Fiedler manifestly couldn't like Eliot's argument, not so much because it differs from Fiedler's (though it does) as because it also doesn't—and the points where it resembles Fiedler are a styptic demonstration of Fiedler's primitive rawness in comparison with the Eliot of sixty years ago. It is not so much that Fiedler doesn't like Eliot's essay on Marie Lloyd as that he doesn't like its existing. Hence the pretense that it doesn't. "From biographical sources, I learn . . . ."

Eager to accuse Eliot and others of condescension, Fiedler affects not to notice that the accusation can itself be condescending. He has no qualms about employing what is certainly the most condescending form of all, the one that is preceded by a drawl: "rather condescendingly" and "a little condescendingly" put in several appearances.

On every important matter in this book, Fiedler is in contradiction with himself. This is not a case of an elaborately scrupulous account such as necessarily includes exact reservations, but simply of political shudderings and judderings. Fiedler might retort that, very well, he contradicts himself, he contains multitudes. They are not multitudes, but mobs.

Part One is called "Subverting the Standards." The contradictions arrive at once, for nothing could be more comfy than our old friend *subverting*. No piece of academic radicalism would feel at home without it. Fiedler, who spurns "the New Critics' cant of the time" (the word "tragic," as it happens), welcomes all the newest critics' cant of our time: "subvert" on every page, flanked repeatedly by the deathly "viable" and the hollow "resonant." Then there are those standards. Fiedler, who knows that some works of art, whether elitist or popular, are better than others, can't do without standards but can't bear the elitist sound of them. So he simply puts the word into inverted commas whenever he is talking about anybody else's criticism, while reserving the right to speak of his own uninverted standards when it suits his book. All the crucial terms of the argument move in and out of inverted commas for polemical convenience: "serious," "classics," "artist," "pornographic," "poetry," and of course "literature."

Is there or is there not such a thing as literature? "What used to be called 'literature,'" and "what used to be 'literature.'" This way of speaking is then to be found untroubled, within the same covers, in the company of such uninverted usages as these: popular literature; the distinction between literature and science; literature cannot be separated from history; the split between High Literature and low; an event in the realm of the marketplace rather than of literature; and not as literature but as myth.

Fiedler is enthralled by his new freedom, his managing to "end up as a Pop Critic" (upper case here, lower case later); he is learning "to speak the language of popular literature." He does nothing to reconcile this claim with the language he actually speaks, a language aloft. The page that announces his pop-ness needs to murmur "iconic," and before long we are meeting such undemotic words as "demotic" and such unpop words as "mythologem," "oneiric," "epigones," and "eucatastrophes."

Again, should there or should there not be a canon? Once more our academic radical runs with the hare and hunts with the hounds. Since half of his book is called "Opening up the Canon," there presumably not only is a canon but will continue to be one. But Fiedler hates himself for being only a reformist, and wants to be an apocalyptic revolutionary. ("The time for a third revolution in English studies is at hand.") He therefore has to dissociate himself from such reformism as would open up the canon. So he disparages those whose efforts ended "by merely substituting a new canon for the old," as if his own enterprise of opening up the canon (to *Gone with the Wind* and *Roots*) were not itself inevitably the creation of a new canon. He expresses his dislike of Kahlil Gibran and Rod McKuen and some of Tolkien, saying of some pop critics that "I myself could not care less whether certain of their favorite printed poems ever make it into the canon or not."

But then he has to pull himself together, or rather apart, since his radical credentials are imperiled by the very idea of a canon, whether opened up or not. Luckily he has at hand the usual evasive formula. "That the very notion of a 'canon' had been called into question by the rise of mass culture I was not yet prepared to grant." So the word canon, which is essential to his arguments, and which must there repeatedly stand straight without inverted commas, is now made conveniently equivocal, and is followed by that other evasion everywhere practiced by radical insinuation: "called into question." The implication is that the very notion of a canon has not only been called into question, but that the ensuing answer is that the notion was cogently exposed as an illusion. But this last bit would actually have asked some work, some sustained argument. Better then to leave it at insinuation merely.

Sometimes Fiedler says that there is, or should be (a different thing), no distinction between high art and popular art. Sometimes he speaks as if there is such a distinction. Sometimes he speaks as if the greatest art satisfied the widest range of criteria. There is obviously something to be said for all of the positions he takes, but nothing to be said for a book that tosses them all in, one by one, to suit its polemical convenience.

The lurches and vacillations reach down even into the matter about which Fiedler cares most. He announces that he is taking the first steps "toward creating a new kind of criticism"; this then turns out to be nothing new either to him or to those who have read him, but his old story that there are writers of "great mythopoeic powers." The story is not the worse for being old, but it should not be billed as new, especially as the need to insist on novelty forces Fiedler into some demeaning disparagements of his earlier, better, work. Fiedler in his prime would not have allowed himself so many of those *somehows* that are exactly what a critic has to convert into a true *how*. One page has "images which seem to exist somehow before and after, outside those words," and "somehow irrelevant"; another page has "somehow laughable," "somehow their own," and "somehow preeminently so"; and elsewhere there is the usual burly cop-out: "yet somehow so magically moving," and "somehow they had remained archetypally inert."

But the nub of the contradiction is the question of whether or not literature is, among other things, to be valued because it does good. Fiedler repeatedly disdains moralists and their claim for art as having "redeeming social values," as educational or pious; he is outspoken in not countenancing any talk of art as enhancing life or as making us more worthy. But his own mythic criticism is itself no less didactic and moralistic, despite its different emphasis. For myth, in Fiedler's view, teaches us. Its literature "teaches us that the impulse [to transgress taboos] preexists in the deep psyches of us all." Fiedler can speak of the value of his beloved myths as being their serving as "psycho-social therapy." Since this is one of the most priggish positions a critic could take, Fiedler naturally can't stand it, and three pages later he can be found jeering at Bruno Bettelheim on fairy tales:

> After all, Bruno Bettelheim has recently given them the psychiatric seal of approval in his *Uses of Enchantment*, assuring us that such childhood classics (he is much less approving of latter-day schlock out of, say, the Disney Studios) are *good* for them, and for us in our relationship with them.

Why this repudiation, those italics? Because Fiedler is pretending that his myths—valued as "psycho-social therapy"—somehow aren't receiving his "psychiatric seal of approval," aren't being offered as "*good* for" us.

He allows himself the laudatory terms of therapy ("it is indeed an essential function of literature to release in us unnatural impulses"), while refusing such terms to those who accept the "clinical assurance that 'privileged insanity' is finally therapeutic and therefore okay." He allows himself that which he denies to, say, any Christian critic: the right to praise things as "refreshing to the spirit." He allows himself the terms of religion ("a recourse to the dark powers in quest of salvation"), while refusing such terms to all those who locate salvation elsewhere.

The untroubled elitist, reading *What Was Literature?*, is likely—turning typically to French—to be troubled by a strong sense of *déjà vu*. What *was* it? Then it comes back. All this about a man's education into the anti-priggish worldly truth; the love of "lucre," and the love of such a word; the knowing little allusions to T. S. Eliot, and the repeated adaptation of D. H. Lawrence's "dirty little secret"; the pseudo-confessions, the self-praises, the air of courageous candor along with the unnaming prudence; the scorn for "the American anti-success story," and the "realizing how in our world nothing succeeds like failure": all this, and that one reiterated turn of phrase, snuffed by the hardest of hard noses: "the American dream of 'making it'," "the guilt we have long been trained to think of as the inevitable accompaniment of making it," "aspiring to make it". . . . Of course! So could it be that in the past Leslie Fiedler has published not only (as he tells us) under the name of "John Simon," but under that of "Norman Podhoretz"?

Donald Davie
Trying to Explain

'**S**ince Byron and Landor, no Englishman appears to have profited much from living abroad.' So said an American who rightly believed himself to be profiting from living abroad, T. S. Eliot in England in 1918, honouring the American who had likewise profited and who had then become—as Eliot would—an Englishman: Henry James. 'The fact of being everywhere a foreigner was probably an assistance to his native wit.'

And Donald Davie, who everywhere has his native wits about him, has he profited much from living abroad? In half-praise of George Steiner, Davie floats 'a tradition of high-flying speculation about litera-ture, which we costive islanders cannot afford not to profit by'. 'Specu-lation', 'afford' and 'profit' put a poet's pressure on 'costive'. Yet should Davie simply say 'we costive islanders'? It is odd that he doesn't openly count the costiveness and the profit of his being stationed abroad.

'Here are some periodical pieces, mostly rather recent, which con-cern themselves with poetry both American and British, from the point of view of a British poet who has, however, resided for the past ten years in the United States.' One word in Davie's preface is uncharacteristi-cally demure. 'Resided'? An Englishman such as he, with his convictions and his angers, would not be likely to profit much, except financially,

London Review of Books (4 June 1980)

from residing abroad. The book's blurb is right to strip away this residual pudeur, and to speak of 'the point of view of a British poet who has lived for the last decade in America'. But then the casualness of Davie's opening—'Here are some . . .'—might mislead. The critic who waited for twenty years before agreeing to a collection of his essays, and who then permitted another to compile it, would not be the man to bring out, only two or three years later, a rag-bag.

Trying to Explain collects its strength, urged on by an exacerbated feeling for the differences between England and America; by a painful reluctance to abandon its hope that each might adopt something of the other's wisdom; and by a confidence that we must newly see the truth of the old sense of things—namely, that the Englishman is the victim-beneficiary of a belief in the artist as amateur, and the American of a belief in the artist as professional.

This wise saw is filled out with modern instances. Davie has lost none of his ability to swoop upon a single fact of singular importance. On Allen Tate's retreat from the factuality of his poems, such that 'Shadow and Shade' is seriously flawed by 'the impossibility of knowing where the two actors in the poem are standing (indoors, that is, or out-of-doors)'; on Ed Dorn's magical misspellings, which are sometimes 'exhuberant' and more often 'queezy', but which can pack a portmanteau which is worth the carriage, as in 'The creatures of ice feignt and advance' (or the truest poetry is the most feigning); on Robert Lowell's achieving what is rare in him, a telling sequence, in his *Selected Poems*, 'Nineteen Thirties', 25 poems formerly scattered and now finding the arc they were meant for—on all these and on much else (Yeats's fascism, and Pound's), Davie can strike sparks and can kindle fervour.

Yet there is much that is strange about the book's movements of mind. There are no fits and starts, but there are leaps and bounds. Take the preoccupation to which very many of the essays recur, which is seen as epitomising the contrast between the English amateur and the American professional: the belief in an *atelier* or studio. The idea of thresholds is crucial to Davie here, and he argues persuasively that below a certain threshold of skilled competence a dedication to the artist as

amateur may issue only in the slovenly and amateurish, and above such
a threshold a dedication to the artist as professional may issue only in
the facile and professionalised. But why does it follow that *ateliers* are
the answer, or even an answer? 'Both Pound and Wyndham Lewis were
American or Americanised enough to have on the contrary a *professional*
attitude to their respective arts, in the quite precise sense that they
saw the continuity of art traditions ensured by the *atelier*, the master
instructing his prentices. The renegade or maverick Englishmen with
whom they allied themselves—Ford, and at another level A. R. Orage—
shared this un-English conviction and habit.' Yet it does not seem from
this book that any of these writers did convert this conviction into a
habit. Where did the studios flourish, who were the masters and who
the prentices? Davie quotes Canto 80: 'For "prodigies" ("Mr Binyon's
young prodigies") surely we ought to read "protégés".' But we shouldn't
delete 'prodigies': to lose the pun would be to lose the lugubrious implication that, in this day and age and art, a protégé would be a prodigy.
Davie is obliged to protect, not prentices, but his own conviction; to
protect it against what he himself then elicits from this Canto: the question about Binyon and Sturge Moore, 'whether the two senior writers
could not have established themselves—at least for some purposes—as
masters of *ateliers* in which the two young hopefuls might have enrolled
as apprentices'. For the answer to the question 'could they not?' is more
no than yes, and the answer to the question 'did they?' is flatly no. That
Pound hungered for such a relationship, that at the age of 48 (in 1934)
he would still have liked 'to enroll in Binyon's seminar if Binyon would
only call it into being': this is delightfully established by Davie. But the
sweet fatuity and credulity of the wish (Pound and Wyndham Lewis,
prenzies to Binyon and Sturge Moore?) ought to make against Davie's
urging us to share it.

For one thing, Davie is markedly short of accounts of such literary
ateliers and their success. For another, he doesn't ask any questions
about the differences between the visual arts and the art of literature,
and how these might render more difficult and even perhaps inapplicable
the concept of an *atelier*. He assimilates it to the 'creative writing' schools

or classes in America (respected there, and complacently despised by the British, it seems), as if the two were not radically different in where they located a very substantial part of their authority. He notices, but does not stay with, the fact that the word *atelier* is foreign not just to British but to American ears. Of his 'consultancy sessions' at Stanford in the writing of poetry: 'Here it seems to me that the relationship is that of a master to an apprentice. I like to think of it being like Ghirlandaio in his workshop. And as we all know, in that workshop (for which for some reason we always use the French word *atelier*), were young apprentices learning at the master's feet.' For some reason? The French word will not be assimilated, and the recalcitrance may have something to do with the thing itself. But then these days 'workshop' won't really do either, even if you don't go as far as Jake of *Jake's Thing*: 'If there's one word that sums up everything that's gone wrong since the War, it's Workshop.'

'The strictly poetical inspiration of our poetry,' said Hopkins, a poet-critic of whom Davie has disapproved but with whom he might here concur, 'seems to me to be of the very finest, finer perhaps than the Greek; but its rhetoric is inadequate—seldom first-rate, mostly only just sufficient, sometimes even below par. By rhetoric I mean all the common and teachable element in literature, what grammar is to speech, what thoroughbass is to music, what theatrical experience gives to playwrights.' But it does not follow that dedication to an appropriate professionalism would have to—or would be likely to—take the form of enrolling in an *atelier*. The teachable element in literature might, after all, be best taught even to poets by an attention not to their own poems or to their master's, but to poets not alive or not in the room. Or it might be taught by the private solicitudes of friendship (Hopkins and Bridges) or by the public educings and adducings of a periodical.

This matters to Davie's book, not just because *Trying to Explain* does not really try to explain how it is guided to this outcome, but because there is entailed a slight to 'the two massive figures of Henry James and T. S. Eliot'. Neither lacked the highest respect for the teachable element in literature; but neither devoted much energy to any *ate-*

lier. 'It was this unrelenting professionalism in Pound that set, and continues to set, Englishmen's teeth on edge.' But before setting our teeth off edge, we should at least ask whether Pound didn't have a less than fully intelligent and imaginative notion of what the truly professional consisted in; should ask whether there is anywhere in sight an even better dedication. It is not clear whether Davie believes Eliot to have been guilty of unrelenting amateurism or of relenting professionalism, but either way Eliot is never to be acknowledged here as any kind of principled differer from Pound. Pound did what Auden says you mustn't do in the company of the English, he talked shop—'(Once again Eliot knew, or soon learned, better).' And this was merely worse? Eliot is introduced as 'that one of [Pound's] erstwhile protégés who had become, surprisingly, a pillar of the English establishment—Eliot, editor of the *Criterion*'. Prodigy, certainly; protégé . . . ? It would not suit Davie's argument to acknowledge Pound's letter in 1914 about Eliot: 'He is the only American I know of who has made what I can call adequate preparation for writing. He has actually trained himself *and* modernised himself *on his own*.' Anyway, why should it be automatically assumed that the mutual respect of Eliot and the English Establishment is something for which they must be disrespected? Is the implication that Eliot abandoned his proper professionalism? Or that he never had it? (Evidence?) In any case, what matters is that the artist should *be* professional, not that he should bristlingly announce his unrelenting professionalism. Davie rightly insists that Pound could not have stayed in an England which was so obtusely hostile to him. But he goes on: 'If Pound had been different . . . ? He would have had to be as different as T. S. Eliot; and there's an end of *that* speculation!' But it isn't the end of speculation about this shriek-mark. For what exactly did Eliot achieve in his difference from Pound in this matter? If Eliot did not merely renege, what did he create as an alternative to Pound's sense of professional dedication?

Davie says that 'on this issue indeed the comparison with Eliot is inescapable,' but the issue is then escaped from, and we hear only the terms of unspecified social offence and not at all the terms of the particular social offence given by that conception of the artist as professional which so disturbs the English. 'Eliot very early learned and bowed to the English rule that social amenity must not be disturbed—alike in his life-style and, after *Poems 1920*, in his poetic style also, he observed this rule punctiliously.' But the life-style of the very young Eliot in America—whether within his family or at Harvard—was no more willing to disturb social amenity than was that of Eliot in England, and so there are reasons to be sceptical of 'Eliot very early learned and bowed to the English rule . . .' The English rule was also the rule of the young Eliot's America (which was not all of America, but then nor was the England which is posited all of England). The life and art of Eliot are underdescribed here by Davie, to put it mildly; concerned and informed patience is given to Pound, whereas Eliot is offered as presenting no honourable alternative to Pound's honourable pugnacity and exile. But then such alternatives are often waved away by Davie. The same page pops this question: 'Is it perhaps true that for many of the English, poetry has never been anything else but a superior parlor game? We might begin to think so if we reflected that in parlor games the rules never change, and then noticed that this year the most accomplished of our poets in their forties published, sixty years after Pound's *Lustra* and Eliot's *Prufrock*, an ambitious poem in the shape of 15 interlinked pentameter sonnets.' (This year? The lecture was given in 1977 but published in 1978.) One desirable rule of literary criticism might be that you should not calumniate the unnamed, or incite parlour-game guess-work about poetry. (Is it Geoffrey Hill? *Fifteen* sonnets doesn't fit, though there would be something boldly winsome about offering Hill as your example of the poet insufficiently dedicated to his art.) Even more important, there is the assertive naivety which does not need even to argue in any way for its belief that a sonnet sequence must today be nothing but a parlour game, a regression in the art of poetry, a sinking-back down some evolutionary scale. All of which would be extraordinary if it weren't that the argument about Pound and Eliot is so badly manned that it needs all the reinforcements which rhetoric's encitements can drum up.

Something else is strange about the book. For Davie is necessarily much occupied with expatriates, and yet at no point does he discuss either the general advantages and disadvantages of this vantage-point or the particular ones which might go with a particular siting. Eliot is 'the American Virgilian expatriate'; Dorn 'has lived in England, has been happy there'; Lowell had 'his withdrawal to England'; Steiner 'has removed himself from the British literary scene to Geneva, for reasons which I understand'; and the publisher of this book itself, Michael Schmidt of the Carcanet Press and of *PN Review* (of which Davie is an editor), is Davie's double-goer off in the opposite direction ('American by conditioning, but Mexican by citizenship and an English resident by preference'). Davie repeatedly speaks of 'my English-conditioned taste', 'my British conditioning', 'my English ear'; he muses 'as an Englishman' about this, and as 'a British reader' about that. But he is not simply a British reader (whether of British or American poetry), he is a British reader who does almost all of his reading, and of his talking and writing, in another country. It is eerie that he is not moved to attend directly to what it means to be an expatriate, having home-thoughts and abroad-thoughts from abroad. The first words of his touching essay 'A West Riding Boyhood' are: 'In California, one summer afternoon in 1971, soon after my 49th birthday, I slept and had a dream.' To move from the title to those first two words is striking and strange; what is no less strange is the way the words 'In California' at once disappear down a concessive oubliette.

'Ezra Pound's long love-affair with England' is Davie's too, except that Pound had shaken the dust of England onto his feet. But can Davie's long love-affair with America be elided so glidingly? Pound, 'that expatriate and maverick American', is the heart of the matter and the heart of the book. Some of the six pieces devoted to him have telling titles: 'Ezra Pound abandons the English', 'Pound and *The Exile*', 'Ezra Pound and the English'. Davie is often persuasive in rebuking those in England who were violent or condescending towards Pound (though the English might reasonably be vexed by the deployment against them, in defence of a Fascist who supported their enemies during the war, of the dictum by Auden that the English are 'persuaded beyond argument that they are the *Herrenvolk*'). But it is perplexing, and it incites a legitimate hunger which the book never satisfies, that Davie will not share his thoughts, in principle or in detail, about expatriation itself.

We are reminded that Pound was not the only one to find that England after the Great War was, for the artist, 'uninhabitable'. D. H. Lawrence found it so, and Graves and then Auden and Isherwood. But the cases don't click. For Pound—like James and Eliot—had previously found America uninhabitable. Davie finds America inhabitable. I should hope so too. But why wasn't it part of his critical obligation, when engaged so much with 'the matter of England', to say just exactly what it is, this 'point of view of a British poet who has lived for the last decade in America'? It cannot be the same as that of a British poet who simply knows and loves America and its poetry but does not live there.

At one point Davie defends Pound's poem *Hugh Selwyn Mauberley*, and his own arguments about it, against an adverse critic. 'For this sort of Englishman, "externality"—to things English—is what any American is condemned to; and per contra "inwardness"—with things English—is what an Englishman quite simply has, painlessly, as a birthright.' Yet it was Pound himself who signed the warrant for some such condemnation, in a book which Davie has wistfully and wittily acknowledged elsewhere but not here, *Patria Mia* (1913). It was Pound who insisted: 'If a man's work require him to live in exile, let him suffer, or enjoy, his exile gladly. But it would be about as easy for an American to become a Chinaman or a Hindoo as for him to acquire an Englishness, or a Frenchness, or a European-ness that is more than half a skin deep.'

Perhaps Davie believes that the sufferings and enjoyments of exile are to be the tissue of his poetry and not of his criticism. Or perhaps the present collection is a stage towards his engagement with the nature of expatriation, its enabling and disabling propensities. Of his one perverse book, *Thomas Hardy and British Poetry*, he good-naturedly acknowledges that 'it never makes up its mind whether it's addressing the American reader or the British reader, and part of the time it is castigating the

Americans for not being British, and the rest of the time it's castigating the British for not being Americans.' But then nor does it make up its mind whether it is castigating the British for living in Britain.

It may be that there is a clue to what is deep in Davie, in one of the best essays, 'American Literature: The Canon'.

> My [American] students stare at me in surprise when I point out that in the 150 years between the landing of the Pilgrim Fathers and the Declaration of Independence very few people of Caucasian race, born and living in the territory of what is now the continental United States, conceived of themselves as anything but Englishmen who happened to live on the opposite side of the Atlantic from most of their compatriots. Yet so far as I can see (I stand ready to be corrected) this was indeed the case. Indeed, those very Americans who themselves created the American nation as a political identity distinct from the British, the very fathers of the Republic themselves—Ben Franklin, John Adams, Thomas Jefferson—conceived of themselves, at least up to 1776, as Englishmen who happened to live overseas. How could they have thought otherwise?

From these pages there rises a weird yearning. Davie, in his modern self-exile, joins in his imagination those who lived in America but were Englishmen, 'Englishmen who happened to live overseas'. To live in America then was to be—as it now can never be—not an English expatriate but an Englishman's compatriot. Englishmen in America, they lived then within a society profoundly attractive and impressive to Davie:

> Eighteenth-century habits of thought and language persist in American public life as they do not in the public life of England. The Constitution of the United States was framed according to 18th-century pre-Romantic ideals, and is couched in 18th-century Enlightenment language . . . Yet that the American should refuse to sympathise with his own pre-Romantic past, to the extent of denying (unless he is a constitutional lawyer or a professional historian) that he has any 18th-century past at all—this cannot fail to astonish us. Pope and Dryden, Fielding and Goldsmith, ought to be *more* your authors than they are mine, simply because the institutionalised public life of your nation has kept open avenues of

access to their imaginative and intellectual world, in a way that the public life of England has not.

Nowhere does Davie speak as if he had access to a time-machine. Yet his words vibrate with a sense of how perfect a home this would have been for him, this 18th-century England which was America. There is a poignancy in this, as there was in Pound's acknowledgment—never to be accepted by Pound himself—that no American could 'acquire an Englishness, or a Frenchness, or a European-ness that is more than half a skin deep'. Eliot too was haunted. 'It is hardly too much to say,' said he, 'that Chaucer is difficult for a Continental because he is an Englishman, and difficult for an Englishman because he is pre-Reformation—because he belongs naturally and quite locally to the main body of European thought.' Eliot, an American writing this on the brink of becoming an Englishman, longs to belong naturally and quite locally to the main body of European thought, back in the days when in Europe the word 'catholic' meant what it said. This poignancy, where you can conceive of a state within time, for ever closed to you, can be heard even in the wit of another of Eliot's great sayings about James: 'It is the final perfection, the consummation of an American to become, not an Englishman, but a European—something which no born European, no person of any European nationality, can become.' Davie writes, tacitly and touchingly, as if it were the final perfection of an Englishman to become, not an American, but a born-again pre-1776 American, an Englishman who happens to live overseas, something which no born American can become.

Stanley Fish
Is There a Text in This Class?

G eoffrey Hartman is not a theorist himself, not even a theorist
malgré lui, but an advocate of theory. Stanley Fish is both advocate and theorist. The blurb to *Is There a Text in This Class?* dubs him 'one
of America's most stimulating literary theorists'; the advertisements have
upped this to 'one of the world's most stimulating literary theorists'.
The blurb alone could occupy a hermeneuticist for some time, especially
with its saying that Fish 'offers a stunning proposal for a new way of
thinking about the way we read'. Not since Nureyev was described on
the BBC as 'a staggering dancer' has there been so soft a sell as this stunning of our thinking. But Fish, who is very lively, does not stun critical
thought, though his theory would, if acted upon, lobotomise it.

His procedure is to reprint a series of his essays in theory, prefacing
the whole with a jokey-titled 'Introduction, or How I Stopped Worrying
and Learned To Love Interpretation'. Fish is indeed the Dr Strangelove
of the theory effort. Most of the essays are further prefaced by some
account of their rectifiable weaknesses, of their imperfect advance upon
the truth. There can be heard a curious hymnlike crooning. Nearer my
God to Me. There is much humour in this, some of it deliberate. Every-

London Review of Books (16 April–6 May 1981), following Ricks's review of
Geoffrey Hartman, *Criticism in the Wilderness*

thing must be set down, for the record, which is the record of a theorist's shucking of successive approximations or falsities. Some of what he shucks it is odd of him to have encumbered himself with in the first place—most notably, a belief that the collusive couple 'subjective' and 'objective' were honest and helpful. Eventually they are recognised to be neither honest nor helpful, but the weaning from them seems needlessly delayed.

Other evacuations amount to the jettisoning of literature and of criticism, so Fish's robustly skilful moves should be declined. He is set to discard, first, the distinction between interpretation and that which is interpreted, and, second (except that it comes to the same thing), the distinction between reading and writing (though not exactly the distinction between writing and reading, on which he is uncharacteristically silent). For Fish, there is no such thing as a text, or as facts, except as constituted by interpretation itself; it is 'interpretive communities' (Fish's bolt-hole, to escape from solipsism and relativism, neither of which he finally decides could possibly exist anyway) which produce meanings; interpretation is the source of texts, which are the products of interpretation. There is much italicising of words like *produce* and *create*. It is 'interpretive strategies' which '*write* [his italics] the text I write when reading "Lycidas".' Each of us reads the poem he has made. 'Interpreters do not decode poems; they make them.' Once again, as in Hartman, the two-handed engine stands ready to smite both non-critic readers and authors: 'Interpretive communities are made up of those who share interpretive strategies not for reading (in the conventional sense) but for writing texts, for constituting their properties and assigning their intentions.' Where does this leave writers, the original writers? Nowhere. And readers, 'in the conventional sense'? In the same place, yet once more.

Now there is an evident objection to all this, and Fish is too intelligent (and too canny) not to acknowledge it. Granted there is an act of interpretation, 'what is that act an interpretation *of*?' But Fish brushes this away like a fly: 'I cannot answer that question, but neither, I would claim, can anyone else.' Well, a fly has the right to decline to enter the fly-bottle, and nobody but a theorist need feel under any obligation to answer such a question other than with the unelaborated answer, 'a remark', or 'a poem', or even 'a text'—something which, despite all the theoretical or philosophical problems, may be pointed out and reproduced. And if, as Fish claims, no literary theorist can give an answer to the crucial question about interpretation, 'What is that act an interpretation *of*?', then literary theory is even more of a Serbonian bog than one had thought. But though it is clear why Fish exercises all his ingenuity on claiming that there is no such thing as anything independent of interpretation, no 'distinction between interpreters and the objects they interpret', it will still not do for him to claim to be no worse off than any other theorist when it comes to answering the leading theoretical question. He dissociates himself from 'our commonsense intuition that interpretation must be interpretation of *something*.' But you are not necessarily saved from nonsense by insisting that you are not gullible about common sense, and the nonsense is there in the fact that Fish's use of the word 'interpretation' disavows not just 'our commonsense intuition' but the very history and meaning of the word 'interpretation'. The one thing about the word 'interpret' which cannot be ignored is its propensity to be a transitive verb. But Fish needs the word 'interpretation' to lend dignity and substance to his enterprise, which is why he has not made up a new word instead (is 'decertainising' his own new word? I trust so); but the word 'interpretation' will not be the self-consuming artifact he asks it to be, will not commit suicide for the illusion that you could have an interpretation that was not of something.

Which is why the advertisement's sentence, plucked from the blurb, is so false to the book, or true to a falsity in the book: 'Arguing for the right of the reader to interpret and in effect create the literary work, Fish skillfully avoids the old trap of subjectivity.' *In effect* create the literary work? Nowhere in this book of nearly four hundred pages do the words 'in effect' qualify 'create' (or 'produce' or 'write' the literary work): rather, 'create' and its variants are repeatedly italicised in order to underline that Fish is *not* genially and permissively saying that the reader only 'in effect' creates the literary work. One sees why it is prudent to foist the words into a blurb and advertisement, since the naked claim is preposterous (before-after, arsy-versy). If the reader really does, and not just 'in effect', create the literary work, what did the author do? He is just a spare pen at the hermeneuticist's wedding. But the trouble is that this is exactly Fish's claim.

Fish never says 'in effect create', partly because he is strong-minded, and partly because for him there anyway isn't any difference between 'in effect' and 'in fact'. The only fact *is* an effect. He says 'in fact' a great deal in fact—oddly for someone who insists that there are no facts *tout court*. He says that even 'Milton', if we say that 'Lycidas' was 'written by Milton', is a 'notion' and an 'interpretation'. His book has no truck with the kindly misguided liberalism of 'in effect'; the acknowledgment would not be a small one at all, but a huge crevice in the argument. Once admit that the reader in effect creates the literary work, and you cannot escape the question: 'What then is *in effect* being contrasted with?' Fish might say that he couldn't answer that question (any more than 'What is that act an interpretation *of*?')—but nor could any other theorist. Yet he couldn't afford to make a habit of not being able to answer such questions. Better do as he does: that is, never allow the question to be raised in effect or in fact, the question of how we can speak of what the author did—as distinguished from what the reader does—once we have appropriated the words 'create', 'write' and 'produce' for the reader's part in the enterprise. The silence here too is deafening in its effrontery, as it was when Hartman was able equably to say that the reader 'becomes at once reader and writer' (though Hartman hedges as Fish does not). The wish to save readers—by which is meant critics—from feeling inferior has led to the rendering of authors superfluous except as somehow the inexplicable occasion for critics to go about their bankrupt business, since there are now no words left with which to describe what authors effected or achieved. Critics, academic critics, are to take over from both non-professional readers and from writers. Fish believes that he is doing the profession a service:

> Perhaps the greatest gain that falls to us under a persuasion model is a greatly enhanced sense of the importance of our activities. (In certain quar-

ters of course, where the critical ideal is one of self-effacement, this will be perceived to be the greatest danger.) No longer is the critic the humble servant of texts whose glories exist independently of anything he might do; it is what he does, within the constraints embedded in the literary institution, that brings texts into being and makes them available for analysis and appreciation. The practice of literary criticism is not something one must apologise for; it is absolutely essential not only to the maintenance of, but to the very production of, the objects of its attention.

Once again, the alternative is travestied: there are other possibilities than megalomania and 'self-effacement'. And notice, for instance, how the alternative to 'the greatest gain' turns out not to be 'the greatest loss' but 'the greatest danger'. More important is the obliteration of the writer—a person who might first of all be thought of as bringing texts into being and making them available, a person who might be thought to have at least some small claim as having humbly contributed to 'the very production' of literary works. Like Fish, I don't think that the practice of literary criticism is something one must apologise for, but if Fish's claims were true, then no apology by academic critics—to authors and to readers—could ever be adequate. Dr Strangelove nukes them out of existence.

The attack on not just the authority of authors but their very existence is inseparable from the attack on intention in literature. Fish is very persuasive on the inescapability of interpretation, and he shows that if you seem to meet an utterance which doesn't have to be interpreted, that is because you have interpreted it already. But it is a fundamental objection to the extreme of hermeneuticism today that, in its adept slighting of authorial intention, it leaves itself no way of establishing the text of a text. To put it gracelessly like this is to bring out that some of the convenience of the word 'text' for the current theorists is its preemptive strike against the word 'text' as involving the establishing of the words of a text and their emending if need be. For on Fish's principles, need could never be. There are no facts independent of interpretation; moreover every interpretative strategy can make—cannot but make—perfect sense, according to its lights, of every detail of every text.

To put it at its simplest, Fish's theory has no way of dealing with misprints. His book happens to be full of misprints. I acknowledge that I call them misprints only by an act of interpretation: that is, I judge that Fish's enterprise in *Is There a Text in This Class?*, unlike Joyce's in *Finnegans Wake*, makes it so unlikely that he intended to call the word 'pleasurably' an 'abverb' that I'd feel bound—if I were his executor and he dead—to change it, to correct it, for the next printing. Of course, he *could* want the word 'abverb' (as in 'pleasur*ab*ly'), but I so much doubt it that I'd bet on it. In other words, we may legitimately judge that we should here read another word ('adverb'), in the most fundamental sense of what it is we should read. The result of my interpreting it as a misprint would be the emendation of the text of this text, and would be the removal thereafter from interpretability at all of the word 'abverb' once so interpreted. Fish didn't mean 'abverb', and so it doesn't make sense to ask what he meant by it. I'd do the same with other misprints here, all of which *could* be in lively creative relation with other words in their vicinity but all of which I am confident are merely misprints: 'distinterested', which might be distantly disinterested, but isn't; 'defintion', which lacks clear definition; 'ambguity', which has one type of it; 'Ftting together', which doesn't; 'innaccurate', which is so (like an Errata-slip which I once saw, headed 'Erata', and which the hermeneuticist might offer as a meta Errata-slip); 'exhilirating'; and—best of all— 'paristic on everyday usage', which would do very nicely as meaning 'parasitic on Paris' yet which is probably not a revealing pun but a misprint such as reveals nothing except that Harvard University Press lacks good proof-readers. Nothing except that Fish, like other extremists of interpretation, is committed to an inordinate and unworkable sacrosanctity for the text of any text. His theory forbids him to emend, since there isn't any thing which he *could* emend, there being no text independent of interpretation, and all interpretation being, on his explicit and detailed account, perfectly self-fulfilling. 'Interpretation creates intention,' so you could not posit an intention outside your interpretation; and since interpretations always work perfectly upon whatever they are given, you can't use intention to emend a misprint.

Yet I don't believe that when Fish refers to Christina Brooke Rose, he is referring to a hitherto-neglected near-namesake of Christine Brooke-Rose, or somehow subtly intimating something about Christine Brooke-Rose by 'subverting' her into a Brooke-Rose by any other name. I think Christina should be interpreted as a mistake or a misprint, and so should be tacitly or physically emended away, out of harm's (hermeneuticism's) way. The same goes for all the other people who are here misnomers: Macauley, and Mark Kinkead-Weakes, and Frederic Jameson, and Philip Hosbaum. These phantoms have in common only that they appear in Fish's book and should be emended into disappearance, as should a nonexistent poem by Wallace Stevens twice called 'Anecdote of a Jar'. At least, I hope that Fish wouldn't claim that this mistitling has called the poem into existence, along the lines of his conclusion to 'Interpreting "Interpreting the Variorum"': 'I was once asked whether there are really such things as self-consuming artifacts, and I replied: "There are now." In that answer you will find both the arrogance and the modesty of my claims.'

The case of the poem which perhaps didn't exist is there in Fish's telling how he left up on the blackboard the list of names from a previous class on linguistics:

Jacobs-Rosenbaum
    Levin
    Thorne
    Hayes
    Ohman(?)

Then, having drawn a frame round it and added a fictitious page-reference, Fish told the incoming class (students of 17th-century religious poetry) that this was a poem. They then exercised their critical faculties on it, and said much that was ghoulishly plausible and imaginative. For Fish, this odious experiment proves that 'skilled reading . . . is a matter of knowing how to *produce* what can thereafter be said to be there. Interpretation is not the art of construing but the art of constructing. Interpreters do not decode poems; they make them.' But his demonstration is flawed in three crucial ways. The first concerns his claim that 'my students did not proceed from the noting of distinguishing features to the recognition that they were confronted by a poem; rather, it was the act of recognition that came first—they knew in advance that they were dealing with a poem—and the distinguishing features then followed.' But when the students came in, Fish 'told them that what they saw on the blackboard was a religious poem,' and therefore to speak of their 'recognition' of it as a poem is to ignore too much about the experiment (and about its replacing of authors' authority by pedagogues' authority and sanctions). Second, Fish cannot himself describe the names on the blackboard without just such a removing of the matter from contestable interpretation as his theory forbids:

> Ohmann's name was spelled as you see it here ['Ohman(?)'] because I could not remember whether it contained one or two n's. In other words, the question-mark in parenthesis signified nothing more than a faulty memory and a desire on my part to appear scrupulous. The fact that the names appeared in a list that was arranged vertically, and that Levin, Thorne and Hayes formed a column that was more or less centered in relation to the paired names of Jacobs and Rosenbaum, was similarly accidental and was evidence only of a certain compulsiveness if, indeed, it was evidence of anything at all.

But the insistence, confident of its own stability, that something in a text 'signified nothing more than' what its writer now declares; the belief that something, several things, in a text can be attributed to accident ('similarly accidental'), and that we can rest assured that something 'was evidence only of a certain compulsiveness if, indeed, it was evidence of anything at all': these are admissions as to accident and as to evidence which are incompatible with Fish's theory of interpretation. For Fish, there is no such thing as evidence distinct from interpretation, and from interpretation's self-fulfilling perfection. Yet he needs here to say that something in a text may not just be explained but may be explained away (away from the need to be interpreted as signifying something); he says that something in a text might be evidence of nothing at all.

How could it, on his terms? Or (it comes to the same thing) how could it *not* be, since on Fish's terms all evidence is evidence *of* nothing at all? In other words (see how he uses 'In other words' there), he can make his classroom experiment real to us, and establish its interest, only by declaring what the listed names really were, really accidental or partly so. Yet for him the idea 'really were' is a delusion, a vacancy. Then at the very end of this essay, he says: 'That text might be a poem, as it was in the case of those who first "saw" "Jacobs-Rosenbaum Levin Hayes Thorne Ohman (?)" . . . but whatever it is, the shape and meaning it appears immediately to have will be the "ongoing accomplishment" of those who agree to produce it.' But there are two questions still. First, what can it mean for Fish to put the word 'saw' in inverted commas since on his terms there could not possibly be a difference between seeing and 'seeing'? Second, why is the order given here for the names different from that on the blackboard as Fish has several times given it ('Thorne' before 'Hayes', not after)? Perhaps, as with the old radio programme and its 'this week's deliberate mistake', Fish is a pedagogue to the last, keeping us on our toes with a last-minute trick. But I doubt it. The difference is not to be interpreted except by being interpreted away (removed from the sphere of interpretation thereafter) as 'accidental'—that is, interpreted as a slip not needing to be further interpreted. But for Fish to acknowledge any such error or accident or misprint, any possibility of wise emendation, would be for him to acknowledge something independent of interpretation, even if it were only the fact that he had meant to give the list once more in the real and authorised version.

Philip Larkin
Required Writing: Miscellaneous Pieces 1955–1982

'How,' asked Dr Leavis, vaulting into his review of T. S. Eliot's *On Poetry and Poets*, 'can a book of criticism be at once so distinguished and so unimportant?' Of Philip Larkin's comparable and incomparable 'miscellaneous pieces', it might be asked: How can a book of criticism be at once so un-'distinguished' and so important? But then how can this Faber book of groans be so exhilarating? The open unsecret is: by being unremittingly attentive and diversely funny. Asked in an interview about his 'secret flaws' as a writer, Larkin levels his reply: 'My secret flaw is just not being very good, like everyone else.' Asked whether he consciously uses humour to achieve a particular effect, he obligingly particularises while generalising: 'One uses humour to make people laugh.' Deprecating untruth, he is a master at combining the Retort Courteous and the Quip Modest. *You didn't mention a schedule for writing* . . . 'Yes, I was afraid you'd ask about writing.' Sometimes things are such that he does have to press on to give the Reply Churlish ('Who's Jorge Luis Borges?'), and the Reproof Valiant (*What do you think about Mrs Thatcher?* 'Oh, I adore Mrs Thatcher'), and even the Countercheck Quarrelsome ('Oh, for Christ's sake, one doesn't *study* poets!'). But like

London Review of Books (1–14 March 1984)

Touchstone, he is not cut out for giving the Lie Circumstantial and the Lie Direct. Like Touchstone, he is independent of mind, prepared to tell people when they are feigning; and, playing the Fool, he is of course licensed by all the authorities whom he banters, cajoles and outwits, countenanced and honest the while.

Larkin clears of cant not only his mind but his mouth, and not only his. Dr Johnson steadies Larkin's mind ('Now one must clear one's mind of cant'), while at the same time encouraging him to heights of irresistible albeit temporary concession which are a comic counterpart to the great verse-paragraphs of 'The Vanity of Human Wishes' ('Yet should . . . Should . . . Should . . . Should . . . Should . . . Should . . . Yet'). Concerned not to be unfair, even to 'The Holy Barbarians' alias the Beats, Larkin musters a crescendo of grantings while biding his time:

> Now one must clear one's mind of cant and admit, firstly, that everyone is free to live as he likes as far as society will let him; secondly, that other people besides Angel Dan Davies enjoy poetry, jazz and sex; and thirdly that, appalling as it would be to have Itchy Dave Gelden coming in one's door 'fidgeting and scratching his crotch' ('Hi, what's cookin'? Are we gonna blow some poetry, maybe?'), he would probably be no worse than a guardee subaltern talking about Buck House, or your father-in-law telling you how his new golf clubs cost more but aren't as good as his old ones. Other people are Hell (I have never seen why Sartre should have been praised for inverting and falsifying this truism), and the self-important spongers of Venice no more so than the rest.

By this time one is yearning for the stubborn *But* against which all these sequent waves of fairmindedness will go up in foam. Larkin's timing is perfect, and his But of a sentence is petrified into a twelfth of his opening one. 'But Mr Lipton's point is that they are a lot less so.' The retorted scorn of this is as unanswerable as a back turned upon you, duly and inexorably.

Larkin's eloquence repeatedly casts itself as retort and ensuing silence. He is in every sense a reactionary writer. *Required Writing* turns the tables on required reading, and its author has a good ear for a retort:

Cole Porter's wife, asked if her jewels are real, asks back: 'Real *what?*' Larkin similarly turns back a turn of speech so that his interlocutor (an interviewer, a critic, a poet or a reader) has to face the prior question about that way of putting it. Sometimes the tone of his manoeuvre is robustly collusive, as who should say: Come off it. There is an apocryphal story afloat of Larkin grumbling to someone about how it is the schoolteachers who are the really lazy sods, whereupon the embarrassed remonstration 'I'm a schoolteacher myself actually' was at once met by Larkin's genial rumbling it as a chance for co-opting: 'Well you'll know just what I mean then.' Sometimes the retorting tone is nannying, along the lines of 'Take those words out of your mouth, you don't know where they've been.' Mostly the tone has the dear grouchiness of Edward FitzGerald, another master of lugubrious comedy and of critical aperçus that weigh more than other men's tomes. Like Larkin a chastening defender of poets against their own incipient inauthenticities, FitzGerald used to groan to good effect. Tennyson had written for his friend Spedding, bereaved of a brother:

> Words weaker than your grief would make
> > Grief more. 'Twere better I should cease
> Although to calm you I would take
> > The place of him that sleeps in peace.

FitzGerald subjected this to a proto-Larkin quizzing: 'I used to ask if this was not *un peu trop fort*. I think it's altered or omitted in future Editions. It is all rather affected.' So Tennyson authenticated the lines as:

> Although myself could almost take
> > The place of him that sleeps in peace.

Larkin has found it—not officiously made it—his business to ask of certain ways of putting it if they are not *un peu trop fort*. To ask it in English, though, lest the very asking be rather affected.

Come off it, or *un peu trop fort*: Auden, for instance, is asked not to come on quite so strong. When Auden contrasts poets ('They can dash forward like hussars') with novelists (who 'must /Become the whole of boredom'), it remains for Larkin to do the de-canting: 'Nobody has ever likened me to a hussar, and I doubt if any novelist has ever quite managed to become the whole of boredom; there is always a little left over for the reader.'

Sometimes the retort courteous will be a matter of giving a reverberation to the most conventional of phrases: 'I never learned to dance in a conventional sense.' Sometimes the turn will be a reminder of how worse-than-provincial the metropolitan vanity can be. *So you don't ever feel the need to be at the centre of things?* 'Oh no, I very much feel the need to be on the periphery of things.' None of his retorts is a put-down, because our author's own propensity to succumb to the lures of plumpness is ruefully acknowledged. Ripeness is all but inescapable. A rhetorical formula like 'If I hesitate to call this such-and-such' is all set to deliquesce from ripeness to rottenness: Larkin stanches it, first by going for the sort of word that ordinarily would not follow this rhetoric ('If I hesitate to call this boloney . . .'), and then by going on to two very different kinds of admission neither of which would usually gain entrance after such an opening—this, plus a vigilant parenthesis: 'If I hesitate to call this baloney, it is partly because I cannot disprove it (any more than he can prove it), and partly because I seem to have said something of the sort myself.'

Naturally it can be replied that these humorous turnings are no less rhetorical than the higher-flying tropes that they trap, but it is central to Larkin's achievement that he should repeatedly create authenticity out of the interrelation of inauthenticities. The balance and sustenance of alternate tones are often in Larkin, as they were in Byron, a balance and sustenance of alternate rhetorics, neither of which is authentic in itself but which in conjunction and mutual critique can be magnanimously right.

It is a feat of this book that, for all its grudging and its grudges, it should feel so magnanimous. Partly this is because it is so open in its antagonisms, its doubts, and its warnings (especially about the cultural entertainment industry and about the 'cunning merger between poet, literary critic and academic critic'). Partly it is that Larkin is so happy to let other people say felicitous things. Many of the best jokes are allowed to be other men's. 'I remember saying once, I can't understand these chaps who go round American universities explaining how they write poems: it's like going round explaining how you sleep with your wife. Whoever I was talking to said, They'd do that too, if their agents could fix it.' Or there is his substantiating Betjeman's tolerance: 'I remember once saying to him, "Churches are all the same really," to which he replied: "Oh, I wouldn't say that."' Even more handsome by way of imperturbable discomfiture is Larkin's telling of an Oxford compliment to him, expecially as it lurks in the hinterland which Larkin has made his own, between inadvertence and acumen. (As when Larkin good-naturedly thinks it is a pity that Donald Davie's poem 'A Sequence for Francis Parkman' doesn't 'tell me who Parkman is: one of his American friends, perhaps'. It is a pity, too, about the expunging of what I had taken to be just such an immersing in the deconstructive element: Sylvia Plath 'was, to use Henry James's well-worn phrase, immersing herself in the destructive element'. I'm afraid this now reads banally 'Joseph Conrad's'.) The Oxford memory is this: 'The highest academic compliment I received as an undergraduate was "Mr Larkin can see a point, if it is explained to him."'

The feeling of magnanimity comes as well from the fact that Larkin's devoting himself almost entirely to writers who are usually condescended to as 'minor' (Housman, William Barnes, de la Mare, Betjeman) is itself a various and sustained argument for inverting the usual priorities and for seeing these poets' virtues as the truly important ones. Indeed, Larkin can retrieve the word 'minor' as an ally not to be underrated, saying of W. H. Davies's sweet resistance to rural domesticity: 'He hit back in minor ways such as neglecting the garden and waving at girls in a nearby laundry.' Larkin's veneration of Hardy rings out the more vibrantly if one hears it against the thin words of T. S. Eliot in 1935: 'Thomas Hardy, who for a few years had all the cry, appears now, what he always was, a minor poet.'

The risk taken by the poet, whom Eliot styptically called 'the practitioner', when writing criticism is that things said about others may be taken to be merely self-regarding, the regard being a squint or an *oeillade*. What Larkin says of Eliot—'one suspects in fact that his account of Marvell's quality is to some extent a description of his own, or what he would like his own to be'—must itself be capable of being retorted upon Larkin, with this reservation: that it is a damaging thing to say only if the word 'suspects' is justified. Larkin says of Betjeman that, like Kipling and Housman, he has proved 'that a direct relation with the reading public could be established by anyone prepared to be moving and memorable.' It would be silly to *suspect* Larkin of thinking of himself as in that company. The gaze is straight, no smirking. Larkin singles out as the 'imaginative note' of Hardy 'the sometimes gentle, sometimes ironic, sometimes bitter but always passive apprehension of suffering'. Nothing implies that Larkin thinks himself Hardy's peer; everything does more than imply that Larkin knows himself Hardy's colleague. What did Larkin learn from other poets? 'Hardy, well . . . not to be afraid of the obvious.' Including the obvious admission that when a poet speaks well of others, he is likely to be speaking, well, of himself. For the poet of 'Self's the man' is the man who declines to be a poet in residence 'because I don't want to go around pretending to be me.' He prefers to be a poet in reticence.

He has for some of us that rare comic force which is a matter of the whole idea of him and his ways and his tones, so that just to imagine his cadences is involuntarily to smile to yourself. There is a sentence in a school anthology the mere thought of which always makes me happy, even though the sentence quotes nothing directly and resembles the flattest exchange of courtesies: 'I consulted Philip Larkin about his inclusion in this volume: Mr Larkin's view was that he would prefer not to collaborate with attempts to make his poetry more accessible to younger readers.' (It is 'collaborate *with*'—not *in*—that does it.) I get the same pleasure from the exquisite flat-tongued opening of a paragraph in a piece here on A. E. Housman—it goes simply: 'Then again, he seems to have been a very nice man.'

'The authority of sadness' is what Larkin respects in the poetry of Stevie Smith. But these flickering counter-impulses of wit and humour are what validate such sadness, in Larkin's poetry as in hers, just as the counter-impulse of sadness deepens the humour of Larkin's prose. Taking a proper pleasure in creating a poem, or in re-creating as a reader its experience, is something quite other than a covert pleasure in sadness itself. Larkin's prose is indeed the humorous relishing of glumness, but his poems, except when they lapse, are not a relishing of sadness. 'Actually, I like to think of myself as quite funny, and I hope this comes through in my writing. But it's unhappiness that provokes a poem.' The achieved authority of sadness is not the same as the inaugurating provocation of unhappiness. Larkin would be suspicious of Tennyson's open arms:

> Immeasurable sadness!
> And I know it as a poet,
> And I greet it, and I meet it,
> Immeasurable sadness!

Meeting it, yes, but greeting it is going a bit far.

Of course there are questions (especially about reconciling this with that) which Larkin need not particularly worry about but which we should. A man may live differently with his own contradictions, not least because he knows both how much they have made possible for him and how little might be left standing if he were to permit himself an Ibsenesque dismantling. But this very lucid writer can be very puzzling. 'It would be death to me to have to think about literature as such, to say why one poem was "better" than another, and so on.' Why should this, when under academic auspices, be more death-dealing than it is when as a reviewer (of Auden, most notably) Larkin is obliged to do exactly this, to say why one poem is 'better' than another? He does it, with stringency and glee. Even better, he goes for better not 'better', having no truck with those prophylactic inverted commas which belong in the unLarkin worlds of high pseudo-philosophical intellectuality or of low cultural egalitarianism. Assuredly Larkin believes—and says—that some poems are better than others, not 'better'. Is the point that if he were in 'the academic world' (or, rather, were there as a teacher, not a librarian), he'd have to go in for inverted commas? Or is there something very different about reviewing? Or should one just say: Come off it?

Then there is the selecting itself. Many reviewers have bemoaned the absence of their favourite Larkin bemoanings. Believing as I do that some of Larkin's best things are very portable, I particularly regret that, once he'd decided he would include items as small as paragraphs, he had no time or space for the following three, all of which exhibit the sentiment (of honesty) with more weight than bulk. From the *London Magazine* (February 1962), on literature, life and death, and on the poet's being 'perpetually in that common human condition of trying to feel a thing because he believes it, or believe a thing because he feels it'. From *Poet's Choice* (1962), on 'Absences', as then his favourite poem: 'I fancy it sounds like a different, better poet than myself. The last line, for instance, sounds like a slightly-unconvincing translation from a French symbolist. I wish I could write like this more often.' And from *Let the Poet Choose* (1973), where his entry is entrancingly timed:

> I looked through my three books of poems, and after some time came to the conclusion that I was subconsciously looking for poems which did not seem to me to have received their due meed of praise. Of course, there were quite a lot of them, and selection was difficult, but in the end I picked 'MCMXIV' and 'Send No Money', both from *The Whitsun Weddings*.
>
> Looking at them, I see that they have a certain superficial resemblance: they are both, for instance, in more or less the same metre. On the other hand, they might be taken as representative examples of the two kinds of poem I sometimes think I write: the beautiful and the true. I have always believed that beauty is beauty, truth truth, that is not all ye know on earth nor all ye need to know, and I think a poem usually starts off either from the feeling How beautiful that is or from the feeling How true that is. One of the jobs of the poem is to make the beautiful seem true and the true beautiful, but in fact the disguise can usually be penetrated.

How clean this comes. But then so does everything actually included in *Required Writing*, except perhaps its no longer being recorded (as it was on magazine publication) that for the *Paris Review* interview Larkin flunked or funked his orals. Gone is the prefatory note which included: 'Mr Larkin did not let down his guard sufficiently to be interviewed in person. He stipulated it be conducted entirely by post: "You will get much better answers that way." He took nearly five months to answer the initial set of questions, stating, "It has taken rather a long time because, to my surprise, I found writing it suffocatingly boring."' Boring it isn't, but it now lacks some of its comedy for those unaware of the exact circumstances which moved the interviewer to deploy as the final ground of his beseeching: 'For someone who dislikes being interviewed, you've responded generously.'

Raymond Williams, writing about *Monty Python*, said not uncheerfully that 'English philistinism has always comforted itself with the half-memory of the man who tried to be a philosopher but found that cheerfulness kept breaking through' (*LRB*, Vol. 2, No 23). Larkin, full-memoried, remembers the difference between breaking through and breaking in, and in his mock-philistinism creates a deliberate variant on those words of Oliver Edwards to Dr Johnson: Larkin tells how, unable to maintain as a reviewer his intended praise for all jazz, the interest of those reviews for him now is in 'watching truthfulness break in, despite my initial resolve'. Truthfulness, cheerfulness, and the authority of sadness: we should gratefully retort upon Larkin the anecdote he tells of William Barnes. 'Nor was his appeal limited to men of letters: "an old Domestic Servant" wrote to him in 1869, having found his poems among some books she was dusting: "Sir, I shook hands with you in my heart, and I laughed and cried by turns."'

Novelists and Poets

Ernest Hemingway
Islands in the Stream

"Y ou're going to write straight and simple and good now. That's
the start." The faded adjuration in *Islands in the Stream* is from
one half of Hemingway to his other half—from the lonely uncorrupted
painter Thomas Hudson to the companionable corrupted novelist Roger
Davis. "That's the start": and *Islands in the Stream*, which is the end, is
not straight or simple or good. Written mostly in 1951, ten years before he shot himself, it is Hemingway's last novel; it comes hard on the
callous heels of *Across the River and Into the Trees*, and it opens up the
Parisian reminiscences (it has its own such) which petrified as *A Move-
able Feast*. It had grown into a four-part enterprise, but Hemingway
salvaged *The Old Man and the Sea*, and what now remains is Part I
"Bimini," Part II "Cuba," and Part III "At Sea."

"Bimini" is Thomas Hudson in the 1930s entertaining the three
sons of his two wrecked marriages; they fish; their love leaves him open
to his loneliness, and then the death of two of them leaves him nothing
but lonely. "Cuba" is Thomas Hudson clandestinely war-efforting in
about 1942; his other son (the eldest) has been killed as a pilot; Thomas
Hudson drinks; he meets his first wife who is all he has ever wanted.
"At Sea" is Thomas Hudson commanding the pursuit of some German

U-boat survivors; the Germans die, and it may be that the wounded Thomas Hudson is about to too.

The three Parts part. According to Carlos Baker: "he hoped to make each section an independent unit. Later he would accomplish the welding job that would unify the whole." But nothing could ever have welded these together—they desperately don't fit, which is both why Hemingway had to write the book and why he didn't publish it. The fissures can't even be leaped, let alone welded. Part III is At Sea and so is the book. "There aren't any answers. You should know that by now. There aren't any answers at all." But when Thomas Hudson says answers, Ernest Hemingway means questions.

Devious and secretive, *Islands in the Stream* is an elaborate refusal to say what is the matter with Thomas Hudson. It calls him Thomas Hudson throughout, which makes the reader's relationship with him at once utterly stable and aloofly unadvancing. The book makes it impossible for us to know what is the matter with him (and so at the same time to know what was the matter with Hemingway) by an ingenious circumvention: it proliferates good reasons for him to be in a bad way. What—it asks incredulously—is the matter with him? Haven't his marriages broken up? Doesn't he still despairingly love his first wife? Aren't all his sons killed? Isn't his work as a painter threatened by drink and indiscipline? Isn't he enduring the joyless dangers of furtive seamanship in a war which seems merely six of one and half a dozen of the other? What more do you want? Well, yes: but apart from the "work" one (which doesn't ring true but does ring revealingly false), all of these stand rather as *ex post facto* constructions than as living pains. The great swordfish here escapes; the mighty fish which Hemingway here most adroitly lands are indeed prize-winning specimens but are red herrings. That Thomas Hudson feels the worthlessness of it all, this comes through. But his creator, with that kindliest of protectings which is usually a self-protecting, decides against any painful exploration of what is the matter: instead, he scatters matters. The gap then yawns—sometimes like a crevasse, sometimes like a yawn. The "sinister acumen" which W. H. Mellers half-praised in Hemingway thirty years ago (*Scrutiny*, 1939) is here bent to not giving anything away—or rather to giving away haystacks with the odd poisoned needle in them. As in the Father Brown story where there are too disconcertingly many murder weapons, so here there are altogether too many things which could have killed Thomas Hudson's spirit. "He did not know what made him feel as he did." Nor did his creator—or if he did, he wasn't telling. The enterprise is intricately self-defeating, at once locally steered and drivingly uncontrollable ("It was as though he were hooked to a moving anchor"). It resembles *Hamlet* as it seemed to T. S. Eliot. Eliot sought an objective correlative, "a set of objects, a situation, a chain of events which shall be the formula of that *particular* emotion"; what he found was pathology and failure:

> Hamlet (the man) is dominated by an emotion which is inexpressible, because it is in *excess* of the facts as they appear. And the supposed identity of Hamlet with his author is genuine to this point: that Hamlet's bafflement at the absence of objective equivalent to his feelings is a prolongation of the bafflement of his creator in the face of his artistic problem. Hamlet is up against the difficulty that his disgust is occasioned by his mother, but that his mother is not an adequate equivalent for it; his disgust envelops and exceeds her. It is thus a feeling which he cannot understand; he cannot objectify it, and it therefore remains to poison life and obstruct action.

Thomas Hudson's three sons are slaughtered for the cruellest of markets: not commercialized sentimentality, but authorial escape. They are thrown off the sled so that Thomas Hudson—alias Ernest Hemingway—may get away. And why the frantic flight? What do you mean, those may not be wolves at all—didn't you see me throw the children to them? It was Fitzjames Stephen who was wittily perturbed about infant mortality in Dickens: in Dickens "an interesting child runs as much risk . . . as any of the troops who stormed the Redan." In Hemingway— a trooper who stormed Redans for all he was worth—the children ought to ask danger-money. Two sons abruptly die in a car, and one in a Spitfire; such things happen, but the book should not make out that this precipitates Thomas Hudson's bitter hopelessness. He does not really want to live whether they live or not.

"But why did I ever leave Tom's mother in the first place? You'd better not think about that, he told himself." Thomas Hudson's favorite form of communication with himself is telling himself. Yet we should apply a remark of Thomas Hudson's about that other kind of telling, the sharing of confidences. "Telling never did me any good. Telling is worse for me than not telling." That is Thomas Hudson manfully not expatiating to others on his grief, but it goes for the plight of the whole book. Instead of telling, telling himself. "Work, he told himself." "You'd better not think about that": was there ever a book so obsessively about not thinking about things? And yet the more often the phrase rings out, the more strangely it rings. Must there not be some quite other thing about which Thomas Hudson cannot bear to think, some deepest vacancy which these self-injunctions are to ward off? Or is it that when Thomas Hudson says he'd better not think about something, he means he'd better not think?

> . . . and Thomas Hudson thought he had never seen a lovelier face nor a finer body. Except one, he thought. Except the one finest and loveliest. Don't think about it, he told himself.

> Let's not think about the sea nor what is on it or under it, or anything connected with it. Let's not even make a list of what we will not think about it. Let's not think of it at all. Let's just have the sea in being and leave it at that. And the other things, he thought. We won't think about them either.

> All right now. Don't think about that either. If you don't think about it, it doesn't exist. The hell it doesn't. But that's the system I'm going on, he thought.

> He knew they [the discovered German bullets] were the rest of his life. But he did not wish to think about them now. . . .

> "You truly think we will have a fight?" "I know it. Do not think about that. Think about details."

Well, it keeps your mind off things. What things? There aren't any things any more. Oh yes, there are.

He knew there was no use thinking of the girl who had been Tom's mother nor all the things they had done and the places they had been nor how they had broken up. There was no use thinking about Tom. He had stopped that as soon as he had heard.

There was no use thinking about the others. He had lost them, too, and there was no use thinking about them. He had traded in remorse for another horse that he was riding now.

Go ahead and drink the rest of your drink and think about something good. Tom's dead and it's all right to think about him. You'll never get over it. But you are solid on it now.

The instances are desolate and desolating—and not the less so for the utter unsolidity of this last sentiment (twenty pages from the end). It is not just Thomas Hudson who so unremittingly fingers his concealed wound as never to reach for his bow. Hemingway had become all wound and no bow.

And the other horse that Thomas Hudson was riding now? A bankrupt duty, that of pursuing those Germans. Gone is Hemingway's old vengeful zest of which Edmund Wilson wrote so piercingly ("indulgence in that headiest of sports: the bagging of human beings")—and a good thing it is gone. But what is left is not the disinterested but the uninterested. "Get it straight. Your boy you lose. Love you lose. Honor has been gone for a long time. Duty you do." But so truncated and impoverished a notion of duty does not do its duty: it—and in both ways—does for duty.

Well, I know what I have to do, so it is simple. Duty is a wonderful thing. I do not know what I would have done without duty since young Tom died. You could have painted, he told himself. Or you could have done something useful. Maybe, he thought. Duty is simpler.

But too much simpler, so much so as to be no stay (even when lacquered with hard-wearing irony) against emptiness and terror. Hence the fierce flashes of the old Hemingway—the boy's blistered struggle with the swordfish, or a bloody gloating fight at the dock. Thomas Hudson's friend Roger—with an excuse but with no real reason—smashes up a meanly abusive man. But it turns sour, and not just for Roger. Roger is the stronger and more skilled fighter. As so often in Hemingway, we are offered a "hideous moral spoonerism: Giant the Jack Killer." That is C. S. Lewis's dismayed evocation of *Tamburlaine*, and Hemingway has things in common with Marlowe. There is the single stylistic feat which is indeed a "mighty line" and yet in both senses of the phrase. There is the reducing of life to the sensation and the sensational. And there is the problem of how much in the end someone can know about men who knows so little about women. It was a disaster for Hemingway that he had no daughters; it might have been a disaster for them if he had.

But Marlowe didn't live till he was sixty, didn't have to find out that his simple (though simply equivocal) code wasn't only inadequate to the complexities of love and of steadfastness but was inadequate even to most of the simplicities of life. It is impossible to read *Islands in the Stream* without thinking of Hemingway's suicide. So much of the book is about suicide, and often the anecdotes are so little to the point as to make it likely that the point is not where Hemingway is pretending. There is the pig which swam out to sea.

> "*¡Que puerco más suicido!*" Thomas Hudson said. . . . "I'm sorry your pig committed such suicide." "Thank you," said Thomas Hudson. "We all have our small problems."

There is the detailed irrelevance of "the suicide gentleman":

> We all called him Suicides by then so I said to him, "Suicides, you better lay off or you'll never live to reach oblivion."

Is it a laugh that (successful) Suicides is good for? And there is the discussion of committing suicide by eating phosphorus, and by drinking dye, and by setting yourself on fire. And there is Roger's mistress, who killed herself.

> "You wouldn't ever do that." "I don't know," Roger said. "I've seen it look very logical." "One reason you wouldn't do it is because it would be a hell of an example for the boys. How would Dave feel?" "He'd probably understand. Anyway when you get into that business that far you don't think much about examples."

But Hemingway did think about the hell of an example which his father had set. John Berryman has set it down as Dream Song 235:

> Tears Henry shed for poor old Hemingway
> Hemingway in despair, Hemingway at the end,
> the end of Hemingway,
> tears in a diningroom in Indiana
> and that was years ago, before his marriage say,
> God to him no worse luck send.
>
> Save us from shotguns & fathers' suicides.
> It all depends on who you're the father *of*
> if you want to kill yourself—
> a bad example, murder of oneself,
> the final death, in a paroxysm, of love
> for which good mercy hides?
>
> A girl at the door: 'A few coppers pray'
> But to return, to return to Hemingway
> that cruel & gifted man.
> Mercy! my father; do not pull the trigger
> or all my life I'll suffer from your anger
> killing what you began.

Ivy Compton-Burnett
The Last and the First

W hat have the following in common: Chaucer, Francis Bacon, Donne, Bunyan, Herrick, Jonathan Swift, Smollett, Lamb, Keats, and Shelley? They are the names of characters in the novels of Ivy Compton-Burnett. In her final novel, now posthumously published as *The Last and the First*, there is even a Miss Murdoch. Yet the pregnant exchange about Miss Murdoch's portentous verbal mannerisms cries out (silently, of course, as always in this mistress of the tacit) to be applied rather to the novels of Miss Compton-Burnett herself, those skeletons from family cupboards which between 1925 and 1963, from *Pastors and Masters* to *A God and His Gifts*, have daunted and delighted with their finely bony family likeness. From beyond the grave—as so often in the novels themselves, where the human will has its last joyless fling when it makes its will—there now comes this disconcerting admonition, a concession which is disarming yet armed; taking the words out of one's mouth and having them as the last word.

> "Miss Murdoch seems in her way an unusual woman," said Madeline.

New York Review of Books (21 October 1971)

"She does," said Sir Robert. "It is a safe thing to say."

"She is not unusual in herself," said Eliza. "She has invented a way to seem so. And I daresay it deceives many people, including herself and Madeline."

"It is true," said Hermia. "And people are perceiving the truth. She may have done better at first, when the method was more alive. Before it was an echo of itself."

Yet those names, Chaucer and others: what is she up to? It is characteristically taunting, a persistent insinuation which we are by no means sure how to take. One way to take it is humbly, as before a goddess and her gifts. Charles Burkhart's book on Miss Compton-Burnett (1965) can hardly bring itself to look her gift horses in the eye, let alone in the mouth. He too much substitutes gratitude, about which the novels happen to be bitterly acute, for thinking, and so feels no qualms about saying simply this: "A minor, quite meaningless, but amusing convention is that many of the characters' names are those of literary figures."

He ought to have taken note of, and not just noted, the somber injunction in *The Present and the Past*: "It is a mistake to ignore conventions. There is always a reason behind them." For as Mary McCarthy observed in her incisively intelligent inquiry into "The Inventions of I. Compton-Burnett" (in *The Writing on the Wall*), such nomenclature is one of the unignorable ways by which the novels establish their uneasy complicity—for better and worse—with the family of authors, a family whose rivalries, closing of the ranks, pressures, and passions are no less intimidating than those of the domestic family. From first to last the novels are alive with writers, professional and amateur (*Daughters and Sons* and *A God and His Gifts* each have an infernal trinity).

The novels—which are tinglingly self-conscious about being novels, and are in important respects about themselves—do not take a blithe or benign view of imagination and of the creative drive, including their own. They brood—a creative process but a glowering stationary one. They ponder the puns buried like time bombs within words like *dictate*. Or deep-rooted derivations, such as affiliate *authors* to *authority* and to *authoritarian*. They speak often of Oedipus—in *The Last and the First* it is said of Jocasta Grimstone and her Osbert that she "felt to him as her son, but had her own view of him as a man, and was in no danger of her namesake's history." But we scent in the novels a doubt whether Oedipus's option was not somewhat on the soft side, since all he had to guess was the answer and not first the riddle.

The Last and the First was complete, though not finally revised, at Dame Ivy's death in 1969, aged eighty-five. It is the mixture as before, the only problem being the usual one that the label is mysteriously missing from the bottle and so there seems to be no telling what the mixture is. Poison or antidote? The constituents, which are at once cool ingredients and close obsessions, are the familiar family ones such as fermented the previous eighteen phials from Dame Ivy's dark laboratory. (There, too, in that odd first novel, *Dolores*, published in 1911, which is a fascinating compendium both of what she subsequently most grasped and what she most came to repudiate.)

"How the first can be last, and the last first!" Hermia Heriot, at thirty-four, braves her stepmother's wrath, and invests her father's money and her own self-esteem in a local school so that she may find scope for her talents. She fails to find it and perhaps even them. A proposal of marriage is no substitute, and is rejected. But her suitor opportunely dies and leaves her all, to his mother's incredulous perturbation. Will Hermia embrace her good fortune or take a high moral line? And will she anyway do the right thing by her father and stepmother, now impecunious? Or will she—a last-minute bolthole—accept a new suitor whose letter had been feloniously intercepted by that stepmother for whom nothing had always been the obvious point to stop at? And if so . . .

What we are reading is another chapter in that long day's dying which is the death of the family (death dealt by it and to it). The opening at a family breakfast which is both lurid and chilling; the setting, assured but vague, within late Victorian England; the domestic tyrants; stepchildren and crossed loyalties; a school in decay; the two households which are in collision and in collusion; the unheralded proposal of marriage; the flabbergasting last will and testament, the purloined letter, the misplaced secret, and the overheard conversation; the self-righteous perfidy and chic chicanery of the powerful, and the witty muttering of the put-upon: these constitute *The Last and the First*, as they have constituted the novels from first to last. Likewise the moral and linguistic preoccupations: with innocence (a steely quality not at all incompatible with its opposite, *nocence*, harmfulness), gratitude, courage, mystery and secrecy, people's sphere, people's place, people's scale.

The atmosphere does not change in this world where few windows are opened and where even the melodramatic smashing of them brings no freshness but merely a revelation of the ingenious triple glazing. It is a heavy atmosphere, in which sayings hang like Damoclean swords, or like unmoving mobiles, or like stale smoke left over from a previous book as from a previous day (one reason why the books begin with daybreak). You don't only hear the sayings, or see them in the dun air sublime, you snuff them. "Nothing goes deeper than manners." "It might be as well to forget it." "That is a thing she will have to face." "Speaking a true word, if hardly in jest." "There are things that have to be said. Or they might really go without saying." "Silence can say more than words." "I have done my best."

As always, there is the preternatural alertness not only to locutions and elocutions, but also to the way we elocute about locutions. "'I suppose this is the thing I should not say,' said Madeline, as she prepared to say it." Or: "'But she would not have accepted him,' said Amy unthinkingly, or rather saying what she thought."

"Hear yourself as others hear you": that renovation intimates a world in which people pay each other the sweetly lethal compliment of listening hard. Ears are cocked, like pistols. For no utterance is perfectly armored, and even pinpricks may with time and luck be fatal. There are some bracing duels in *The Last and the First*. The housekeeper, Mrs. Duff, exacts her revenge, her pound of flesh made word, by remorselessly describing as a "lodge" the smaller house near to the main gates (or lodge, indeed) to which the newly impoverished family will now have to move. Again, Mrs. Grimstone and her grandson are out to slice more than the literal breakfast ham—logic finds itself not chopped but sliced. ("Do you expect other people to eat the fat you have left?" "Is it any good to expect it? Do you think they would?") Again, Eliza rebukes her thirty-four-year-old stepdaughter:

> "Did you have a fire in your room last night, Hermia? I saw the ashes in the grate as I passed the door."
>
> "Then you know I had one. And you must have opened the door. I shut it when I came down."
>
> "I open any door in my house when and where I please. That is not what I said. I asked if you had a fire in your room, and I am waiting for an answer."
>
> "There is no need of one. You have seen that I did. It was too cold to be without one."
>
> "Did you ask me if you could have a fire? You know my rule."
>
> "The words would have had no meaning."

Or there are the novel's opening words; Miss Compton-Burnett has always been exquisitely courteous to her readers, giving them ample warning not to expect the ample.

> "What an unbecoming light this is!" said Eliza Heriot, looking from the globe above the table to the faces round it.
>
> "Are we expected to agree?" said her son, as the light fell on her own face. "Or is it a moment for silence?"
>
> "The effect is worse with every day. I hardly dare look at any of you."
>
> "You have found the courage," said her daughter, "and it is fair that you should show it. You appointed the breakfast hour yourself."
>
> Lady Heriot did not suggest that anyone else should appoint it.

Ivy Compton-Burnett was given her cult—an ambiguous gift, as what gods give must be. She was rather toadied to, and it is no accident that probably the best pieces of criticism are by writers in whose throats toads would especially stick: Mary McCarthy, and Kingsley Amis (in *What Became of Jane Austen?*). As often, cults interlock: her affinities with Jane Austen (of which too much is made if almost anything is made—the novels of George Meredith would be more like it) have hinderingly helped to give her loyaler attendants even than the Janeites, and she shares with the cults of, say, Sherlock Holmes and of P. G. Wodehouse's Jeeves some features which too much lend themselves to charades and chortles. Still, though her admirers tend to be snobbish about her books, her books are not snobbish.

How good are they? As with Jane Austen, the answer often takes the form of coming out for a particular novel by means of some quasi-judicious comparisons; and in those terms I'd plump for *A House and Its Head* (1935) and *A Family and a Fortune* (1939), adding that *The Last and the First* now forms an honorable unstartling pendant to the whole sequence and glimmers with a wintry generosity. But such comparisons within the oeuvre don't get far. They don't, for instance, help with the crucial question of range. Her books are not without intense joys and sorrows, and if the events are cloistered it is with the full-blooded hatreds of a soliloquy in a Spanish cloister.

But it remains true that there are a myriad ways in which human beings think, feel, and act such as never gain entrance to the Compton-Burnett world—not even as haunting absentees. To those who offer as a retort or critical argument the name again of Jane Austen, an answer might begin in the belief that Tolstoy is a greater writer than Jane Austen, among other reasons because range, scope, amplitude are rele-vant—though not punitive or dismissive—critical considerations.

It is true that special effects—of allusive economy, of taunting sobriety—are achieved by Miss Compton-Burnett's very exclusions. She earns much by her basic decisions about how to make her artistic living (decisions which are of course human and not merely technical)—and she pays a price. Of certain poets it may be said (and has best been by Donald Davie) that they command a diction, with the accompanying sense of otherwise feasible words being fended off from the poem, not given admission but making their absence felt; of other poets, that the whole resources of the language are newly open to them and through them, and that they have a language, not a diction. Justice and a proper pleasure ask that we see how much a diction can truly effect, which is a great deal.

Nevertheless the greatest writers have a magnanimity and width which are less predictable while yet involving the greatest expectations. One can be confident that Miss Compton-Burnett's gifts were original, altogether genuine (genuinely obsessional), strictly inimitable, and distinctively exhilarating, without averting one's eyes from the severe limits within which such severe excellence was achieved. She is to the modern novel as A. E. Housman is to the modern poem; we should be sufficiently grateful to such finely frugal artists as not to visit upon them the specially unbecoming gesture of being inordinate on their behalf.

The stubborn puzzle, though, is that of the relationship of the books' manner to their matter. Is the novels' substance—family feelings and what they imply and implicate—affected by the weird means by which it all is brought to our attention? In art, the how and the what together create the why; and it is the why of Ivy Compton-Burnett that is centrally enigmatic.

Much of the dialogue is unearthly; her admirers intone the word "stylization" and pace on. But what is the point of such stylization, and what does it do to—or for—the meaning of what such novels say? Most of the characters are character types (autocratic stepmother, feckless drawler, bright child, and so on). What do the novels mean to say to us about the relationship of the idea of type to psychological truth?

Is one of their reticent insistences the embodied proposition that—despite the implicit claims of most novels—we can know a great deal about how people feel and think without much knowing them as people? Certainly the novels stand in a bizarrely antithetical relationship to those Victorian novels, unwearyingly patient in the exploration of individual psychology, which the Compton-Burnett settings and subject matter cannot but summon up. And the plots: how are we to take their fantastic coincidences, their bolts from the blue, their unremitting confidence that every machine will have its attendant god waiting to come down and sort things out? Does such a method of construction ask us to put upon what the novel seems to say a different construction?

Dialogue, character, plot: in each case there springs to every critic's mind the word "convention." But this word, though an essential start to the critical argument, is hopeless as any kind of useful conclusion to it. There are three distinct positions once improbability is admitted to burgeon in these novels. (The admission is often grudging, and critics wriggle in order to make out that such things do happen but don't much come to light. True, but arguing about undiscovered murders is a cloudy business, and it is not only myopic realists who find the events in Compton-Burnett strange beyond belief.)

You can claim that in Compton-Burnett the plot, for instance, is blankly neutral. "The novels employ the Greek paraphernalia just as they employ any other convention, as a vehicle not as an end" (Burkhart). The "vehicle" simply, and not the artistic medium; the medium, after all, affects the message, whereas a vehicle delivers the goods. So Burkhart's critical epilogue says of *The Last and the First*: "The plot, never very important in these novels, seems as usual arbitrarily imposed, a mere mechanical framework for the ceaseless talk." Such a conception of plot—or indeed of any of the elements that together constitute a work of art—is radically mistaken, though one often despairs of curing anyone hooked on it.

Secondly, you can simply deplore the incongruity by which these novels yoke together truth of feeling with falsity (that is, laxity) of convention. Kingsley Amis candidly praises the realistic passions of hatred and pity, while candidly deploring the means by which these passions are mediated: "They work not through, but alongside and apart from, an arbitrary method of construction and a technique of dialogue which is too often de-individualizing and at times undisciplined."

Third, you can accept Amis's description of the disjunction (Miss McCarthy similarly remarks that the novels "do not 'relate' to their material in the ordinary literary way, but crab-wise"), but then ponder whether such a disjunction is necessarily a bad thing—that is, whether it cannot make its own point. The ambition both of comedy and of melodrama (mingled in Compton-Burnett, as in Wilde or as in Shakespeare's last plays) is to hold up to nature not just a mirror but a distorting mirror. That the mirror does indeed distort is not something that one is supposed, with misguided magnanimity, to avert one's eyes from. Do Miss Compton-Burnett's extraordinary novels really think of themselves as showing us the way that things are, or even were? Or are they not meant to tease us into thought, by a cryptic combination—as in surrealism—of lifelikeness and lifeunlikeness? "'Well, it shows that all things are possible,' said Madeline. 'And it is sometimes hard to believe that that is true.'"

But comedy, though rooted in our wish to believe that all things are possible, is committed to assisting us, gently, not to succumb to such a wish. "We have art that we may not perish of the truth"; we have comedy that we may not perish of the truth that not all things are possible. A comedy in which a character (or, implicitly, the plot) says otherwise is not necessarily asking to be believed. Ivy Compton-Burnett was not naïve but properly deep when she said oracularly (and oracles act out their truthful comedy) that "as regards plots, I find real life no help at all. Real life seems to have no plots, and as I think a plot desirable and almost necessary, I have this extra grudge against life." Such umbrageous comedy as hers is to help us not to take such umbrage against life.

Christina Stead
The Man Who Loved Children

"An Unread Book" is Randall Jarrell's title for his first-rate Introduction to Christina Stead's *The Man Who Loved Children*—so it seems that none of us needs to feel personally ashamed of somehow never quite having heard of the book. The literary world as a whole, though, ought to be ashamed. A few critics, most notably Elizabeth Hardwick, stood up to be counted—on the fingers of one hand. But even now, twenty-five years after its first publication, one can't help thinking that there is probably as much good luck as good management in its reissue and acclaim. Our grateful excitement at discovering a marvelous neglected novel oughtn't to relax us into all's well that ends well. *The Man Who Loved Children* must now be safely home, but it only scraped there. Who can now be so sure that achievement is bound to win in the end? The history of this one book is a piercing accusation against that part of the literary world which is bemused by modernisms and insatiably demands not that books be kept alive but that more books be born. *Et dona ferentes* . . . Continue to beware of publishers even when they come bearing gift-horses.

The Man Who Loved Children is superb as both a telescope and a microscope. It sweeps horizons as confidently and commandingly as

New York Review of Books (17 June 1965)

it sweeps to bacteria. As Mr. Jarrell says, no other novel makes so scrupulous, so passionate, and so convincing a study of a family—and with such generalizing force that one immediately expands that to *the* family. Samuel Clemens Pollit, who loved children, and his wife Henny, who often did not love children at all but yet almost always respected them as Sam never does: this marriage is rendered with brilliant specificity and sense of context. The seven children are a living, changing family—not, as so often, an artful background. Instead of "realistic" eruptions of child-life which then relapse (out of sight, out of the author's mind), Miss Stead shows that the children are the element in which the family lives and moves and has its being. Children should be seen and not heard?—a canny precaution for the mediocre novelist. But here the children are not only seen and heard, they are felt, smelled. We blush for them and we instinctively react as their parents. And all this with wit:

> "Ernie's nuts," said Little-Sam, "he's always studyin'; he's a fairy."
> "What did you say?" cried Henny. Little-Sam grinned foolishly while the other boys (except Ernie) looked pleased. After a devious discussion which revealed that Little-Sam used the word for anyone but a football hero, Henny suddenly cried,
> "Now pack up, kids, and go to bed."

The immediately obvious triumph of the book is its sense of speech. The language or rather languages of childhood are caught with brilliance and humor, with a warm response to what is supple and untamed and yet without that romanticism which believes that only wisdom comes out of the mouths of babes and sucklings. Not knowing how to use words is one of Miss Stead's central subjects, and this ranges all the way from our start at "fairy," up through the sensitive recording of children's attitudes to metaphor and cliché (Ernie, who lives for money, flinches when his mother speaks of his "bottom dollar"), and culminates in the wheedling rhetoric used by Sam. His blood-chilling jocularity, his simulated baby-talk which we cannot but hear as more a relapse into his true babydom than a simulation, his insane energy ("Bounding Health"): all this is heard by Miss Stead—or rather, listened to, since hers is much more than the art of the tape-recorder. "Quiet, kids," said Sam, "perpend, give ear: Jo will play us a toon, a little moozic." Even more important than this is Miss Stead's sense of convincing falsities of speech. Like George Meredith at his best, she is fascinated by the way we speak to ourselves in the privacy of our skulls, and she is able to remind us of what we would rather forget—that we are all continually employing, to ourselves and to others, a false rhetoric, overblown, indiscriminately theatrical, and yet indisputably ours. Hard for the novelist to differentiate the two ways in which we might use the word "unconvincing." But Sam's words ring true in their very hollowness, whether it is the rhetoric of noble anger ("I will not tolerate this everlasting schism"), or of sentimental idealism:

> It is just like our poor little silly, funny human life, but it comes to a good end because they are good people underneath all their poor willfulnesses and blindnesses. They really love each other, although they *do* show a tendency to scratch out each other's eyes at moments: and then they find they don't hate each other as much as they thought. People are like that, my *Troglodytes minor* . . .

The endless bitter war between Sam and Henny is one in which we are totally involved not simply because we know and care a great deal about them. Certainly their natures, their circumstances, their common pains and hatreds, are all before us—Miss Stead succeeds amazingly in holding all this not only in her head but in her heart. Yet the quarrels, the vituperations, the lunacies, ripple out to become a clash of two distinct systems of judgment. Henny is in some obvious ways crueler than Sam, and especially in her treatment of her stepdaughter Louie. And yet everything that she says and does, however appalling, is evidence that tragedy and suffering mean something to her, can find a place in her heart. Sam is the opposite: "tragedy itself could not worm its way by any means into his heart. Such a thing would have made him ill or mad, and he was all for health, sanity, success, and human love." All the words which we want to hurl at him—he is impossible, intolerable—are not quite words of moral judgment, or else they are so total an accusation against his whole being that we hesitate to use them. *The Man Who Loved Children* is not a title of simple irony, because after we retreat from such a "love," we still have to concede that Sam really did love children. He was "wonderful" with them, with all the irony and non-irony which the word has to include. His first wife had written of him, gently, "He is such a good young man, he is too good to understand people at all"—and we will underrate both him and the book if we take this too as a simple irony. Sam is a Feiffer character, but living in a fully realized world of tragedy. Not a hypocrite at all, but a classic case of the softly aggressive victim. It is all very well that the meek shall inherit the earth, but Sam, disconcertingly, seems to be doing it here and now, his other cheek turning like a top. Miss Stead catches this in five words: "A smile bared his teeth." Driven unjustly out of his job, pruriently chaste while his wife commits adultery, steeped in unexpected poverty, he yet responds to it all with an energetic unconcern which is at once super-human and subhuman. When Henny speaks, we wince; when Sam speaks, we blush. When she is at her worst, we wish she were dead; when he is being most himself, we wish we were dead. She lacerates our heart, he makes our heart turn over. It is not easy to pity his immature in-sensitivity as much as her morbidity, but Miss Stead manages it—she, odd though it may seem, is the woman who loved the man who loved children.

Everything in the book deserves notice. Its narrative skill; its sense of how much it matters to have money; its creation of locality (Wash-ington, Baltimore); its pained insistence on the rights of women and children; its political acuteness, especially in its feeling for what under-lies those people and those moments which protest that they are non-political; its presentation of a religious soft-soaping secularism: these are not extraneous but the fiber of the book. The eldest girl, Louie, is won-derfully drawn, so much so that one ought to invoke *The Mill on the Floss*. And a real feeling of how a family grows and changes is conveyed by the way in which Louie gradually comes to assume more and more of the family's life and of the book's meaning. In its sense of growth and of generations, in its generality and specificity, above all in the central place which it accords to feelings of indignation and embarrassment, *The Man Who Loved Children* is in the best tradition of the nineteenth-century novel.

Brian Moore
The Emperor of Ice-Cream

The singular strength of Brian Moore's novels is manifest in their abolishing brow-distinction. Their way of doing so is not by what is essentially a highbrow strategy: the offering of different 'levels', with its implicit condescensions (they read it for the story, we read it for the symbols and themes). Mr Moore's new novel, like its predecessors, makes itself accessible to everyone, not by offering different things to different men, but by concentrating simply, directly and bravely on the primary sufferings and passions that everybody feels. Of all our present novelists, he is for me ('for me', not because of any hesitation, but because of the nature of the praise) the one whose books most immediately evoke and touch my private feelings and fears, memories of what it was, when one was like that in the past— dismay at what it will be, when one is like that in the future. Kingsley Amis, not a lachrymose man, once paid R. S. Thomas's poems a tribute such as few reviewers feel it quite proper to pay: 'It is enough to say he often moves to tears.' The best moments in these novels have such a power—you have to pull yourself together. Agreed, it is a power that can often be felt strongly enough in bad films, but few good novels can do any such thing.

New Statesman (18 February 1966)

Sentimentality, some will say. But a novel such as Mr Moore's first, *The Lonely Passion of Miss Judith Hearne*, does not move us by any kind of illicit manipulation. Humphry House spoke of sentimentality as 'the imposition of feeling as an afterthought upon literalness'. But that wouldn't apply to *Judith Hearne*, where the emotion is intrinsic to the description, itself a matter of sharp delineation. It is natural that it should have been a literary critic of the Victorians who found so good a definition, and Mr Moore's novels belong without any embarrassment in the tradition that the Victorians magnificently established. He is, if you like, a 'conventional' novelist, quite without experimentalisms and gimmicks. In none of the novels is anything concealed except the art by which they transmute 'an ordinary sorrow of man's life' into something we care about. He does not, in fact, need the services of a literary critic, which may be one reason why the learned journals and the little magazines—despite the boom in modern fiction studies—are content to ignore him.

He writes transparently, in a style which differs from ordinary speech only in being more tellingly economical, less muddled and less afraid. 'A prose such as we would all gladly use if we only knew how'— that is how Arnold praised Dryden's style. The words do not half reveal and half conceal the soul within—they altogether reveal it. In reading Mr Moore, your mind and heart are entirely set on his events and people, and what is touching is the direct contemplation of the predicaments, predicaments which are unique in their particulars but commonplace enough. One can quote George Eliot without name dropping and without implying that Mr Moore is her peer: 'Pity and fairness embrace the utmost delicacies of the moral life.' 'That element of tragedy which lies in the very fact of frequency.' If in the end we are not moved so profoundly—though we are indeed moved—by the break-up of the marriage in *An Answer from Limbo*, we are at any rate moved in something of the same way as by the desolating marriage of Rosamond and Lydgate in *Middlemarch*.

In *Judith Hearne*, we realise what it is to be a middle-aged spinster in Belfast, not yet having utterly capitulated to alcohol or self-deception, dignified in her pained understanding that she is of no importance or use to anyone whatever. Mr Moore suppresses nothing: her snobberies, her prejudices, her preposterousness, they are all there, all relevant, and all as nothing compared to her sufferings. Hers is not only a lonely passion, but also a lonely Passion. And she chooses it, in that foolish, honourable moment when she lets herself be persuaded not to commit her desperate aunt to an asylum:

> She had given her word: she did not go back on it. Her aunt lived five years after that promise, fighting and raving her way through every ghastly day, until one Sunday morning in 1947 Judy found her sitting straight up in bed, eyes open, her bloated hawk face fixed in its habitual frown of reproof as life suddenly deserted her.

The second novel, *The Feast of Lupercal*, now a paperback as *A Moment of Love*, makes us understand what it is to be a 37-year-old schoolmaster in Belfast: a good, weak, losing man who is still a virgin. 'In fact a hell of a lot of people are.' Pitiful, funny, and true. 'The trouble was, none of us knew how to talk to girls at all, he thought.' What this remarkable novel brings out is Mr Moore's gift for understanding and presenting the moments of moral decision, of what—in a quite unheroic setting—is simply heroism. Una, the girl whom Devine loves and who slightly loves but mainly pities him, has spent the night with him. They both remain virgins. And yet Una is now in such a tangle with her family, so distraught and vulnerable, that the only way in which he can help her is by telling her family the truth about that night. He refuses, afraid of the humiliation if they don't believe him, and even more afraid of the humiliation if they do. Then, after all, he suddenly does tell. He has already certainly lost Una; he certainly gains incredulous sniggers. But how could we fail to be moved by what he is and does? As an act of courage—and with far more of vital self-esteem at stake—it ranks with the end of *Our Mutual Friend*, when the good worm Twemlow turns and slays Podsnap.

The Luck of Ginger Coffey, is, I think, the slightest of the novels. This may be an imaginative failure in me: the concerns of the book—

expatriation (an Irishman in Canada), unemployment, wrong employ-
ment—are real and central enough, but I see not feel how relevant they
are. Yet I can imagine people responding with exactly that personal involvement, that necessity to think about one's own life as well as about
the life lived in the book, which constitutes Mr Moore's simple excellence. But for all the pathos and the sullen ludicrousness, there is something undirected about the book, as there is something unrealised about
Ginger Coffey himself. If I am right, it may be because here Mr Moore
(who was himself a proof-reader and then a reporter for four years in
Canada) is a little too near his material. Imagining what it is like to be
Judith Hearne was both harder and more rewarding than imagining
himself Ginger Coffey.

In *An Answer from Limbo* he wrote like an angel—a recording angel, in the sorrowing acuteness of his observation. Here is a marriage,
still polite, affectionate, and altogether possible, and here are its reluctant enemies: casual selfishness, a not ignoble ambition (Brendan wants
to be a real novelist—he has talent, but the time and energy will have to
be found at the expense of something), and a mother-in-law. It is characteristic of Mr Moore that he can take the comic stereotype of the
mother-in-law, acknowledge what is true about it, and then use it in the
interests of a delicate and memorable tragi-comedy. The arrival in New
York of Mrs Tierney is the meeting of two utterly different worlds of
taste, temperament and values. The tragedy—despite everything which
continually whispers that surely these are just trivial misunderstandings,
and all so silly—cannot but come. Jane Tierney's despairing, mindless
adultery, which she schizophrenically watches with mild surprise, is
laceratingly convincing.

The new novel, *The Emperor of Ice-Cream*, lacks the concentrated
force, the finality, of *Judith Hearne* and *An Answer from Limbo*. This is
not because of a loosening in Mr Moore's grip—it is the consequence
of his refusing to write the same novel twice. Judith Hearne is not going
to change, nor is her world. Devine in *The Feast of Lupercal* is not
doomed, but he will be unless he is very lucky—in any case his nature is
now what it is, and there can be no confidence that he will ever again

have the chance to remake himself. In *An Answer from Limbo* the finality is at its most hideous. The mother has died, the wife has gone, Brendan will write novels; but, in his closing words, 'I have altered beyond all self-recognition. I have lost and sacrificed myself.'

The Emperor of Ice-Cream is the first of the novels to be about the creation of a self. Gavin Burke is 17; he has left school to join the Belfast ARP (it is November 1939), much against his parents' wishes. The novel shows how he finds out what he is and sets about making himself what he wishes to be. It is, quite straightforwardly, about growing-up, and it is inherent in such a subject that it can have no such conclusive thrust as has characterised the earlier novels. The book is outwardly fragmentary, because it shows how fragmentary the world is to a 17-year-old. It is not that Mr Moore merely and inertly reproduces fragmentariness, rather that the continual glimpses of the peripheral adult worlds are an essential part of the artistic concern. A simple instance is the way in which some of the ARP wardens talk about murdering the hateful officer Craig if an air-raid comes. They mean their hatred, and quite possibly mean to act; Gavin is drawn into mute acquiescence. But when a dreadful air-raid devastates Belfast, Craig is still bullyingly alive. A loose end? No, because the uncertainty is that of life itself. We have no indication that Craig is safe for ever. And being able to live with such uncertainty is what is implied in the adulthood which comes to be Gavin's by the end of the book. For most of the time Gavin can make nothing but sorties into the innumerable adult worlds that lie all round him. There is the world of the ARP post, with its apparently futile exercises, its glimpses of the alcoholic, the randy, the old pretending to be young enough for the job. Elsewhere there are the worlds of the piggishly rich, of those who—not without reason—are politically blind. (By the end, Gavin's father has reversed his old assertions into 'the German jackbook is a far crueller burden than the heel of old John Bull.') These are the forces that are making and breaking Gavin: the ARP post, Belfast and his family, and his inconclusive, half-understood calf-love for a young nurse. The strange elation of Gavin and of much of the book comes from the congruence of the adolescent flux with the larger flux that is about to engulf Europe.

In the course of the novel everything changes, yet not into stasis. Everything that was at the edges gradually moves into the centre, into an adulthood which acknowledges circumspection and which involves the recognition that there are worlds that one will never really penetrate. It involves abandoning so much of what there was once room for at the edges. Even the Wallace Stevens poem which gives the book its title shifts its emphasis. At the start, it is part of Gavin's naïve but genuine feeling for poetry, its force mainly inhering in the erotic stanza about the 'concupiscent curds'. By the end of the book the poem has found its true centre of gravity:

> If her horny feet protrude, they come
> To show how cold she is, and dumb.
> Let the lamp affix its beam.
> The only emperor is the emperor of ice-cream.

But although Stevens's poem is integral to the novel, it is not at all the kind of poetry most akin to the manner and matter of *The Emperor of Ice-Cream*. For the heartfelt directness of Mr Moore's novels, we must look rather to the Larkin of 'Mr Bleaney', or the Austin Clarke of 'Martha Blake at Fifty-One'.

Brian Moore
The Mangan Inheritance

J amie Mangan, left at 36 by his wife and then suddenly left all her
money, takes it into his heart to go off from New York to Ireland to
find out whether or not he is the great-great grandson of the poet
James Clarence Mangan. Jamie's father had once half-heartedly tried
this, but he wasn't prey to a sufficiently insatiable hunger for the quest.
But then it is Jamie, not his father, who bears an uncanny resemblance
to the man in an heirloom daguerrotype which has 'J.M. 1847?' on the
back of it. The resemblance—a newly missing tooth, for instance—
eerily increases once Jamie is in Ireland, entangled with disreputable
Mangans who are probably his cousins (ah, how treacherously and
sluttishly lovely, and how erotically practised, is 18-year-old Kathleen
Mangan), and likewise with respectable Mangans who are very guarded
(and what are they guarding?). Jamie starts to sense that the daguerrotype is not so much a passport to a past world as a death-warrant in a
present world.

'We are the same, all of us. We look the same, we write poetry, and
we come to a bad end.' For his double or *Doppelgänger* monstrously
multiplies. It is not just that Jamie has the face of James Clarence
Mangan (and the poetic aspirations, and so the bad end?), but that the

London Review of Books (6 December 1979)

face is also the face of two more Mangans along the line, a line which is cursed with their lineaments, with their versifying lines, and with their palm-lines of violence and death. What, will the line stretch out to the crack of doom? Jamie, though, looks like being the end of the line. Meanwhile the double-goers double into triple- and quadruple-goers.

So the jacket of the English edition of Brian Moore's latest (tenth) novel, the blurb of which is superior to that of the American edition in that it doesn't betray the plot, is inferior in that it limns the daguerrotype and then splits the face down the middle, tonsorially and sartorially, as if the novel were your usual Caledonian-type antisyzygy, the story of a contrastive double rather than of a double double. What the Mangan face beseeches is recognition, of itself and for its writings.

At the centre of *The Mangan Inheritance* is a person who has—as yet?—no centre. As long as Jamie Mangan was married to the very famous filmstar Beatrice Abbot, he had no other identity than that of her husband. Karl the doorman equably calls him 'Mr Abbot', and in the anger of a quarrel Jamie rams the truth of Beatrice's words into his head: 'I'm your husband. That's it, isn't it? That's what I am. That's exactly what I am. In fact, it's all I am.' Yet when she walks out on him, he is released only into a different sense of the same vacancy of self: 'Nothing happens. It's as though I'd ceased to exist.' And what has he ever achieved? 'At 36 I'm nothing.' But then the quest to Ireland cannot simply restore him to being someone. 'Like the man in that photograph, he had once been someone, was now no one, and might here, in this small wild country on the edge of Europe, discover who and what he would become.' Yet to find oneself the latest incarnation of the Mangan face, the Mangan ill-fortune, and the Mangan poetic itch: this is to find an identity, perhaps, but not to find one's own identity or individuality, even apart from the fact that the face which later beetles into his, the face of his aged double, is that of a wheedling pervert and poetaster.

When Mangan arrives in Ireland, he thinks of himself as 'reborn but not renamed, searching a new identity'. At first, comparatively blithely, that *searching* means 'searching for' or 'seeking': the climax of his search, though, is not his searching *for* a new identity but his searching it. He searches it, through and through, and what he then diagnoses looks like a disease in his blood. Perhaps he will be saved. For, off the end of the book, beyond its chastened close, there is at last a duty for Jamie Mangan, and duty is nothing like so stern and jealous a god as is the dearth of duty. Someone yet unborn is going to need this man who, now knowing what is the blight Mangan was born for, might otherwise wish that he had never been born.

It cannot be simply a stricture on this novel, then, that its hero is something of a zero. Nothing in himself, he yet multiplies into other selves; and he multiplies the scale and the stakes of all those with whom he engages. If he is a cipher, this, too, he multiplies into both of the senses of a cipher. Certain honourable satisfactions are therefore honourably not forthcoming from this novel, and the would-be poet Mangan is not himself a centre of interest in the way in which the would-be novelist Brendan Tierney is, in Moore's earlier superb novel *An Answer from Limbo*. Yet this isn't a defect in the book, it is the ground (grounds constituting limits, true) of its success. The nature of that success can be glimpsed within the 'glassed-in bookcase with leather-bound books on its shelves', there within the scrubbed cottage which belongs to the respectable branch of the Irish Mangan family. Pride of place within that sentence, and so within the bookcase, is given to 'the Waverley novels of Sir Walter Scott'.

It is *Waverley* itself which defines the kind of success gained here, for it is *Waverley* which Donald Davie celebrated in these terms in *The Heyday of Sir Walter Scott*: 'The hero in the lost-father fable *has to be* what Scott and the others have made him—wavering (there is a sort of pun with "Waverley"), inconstant, mediocre, weak. How else should he behave, since, not knowing his father, he does not know who he is, nor where his allegiance lies?' For *The Mangan Inheritance*, too, is a lost-father fable. Jamie is credulous when he finds the demonic hermit, 'this poet who bore his face, his true spiritual father'. Yet he is inconstant—fortunately, since he is thus able to recognise where his allegiance lies, acknowledging that his true spiritual father is . . . his father. In the words of the book's last page: 'Through his father—who knew nothing of Gorteen, Duntally, Norman towers, and lonely headlands—the uncanny facial resemblance, the poetry, the wild blood had been transferred across the Atlantic Ocean to this cold winter land, to this, his father's harsh native city in which he now lay dying. He looked at his father's face and wished that those features were his own.'

Much of Davie's spirited salute to *Waverley* ('one of the greatest novels in the language') would constitute a firm basis for a true reading of Mr Moore's markedly good novel. Like *Waverley*, *The Mangan Inheritance* 'shows the victory of the un-heroic over the heroic': '"Heroic" and "un-heroic" may both be misunderstood, unless we admit that for "heroic" we may substitute "barbarian", for "un-heroic", "civilised". The second pair of terms tilts the scales of approval towards the English, as the first pair towards the Scots; the novelist's achievement is in tilting neither way, but holding the balance scrupulously steady.' For 'English', we may substitute 'North Americans', and for 'Scots', 'Irish'.

Likewise, if Mr Moore's presentation of Mangan is, like Scott's presentation of Waverley, 'a strong portrait of a weak or weakish character', the perceptive critic has brought out what the strength is for:

> Thackeray, when he subtitled *Vanity Fair* 'a novel without a hero', meant by that something very interesting but quite different from what it may mean as applied to *Waverley*. The formula fits the Scott novel just as neatly. And the enormous advantage of the Scott method in this particular is that it makes of the central character a sounding-board for historical reverberations, or else, to change the metaphor, a weathervane responding to every shift in the winds of history which blow around it. This device, and this alone, of a weak hero poised and vacillating between opposites allows the historian to hold the balance absolutely firm and impartial, giving credit everywhere it is due. If the central figure is exempted from judgment, this is not from any moral laxity in the storyteller; but is designed to permit judgment of the parties, the ideologies, the alternative societies which contend for his allegiance.

Jamie Mangan is the precipitator, not the passer, of judgments. He is no longer the person he was: 'That person would have made guilty judgments on this girl'—a beautifully equivocal use of 'guilty', one which is the disconcerted counterpart to Beatrice's hideously undisconcerted use of the word when she announced her defection: 'I realise that I'm the guilty party, so to speak.' Jamie in the end believes himself incapable of judging his odious double's poetry, but he judges it all right: 'I can't judge it. I'm completely hostile to its content.' Poetic justice? The phrase is one which the blackguard poet uses twice—'If there was any poetic justice, which there's not, I'd be as well known as James Clarence himself': this, with a smirking disregard for the nemesis which is part of this locution for ideal rewards and punishments.

Henry James said that '*Waverley* was the first novel which was self-forgetful.' No modern novel can be thus self-forgetful, and *The Mangan Inheritance* is instinct with conscious memory of itself, and of its proceedings. But its life as a novel is a matter of its having at its heart a strong portrait of a weak character, naggedly unable to be self-forgetful, the more so as his doubts increase as to whether he even has a self to forget—and yet finally becoming capable of the strong form of self-forgetfulness which is self-abnegation.

The Mangan inheritance is a double one, as befits its involving a search for a double. The literal inheritance of money is what makes possible the search for the heritage of blood. But it is one of the lacerations within the book that though 'the Mangan inheritance' is a straight description in that it is Jamie Mangan who inherits all that money (about $800,000), it is askew in that the money could as well be called the Abbot inheritance: Mangan inherits it from his wife Beatrice Abbot (who assuredly is not known as Mrs Mangan), and moreover she had inherited half of it from her father. Mangan knows that the honourable thing to do would be to renounce the money, left to him by a wife who was cutting him dead but who had not yet had time to cut him out: but his urge to discover his forbear makes forbearance impossible. In the bitter end, though, he cuts his ill-gotten losses. The vital and honest spending of the Mangan inheritance will be its caring, not for Mangan, his father's child, but for another child of his father. Jamie Mangan has inherited, from someone not of his blood, blood-money. He has inherited too the wild blood and the poetic lust of the Mangans, the line running back to 'the first *poète maudit*'. For James Clarence Mangan 'was the prototype of that sort of poet. Before Baudelaire or Rimbaud. Before the term itself was invented.'

Jamie often wonders what to wear, and Beatrice used to unleash a psychiatrist on to this: 'Narcissistic, wouldn't you say? Or perhaps, said Dr H., some deeper problem of identity. Beatrice could quote an analyst to suit her purpose.' Devilish. But then someone is citing Shakespeare to his purpose. The book's purpose brings out the way in which quotation and allusion are intimate with the deep problem of identity. An earlier novel of Mr Moore's, *The Emperor of Ice-Cream*, had made serious play with the Wallace Stevens poem, gravitating from the delicious chill to the coldness of death. But it is inheritance which makes allusion central and indispensable, since literary allusion is itself an act of inheritance. To use the wording of previous writers is to acknowledge oneself an heir. But heir to what?

For the Augustan poets, the crucial acts of allusion were those which alluded (with a witty self-reflexiveness which was not narcissism) to inheritance royal, legal and literary. For Wordsworth, the previous poetry which was now his heritage was alive with a sense that the central human inheritance was perceptual, being the human senses, especially the eye and ear. The great achievements of allusion, in this sense of inheriting the words and phrases of previous poets, are precipitated by a coinciding of whatever is seen in life as the central or crucial inheritance with those particular acts of literary inheritance which are allusion itself. *The Mangan Inheritance* is in this tradition— a most intelligent, resourceful and surprising quest for a family inheritance which is at once an uncanny facial resemblance, poetry, and wild blood. The black blood of the Tennysons, you might think of murmuring, except that James Clarence Mangan was secured neither within the laureateship nor within genius.

The first explicit allusion, half a dozen pages into the novel, comes when Jamie reflects from Byron:

> Man's love is of man's life a thing apart,
> 'Tis woman's whole existence.

'He picked up the coffee-pot. By Byron's standards, he was not a man.' But is he even an existence? Twenty pages later, and now in that foreign country from which he had emigrated, Canada, his rage splutters into the murder of rhythm:

> Time to rewrite Byron's lines:
>
>> Her love was of her life a thing apart,
>> 'Twas my whole goddamned existence.

What looked like salvation from this, namely the Mangan quest, turns into the damnation of Mangan look-alikes. 'Be damn and you have the look of a Mangan, so you have.'

But Byron's wise levity had early been replaced by T. S. Eliot's wise gravity. Jamie does not know how to be himself once Beatrice is glitteringly back in the apartment for some divorce-chat:

> Eliot's lines came into his head:
>
>> Who is the third who walks always beside you?
>> When I count, there are only you and I together
>> But when I look ahead up the white road
>> There is always another one walking beside you.
>
> In the three weeks since she left me another one walks always beside us.

It is a great stroke, to turn Eliot's mysterious third person into the adulterous lover who has created a triangle which will now be collapsed back so that it will be Jamie who is to become the third person, left behind. A true stroke, too, not only in that *The Waste Land* is (among other things) a poem of marriage misery, but also in that it is a masterpiece of allusion, including the uncrystallised allusiveness at this very point, with Eliot not altogether sure who is the other one to whom he is indebted for this evocation of another one: 'The following lines were stimulated by the account of one of the Antarctic expeditions (I forget which, but I think one of Shackleton's): it was related that the party of explorers, at the extremity of their strength, had the constant delusion that there was *one more member* than could actually be counted.' From one point of view, the third person is the poet Eliot himself, who provides Jamie with the painful solace of these lines, with their companionship in grief and loss. Again, given the hideous amputation at the novel's climax, the novel might be seen as a nightmarish perversion of Eliot's italicised words: *one more member*.

Allusion plays throughout the novel, with cunning and versatility. Not only does it embody a great variety of inheritances—guilt, disease, talent, money, physiognomy, property—it also allows James Clarence Mangan's work to figure in the book with a substantial solidity and yet with an acknowledged insubstantiality. What is so right about the choice of the poet James Clarence Mangan is exactly that you can be happy neither simply to grant him, nor simply to withhold from him, the name of poet. Lines of his keep recurring:

> O, the Erne shall run red,
> With redundance of blood . . .

Are they any good or not? Jamie Mangan, goaded by praise of his forbear which comes from lips which he loathes, lips of Mangan's kin and his, is driven in the end to total rejection:

> Oh, for God's sake, you stupid old fool, who in hell do you think Mangan *was*? Nobody ever heard of him, outside of a few English professors and the people who live here on this godforsaken island. Mangan's not a world poet. He never *was*. He's dead, buried, and forgotten. Second-rate, rhyming jingler, doing translations from languages he didn't understand, dull, and pathetic, just like the crap you showed me today.

But the book doesn't endorse the judgment. Not only was there, as it happens, a last-minute revision to the last page of this novel's proof-copy, so that 'the bad poetry, the bad blood' became, with studied abstinence from conclusive judgment, 'the poetry, the wild blood', but James Clarence Mangan's poetry remains memorably bizarre and hauntingly apposite:

> Would give me life and soul anew,
> A second life, a soul anew . . .
>
> My royal privilege of protection,
> I leave to the son of my best affection.

T. S. Eliot is by no means the only poet to haunt the book and the consciousness of Jamie, but it is his art which walks beside all of the art called up, whether actual, like James Clarence Mangan's, or imagined, like that of other Mangans.

> *Mangan, James Clarence* (1803–49), Irish poet and attorney's clerk, whose life was a tragedy of hapless love, poverty and intemperance, till his death in a Dublin hospital. There is fine quality in his original verse, as well as in his translations from old Irish and German.

The entry in *Chambers' Biographical Dictionary* is as recent as 1974, and yet how right of it to speak with that touch of archaic falsity about a true suffering, as 'hapless love'. Mangan himself, in 'The Nameless One', was happy to tell of his miseries:

> Till, spent with toil, dreeing death for others,
>   And some whose hands should have wrought for him;
> (If children live not for sires and mothers),
>   His mind grew dim.
>
> And he fell far through that pit abysmal,
>   The gulf and grave of Maginn and Burns,
> And pawned his soul for the devil's dismal
>   Stock of returns.

Abysmal, yes, and dismal; the rhyme has something of the demented unignorability of Tennyson's rhyme of 'abysm' with 'Zolaism'.

The first page of the introduction to John Montague's *Faber Book of Irish Verse* moves at once from saying that 'the true condition of Irish poetry in the 19th century' is 'mutilation', to 'Loss is Mangan's only theme,' this sentence then speaking of castration in a way which is grimly germane to Brian Moore's novel. But there is another shadowy name which looms unnamedly large in the book, that of the bland charmer who had all the graces which were denied to the *poète maudit* who yet perhaps was man enough for damnation:

> Oft in the stilly night,
> Ere slumber's chain has bound me . . .

The lithe and lying Kathleen sings all of this, with great beauty, at a very important moment of the book. Thomas Moore's lines are alive as part of the Moore inheritance.

Kingsley Amis
One Fat Englishman

K ingsley Amis's heroes have got progressively more nasty, though
the main complaint against him has been that he hasn't sufficiently realised just how nasty they are. One doesn't have to subscribe
completely to the gentleman's code to feel that it was not good form of
Patrick Standish, the hero of *Take a Girl Like You*, to deflower Jenny
Bunn when she was very drunk—though there is room for dispute as to
how much she was to blame. The argument is about an author's being
in collusion with one of his characters, a charge which Mr Amis himself
has brought against *Mansfield Park*, arguing, and not weakly, that it is a
morally corrupt book. But collusion is of all charges the hardest to prove
or disprove, since it so easily gets caught in a circle. Where do we find
our evidence that Standish is a bad man except in Mr Amis's novel?
Then why should we assume that he is unaware of the significance of
evidence which he himself has provided? Some critics have talked as if
it were Mr Amis himself who drives about taking delight in splashing
poor old chaps standing by the gutter. That would be very wrong of
him. But it is legitimate to have doubts about the self-knowledge of
those who speak of such goings-on with a whey-faced rectitude that
pronounces on how totally and farfetchedly hateful such behaviour is.

New Statesman (29 November 1963)

A crowd of people is waiting for a door to open; up comes a man who boldly, naively, tries the door; a tremor of disinterested glee runs through those waiting. Mr Amis, and rightly, is less worried by those who are gleeful than by the mature onlooker who is shocked and mutters his thanks that he is not as other men.

But *One Fat Englishman* makes it look as if Mr Amis feels he has had enough of being told off for being in cahoots with his heroes. The fat (16-stone) Englishman is Roger Micheldene, in America on publishing business. Certain episodes in the book—and this is one reason why it is a failure, though a very interesting one—seem to owe their presence mainly to the necessity that the author should be seen to dissociate himself from his hero. Mr Amis has publicly attacked anti-Americanism; his hero is bitterly anti-American. All the world knows that Mr Amis likes jazz; there is therefore an extraneously overelaborated bit where we find out just how much Roger dislikes jazz. He also dislikes Jews and African politicians, while liking snuff, which he is oppressively and snobbishly discriminating about. He is spiteful: he throws into the long grass a toy belonging to a disliked child. Lecherous: he is throughout pursuing Helene, the Danish wife of his friend Ernst Bang (she has been his mistress before); he has a short unlovely affair with a hungry American wife. He is aggressive. And above all he is angry: 'Of the seven deadly sins, Roger considered himself qualified in gluttony, sloth and lust but distinguished in anger.' This irritability comes out in gusts of hatred for almost everybody who crosses his path; sometimes it looks as if he will be an amuck elephant. And yet, and yet. It certainly seems to me that in the end the author likes the character. I did too.

You can say that all that happens is Mr Amis backslides into his old fraudulent confusions, that the hands are the hands of Roger, but the voice is Amis's voice. Even so we ought not be swept along by the dominant usage of 'moral' to mean 'severe and unrelenting in judgment'; mercy is a moral quality too, and traditionally the one fostered by comedy. William Empson has sharply shown up those critics of *Volpone* and *The Alchemist* who feel morally cheated because the characters are let off so lightly at the end. Jonson was not in collusion, he simply wasn't vindictive. *One Fat Englishman* certainly seems to me a very odd and puzzling book, but there is not necessarily anything corrupt about its asking us to believe, and (more difficult) to feel, that in spite of everything that is terrible about Roger he is not for hating. Dr Johnson praised Samuel Richardson for his portrayal of Lovelace (a character who has obviously fascinated Mr Amis):

> It was in the power of Richardson alone to teach us at once esteem and detestation; to make virtuous resentment overpower all the benevolence which wit, elegance and courage naturally excite, and to lose at last the hero in the villain.

But 'virtuous resentment' can take unworthy forms. And, given a somewhat different man from Lovelace, why is it a less admirable thing to do, to lose the villain in the hero?

My qualms about the end are not moral but technical. Roger is sailing back to England, having lost Helene to a younger rival and having found out at last that she has never really felt more than pity for him. But it is as if at the last moment Mr Amis became anxious, fearing that after all we will be simply pleased at Roger's discomfiture. 'Then he wanted very much to cry and started to do so. This was unusual for him when sober and he tried to work out why he was doing it.' It is not that people like Roger don't cry; it is rather that the moment seems to have too much of a palpable design upon us. There is nothing maladroitly embarrassing about it; it is just that it has the air of trying to intercede on Roger's behalf, of doing something which ought to have been done earlier, and which for me in a way had been. In other respects, the glum bathos of the ending seems right. Flat but faithful, it is agreeably unlike the ending of *That Uncertain Feeling*.

All the same, it is true that the novel is pervasively equivocal, so that the problem is whether or not it is dealing with matters on which it is proper to be equivocal, indeed improper to be anything else. There is a certain sense in which, like much of Swift, it is less a novel than a trap. Swift knew that 'satire is a sort of glass wherein beholders do generally discover everybody's face but their own.' Mr Amis, to counter this, has devised a novel your reaction to which inescapably publishes your own prejudices, displaying as it were your own face on the screen. It is true that in reacting to any book we proclaim or let slip things about ourselves, but few books have been written quite so insinuatingly about, and to elicit, prejudice.

The book itself describes innumerable ways of being nasty and silly. There is the snobbish ostentation with which Roger crushes out an expensive cigar on the grounds that it is imperfect. There is the novel called *Perne in a Gyre*. There is the other novel *Blinkie Heaven*, written by Roger's sexual rival, about a strip-club for the blind, where the MC taunts them unbeknown with hideous women: 'It's just when the girl with the biggest squint and the most acne is taking off her G-string that the hero gets his sight back.' ('Perhaps one of the four most poised and authoritative contributions of the New York neo-Gothic meta-fantasy school'—*TLS*.) There is the anti-British prejudice, equating 'Britishly' with 'effeminately'. There is Anglophilia:

> An Englishman. Another goddam Englishman. I like that. I do like that. I'm a horrible Anglophile, you know. And believe me there aren't too many of them around these days, brother.

Even Roger's anti-semitism, which doesn't in fact come to much, looks different when we see it flanked by 'Brilliant young Jewish kid from New York. They don't come any smarter than that'; and by the fact that it is this kid himself who has the bright idea, for *Blinkie Heaven*, of dark-glasses for the blind with light-up slogans inscribed on them: 'an assortment of, oh, *God Damn All Kike Filth, Death to Lousy Irish Micks* and so on, depending on the minorities situation in the district the guy comes from.'

The effect of Mr Amis's extraordinary and various culling of prejudices is to make *One Fat Englishman* a work from which we are pretty sure to select just our own, giving ourselves away as we do when doodling. Reviewers are obviously the first to show themselves up. So that we have already been told that the book shows us how awful the affluent society is, whereas in fact there is an interchange which brings out just how awful it is to use the phrase 'affluent society'. Similarly, we've been told that it shows how terrible a certain kind of Englishman is, 'the vulgar aesthete, the petulant intellectual' (*TLS*). But it isn't clear that the book is so convinced that vulgarity is a deadly sin, just as it is hard to use the word petulant without sounding petulant. The book is said to plant its fist 'square in the belly of the fat English publisher', but if I were you, sir, I wouldn't be so sure about where that fist is aiming. Mr Amis is well aware that satire is a sort of fist which beholders do generally see aimed at everybody's belly but their own.

What happens, by design, is that it becomes almost impossible to deplore certain attitudes or prejudices manifested by the characters without by the same token endorsing other ones—and those too having a pretty unpleasant ring. Compare the epigraph for Mr Amis's stories, 'My enemy's enemy is my friend,' a wish to know where you stand which this novel shows to be both natural and a bit crazy. As when an unimpressing Englishman, Pargeter, calls England 'that bloody awful dump', gets rebuked by Roger ('when the Queen and Prince Philip were here and drove through New York or Washington or one of these places they had more of a reception than that frightful man General MacArthur'), and then at once retorts that of course he knows that America is terrible too ('the John Birch Society and muggings in Central Park and no Jews in the golf club'). Certainly it is all confusing: 'A tricky regrouping seemed in store for Roger.'

The whole novel is about prejudice; the very first conversation includes: 'Not much sense of humour, though. He's a bit fiercely Danish.' 'You mean that's why he doesn't have much sense of humour?' But then it is possible that presenting such a vast array of prejudices colliding with each other (not hurting, since really nobody gets hurt unless it be Roger) is not a nihilistic undertaking. One is left with a very powerful feeling of the extraordinary futility of anger. Granted, it is wrong of Roger to react to the showing-off of Irving Macher by thinking of him as a 'Hebrew jackanapes'. But then it would be wrong, too, of us to think that all such irritabilities come to the same thing as the extremes of anti-semitism; it would be wrong to suppose that this unpleasant trait settles the matter of whether or not Roger is worth liking. Most of the situations which crop up in the book, or most of the characters holding opinions, turn out to be cases of six of one and half a dozen of the other, and it is only a form of sentimentality to suppose that life is not full of such situations and such characters. (The *opinions* are another matter.) That uncertain feeling is sometimes better than any available certain one.

Roger, for example, is not the breaker-up of a happy marriage or even strictly speaking Helene's seducer; the origins of the affair remain distant, and her husband knows perfectly well that she has lovers and says he doesn't mind. Who are we, to be more indignant than he is? People in glass-houses shouldn't throw stones, and here we all manifestly are, in glass-houses. It is impossible to talk about the book without (unless you are very deaf) hearing breaking glass. That may let in fresh air. Anyway it is a feat of virtuosity to have written a book which ought to induce so much unease at the idea of pronouncing on its moral judgments.

Where the book fails for me is quite simply in its presentation of character. It is too short for Mr Amis to have a real chance to develop characters in any detail, so that we end up with curiously little sense of how Helene and her husband, say, really spend most of their time. Mr Amis has always been masterfully economical with minor or minimal characters, but those he places in the centre do need the space he gave them in *Take a Girl Like You*. The new novel is bold and original in its purpose, but tantalisingly inadequate in other ways; what, for instance, are we to make of the fact that Roger is a lapsed homosexual? Either more ought to have been made of that, or less. Still, it is a remarkable trap for shaming us, and not a squalid one, because Mr Amis doesn't shrink from shaming himself. He would agree with Byron:

> The Cant is so much stronger than the *, nowadays, that the benefit of experience in a man who had well weighed the worth of both monosyllables must be lost to despairing posterity.

The cant he has excluded.

V. S. Naipaul
The Enigma of Arrival: A Novel in Five Sections

The Enigma of Arrival: V. S. Naipaul's title is the one at which Apollinaire enigmatically arrived, for the painting by Giorgio de Chirico. A detail of it illuminates Naipaul's cover and his book: making their huddled way from a classical quayside (the scene bathed both in shadow and in sun), two stoled figures have their obscured faces towards us and their backs to a wall. Above the wall billows the sunlit summit of a sail.

Naipaul's novel broods upon this arrival, and even more upon what the departure might then be. For he has long been haunted by the fabled sense that upon return to the quayside from this visit to the ancient city, a traveller is to find that the sail has gone. The life will have been lived out. Life is a readying for that which will then be too late. The readiness is all. This is contemplated not with indignation but with dignity, and Naipaul's ample unfolding book is of great beauty, delicacy and courage.

There was no enigma in Naipaul's arrival on these shores nearly forty years ago, for with all its faults England offered the best opportunity for a very intelligent and very sensitive 20-year-old Indian from Trinidad with ambitions to be a writer, and a metropolitan writer at

London Review of Books (2 April 1987)

that. No enigma, but something of a miracle. For Naipaul, by coming to see—with the depth and passion of his earnest glance—the real nature of his gifts, of his self, and of his truest material, has become able to transmute his very misunderstandings into art of a crystalline honesty. *The Enigma of Arrival* newly constitutes Naipaul's claim to be, as a novelist and critic of societies, the most important import since Joseph Conrad and Henry James. Not least because he so extraordinarily combines their traditions, right down to following James in this book to where T. S. Eliot was mildly shocked to find him, seeking spiritual life in English country houses. Conrad's pertinence to Naipaul is written not all over, but all in, the novels of the Seventies, and 'Conrad's Darkness' was enlightened by Naipaul in an essay of 1974. This new novel might seem to have moved elsewhere, since the fiction within the book creates quite another world, one of Wiltshire dailiness, of neighbours and their ordinary sorrows, of small prides and predations, of a great estate that has run to seed. The course of empire is another thing. Or is it? For Naipaul is there, from the other ends of the earth (both the Indias), there in his cottage upon the estate, because of empire; and the estate itself is the creature of empire, an empire that is now grudgingly bowing to yet more imperious necessities.

Some of Naipaul's most subtle, most perfectly calibrated and least sentimental understanding of empire is to be found in this deep book. 'The imperial link' coheres with the word that is Naipaul's bond. And then the world of quiet Wiltshire is not an idyll, unaffected or uninfected. The military ranges of the downs reverberate to war, past, present and future. Domestic humiliation spills over into a killing. There is a dictator and his name is solvency.

Naipaul is grateful for the retreat, the privacy which is respected (others' and his own), the distant courtesy of his unseen landlord (twice-glimpsed only, in all the years). Hovering above the whole story of the great estate, its owner and its gardener, its steward and its tenants, is the admonition by Conrad to which Naipaul has elsewhere so recurred, the warning which no one can afford to be above: 'Few men realise that their life, the very essence of their character, their capabilities and audacities, are only the expression of their belief in the safety of their surroundings.'

For security is still Naipaul's occupation. The insecurity of himself as a pessimistic young hopeful, prompt to resent and unhumbled by humiliation; the insecurity of the young writer, alert in Earl's Court to everything except what would prove to be his real material, and setting himself to be a knowing writer, socially knowing and wink-tipping, when all the time his true comprehension (of the unknowing) lay in wait for him; the insecurity that is racial, and sexual, and financial (as if these were distinct even though they are distinguishable): these are only some of the insecurities which were to be cooled, calmed and even cured when, after twenty years in England, Naipaul entered the peace, the refuge, of his cottage and his neighbours.

Not that he got his new world right at once, either; the progress of his understandings and of his affections is beautifully told. No beating of the breast, simply (authentically) some shaking of the head, in the incremental realisation of how deliberated, how contrived, how endangered, how hopeless even, was this world which at first looked to be rooted, natural, all all of a piece throughout. 'My landlord' (his name we never hear, and that is right, since he is *sui generis* in the world not only of the book but of the life it records)—the landlord is a recluse, damaged and sometimes disabled by accidia, and confirmed in his grand sloth by the very circumstances which are failing to protect him against decay: 'There was nothing in that view (of ivy and forest debris and choked water meadow) which would irritate or encourage doubt; there was nothing in that view which would encourage action in a man already spiritually weakened by personal flaws, disappointments, and, above all, his knowledge of his own great security.'

The progress of the book is towards an ever graver sympathy with the all-but-unknown person of the landlord, a progress towards the acknowledgment that the dereliction (stubborn repeated word) of the estate need not constitute a dereliction of duty. There is nothing morbid in Naipaul's admission, 'I liked the decay, such as it was'; and there is something admirable in the landlord's self-satisfying (more than self-satisfied) realism, his power to give to the decay of a great house in its due season the calm which Wordsworth saw in a season's decay, 'clothed in the sunshine of the withering fern'.

> Ivy was beautiful. It was to be allowed to grow up trees. The trees even-tually died and collapsed, but they had provided their pleasure for many years; and there were other trees to look at, other trees to see out my landlord's time. So too it had been with people. They had been around; when the time came they had gone away; and then there had been other people. But it wasn't like that with Mr Phillips. He had been too impor-tant to my landlord.

'Security' was once the wrong kind of over-confidence, or careless-ness. 'And you all know security/Is mortals' chiefest enemy.' The old sense of the word lurks within the new, as a warning. Naipaul makes much of this while saying nothing of it; his sense of the ancient mean-ings is at one with his pleasure in happy misprisions. There is no con-descension in his savouring the comedy and the pastoral and the tragedy of such turns of speech. '"You know me," he would say. "I'm a down-and-out Tory." Running together "down-right" and "out-and-out".' Or: 'To pick the pears *in*—I liked that *in*, I played with it, repeated it.' Or: '"Of course it's an old wise tale." "Old wise tale"—it was what he said; and the idiom, as he spoke it, with its irony and tolerance, sounded original rather than a corruption.' But the most fecund of these vegeta-tions is at the heart of the book:

> This vegetable graveyard or rubbish dump Pitton described as a 'gar-den refuge', and a certain amount of ingenuity went into finding or creating these hidden but accessible 'refuges'. That was how Pitton used the word: I believe he had two or three such refuges at different places. Refuse, refuge: two separate, unrelated words. But 'refuge', which Pit-ton used for 'refuse', did in the most remarkable way contain both words. Pitton's 'refuge' not only stood for 'refuse', but had the addi-tional idea or association, not at all inappropriate, of asylum, sanctu-ary, hiding, almost of hide-and-seek, of things kept decently out of sight

and mind. He might say, of a fallen beech branch on the lawn, or a heap of grass clippings: 'That'll be going to the refuge.' Or: 'I'll take it down to the refuge presently.'

What saves these incorporations from being lordly is their respectful saltiness—that, and the way in which Naipaul is perfectly willing to pounce upon locutions which deserve it. There is Alan the arch literary type: '"All this is going down in the diary," he would say, or, personalising it, "This is for Diary," or "Diary will take due note."' And there is the repudiation, in everyone's interests, of the terms of the angry confidence suddenly vented at the bus-stop. 'She waited until the bus almost stopped. She said, "It's that fancy woman of his."'

The strength and loveliness of Naipaul's book are in every sentence; it has what Shelley yearned for when he acknowledged that there was in his work an absence of that tranquillity which is the attribute and accompaniment of power. Yet the unmistakable triumph is against such odds and is in its way such a surprise. In time, and with time, a critic rather than a reviewer may go some way towards unfolding how Naipaul manages it. Manages to write something which is at once a *Prelude* autobiography (the growth of a novelist's mind) and a fiction—this, without Naipaul's succumbing to the usual temptation of cannily sheltering behind the responsibilities of the one whenever the responsibilities of the other prove irksome or inconvenient. Naipaul ducks nothing; he prettifies and philosophises nothing. There is nothing fancy here for those who are delectably teased by some theoretical imbroglio about facticity and the fictive.

Then again, how does he create such suspense, given that he permits himself so little plotting? He has what Eliot praised in Jonson, 'immense dramatic constructive skill: it is not so much skill in plot as skill in doing without a plot.' What is it, too, that so brings to life his characters? Or rather, the people, who are indeed not brought to life by the book but who bring their life and lives to the book. There is no mistaking, and no forgetting, the reality of Mr Pitton the gardener; of Jack, a gardener (his own garden, a very different thing); of Mr and

Mrs Phillips, overseeing; of the landlord, overlooking. These are people, of worth, frailty, idiosyncrasy; none of them fudged into being either 'a one' or a type, and all of them diversely seen by quick-eyed love. And by slow-paced judgment.

Timing is a nub. Naipaul takes his time, and he takes others' time as he finds it. He can speak of his own past folly without self-congratulation, and of his achieved understanding without mock-modesty.

> Oft times nothing profits more
> Than self-esteem, grounded on just and right—

Milton is right, and the more so because when you round the corner into the next line you meet the salutary admonition

> Well managed—

itself very well managed. Naipaul's self-esteem is grounded on just and right, and it is well managed, both as duly curbed and as duly given play.

Naipaul has long possessed what Matthew Arnold praised in Dryden and himself manifested in the moment of praise: 'a prose such as we would all gladly use if we only knew how'. But the prose of *The Enigma of Arrival* is a new departure and arrival, though entirely continuous with the old strengths. It is more simply beautiful and more beautifully simple; the book speaks often of versions of simplicity (Dickens's, for one), and of how easy simplicity isn't. 'The simplicity and directness had taken a long time to get to him; it was necessary for him to have gone through a lot.' There 'get to' and 'gone through' are perfectly idiomatic but have their unexpected poetry in their sense of each going half-way to meet the other, the simplicity and the he. Naipaul would concur with Eliot: 'Great simplicity is only won by an intense moment or by years of intelligent effort, or by both.'

For Eliot is a presence throughout this book, as he could not help being for Naipaul, another expatriate radical of the right. 'The fact of being everywhere a foreigner was probably an assistance to his native wit' (Eliot, on Henry James). Eliot's elegiac scrupulosity; his sense of not just historical but geological strata; his feeling for gardens, and for civilisation as coming to mean both what has been gained and what has been lost; his unsentimentality, wronged as coldness; his apprehension of empire; his religious gravity; his dismay at histrionic vanity: all of these are alive in Naipaul's book, and there is much in Eliot's essay on Kipling (especially the Kipling of Sussex) that is newly earned by Naipaul in his Wiltshire.

Eliot might even help with the most manifest and most mysterious fact about Naipaul's style here: its being utterly untroubled by repetition, its happiness in saying everything several times, here and now and then and in its own good time. Nothing is said that is not said again; scarcely an anecdote or an observation but is offered anew. With slow rotation suggesting permanence.

Naipaul knows the vexation that a reader might feel, and is expert at reassuringly evoking the wrong sort of repetition: 'The little aeroplane droned on and on. The repetitiveness of this form of travel was an un-expected revelation.' Expert, too, at evoking the quasi-difference which amounts to nothing: 'In the late afternoon we took off again, and the aeroplane flew and flew into the night and then it flew around in the night.'

Naipaul makes good on his book's every promise. I am aware of falling short of making good on my saying so. But I am sure that the central achievement is one of tact, alive in the shaping both large and local. Since the story is both that of the inner development of a writer's conscientious consciousness (*not* his sensibility) and that of a world which he entered and affected, Naipaul's duty is to the interdependence of two independent realities, to be equally respected. *The Enigma of Arrival* is 'A Novel in Five Sections': 'Jack's Garden', on a dying man's tending and courage; 'The Journey', on Naipaul's emigration and then his younger London days; 'Ivy', on dereliction, decay and oustings; 'Rooks', on breakdown and illness; and 'The Ceremony of Farewell', on Naipaul's return to Trinidad for the religious ceremony upon the death of his younger sister. Five sections—and then tacitly six, since the dedication creates its painful symmetry across the book:

*In loving memory
of my brother*
SHIVA NAIPAUL
*25 February 1945, Port of Spain
13 August 1985, London*

The dedication itself is both independent of the sections and interdependent with them.

Naipaul has perfectly judged the demands of respect, again both separate and mutual, in the large sequence. The blurb, though honourable enough, does less than justice to Naipaul's exact art when it says that 'the outer story concerns the writer's special journey' (both from Trinidad and as an interior development), and that 'within that account is a fiction, about England.' For Naipaul has so constructed the book as to leave open this crucial question of which is the outer story and which is the inner one, since what is outer is always in danger of being slighted into mere frame, and what is inner of being slighted into, oh dear, yes, a story. In one sense, the fiction can be understood only within the context of Naipaul's having come to understand, not just what he can do as a writer, but why it truly matters that he do it: but unless a different kind of primacy attached also to that world which was at first independent of him, he would be as a novelist all mill and no grist. Which is why the 'outer story' of the writer is not what we first meet, but instead the differently outer story of Jack's garden: from which we work backward through time and space before taking up the present and the future.

Again, the blurb sells Naipaul short in concluding with this: 'While this is a novel about a specific time and place—Britain in the aftermath of Empire—at a deeper level it is an exhilarating exploration of a writer's world.' At a deeper level? It wouldn't do simply to reverse this and insist on the opposite half-truth that the deeper level is not that of the writer's world but of the world that is not of his making: the truth is that Naipaul, who is not reluctant to pass judgments when he has to, is wisely declining any invitation to judge one or the other to be the deeper level. The book's artful structure embodies the reciprocity of respect, the power of equipollence.

Such a dual respect, for its own arrivals at understanding as well as for those other lives at which it arrived (whether in fact or as fiction), is likewise the special triumph of Naipaul's style, and of the double beauty which it has, acutely perceptive at once of the world elsewhere and of its own world of the words' enactments. At its simplest, this may be a matter of exactly catching a talkative reiteration in a woman newly widowed while at the same time practising a form of such reiteration oneself, so that 'She was repetitive'—said twice—is free from condescension's sigh. Naipaul simultaneously listens to others' thoughts and to his own thinking about this: so we need to hear, for instance, the repetitions of the words 'the ivy' as they come to twine themselves obdurately about his sentences, on the landlord's refusal to be intimidated into preferring another kind of power to ivy's: 'Did he see the ivy that was killing so many of the trees that had been planted with the garden? He must have seen the ivy. Mrs Phillips told me one day that he liked ivy and had given instructions that the ivy was never to be cut.'

Naipaul no more does any pruning than 'my landlord' does. There is one serious misguided literal act of pruning reported in the novel, when Mrs Phillips takes it into her head to rebuke both the gardener Pitton and nature by 'cutting right back' the roses. Reduced to briars thereafter, they may one day, Naipaul darkly suggests, prompt the mistaken reflection that this is what happens to roses if you don't prune them.

Or there is the beautifully judged movement, itself all backings and trackings and pressings-on, in a paragraph like this, which is completely faithful both to the external setting or circumstances which it catches and to its own movements of mind or powers of development, its own 'lateral lanes':

> It was his father-in-law I noticed first. And it was his father-in-law I met first. I met him quite early on, while I was still exploring, and before I had settled on a regular daily route. I walked or picked my way down little-used lateral lanes on the hillsides, lanes deep in mud, or overgrown

with tall grass, or overhung with trees. I walked in those early days along lanes or paths I was never to walk along again. And it was on one of those exploratory walks, on a lateral lane linking the steep rocky road beside the windbreak with the wider, flatter way, it was on one of those little-used, half hidden lanes that I met the father-in-law.

Repetition in style can so easily become a failure of tact that it is both a revelation and a delight to meet such persistent felicity. The enigma of arrival is a stylistic as well as a narrative feat, instinct with regressions and progressions. So that Naipaul comes to deserve two supreme tributes. First, Coleridge's: 'The reader should be carried forward, not merely or chiefly by the mechanical impulse of curiosity, or by a restless desire to arrive at the final solution; but by the pleasureable activity of mind excited by the attractions of the journey itself. Like the motion of a serpent, which the Egyptians made the emblem of intellectual power; or like the path of sound through the air; at every step he pauses and half recedes, and from the retrogressive movement collects the force which again carries him onward.' And second, Eliot's tribute to Lancelot Andrewes: 'In this extraordinary prose, which appears to repeat, to stand still, but is nevertheless proceeding in the most deliberate and orderly manner, there are often flashing phrases which never desert the memory.'

Ian McEwan
The Comfort of Strangers

I an McEwan's tale is as economical as a shudder. It never itself shud-
ders, which is one reason why it makes you do so. By staying cool in
the face of the murderous madness which it contemplates, it precipitates an icy sweat. What it does even with equanimity is not to *display*
it. A characteristic McEwan sentence is one of which it might be said
(here in Venice revisited) that the law allows it and the court awards it.
'She loved him, though not at this particular moment.' This means what
it says, exactly. It is not a warrant for sarcasm's burliness, for inferring
that she didn't really love him at other moments, or that she really disliked him at this particular moment. Grim, laconic and humorous, it is
a bracing sentence, a short, sharp shock.

A modern couple, unmarried and unattached, is in ancient Venice.
They meet a couple, married and detached, by whom they are fascinated. The fascination turns out to be the lethal hypnosis which the
snake bends upon the rabbit. Best not to reveal in a review just what
happens. Not that other reviewers have been continent, and not that the
book's suspense is of the thin kind which aims at the suicidal success of
extinguishing in a surprised spasm the pity and terror which it has
raised: but a second reading of the book is intensely different from a first

London Review of Books (21 January–3 February 1982)

reading, and to abridge this by an unwarranted revelation is to cause some such waste as is here poignantly engraved within an extremely wasteless art.

McEwan is drawn to images of intense negation. Sometimes they incite a sigh, as they do in Philip Larkin's line: 'Such attics cleared of me! Such absences!' 'The word "relationship" was on their lips so frequently they sickened of it. They agreed there was no reasonable substitute.' Sometimes the negations incite a cry, but a cry such as never actually escapes the tightened lips of a proud sufferer. A child is being punished: 'No one spoke. It was like a silent film. My father took a leather belt from a drawer and beat my sisters—three very hard strokes each on the backside—and Eva and Maria did not make a sound.' Or a wife is being punished, it may be: 'As they descended the first flight of stairs, they heard a sharp sound that, as Mary said later, could as easily have been an object dropped as a face slapped.'

Such negations are alive, everywhere and diversely. 'For reasons they could no longer define clearly, Colin and Mary were not on speaking terms.' We are never properly introduced to this couple; the first sentence of the book presses upon us an ignorant intimacy with them such as characterises a first-naming world for which the old formalities are unthinkably vacant and the new informalities unutterably hollow: 'Each afternoon, when the whole city beyond the dark green shutters of their hotel windows began to stir, Colin and Mary were woken by the methodical chipping of steel tools against the iron barges which moored by the hotel café pontoon.' Colin and Mary Who? Or rather, since they turn out not to be married, Colin Who and Mary Who? There is much that we learn about them, but never these simple assurances. *The Comfort of Strangers*: this, and the discomfort of being lured into an unknowing intimacy with strangers, into a meeting-place which is fiercely lit and surrounded by shadows.

When Colin and Mary meet Robert, he drily pumps them:

> Robert began to ask them questions and at first they answered reluctantly. They told him their names, that they were not married, that they

did not live together, at least, not now. Mary gave the ages and sexes of her children.

Does 'their names' mean one each or two each? How deftly and equivocally servile the language can be. We never learn the names of those children of Mary, or the surname of Robert and his wife Caroline, and we feel the pull of collusive intimacy, as if an offensive had been launched so irresistibly forward into acquaintanceship as now to leave life too short for the main body of relationship ever to catch up. Names are not taboo here, but they are mythologically chastening.

> 'How long have you known Colin?'
> 'Seven years,' Mary said, and without turning towards Caroline, went on to describe how her children, whose sexes, ages and names she explained in rapid parentheses, were both fascinated by stars, how they could name over a dozen constellations while she could name only one, Orion, whose giant form now straddled the sky before them, his sheathed sword as bright as his far-flung limbs.

For a moment there is the chance to breathe a larger air, but soon the frightening factitiousness of first names has coagulated into its own level rituals:

> Colin and Caroline stood up, and Robert opened the door and turned on the light above the stairs. Colin and Mary thanked Robert and Caroline for their hospitality. Robert gave Mary instructions how to reach the hotel.

When the horror is about to reach its hideously playful climax, it is not just a warning but the loved name itself which Mary cannot utter. Drugged as though her tongue had been cut out, and soon to be forced to see a sight such as would put her eyes out, Mary 'mouthed Colin's name. Her tongue was too heavy to lift round the "l", it needed several people to help move it, people whose own names did not have an "l". Caroline's words were all about her, heavy, meaningless, tumbling objects which numbed Mary's legs.' When all is over, except that it will never be over, and when anguish has dulled to ache, the last page will urge us once more to imagine what we cannot hear, Mary again mouthing Colin's name several times without uttering it. So little time has passed since they felt their normal passion tingle and burgeon because of their having brushed the eerie passion of the odder couple: 'Mary talked of herself as a parent, Colin talked of himself as a pseudo-parent to Mary's children; all speculation, all anxieties and memories were marshalled into the service of theories about their own and each other's character as if, finding themselves reborn through an unexpected passion, they had to invent themselves anew, name themselves as a newborn child, or a new character, a sudden intruder in a novel, is named.'

There is no way of talking about this novel without saying Venice, and yet the name is never said. The dust-jacket may give us a Turner water-colour of Venice's waters, but the blurb says not one word about the novel, and the novel never says the word 'Venice'. The scene is unmistakable, and is just the setting within which to make the mistake of your life.

McEwan has said that travel is very important to him:

> I rather like to travel alone. Travelling rather puts you in the role of author—you're passing constantly through situations without any real responsibility towards them. I do find that very exhilarating.

But his Colin and Mary, to whom he does feel responsibility (though not for whom, since they're not his creatures but his creations), are travelling together, not alone. As a couple they will find themselves accursedly alone; before that, they cannot feel blessedly alone, cannot feel any of the blithe jettisoning which delighted Clough's Claude in Rome:

> It is a blessing, no doubt, to be rid, at least for a time, of
> All one's friends and relations,—yourself (forgive me!) included,—
> All the *assujettissement* of having been what one has been,
> What one thinks one is, or thinks that others suppose one.

The Comfort of Strangers, or *Amours de Voyage*. But McEwan's crucial jettisoning is of the name Venice.

When Henry James, a hundred years ago, set himself to be yet another lauder of Venice, he launched himself immediately from his title 'Venice': 'It is a great pleasure to write the word; but I am not sure there is not a certain impudence in pretending to add anything to it.' The positive and irresistible pleasure meets those immovable negatives. I am not sure there is not a certain emulation in McEwan here, a rising to James's challenge:

> Venice has been appointed and described many thousands of times, and of all the cities of the world is the easiest to visit without going there . . . There is notoriously nothing more to be said on the subject. Every one has been there, and every one has brought back a collection of photographs. There is as little mystery about the Grand Canal as about our local thoroughfare, and the name of St Mark is as familiar as the postman's ring.

The postman always rings twice, and there is much mystery in McEwan. The name of St Mark does not ring once, despite his elaborated descriptions of 'one of the great tourist attractions of the world . . . a triumphant accretion, so it had often been described, of many centuries of civilisation'.

For it is not James who contributes most to the familiar compound ghost which haunts Venice here, it is the man whose name James at once proceeded to utter and which McEwan refuses to utter once: Ruskin. McEwan's unnamed and unmistakable and not unreal city is haunted by the unnamed, unmistakable and real Ruskin. He is the only person on the scene missing. In him, all the trapping threads of this web-work of a novel are concentrated: his passion for Venice; his urge to distinguish there the true grotesque from the false, and a true terror from 'a manufactured terribleness'; his sharp dark sense, again there in Venice, of 'this great art of killing'; his appalled understanding of the relations of the modern novel to violent death; his fierce and grand forays into the politics of sex; the bitter failure of his private personal sexuality, and of his mind; even the fact of his being, of all our cultural critics, the one to whom names mean most. 'There is a curious providence in the names of many great men.' But the name of this particular great man is not to be uttered within the world of McEwan's curious providence, though Ruskin's presence is not to be put by. There in McEwan's St Mark's is 'the roofline of the cathedral where, it had once been written, the crests of the arches, as if in ecstasy . . .' Et cetera, the most important of the other things being the name of the man who wrote that description.

Ruskin created his St Mark's in contrast to England: 'And now I wish that the reader, before I bring him into St Mark's Place, would imagine himself for a little time in a quiet English cathedral town.' 'Think for a little while of that scene, and the meaning of all its small formalisms, mixed with its serene sublimity. Estimate its secluded, continuous, drowsy felicities'; and, having done so, enter St Mark's Place, where 'there rises a vision out of the earth,' and where Ruskin rises to thrilling heights, up and up, to his climax: 'a confusion of delight, amidst which the breasts of the Greek horses are seen blazing in their breadth of golden strength, and the St Mark's lion, lifted on a blue field covered with stars, until at last, as if in ecstasy, the crests of the arches break into a marble foam, and toss themselves far into the blue sky in flashes and wreaths of sculptured spray, as if the breakers on the Lido shore had been frost-bound before they fell, and the sea-nymphs had inlaid them with coral and amethyst'. Now, more than a century later, the merely human Colin and Mary are to be found here. In McEwan's prose, there is no confusion of delight.

> They released their hands and sat back. Colin followed Mary's gaze to a nearby family whose baby, supported at the waist by its father, stood on the table, swaying among the ashtrays and empty cups. It wore a white sun hat, a green-and-white striped matelot vest, bulging pants frilled with pink lace and white ribbon, yellow ankle-socks and scarlet leather shoes. The pale blue circular bit of its dummy pressed tight against and obscured its mouth, giving it an air of sustained, comic surprise. From the corner of its mouth a snail's trail of drool gathered in the deep fold of its chin and overflowed in a bright pendant. The baby's hands clenched and unclenched, its head wobbled quizzically, its fat, weak legs were splayed round the massive, shameless burden of its nappy. The wild eyes, round

and pure, blazed across the sunlit square and fixed in seeming astonishment and anger on the roofline of the cathedral where, it had once been written, the crests of the arches, as if in ecstasy, broke into marble foam and tossed themselves far into the blue sky in flashes and wreaths of sculptured spray, as if breakers on a shore had been frost-bound before they fell. The baby emitted a thick, guttural vowel sound and its arms twitched in the direction of the building.

Colin raised his hand tentatively as a waiter whirled towards them bearing a tray of empty bottles; but the man had passed them and was several feet away before the gesture was half-complete. The family was preparing to leave and the infant was handed round until it reached its mother, who wiped its mouth with the back of her hand, placed it carefully on its back in a silver-trimmed pram and set about securing with sharp tugs its arms and chest into a many-buckled leather harness. It lay back and fixed its furious gaze on the sky as it was wheeled away.

Given McEwan's art of giving and rescinding names, it is not surprising that Ruskin's 'the Lido shore' has become 'a shore'. What is surprising, a stroke of frosty challenge, is the meeting of that so-described baby with Ruskin. Things feel safer once its infantile fury is secured within that many-buckled leather harness: yet who knows what later fury those buckles will have launched? Ruskin's 'ecstasy' has had restored to it something of its original intensity of pain, rather as another of his evocations of Venice—'Amid the spires of the glorious city rise indistinctly bright into those living mists, like pyramids of pale fire from some vast altar'—may be darkly acknowledged by McEwan. These are altars which see human sacrifice.

St Mark's is, as they say, Ruskin's epiphany, and one of those who have best said it—Richard Stein, in *The Ritual of Interpretation*—is drawn just here to the word which McEwan so much needs, 'ritual'. Again, it is in pondering Venice that Ruskin is driven to seize and to elaborate that distinction between the true grotesque and the false which is where any fundamental disagreement about McEwan's work must lie. There, and in the related question of true and false terror. Does McEwan play with terror? 'The mind,' says Ruskin, under certain phases of excitement, *plays* with *terror*, and summons images which, if it were in another temper, would be awful, but of which, either in weariness or in irony, it refrains for the time to acknowledge the true terribleness. And the mode in which this refusal takes place distinguishes the noble from the ignoble grotesque. For the master of the noble grotesque knows the depth of all at which he seems to mock, and would feel it at another time, or feel it in a certain undercurrent of thought even while he jests with it . . .

It is not a manufactured terribleness, whose author, when he had finished it, knew not if it would terrify any one else or not: but it is a terribleness taken from the life; a spectre which the workman indeed saw, and which, as it appalled him, will appal us also.

Ruskin was himself appalled by a pathology of the novel of which this novel would have been to him a hectic symptom. In 'Fiction, Fair and Foul' he writes:

The thoroughly trained Londoner can enjoy no excitement than that to which he has been accustomed, but asks for *that* in continually more ardent or more virulent concentration; and the ultimate power of fiction to entertain him is by varying to his fancy the modes, and defining for his dullness the horrors, of Death. In the single novel of *Bleak House* there are nine deaths (or left for death's, in the drop scene) carefully wrought out or led up to, either by way of pleasing surprise, as the baby's at the brickmakers, or finished in their threatenings and suffering, with as much enjoyment as can be contrived in the anticipation, and as much pathology as can be concentrated in the description.

For Ruskin, there is not only a moral question (of innocence) but a class question (of respectability): 'It is not the mere number of deaths . . . that marks the peculiar tone of the modern novel. It is the fact that all these deaths, but one, are of inoffensive, or at least in the world's esteem, respectable persons; and that they are all grotesquely either violent or miserable, purporting thus to illustrate the modern theology that the appointed destiny of a large average of our population is to die like rats in a drain, either by trap or by poison.'

When McEwan's couple is trapped, there is much less confidence that they are either entirely inoffensive or entirely respectable persons, but the cutting force of the story is in its laying bare how ineradicable is this shock that it should be the mostly inoffensive and mostly respectable whom such horrors befall. If it should be wondered whether McEwan is irresponsible or evasive in not making it clear just how much Colin and Mary invited their doom (even, in the brutally superstitious and self-protecting phrase of modern city-life, 'asked for it'), one answer would be that it is of the nature of tragedy that it will not abide this question.

'We didn't exactly plan to come, but it wasn't completely accidental either.' Did King Lear invite exactly his exacted fate? Did he ask for it? Do Colin and Mary? The Venetian police have their unprepossessing prepossessions.

> While they clearly did not believe she had committed any crime, she was treated as though tainted by what the assistant commissioner himself had called, and had translated for her benefit, 'these obscene excesses'. Behind their questions was an assumption—or was this her imagination?—that she was the kind of person they could reasonably expect to be present at such a crime, like an arsonist at someone else's blaze.

For McEwan has undertaken a tragedy. Tragedy acknowledges that the injustices of life are sometimes corrigible. *The Comfort of Strangers* is alive with anger at the injustices, for instance, of the politics of sex, and it includes some vivid conversations on these wrongs and rights; here, the Ruskin who penned 'Of Queens' Gardens' is an adversary (as he is in Kate Millett's *Sexual Politics*). But tragedy has also to acknowledge that the injustices of life are sometimes incorrigible. The longing to explain is not annulled by, but it is chastened by, the inexplicability of evil and the irremediability of suffering. 'Is there any cause in nature that makes these hard hearts?' Many possible causes lurk within the retailed sickness within the past lives of the murderous Robert and Caroline. Yet it may be that there is no cause that makes these hard hearts, or perhaps that there is a cause outside nature.

The last page of the book grants access to Mary bewilderedly 'in the mood for explanation'. 'But she explained nothing.' There is great pathos in this ending, and it comes from the coinciding—perfectly honourable—of Mary's doubleness with McEwan's. He too is in the mood for explanation, but is willing, at least for now and at least in the face of the pain which he has imagined, to explain nothing.

Meanwhile, he has intimated a very great deal. Just how much, within that trodden Venice which Henry James said was in danger of becoming 'the supreme bugbear of literature', can be seen if you think of the new abridgment of Ruskin's *The Stones of Venice*, docked and decked by Jan Morris; and of her *Venice* of 1960, which manages, in innumerable ways that are apt to McEwan's taut enterprise, to soften fierce eroticism into the cosily comfortable ('Venice remains a sexy city still, as many a ravished alien has discovered. It is a city of seduction'), and manages to tame terror into a Petit Guignol giggle: 'If you have a taste for Grand Guignol, Venice has much to offer you: for here, to this day, the spirit of melodrama lives on in shrouded triumph, if you care to rap the tables and seek it out.' For 'the hushed and sudden methods of the Venetian security agencies . . . have left behind them (now that we are quite safe from the strangler's cord) an enjoyable aftermath of shudder.' *The Comfort of Stranglers*.

Donald Davie
Ezra Pound: Poet as Sculptor

'A barbarian on the loose in a museum'. 'A village loafer who sees much and understands little'. Such are the terms in which Yvor Winters passed judgment on Ezra Pound's poetry. These particular pungencies are not quoted by Donald Davie in his study of Pound, but the great strength of his book is its insistence that this general critique of Pound not merely deserves but demands the compliment of rational opposition. Most admirers of Pound truckle to his terms; Professor Davie succeeds most usefully in describing and elucidating those terms, but he maintains our right to judge the terms themselves, to define the limits of what inherently could be accomplished given Pound's mode. The artistic case against Pound is a real one, both internally in his frequent failure to carry out his own poetic principles, and externally in the limitations of the principles themselves.

Mr Davie's praise of Pound is far more convincing than anyone else's, for two reasons. First, that he actually discusses how Pound uses words and rhythms—instead of paying the usual perfunctory tribute to Pound's 'technical mastery' and then scampering on. Whether Pound is a master of words or not, his is certainly not the kind of mastery which stamps itself at once and self-evidently on our minds and hearts, and the question 'What is Pound at?' is as needed for the style as for the larger concerns. The second source of Mr Davie's authority is his reluctance to exculpate Pound, technically or morally. The callous bigotry of Pound's politics is not evaded, and its appalling poetic consequences are conceded. Mr Davie's position has a strength similar to that of Harold Nicolson's *Tennyson*: indiscriminate adulation is seen as one of the poet's worst enemies, so that whole limbs have to be lopped off. When Pound's work is offered as a package-deal, most people will (rightly) mutter 'Return to sender'. But Mr Davie is not afraid of getting a harsh review in the *Pound Newsletter*. *Hugh Selwyn Mauberley* 'falls to pieces'. The Malatesta cantos are 'dusty historical debris'. Those on Chinese history and on John Adams? 'There is no alternative to writing off this whole section of Pound's poem as pathological and sterile . . . His method, ruinously wasteful and repeatedly arbitrary, blurs all distinctions.' No claims whatsoever are made for the unity of the *Cantos*—indeed, Mr Davie goes so far as to speak of 'the lawless world of the *Cantos*'.

There is fervent admiration for Pound's translations, especially from the Chinese, for the *Pisan Cantos* and *Rock-Drill*. The admiration gains from the evidence that the critic is not selling Pound or sold on him. When, for instance, Pound mistranslates, Mr Davie is witty about it, instead of frothing like a pedagogue or claiming that Pound is being superbly 'creative'. He is prepared to offer arguments that are at once precise and tentative. He has the virtue which he praises in Pound, 'the ability to change opinion and confess as much'. At one point a good-natured footnote refers us to the *Pelican Guide*: 'For a more generous as well as more detailed examination of *Hugh Selwyn Mauberley*, see Donald Davie . . .' As a critical study, the book is notable for its habits of mind—and for its sense of fact, its ability to offer a plausible description of the works in hand. The subtitle, 'Poet as Sculptor', is justified by a very informative account (drawing impressively on the work of Adrian Stokes) of just exactly what Pound meant by invoking the analogy. The twists and turns of the prose works, especially the *Guide to Kulchur* and the translation from Confucius, are traced with a pertinacity that is possible only to the well-informed. A strong case is made that Pound's main poetic intention is to create 'a state of mind in which ideas tremble on the edge of expression.' Recurrent, though not repetitive, use is made of the insight that in metre and rhythm Pound was preoccupied with composition by verse-line rather than by larger units such as the verse-paragraph. One thing saves all these diverse matters from flying apart into just such *bric à brac* as the *Cantos* themselves: Mr Davie's remarkable gifts (apparent in all his books) as a commentator on style, his ability to say something both new and true about the lines of verse there before our eyes. What we are given is a convincing account of what Pound wished to do, how he wished to do it, and how—intermittently—he did it.

And yet . . . To me it still seems that Mr Davie has been, though not soft, softish on Pound's basic poetic decisions and principles. Why is the translation from Cavalcanti in Canto 36 so impenetrably obscure? Because there are surviving phenomena that are impenetrably obscure, and 'in such cases the most faithful translation is the one making least sense.' This book, it is true, contains what can be said against as well as for Pound, but it does not admit quite how damagingly radical its own objections are. The case is somewhat like that of A. J. A. Waldock's *Paradise Lost and Its Critics*, with Waldock replying to Dr Leavis that of course he hadn't drawn the conclusions, he was perturbed enough about what he *had* done. In a similar way, though to a much lesser extent, Mr Davie seems to have refrained from drawing the (harsh) conclusions that really follow from his own arguments. Take the basic topic of 'Poet as Sculptor'. True, 'no other vocabulary can render the method and the effect of Pound's late cantos,' and true again that for Pound 'a poem could be almost as much a composition in the space of the printed page as a shape emerging out of the time it takes in the reading.' But then:

> A poem's existence in real or imagined space can never be on a par with its existence in time, since a poem's existence in time, which brings poetry near to music, is a fact of another order altogether . . . Poetry is an art that works sequentially, by its very nature; therefore, it inhabits the dimension of time quite literally.

But surely this is a radical—and unanswerable—objection to Pound and 'Poet as Sculptor'? The limitations of Pound are radical because so much of his poetry, in this one vital respect, denies the intrinsic nature of poetry itself: that one word is read after another. Mr Davie accepts this (we owe to him one of the best formulations of the matter), and yet Pound is somehow not really pressed on the point.

Again, Mr Davie shows how capricious, careless and confused is Pound's use of history. And he rightly insists that this is a poetic disaster. What then can it mean to salvage things in these terms?

> At least we perceive that the poet is once again in command of his material, not only keeping a calculated proportion between history-material and myth-material but balancing one against the other artistically, by contriving parallels between them.

If the 'history-material' is intrinsically hollow, how can there be any kind of poetic achievement in balancing it against myth? Moreover, the failure of most of the historical cantos, together with the lack of any structure other than a thematic one, greatly weakens the effectiveness of the thematic cross-links. Things connect with other things simply because Pound has put them there. Mr Davie remarks that

> the only myths we apprehend and enter into with all seriousness are those that raise as it were to a new power, or into a new dimension, perceptions we have already arrived at by other means.

In Pound, the 'other means' are either feeble or non-existent, so that the myths remain uncorroborated (like those of *The Faerie Queene*, another hamstrung white elephant). 'What began as random associations are seen to organise themselves into constellations ever more taut and brilliant.' Organise themselves? On the contrary, they owe their presence or their return simply and entirely to Pound's imperious organisation— no narrative or history makes their return necessary as well as beautiful (and therefore truly beautiful, true as well as beautiful).

Another leniency is that Pound is often allowed to escape under cover of an antithesis. If Pound were to be praised simply as a talented minor poet, there would be no harm in saying without comment that he gives us *this* rather than *that*. But such antitheses are regularly those which we are not forced to make on behalf of major poets, those poets whom Pound insists that we shall consider his peers. To combine what would seem incompatibles, to unite polar opposites such as novelty and nature—these are the terms of a major poet. So that to defend Pound by quoting his attack on 'those who mistake the eye for the mind' is to admit the smaller standards appropriate to smaller poetry. Why not both the eye and the mind?

The antithetical excuse affects even the admirable account of Pound's insistence on the verse-line. 'Only when the line was isolated as a rhythmical unit did it become possible for the line to be rhythmically disrupted or dismembered from within.' Why 'only when'? It is true that *Pound* was able to achieve an effective internal disruption within the line only by eschewing both enjambment and any larger verse-unit than the line. But the antitheses (verse-member versus verse-line versus verse-paragraph) are exactly those that it is not necessary to invoke for a true master of verse. In Shakespeare, Milton, Wordsworth (and many others), the verse does not find itself having to sacrifice large units in order to achieve small ones, or vice versa. 'For the members of the line to achieve some rhythmical independence of the line, it was essential that the rhythmical impetus through the line as a whole be slackened.' Essential for Pound, yes—but to say so is to deny Pound's claim to high technical mastery. In the work of a real master, impetus would surprisingly coexist with poise, just as local effectiveness would fight not against but alongside larger effectiveness. Pound's terms, the terms on which Mr Davie correctly asks us to discover what is best in Pound, are by their nature an implicit admission of Pound's drastic limitations.

Donald Davie
Czeslaw Milosz and the Insufficiency of Lyric

Davie is nothing if not argumentative, and *Czeslaw Milosz and the Insufficiency of Lyric* is characteristically bracing and pugnacious. In Milosz, Davie has a match, as he seldom does in arguing with or about the poets and critics of his day; it isn't that Davie meets his match but that he meets someone whose substance and stance are similarly strong and independent. It has sometimes seemed with Davie's instanced poets, as with all of ours at times, that they matter less in themselves than as furnishing the perfect polemical *points de repère*; over the years the poems of Christopher Middleton, of J. H. Prynne, and of C. H. Sisson, have all found themselves not so much constituting the grounds of Davie's argument as figuring in it. But Milosz is too stubborn and faceted to be functionalised, even in the most high-minded way, and the result is a disinterested energy in Davie's book in no way diminished by the book's also having an axe to wield.

It is one of the strengths of this lean essay (forty pages ensconced within a further forty comprising Preface, Introduction, Postscript and Appendix) that it makes room for principled dissent from Milosz, especially at those moments when, like Davie on occasion, he cuts corners. The respect for Milosz is more than warm, but the respect for justice is

London Review of Books (4 December 1986)

fervid. Fortunately the force of Milosz's convictions and the unsentimental passion of his poetry mostly permit Davie to be at once acclamatory and just. This, with the exact apprehensions which always animate Davie's critical proceedings. There is, for instance, an unfolding of 'Father explains' which is itself a beautiful fatherly explaining of the poem, an education in this loving poem about education where the poetic imagination, bent over a map, poring yet disciplined, is 'managed by father-as-teacher'.

This may be Davie's first extended argument in genre criticism, from a critic who has been so innovative and so consolidatory under the aegis of diction, syntax, medium, context and more. But the argument itself is distinctly odd, not because one is moved to disagree with it, but because one can't imagine how anyone would disagree with it, the lines of it. Milosz has compelled Davie 'to re-think the nature of poetic discourse'. For Milosz manifests an 'indifference to lyrical purity'. He is not content to remain within the lyric's privilege of saying things that are true—'If true, here only,' only at this time in this place: he needs, and builds, a poetic art which incorporates matters of speculation, argument, and wisdom, together with historical, philosophical and political hard terms. This is all handsomely exemplified, and anyway strikes immediately as true of Milosz; nobody will doubt it who has read Milosz or even read about him. But the thing which is dubitable to the point of making me doubt whether I can have understood Davie's contention, reiterated lucidly though it is, is the assumption—entailing this re-asseverated counter-statement—that we live in days when the lyrical standpoint, the lyrical stance, the lyrical purity and privilege, are believed to be sufficient or all or all-sufficient.

Davie's 'principal and governing insight' is that 'Milosz characteristically seeks poetic forms more comprehensive and heterogeneous than any lyric, even the most sustained and elaborate.' But is Milosz anywhere near being alone or even unusual in this? Davie concedes that the truth about the lyric's being insufficient (insufficient both to the most comprehensive art and to comprehending the modern world—the 'insufficiency of the lyric mode for registering, except glancingly, the complexity of 20th-century experience') is a truth which used to be both acknowledged and grappled with. Milosz is indifferent to lyrical purity: 'But this of course is just what worried and diffident readers have said over two generations about Eliot and Pound, Charles Olson and Basil Bunting—an important point, since it reminds us that, if C. H. Sisson mostly chooses to stay within the conventions of the lyrical standpoint, there were English-language poets before him who had not.' But C. H. Sisson, irrespective of the insufficiency of lyric, is comically insufficient as an epitome of the last twenty years of poetry. Did Robert Lowell and John Berryman, like Sisson— and Milosz—poets of the Sixties and Seventies, rest within the lyric's privilege? Does Ted Hughes, or James Merrill? Does Geoffrey Hill, in *The Mystery of the Charity of Charles Péguy?* Does Donald Davie? As critic, Davie is 'chiefly arguing' for this: 'that Milosz, like a few other ambitious poets of his time, refuses to be restricted in his poetry to the lyric genre or the lyric mode.' How few is few?

As history, whether of the recent past or of the present, the thesis of this book, then, is very peculiar. 'I have suggested, going for support to the writings of Milosz, that no concerned and ambitious poet of the present day, aware of the enormities of 20th-century history, can for long remain content with the privileged irresponsibility allowed to, or imposed on, the *lyric* poet. This is not a contention that will be readily accepted: for less earnest poets are grateful for this privilege, and jealous of it, and their publics are ready to ensure it for them, since it absolves the reader from ever taking his poets' sentiments to heart, except as the poignant expression of a momentary mood.' I see no reason to believe that the sentiments in, say, the lyrics of George Herbert need not be taken to heart except as the poignant expression of a momentary mood; Yvor Winters's supreme accolade for the meditative lyric may have been extreme, but then so is Davie's revulsion from it. But in any case Davie's contention, though it is both roundly and squarely said, cannot square the circle or square with the facts. Which is not to say that the lure of pure poetry, at its purest since Romanticism in the lure of that purity sought by a certain kind of lyric, cannot be felt in the recent past or in the present: simply that capitulation to this lure has been the unusual, not the usual thing. 'For "personal lyric" is the sort of poetry that most of us look for, to the point where some of us forget that other sorts of poems are possible and are still being written.' Some of us? You guys, or not even that but hooded hordes.

But then there is a further difficulty. Davie is writing about genres—and about the 'insufficiency' of a particular genre—without ever engaging directly with the fact that it is inherent in the idea of any genre that it be insufficient. Eliot's poetic repudiation of lyrical confinement is respected by Davie, but then so should be Eliot's own principal and governing insight into the insufficiency of any genre or form. Eliot contended with Middleton Murry:

> I question one assertion of a more general kind: on p.135 Mr Murry affirms that 'drama is the highest and fullest form of poetry.' I should say that in the highest and fullest forms of poetry there is a dramatic element; but I doubt whether the highest and fullest poetry has to take the form of drama. For any form of poetry restricts one's liberty; and drama is a very peculiar form: there is a great deal that is high and full poetry that will not go into that form. Drama was, I think, less of a restriction to Shakespeare than it has ever been to any other dramatic poet; but I do not see how we can assert that it is a higher and fuller *form* than that used by Homer or that used by Dante.

Even the most capacious of the ancient genres, epic and tragedy, are vantage-points from which certain things—and only certain things—can be seen and shown; other vantage-points, those of epigram or comedy (or lyric), are living reminders that the idea of sufficiency—whether sufficiency as achievement or sufficiency to life—is itself insufficient, not even a chimera but a will of the wisp. To write a lyric is to not write something else—but some such thing is true of even the most capacious genres. 'The diminution of all poetry to the lyric' has not, in my view, taken place or even been substantially advocated: but it is in any case no more lethally a diminution than would be effected if the dithyramb (one of Milosz's genres extolled by Davie) were to queen it. Every genre has not only its insufficiencies and limitations, but its temptations and propensities; some genres are more ample than others, true, but none is— in the fundamental sense posited by Davie—sufficient, and moreover the *sequence* of lyrics has shown itself endlessly resourceful in creatively resisting the single lyric's privileged purity. There is something narrow about a notion of the lyric's narrowness which would be so little able to deal with, say, *In Memoriam*. But then the book that some of us most hope that Davie will write is one that will newly do justice to the greatest Victorian poetry.

Seamus Heaney
Death of a Naturalist

L iterary gentlemen who remain unstirred by Seamus Heaney's poems will simply be announcing that they are unable to give up the habit of disillusionment with recent poetry. The power and precision of his best poems are a delight, and as a first collection *Death of a Naturalist* is outstanding. You continually catch yourself wanting to apply to the poems themselves their own best formulations. He remembers his father digging:

> He rooted out tall tops, buried the bright edge deep
> To scatter new potatoes that we picked
> Loving their cool hardness in our hands.

And 'their cool hardness in our hands' is just what we love in the words themselves—an unsentimental clarity which impinges with a sense of the physical and yet never becomes obsessed (in Peter Redgrove's way) with physical impingement. 'Digging' is even able to risk mentioning rhythm ('Stooping in rhythm through potato drills'), and then to manifest the very firmness of rhythm which it speaks of:

New Statesman (27 May 1966)

> The coarse boot nestled on the lug, the shaft
> Against the inside knee was levered firmly.

The extra syllable in 'firmly' braces itself—it sees the line through by skill and will. And the way that the skill of digging combines strength with delicacy is caught in the felicitous play of 'coarse' against the unforeseen but altogether apposite 'nestled'.

Again, 'Follower' is able to evoke the taut accuracy of the ploughman by itself evincing just such an accuracy: the poem tells how the memory of his expert father now stumbles behind him just as he himself once stumbled as a boy behind the plough. The wheel has come full circle, and the poet needs to manifest an expertness which is a counterpart of that skilled authority which he so poignantly remembers from childhood. Needs to, not merely in order to write the poem, but because self-respect and mutual respect insist that working with words is no less dignified, no more prissy, than working with earth.

'The Diviner' presents the intuitive skill of the water-diviner in a way which manages—without narcissism or sidelong glances—to imply that just such a skill is needed here and now by the poet too. One striking moment in the poem takes the kind of risk which the diviner has to, and then pulls it off: the twitch shows

> Spring water suddenly broadcasting
> Through a green aerial its secret stations.

Too clever, too *outré*? No, because 'stations' has a simple and honourable place in traditional praises of nature (the stars in their stations), and because 'broadcasting' did originally mean scattering seed: the modern sense is the metaphorical one, borrowed from country life, and so when Mr Heaney rotates the metaphor, he repays the debt or the compliment to country life. The wheel again comes full circle.

'Churning Day' is not only a finely evocative and unaffected description of how butter is churned from milk, but the poem itself follows the arc of those processes. It gradually becomes 'heavy and rich, coagulated sunlight', and then finally, itself a memory, remembers how the household remembered the recent churning:

> And in the house we moved with gravid ease,
> our brains turned crystals full of clean deal churns,
> the plash and gurgle of the sour-breathed milk,
> the pat and slap of small spades on wet lumps.

What is surprising is the dignity with which Mr Heaney invests such simplicities, such wet lumps. His subject is those things which are inherent or inherited. What he praises is to be praised in his own work.

The central subject is growing up. Wordsworth grew up 'fostered alike by beauty and by fear', and Mr Heaney writes with vivid strength about both. The beauty he finds in unexpected places—the farm machines glinting in the dark barn, the soft mulch at the bottom of the well. The fear he never exaggerates into that sensationalism, that sedentary violence, which currently passes for manly sensibility. Some of the poems present an adulthood achieved once and for all—say, a moment that conquered the fear of rats. Others show us an adulthood won in retrospect, not then. Frog-spawn was quaint, but the multitude of frogs is suddenly terrifying. 'Death of a Naturalist'? Long live the naturalist, since Mr Heaney's powers enable him to transcend the limits of anecdote without kicking the anecdote away from beneath him.

The piercing nostalgia of 'Blackberry-Picking' does not cease to be literally itself in becoming furthermore a type of all that transitoriness for which we have all wanted to weep. The hoarded blackberries rot:

> Once off the bush
> The fruit fermented, the sweet flesh would turn sour.
> I always felt like crying. It wasn't fair
> That all the lovely canfuls smelt of rot.
> Each year I hoped they'd keep, knew they would not.

'It wasn't fair' calls across the years in the accents of childhood—only to be answered by the concluding and conclusive rhyme of 'rot' and 'not', so uncompromising after the half-rhymes of the previous lines.

The deploying of rhymes and half-rhymes, the subtle taking up of hints, the sardonic pitying puns—there can be no doubt about Mr Heaney's technical fertility, and it gains its reward in a directness, a freedom from all obscurity, which is yet resonant and uncondescending. The two poems on Ireland's great hunger are masterly. Only in some of the love-poems is there a note of mimicry (Robert Graves?).

Seamus Heaney
Door into the Dark

It is the man's second volume which fixes him. Then we can reassuredly know where we are, for the poet can be ensconced in a mythical landscape—Philip Larkin for ever riffling through photograph albums, Ted Hughes alone with the red in tooth and claw, Thom Gunn riding with his leather-jacketed counter-posse. No amount of poems to the contrary will prise the poets from such imaginary vicinities. So three years after his *Death of a Naturalist*, Seamus Heaney is going to have to reconcile himself to the fact that *Door into the Dark* will consolidate him as the poet of muddy-booted blackberry-picking.

He is not the sort of poet who jettisons. It is impossible to imagine him trying out styles and poetic kinds for size and colour, and so there is a natural and responsible continuity with the earlier book. His preoccupation—nothing as inflamed as an obsession, nothing as indifferent as 'subject-matter'—is still with whatever lasts, with everything of which he can say (the word is crucial to him) that it is *founded*: skills like thatching and salmon-fishing; grievances and injustices like those whose seepage still stains Irish living ('Requiem for the Croppies'); the seasons and the hours; the farm-lunch in the field, the scene Horatian—

> But they still kept their ease
> Spread out, unbuttoned, grateful, under the trees.

The Listener (26 June 1969)

—and yet unsentimentally stubbly, in a poem which has the real dignity, the dignified reality, of Clare. With such concerns, it is not surprising that there is no drastic break with his previous book, no thrilling repudiation. Only one kind of poem has disappeared: the love poem which deployed an emblematic conceit in the manner of Robert Graves. That tone of voice and that way of proceeding were not Mr Heaney's own. There is only one love poem in *Door into the Dark* (though there are many loving poems, and two poignant erotic poems), and 'Night Drive' is a darkened landscape of love, not a brightly lucid diagram of it.

What is new is signalled by the first poem in the book, 'Night-Piece'. For this is a cryptic poem—'Must you know it again?' it asks at once with sharp dismay, and what exactly that moment of terror is at which the horse draws back its lip ('A sponge lip drawn off each separate tooth') remains tantalisingly unspecified. The point is not that 'Night-Piece' is typical of the poems; there is much that is fine in the old manner, shiningly transparent and open ('Thatcher', 'The Forge'); rather, that the placing of 'Night-Piece' points to the new vein which the poet has struck. The earlier poems had their resonance, but it was without this riddling insidiousness. There is often a calculated—yet not calculating—moment in which we are simply not sure how to construe a striking phrase, and then the phrase suddenly illuminates itself. Beckett's 'Vent the pent' lights up as soon as it dawns on us that the words are an injunction. Mr Heaney's poems now meet riddles with such riddles.

> Birch trunks
> Ghosting your bearings . . .
>
> Stun a stake
> To stalagmite . . .

In what sense are we to take the words? Even in context there is a delighting pause during which we are taking these phrases to ourselves, waiting to comprehend them. Between the stirrup and the ground we find them mercifully solving themselves.

Sometimes the riddling effect is like that of 17th-century poetry, setting itself to create a bizarrely commanding circumlocution for something bizarrely fearsome in nature. So the eel is sinuously, intricately, described as

> a muscled icicle
> that melts itself longer
> and fatter.

'The eel describes his arcs without a sound': the 'Lough Neagh Sequence' (Mr Heaney's most remarkable achievement yet) itself offers a submarine pun on what it truly is to describe. Much as the last poem in the book—'Bogland'—sees the bog as a threat to creation, sees it as

> Missing its last definition
> By millions of years.

The mightier riddles are myths, and Mr Heaney has a new way with them. 'Rite of Spring' is about a frozen pump, and 'Undine' is about irrigation. They are both lovingly specific and specifically loving. The frozen pump is lapped with straw, set in flames, and melts. It is a warm poem about frigidity, about sentimentality as a cold force not a warm one, and about unresponsive angularity—and in being all this it is not any the less about the coming of spring and about a frozen pump which is lapped with straw etc. It is good that Mr Heaney freed it from the title 'Persephone' (as he first printed it); it is even better that he changed 'but' to 'and' in the last line, a small change of very great moment indeed, in terms both of physiology and magnanimity.

Seamus Heaney
Field Work

Those of us who have never swallowed an oyster have presumably never lived life to the full. The Augustan poet was not merely mocking the heroic when he said that the man must have had a palate coated o'er with brass who first risked the living morsel down his throat. Seamus Heaney offers 'Oysters' ('Alive and violated') as his opening. Opened at once are the oyster, the mouth, the meal and the book. It is at the start a delicious poem, not least in its play of the obdurate against the liquid:

> Our shells clacked on the plates.
> My tongue was a filling estuary,
> My palate hung with starlight.

'Clacked', for once, does not rebuke the 'tongue' of other people; 'plates' finds itself soothed out into 'palate', rather like 'oysters' into 'estuary'.

But indignation flickers, and though it is appeased it is not expunged.

> Bivalves: the split bulb
> And philandering sigh of ocean.
> Millions of them ripped and shucked and scattered.

We are not to sigh Shucks. For even the happiest recollection is liable to be blandly tinged with snobbery, as if memory were a fine cellar:

> And there we were, toasting friendship,
> Laying down a perfect memory
> In the cool of thatch and crockery.

So in the end, having next riddled the oysters (they are something of a riddle themselves) as 'The frond-lipped, brine-stung/Nuts of privilege', the *poem* is stung too:

> And was angry that my trust could not repose
> In the clear light, like poetry or freedom
> Leaning in from sea. I ate the day
> Deliberately, that its tang
> Might quicken me all into verb, pure verb.

The anger is real, but is headstrong. Instead of the nouns of privilege (property and possessions), there is to be the imaginative activity that is alive only as verb. At least since Ezra Pound, this has been a lure for poets, a thrill and a delusion. For as Heaney's last line acknowledges, 'verb' is indissolubly a noun. And the word which matters most is 'trust'.

When we come to close this book which opened with 'Oysters', we have finally contemplated the hideous devouring of a living morsel through all eternity. For the book ends with 'Ugolino', Dante's insatiable avenger, gnawing undyingly and unkillingly upon the head of the man who had starved to death his children and him:

> That sinner eased his mouth up off his meal
> To answer me, and wiped it with the hair
> Left growing on his victim's ravaged skull,
> Then said . . .

The 'eased' is cause of wonder; and of horror, like the serviceableness and decorum of that napkin of hair. 'Ugolino' too is in part about trust:

> how my good faith
> Was easy prey to his malignancy . . .

The word 'prey' feels how intimate may be the bonds between trusting and tasting. Both the first and this last poem in the book speak of 'my tongue'.

Field Work is alive with trust (how else would field work be possible?), and it could have been created only by an experienced poet secure in the grounded trust that he is trusted. Heaney is the most trusted poet of our islands. (Larkin is now trusted not to produce bad poems, but not necessarily to produce poems.) *Field Work* is an even better book than *North*, Heaney's last collection, in that it is more profoundly exemplary. One poem is admittedly sceptical of the word 'exemplary' when applied to poets, as is clear from the question which the poet, lodged in the ninth circle of Hell, puts to his wife when ('Aided and abetted by Virgil's wife') she visits his damnation. About the poets now alive, he asks:

> whose is the life
> Most dedicated and exemplary?

But Heaney's art is urgently exemplary while being aware that urgency may easily be in collusion with violence and threats. A landscape's peace of nature, a person's peace of mind, a land's peace: '*The end of art is peace*' could be, we are told, the motto of the woven harvest bow.

North, by bending itself to deep excavations within the past of Ireland and of elsewhere, achieved a racked dignity in the face of horrors. The poems were truly enlightened. But *Field Work* shows, more variously and with high composure, that there is something more primary than enlightenment. Henry James said of Eugénie de Guérin and her piety, what could not be said of Heaney and his, that she 'was certainly not enlightened'. Yet when James went on, 'But she was better than this—she was light itself,' the respectful directness of this does itself have something of light's unarguable presence. Its presence is not sentimentalised in Heaney's poems. 'I think the candour of the light dismayed us.'

Ungullible trust will always be of value, but especially so in Ireland torn by reasonable and unreasonable distrust and mistrust. The resilient strength of these poems is in the equanimity even of their surprise at some blessed moment of everyday trust. So the book's second poem,

'After a Killing', likewise gives us food for thought, but this time the food is not outré like oysters. What hope is there, after a killing? Only this—and if we insist on prefacing it with 'only', we have already sold the pass:

> And today a girl walks in home to us
> Carrying a basket full of new potatoes,
> Three tight green cabbages, and carrots
> With the tops and mould still fresh on them.

Such an ending, in its tender hope, looks cynicism's desperation levelly in the eye. The gait with which the line itself 'walks in home to us' is simply sturdy. There are no exclamations, even of gratitude, just a sense of gratitude. What could be less novel than those new potatoes? Some may think that this is bathos, but the presence within these poems of William Wordsworth (Dorothy and he at one point make a fleeting appearance, grave comic spectres not lightly to be called up for comparison) is a reminder that after the Augustans had derided it there really was discovered to be such a thing as the art of sinking in poetry.

Art practises what it preaches, and it turns into substantial worth what might be unworthy in both of those verbs. Heaney's poems matter because their uncomplacent wisdom of trust is felt upon the pulses, his and ours, and they effect this because they themselves constitute a living relationship of trust between him and us. He trusts you not to snigger at surprising simplicities:

> trusting the gift,
> risking gift's undertow,

says Heaney of a man with a musical gift, and it is brought home that there may be as much wisdom in trusting your own gifts as in trusting those who bear gifts.

What saves the poems from cadging is their supple legitimate preemption, their conscious, resourceful and bracing acknowledgement of what is at stake. Braced to, not against, as in the description of the sunflower as 'braced to its pebble-dashed wall', where even 'dashed' is secure and stable and not destructively hasty. A great deal of mistrust is misconstruction, and like the acrobat half-feigning a faltering Heaney's poems often tremble with the possibilities of misconstruing and misconstruction which they openly provide but which only a predator would pounce upon.

It is there, for instance, in the play of 'mould' against 'fresh':

> and carrots
> With the tops and mould still fresh on them.

After all, one near-fetched sense of the word 'mould' would bring it into contention with 'fresh'. Heaney's sense of the word here (the brown earth, not the green mildew) is manifestly unmistakable, but the force of the line is partly a matter of the other sense's being tacitly summoned in order to be gently found preposterous. Nothing can more bring home the innocent freshness of carrots with the earth still on them than the calm rejection—utterly unutterable—of the dingier sense of 'mould'.

Heaney practises this beneficent sleight throughout the poems. It is there earlier in this same poem in the line, 'As if the unquiet founders walked again', where the faltering sense of 'founders' is felt under the feet of the line, a line which walks so differently from 'And today a girl walks in home to us.' The founder of modern Ireland may perhaps founder. Or here:

> And as forgotten water in a well might shake
> At an explosion under morning
>
> Or a crack run up a gable,
> She began to speak.

It is unthinkable that Heaney just didn't notice the subterranean ripple of 'well might'. It is not an unfortunate oversight: it is a fortunate overseeing, and its point is to 'shake' our sense of these relationships without shaking our trust. If you were to notice nothing, you well might be impervious to the unseen ripples.

The ripple has, even in this sardonic poem ('Sibyl'), an affinity to comedy. Indeed, 'well might' is a comic counterpart to Kingsley Amis's satirical shaking of the word 'just'. Amis invoked Shirley:

> Only the actions of the just
> Smell sweet and blossom in their dust.

And in doing so expressed his settled distrust:

> Which does the just about as much
> Good as a smart kick in the crotch.

Just about as much.

Heaney's comedy, like all the best comedy, is a matter of trust. So 'The Skunk' is an exquisitely comic love-poem, and you have to love your wife most trustingly, and trust in the reciprocity, before you would trust yourself to a comparison of her to a skunk. No offence meant; no offensive launched. Then the poem is at once followed by 'Homecomings', where the loved woman is a clay nest and the man is a martin. Affectionate, delicate, calmingly dark, and as confidently trusting in its own arc as is the bird in its flights nimbly and repeatedly home, the poem goes out of its way (except that this is how the martin skims and veers) to speak in ways which would lend themselves to misconstruction if it weren't that love is a nesting trust. 'Far in, feather-brains tucked in silence'. For in this sweet evocation of the bird within the nest of the woman's head, nothing could be more remote than any accusation that anyone is feather-brained. How could we appreciate such trustful remoteness except by calling up the sheer ludicrousness of its possibility?

> Mould my shoulders inward to you.
> Occlude me.
> Be damp clay pouting.
> Let me listen under your eaves.

The tucked-in pressure is there in the way in which 'mould' wants to expand into 'shoulders'; and the mouth of the clay nest may be 'pouting', but in the confidence that no other pouting is going on (pure Keats, this). Nothing could be more unmisgivingly an act of loving inclusion than the stern word 'occlude' here, just as nothing could be less furtive, more openly trusting, than the final eavesdropping.

No need of manna when the actual is marvellous, our conversation

> a white tablecloth spread out
> Like a book of manners in the wilderness.

Likewise, the word 'implicated' is consciously innocent in Heaney: implicated, not in wrong-doing, but as the plaiting of the harvest bow. Heaney's resourcefulness is astonishing, not least in that astonishment is not then something which the poems incite. This pacific art has learnt from the poet to whom Heaney offers here an elegy, Robert Lowell, but the effect is altogether different from Lowell's Atlantic astonishments. But then Heaney's trust in other poets is itself part of his art, as in the rueful comfort to be divined within the conclusive line: 'Our island is full of comfortless noises'. Be not afeard, the isle is full of noises . . . And that's true too.

Other Arts

Marshall McLuhan
Understanding Media

T he importance of *Understanding Media* has nothing to do with worth. Marshall McLuhan is now a power in more than one land, and not only as Director of the Centre for Culture and Technology at Toronto. Since a great many people are concerned about the effects of TV, films, advertisements and the press, they will turn more and more to a praised expert. And there is, too, a market for heady prophecies, especially those which skilfully and at the last moment substitute a sermon for a forecast. Like Jacques Barzun, Mr McLuhan has the suspenseful air of being about to lift the veil. Does Telstar bode? Yes, indeed, and we may expect (excitement mounts), we may expect that

> the time factor in every decision of business and finance will acquire new patterns. Among the peoples of the world strange new vortices of power will appear unexpectedly.

'Unexpectedly' is about right, for all the help we actually get from Mr McLuhan's clutch of crystal balls. The car has altered everything, 'and it will continue to do so for a decade more, by which time the electronic successors to the car will be manifest.' Nostradamus redivivus? A reader who crosses Mr McLuhan's palm with two guineas may feel gulled.

New Statesman (11 December 1964)

Three themes cohabit, not very fruitfully. First: electronics and 'electric speed' are different in kind from the mechanical (which is linear, typographic, uniform and repeatable). Our present culture partakes of both. The mechanical or typographic culture necessitated sequence, fragmentation and specialisation; but the new electronic culture 'retribalises', makes the world a village, and is organically instantaneous.

> Man can now look back at two or three thousand years of varying degrees of mechanisation with full awareness of the mechanical as an interlude between two great organic periods of culture.

The second theme is 'The Extensions of Man':

> Whereas all previous technology (save speech, itself) had, in effect, extended some part of our bodies, electricity may be said to have outered the central nervous system itself, including the brain.

Third:

> Political scientists have been quite unaware of the effects of media anywhere at any time, simply because nobody has been willing to study the personal and social effects of media apart from their 'content'.

These are important themes, but they are altogether drowned by the style, the manner of arguing, the attitude to evidence and to authorities, and the shouting.

Any medium has an effect *qua* medium, over and above its content. To have said so would have been to have written a sadder and a wiser book (and a shorter one). But Mr McLuhan's contempt for people who attend to the 'content' leads him to deny that content plays any part at all. 'The medium is the message,' he intones again and again. 'The effects of technology'—and by technology he means all 'extensions of man'—'do not occur at the level of opinions or concepts, but alter sense ratios or patterns of perception steadily and without any resistance.' If he had said 'do not occur *only* at the level of opinions'—but no, for him the sole effect is that of the medium itself. Literacy creates individualism, and 'this fact has nothing to do with the *content* of the alphabetised words.' 'The effects of radio are quite independent of its programming.' TV creates 'total involvement in all-inclusive *nowness*', and 'this change of attitude has nothing to do with programming in any way.'

All of which means that *Understanding Media* cuts off its extension of man to spite its face. How can Mr McLuhan possibly use the medium of the *book* (typographic, linear, fragmented) in order to speak in this way about the electronically instantaneous? On his own terms, a book cannot but enforce the typographical attitudes which he insists are cramping Western man. If his arguments are true, how silly to annul them by using a medium which has no option but to annul them.

He wriggles in this unmentioned predicament, and does his best to escape by abandoning all the sequential virtues of a book. He says the same thing on every page, and repeats whole chunks when he feels like it—which is perhaps one kind of instantaneity. He praises the Eastern ('oral') mode of thought: 'The entire message is then traced and retraced, again and again, on the rounds of a concentric spiral with seeming redundancy.' But if this 'oral' tradition could be incorporated in a book, his arguments would all collapse. The attempt may be pluckily preposterous, but the outcome is not just 'seeming' redundancy. The moral position, too, is shaky, and not even the quotation from Pope Pius XII about media quite manages to shore it up. Mr McLuhan may insist that he is 'withholding all value judgments when studying these media matters,' but in fact his terms are about as neutral as a bigot. Who will be found to speak for literacy (which has 'fragmented' and 'mutilated') when the electronic culture is described in these terms—humble involvement and deep commitment, participation, heightened human awareness and unifying the life of the senses? 'Contemporary awareness had to become integral and inclusive again, after centuries of dissociated sensibilities'—does that withhold value judgments? And is it an act of neutrality to give a chapter to each of 26 media, but no chapter to the theatre?

Very well—people were wrong to ignore the nature of a medium. But that doesn't beautify the airy hauteur to which the arguments rise whenever they confront facts, earthy political facts. Possibly radio does inevitably inflame, and TV does cool, but the authorial tone is too epigrammatically Olympian. 'Had TV occurred on a large scale during Hitler's reign he would have vanished quickly. Had TV come first there would have been no Hitler at all.' Vanished? Like a Walt Disney ogre? So confident a magic wand does not like the fact that there are facts. Can we be quite so sure that Nazi TV would have had no choice but to intervene so coolingly and so effectively? Is 'content' (even anti-semitic content) really a matter of total indifference in comparison with 'the medium proper'? Mr McLuhan may perhaps be right, but Hitler seems to me a subject where too serene a confidence in one's own theories can easily look unfeeling. After all, there are those of us who would have traded all of Pope Pius's words about mass media for just a word or two about the massacre of the Jews.

Mr McLuhan's confidence, quite without irony, sees the computer as a type of the Holy Ghost: 'The computer, in short, promises by technology a Pentecostal condition of universal understanding and unity.' So much for greed, crowding, hunger, and all the hard facts which make universal understanding and unity a matter of intractable things as well as of language and media. When Mr McLuhan invokes his Pentecost, there is no doubt about the mighty rushing wind, but where are the tongues of fire?

It seems that we have been fools, but now at last we will be put right about it all, though our patient teacher can't quite prevent his eyelid from drooping disdainfully. 'It is not the increase of numbers in the world that creates our concern with population,' rather it is 'our electric involvement in one another's lives'. Our 'concern' may well have been pricked by the media, but it is not entirely evolved from them, since there remains the glumly objective fact of the increasing population, a fact which to any man who wants to live as something more than 'a student of media' is in itself a cause of concern. Could it be that Mr McLuhan averts his eyes from the fact because the Catholic Church wishes it weren't a fact? When the facts would be embarrassing, Mr McLuhan passes by on the other side. It seems that 'literate man' is a warped creature, 'quite inclined to see others who cannot conform as somewhat pathetic.' And then, without a pause: 'Especially the child, the cripple, the woman, and the coloured person appear in a world of visual and typographic technology as victims of injustice.' But in this world, the world of facts as well as of media, coloured people do not merely *appear* (thanks to tricksy typography) to be victims of injustice, they *are* such. Not every single individual, of course, but quite enough for Mr McLuhan's enlightened detachment to get tarnished. He long-sufferingly tut-tuts—how naive of people to be upset by circumstances, instead of realising that it is all just the built-in preconceptions of media.

Media, apparently, and not moral convictions, get things done: 'the real integrator or leveller of white and Negro in the South was the private car and the truck, not the expression of moral points of view.' Notice 'was', as if it were all a thing of the past, so that now the historian can bask in equanimity. Notice, too, that it isn't said that the truck was in the end the most effective or most important integrator or leveller—no, it was 'the real' one, which leaves 'moral points of view' (a prettily placid piece of phrasing) as merely unreal. As if there weren't enough people willing to be told that justice in the South (a) has been achieved, and (b) is no moral concern of theirs, without our author handing them warrant (don't worry, the truck'll change all that). This may all be unwitting, in which case it is the consequence of Mr McLuhan's furious rebound. Since everybody else will talk about nothing but 'content', he will talk about nothing but media—nice, neutral, omnipotent media.

There is a similar stoniness when he discusses 'labour-saving' devices, toasters or washing-machines or vacuum cleaners: 'Instead of saving work, these devices permit everybody to do his own work. What the 19th century had delegated to servants and housemaids we now do for ourselves.' Oh no we don't. When we switch on the automatic washing machine, Mr McLuhan and I are not in any meaningful sense doing the same *work* as servants used to do. There is something unimaginative about a deftness that is so very interested in 'devices' and so little interested in how 19th-century servants really did work. 'Today, in the electronic age, the richest man is reduced to having much the same entertainment, and even the same food and vehicles as the ordinary man.' Try telling that to the many ordinary men who live in 'the other America', let alone three-quarters of the globe. Mr McLuhan may claim the licence of a prophet, but even a prophet will be the more humane if he does not state as today's fact what may perhaps one day come to pass.

Such indifference to fact is not always politically disagreeable, but it is always absurd. Literate societies don't like B.O.? That must be because the odour 'is far too involving for our habits of detachment and specialist attention.' But why shouldn't it just be that we don't like the smell? Ah, but what about 'the strange obsession of the bookman with the press-lords as essentially corrupt'? That must, it seems, be due to the antagonism of the book to the newspaper as a medium. Yet what if it weren't a strange obsession, but a fact, that press-lords are corrupt?

The style is a viscous fog, through which loom stumbling metaphors. And Mr McLuhan's subject, after all, is the imagination and the emotions. Nothing could be less imaginative than all this talk of 'a complex and depth-structured person', especially as the depth resembles a sump: 'people begin to sense a draining-away of life values.' What we need is 'the mosaic of the press' which 'manages to effect a complex many-levelled function of group-awareness.' Fortunately 'the tactile mesh of the TV mosaic has begun to permeate the American sensorium'—hence the 'complex togetherness of the corporate posture'. What makes it all so grisly is that this unfelt, unfeeling and nerveless style is forever insisting on how media grip, how they touch, how they create.

The tastes are of a piece with the style. He asserts that ours is 'one of the greatest ages of music, poetry, painting, and architecture alike.' Later he comes to think that this was a bit half-hearted, so he steps it up: 'the arts of this century' have an 'ascendancy over those of other ages comparable to that which we have long recognised as true of modern science.' And the justification for such a claim? Well, there is the 'extraordinary intensity' of Agatha Christie's *Labours of Hercules*. And there are advertisements.

> The ads are by far the best part of any magazine or newspaper. More pains and thought, more wit and art go into the making of an ad than into any prose feature of press or magazine.

Anybody who thought that advertisements have as much ugly lying as witty art would simply be exposing himself as one of the 'media victims, unwittingly mutilated by their studies'. 'Ads are ignored or deplored, but seldom studied and enjoyed'—as if enjoyment could not but follow study, as if it weren't even a possibility that one might study and then deplore. Since he so admires advertisements, it is not surprising that he uses them as evidence. Is Mrs Krushchev's plain cotton dress an icon of thrift? Yes—a 'very ingenious ad' has said so. Are the Greeks more sensuously involved? Yes—a travel guide has said so. *Vogue* proves one fact (and I don't mean about *Vogue*), and *Life* another, as if they were irreproachable works of history.

Mr McLuhan uses his authorities about as convincingly as his evidence. No doubt there is still a lot to be said for Bergson and Toynbee, but it is not now possible to plonk down their names as if they settled a matter. Mr McLuhan invokes Lynn White's *Medieval Technology and Social Change* for its argument that at a particular time the stirrup profoundly affected ways of life—but he does not mention that there are unridiculous historians who believe that the arguments are important but the evidence (especially as to dating) far from complete. Similarly, great play is made with that dread 'dissociation of sensibility' which at some unspecified date overtook Western man—as if any scrupulous cultural historian now thought the phrase anything but a faded bright idea. It is not only those who have been twisted by literacy who will find all these arguments short on evidence. Perhaps Mr McLuhan's history is more accurate than are his literary quotations. The audacity is impressive, as when he takes E. E. Cummings as a type of the poet whose work is for the ear and not for the eye: Cummings must be 'read aloud with widely varying stresses and paces', since 'people who feel that poetry is for the eye and is to be read silently can scarcely get anywhere with Hopkins or Cummings.' I would like to hear Mr McLuhan rendering

Cummings's '.gRrEaPsPhOs)'. But even so great a vocal skill would not be a substitute for cogency or clarity of argument. Or for an accurate text of Cummings—Mr McLuhan does not give us Cummings's spelling, capitalisation, hyphenation, lineation or spacing. The masters of the subtle schools are controversial, polymath. Mr McLuhan shifts from ham to ham, stirring the water in his bath.

Richard Whelan
Robert Capa: A Biography

B Y 1943 "The Greatest War-Photographer in the World" had
reached his third war. After the Spanish Civil War and the Chinese-
Japanese War, Robert Capa was with the US Army in Tunisia: snatching a moment for a call of nature in the desert, he suddenly realised that
he was in the middle of a minefield. More than ever he needed to relieve himself but didn't risk even that movement; it seemed an age till
the mine removal squad relieved him. In 1954 Capa was on his fifth
war: after Palestine/Israel in 1948, he was with the French troops in
IndoChina. He stepped on a Vietminh mine. He was 40.

He was a brave man, skilled, wily, charming and ruthless—though
his photographs are full of that old-fashioned quality for which we have
mislaid the word: ruth. He stands with Wilfred Owen as one whose art
was itself able to distil "the pity of war, the pity war distilled". The soldier falling in Spain, shadowed by death; the fighter ace in Tunisia, with
his sidelong glance and his direct notches swastika'd on the fuselage; the
D-Day landings, awash and beached; the shaven heads of French col-
laborators, shamed, shameful; General Omar Bradley with his nose
comically (not ridiculously) plastered for the miniature wound of a
lanced boil: these are the witnesses to Capa's greatness as a witness.

Though a photographer's sufferings are never exactly those that he faces, the photographer is the heir to the great cry of the poet who knew the American Civil War in more than its haunting photographs: Walt Whitman, with his words. "I am the man, I suffered, I was there".

If you have £15, spend it on Robert Capa. Spend it, that is, as writing this review made me happily spend the money, on *Robert Capa: Photographs*, issued by Faber to coincide with the publication of *Robert Capa: A Biography*. You can wait to spend your next £15 on the biography.

Capa's was a disturbed life. Born Endre Friedmann in Budapest in 1913, restless, gifted and unrooted, he was to find himself gradually becoming not a journalist (he spoke umpteen languages, all badly), but a photographer. He haunted many an Unreal City of the gathering storm: the Berlin of swelling Nazism, the Paris of clash and counterclash, the Madrid of the doomed Republic, the London of the Blitz.

His first scoop was Trotsky in 1932 addressing Danish students on the Russian revolution; late ones were the polyphilogenitive Picasso, Matisse at work compactly crouching, Hemingway slumped and porcine, Gary Cooper exquisitely swaying across a treetrunk with a fishing rod, and Ingrid Bergman cool. He became an American citizen, the better to be a world one. He loved and was loved and was lonely. He founded the photographer's cooperative Magnum—champagne, not sham pain. When he was killed he had for a while been in a bad patch which might have proved much more than a patch.

Yet the greatest interest of Richard Whelan's biography is not that which happened (fascinating though it all is) but that which did not. For this compelling photographer was a compulsive liar. A *Pathé* logical one. His biographer expresses no shock or dismay, and since he clearly not only admires but likes Capa, it is all the more telling that on almost every page he has to warn you not to believe Capa. Capa claimed . . . but in fact . . . : this is the genial litany. Capa invents, embroiders, co-opts. It may be a question of whether he did indeed see, poignantly there on the prison wall in Hungary, the pencilled names of two young

Communist martyrs (he didn't—they weren't arrested till a year after he left Hungary). The woman he loved, Gerda, was killed in Spain in a hideous accident; Capa said she was his wife, which she wasn't, and said he was with her at the time, which he wasn't.

Now it is true that the magazines for which he worked also regularly told untruths, to put it mildly. *Life* claimed that he had waded across the Segre river with troops in Spain when he had really been at a party with Hemingway and Malraux. But Capa caps the lot. His autobiography, *Slightly Out of Focus,* is apparently more a work of fiction than of fact. Again and again his claims are shown to be false. "The only elements of truth in the entire story . . .", sighs Whelan good naturedly; and again, "So there may be an element of truth in his account". May there, now.

What is bizarre is this vision of the photographer as liar. Perhaps the truth-claims made by and for the camera are so hard to live always with that a great photographer starts especially to crave freedom from truth's imperatives. But the really disconcerting part is the doubt as to whether Capa's personal untruthfulness seeped into his professional conscience. For it would be odd to claim that his photographs would be the same, would be as moving or moving in the same way, if we were to learn that they were in fact film-stills, and that those were not prisoners of war at all, or corpses, but film-extras and set-up sets.

Photography, or at least such war-photography as Capa's, has a contract with its contemplators. Once all the deductions have been made that acknowledge the photographer's inescapable selection, placing, timing and so on, the war-photograph says, not that this is how it looked, but this is how it was. It happened. Which is why I, for one, find it appalling that Richard Whelan can in the end brush aside the question of whether Capa's most famous photograph, the falling soldier in Spain, was faked or not. (There have long been known to be problems about the place, the time, and the sequence, all calling in question the photographer's fidelity, his trust-worthiness; and there are other instances too.) "The fact is that we shall probably never know exactly what happened on that hillside", says Whelan with relief.

To insist upon knowing whether the photograph actually shows a man at the moment he has been hit by a bullet is both morbid and trivialising, for the picture's greatness ultimately lies in its symbolic implications, not in its literal accuracy as a report on the death of a particular man.

No, this is irresponsible and itself trivialising. Would the photograph really have effectively, affectively, the same symbolic implications if Capa had hired an actor for his shot? Such a photograph as Capa's moves us as it does because it is offered not as a film's fiction but as a war's fact. We take the force of it because we take the photographer's word for it. Our understanding of war shown here is based on an understanding, and faith misplaced would be art evacuated. It is terrible to think that Capa may have been corrupted by the devilish imposture advocated by Henry Luce as "fakery in allegiance to the truth". "Capa arranged a whole attack scene: an imaginary fascist position was stormed . . ." What was that about "the first casualty"?

Samuel Beckett
The Theatrical Notebooks of Samuel Beckett: The Shorter Plays,
edited by S. E. Gontarski

Samuel Beckett's originality is of the highest kind: one aware that the word *original*, comprehensively comprehended, takes up within its history not only "existing now for the first time" but also "having existed from the first." Not only original as being—now and in prospect—a way forward, but also as acknowledging in retrospect its having come from way back. The balance and reconciliation of these deep claims will be found to furnish the grounds of any lasting originality.

More than forty years ago, when I was a student at Oxford (and already a votary of Beckett), I heard a memorable talk by the Johnsonian scholar Matthew Hodgart. It brought signally together two great writers: Beckett and Wordsworth. A surprise, and one that was then made good. "Resolution and Independence"; "Old Man Travelling"; "Animal Tranquillity and Decay"; "Argument for Suicide"; "Beggars"; "Incipient Madness"; "The Recluse" . . . : the Wordsworthian titles speak of, and to, the lasting apprehensions that these visionary writers share, apprehensions of solitude, ageing, exacerbation, induration, distance,

New England Review (Summer 2000)

and distaste. True, there are urgent differences: Beckett is inconceivable without a sense of humor, and Wordsworth inconceivable with one. But then John Berryman knew how bizarrely these things may work:

> Churchill was ever-active & crammed with glee,
> Henry was morbid, inactive, & a child to Angst,
> there the difference ends.
>
> (Dream Song 323)

Everybody knows (we are no longer in Macaulay's world of "Every schoolboy knows who imprisoned Montezuma and who strangled Atahualpa")—everybody knows Wordsworth's conclusive thought about originality and literature:

> If there be one conclusion more forcibly pressed upon us than another by the review which has been given of the fortunes and fate of poetical Works, it is this,—that every author, as far as he is great and at the same time *original*, has had the task of creating the taste by which he is to be enjoyed: so has it been, so will it continue to be.
>
> (Essay, Supplementary to the Preface, 1815)

"So has it been, so will it continue to be": what a lovely turn upon originality. Where it was that Wordsworth then moved is less often remarked. For what crowns this supreme apophthegm is Wordsworth's at once acknowledging that this thought about originality and creation is not original to him, is not his own creation: Coleridge is immediately given—and duly takes—a bow. Wordsworth's greatness is at one with Coleridge's.

Beckett's fiction, he believed (and many of us share his belief), is greater than his drama. By and large. And how large his achievement is under both heads, by the bye. But the originality of his drama was and is more immediately manifest. The course of the early fiction, though unpredictable, was not exactly startling. *More Pricks than Kicks* (1934) is a book of short stories with a continuing protagonist-agonist, a book that mounts to a novel of a kind. *Murphy* (1938) is a novel of a kind, complete with a hero, of a sort, and a heroine, ditto. And then in the early fifties there is the slow-motion marathon-run of endurance, of enduring power, the three increasingly outré novels that were at first in French (becoming *Molloy, Malone Dies,* and *The Unnamable*), with *Watt,* written during the war—in France in English—at last achieving publication in 1953. Granted, originality was there, to hand, in spades, but not with quite the shock of the more-than-new that invested *Waiting for Godot* in those same early fifties. It was the dramatic originality, in both senses of dramatic, that created the taste by which Beckett came to be enjoyed (always a curious way of enjoying oneself, it may be granted . . .)—and by which not only the plays but the fictions have long been enjoyed.

It is a blessing that the Parisian director Roger Blin preferred—for a host of reasons, some of them being sensible ones of costs and resources—*Waiting for Godot,* or rather *En Attendant Godot,* to the other play that Beckett had to offer then, a sprawling domestic drama about the loopiness of straightforward life and about diverse cravings for freedom: *Eleutheria.*

Eleutheria—no acute accent on the third *e,* please, whether in French or English—was published in the original French, six years after Beckett's death, in 1995; it has been very well translated into English, by Barbara Wright (London, 1996), having been very ill translated into, I suppose, English, by Michael Brodsky (New York, 1995). In his touching life *Samuel Beckett: The Last Modernist,* Anthony Cronin attributes the translation to a markedly different Brodsky, Joseph. Sometimes it is a pity that one cannot sue for libel on behalf of the dead. For a hilariously lethal exposé of M. Brodsky's *Eleuthéria,* see Gerry Dukes in the Journal of the American Irish Historical Society, *The Recorder* (Fall 1995). "*Ton canotier avait un couteau*" (Beckett). "Your oarsman had a knife" (Brodsky). "Your boater had an osprey in it" (Wright, right). A feather in Beckett's play, and in his and Dukes's and Wright's hat. Your oarsman had a knife? Beckett might stroppily sharpen his *No's Knife.*

Professor S. E. Gontarski supplied an introduction to the débâcle that is Brodsky's *Eleuthéria.* But it is never too late to make amends.

Professor Gontarski does so with the dedicated editorial scholarship that he continues to devote elsewhere to Beckett. Which brings us to the occasion for the present essay: the completion of the series of Beckett's theatrical notebooks. The latest, and the last, volume is *The Shorter Plays*.

The series is simply indispensable, a treasure-house of that which in the fullest sense *informs*. Beckett, as the world knows, became an indefatigable and indeflectible director of his own plays. His theatrical notebooks record his thinking, his feeling, and his refusal to reduce his works to matters solely of either thinking or feeling. His intense self-discipline and self-criticism were keen to inculcate in his actors exactly these qualities, such true training. Self-punishing (not, it seems to me, masochistic), self-mortifying, he judged it his duty to be exact and exacting. For Billie Whitelaw, probably the greatest of his actors in English (one used to be able to say actresses, since it used to be understood that bearing a marked term was not intrinsically demeaning, the suffix -ess doing no wrong to a princess), not only rehearsals but performances were a form of torture. An artistic form. Not the harshest thing of all, an inferno; no, purgatory only (only!), for it does come to an end, and one is supposed to be the better for it.

In this series of thoroughly handsome (thorough and handsome) volumes, we have the working thoughts—the quick forge and working-house of thought and of more than thought—of one of the world's great dramatists. What would we not give for such resources, such records, for one of the great dramatists of the past, for Wilde, say, or Shaw? Whereupon one immediately realizes that apparently there has never been a dramatist who gave such unremittingly attentive and imaginative energy to the realization on stages of his pages.

The general editor of the series, James Knowlson, has already given the world a first-rate biography of Beckett, *Damned to Fame*, subtly mastering the entire French context (of life and letters), and combining a duly investigative spirit with a profound respect for Beckett's reticences and privacies. He has behaved with characteristic modesty in not claiming within this series of theatrical notebooks his own edition of the one for *Happy Days*. This appeared in 1985, in a smaller format than the subsequent volumes, and without a revised text (or a text) of the play. Despite its not forming part of the series (subsequently volumes are numbered I–IV), it is much more than a mere forerunner of them; it is rightly listed with them though not as one of them; and it remains one of the most valuable of these compelling compilations. For Beckett's notebook for *Happy Days* contains some of his most illuminating, and indisputable, acknowledgements of the literary allusions within one of his plays.

The series proper opened with *Endgame* and with *Krapp's Last Tape* in 1992, and then *Waiting for Godot in* 1993, all three including a revised text of their play. *The Shorter Plays* now furnishes not only the notebooks but revised texts of *Footfalls*, *Come and Go*, and *What Where*, plus the notebooks for *Play*, *Eh Joe*, *That Time*, and an appendix on *Not I*. Every page has something to be grateful for, to pore over, to marvel at. Beckett's obduracy is oddly liberating, for it makes so clear exactly what he saw himself as up against, and so makes possible a well-informed and principled disagreement with him. Repeatedly he asked for, and mostly managed to secure, a discipline as severe as that of ballet, a profound self-abnegation.

His strict regimen is continuous with T. S. Eliot's understanding of what had gone grievously wrong with drama in performance. Judging a production of *The Duchess of Malfi* in 1919, Eliot wrote of Miss Nesbitt that she

> continued to make the part, and ruined the lines. We required only that she should transmit the lines, but to transmit lines is beyond the self-control of a modern actor, and so she did what the modern actor does: she "interpreted" them.
>
> As *Hamlet* is performed, only the plot is Shakespeare's; and the words might as well be the flattest prose. For poetry is something which the actor cannot improve or "interpret"; there is no such thing as the interpretation of poetry; poetry can only be transmitted; in consequence, the ideal actor for a poetic drama is the actor *with no personal vanity*.
>
> (*Arts and Letters*, iii, 1919–20)

319

Beckett put into practice, and made others put into such practice as made perfect, the injunction behind Eliot's stringency. If you want a less sharply italicised way of putting it, you could settle for the old urging cited by one of Beckett's best theater-reviewers, Kenneth Tynan. Advice to the actor: Don't just do something, stand there.

Beckett wrote to Alan Schneider (17 August 1961) about Winnie in *Happy Days*, Schneider having asked what "tone you want": "No, just say lines, same tone throughout, polishing mechanically, no emotion on 'blaze of hellish . . .' What tone? This of course is *the* problem. I can find no better word for it than 'mild'."

"Process of elimination": this is a minatory jotting by Beckett in the notebook for *What Where*. There was so much that needed to go through, or rather to be put through, the process. Beckett praised to Schneider "your aversion to half-measures and frills, i.e. to precisely those things that 90% of theatre-goers want" (11 January 1956).

Among the valuable provocations of these volumes is their pertinence to so many of the debates, the matters of critical principle, of our day—and of every age. The unsettling debates will not be settled by reference to Beckett's own accounts of what he sought and found, but no true engagements with the points of principle will be able to ignore the evidence that has been thoughtfully brought together here.

Is a playwright necessarily the best director of his or her work? Might it even be that he or she is necessarily not the best? No general answer could exist, not even a general answer to cover the works of one playwright. Cases are all. Beckett did work wonders; respect for his genius, and awe at it, moved his actors (and his technicians and all the others whose collaboration comes to compose a production) to extremities of dedication and patience. And, yes, obedience. But did the plays under his direction breathe as freely as they might or should? Kenneth Tynan precipitated a crucial controversy when he wrote to George Devine at the National Theatre: "The point is that we are not putting on *Play* to satisfy Samuel Beckett alone . . . I trust the play completely, and trust your production of it—up to the advent of the author. What I don't especially trust is Beckett as co-director." In the event, for "don't especially" read "especially don't". How much more, by which of course I mean less, would Tynan trust Beckett once he was no longer only co-.

It is not that Beckett was simply the man in the iron sweater. How hard, though, he found it to delegate. In early days he would write to Schneider (26 October 1957), "Sorry I wasn't of more help about the play, but the less I speak about my work the better." He stuck resolutely to this when it came to exegesis. The plays meant what they said and showed. Up front. He the author was not privy. Ralph Richardson didn't want—and Beckett didn't then want him to want—the part of Pozzo. Beckett brought this up later when he was being quizzed by Schneider about Mouth in *Not I*. Schneider: "We're assuming she's in some sort of limbo. Death? After-life? Whatever you want to call it. OK?" Beckett (16 October 1972):

> This is the old business of author's supposed privileged information as when Richardson wanted the lowdown on Pozzo's background before he could consider the part. I no more know where she is or why thus than she does. All I know is in the text. "She" is purely a stage entity, part of a stage image and purveyor of a stage text. The rest is Ibsen.

The rest is . . . Silence, please.

Manifestly this is unjust to Ibsen and to all those artistic triumphs possible only to his form of drama; it would be an impoverished world in which the only plays that had a claim on us made Beckett's claims. But how much Beckett was released into effecting by being able to say so roundly "The rest is Ibsen."

Dismissive, this ("the rest is" as "anything else is only . . ."), but perhaps the wording is open to something positive. For *Not I* might itself be a quintessence of Ibsenism, a woman haunted and haunting, A Doll's Mouth, or Head a Gabbler.

Fortunately several things protected his directing of his plays against hardening into the tyranny that the plays themselves regularly put before our wincing eyes. The first is his understanding that the plays, though he wrote them, inevitably escape him and his commands. William Blake could say of his works that though I call them mine, they are not mine.

Beckett could offer his own rueful counterpart, writing of *Happy Days* with a straight face and a flat tongue, "Often wonder who wrote that play and why" (9 June 1971).

The second prophylaxis against over-insistence, against a directorial rigidity, is Beckett's willingness to change his mind. He had, what is always a help in such matters, a mind to change. Resisting the Lord Chamberlain's censoring of *Waiting for Godot* (out with "The bastard! He doesn't exist!", a blasphemy against our creator), Beckett had recourse to some happily inverted commas in mentioning "the hope of getting him to change his 'mind'." Beckett was happy—no, that won't do, for happiness is not it—was prepared to change his mind. The urging to do so came more often from within than from without. He was sincere when he wrote to Schneider (21 November 1958): "Don't feel I want to interfere with your interpretation or that I think there is no other way of doing it but ours." An honorable swerve at the very end: not mine but ours.

The third thing that Beckett possessed to protect his plays against their creator was a generous receptivity to chance, to that which happened to happen. *Krapp's Last Tape* twice found a life of its own that Beckett then blessed. There was the accidental striking of the lamp by Pierre Chabert, the swinging lamp then swirling the light and dark on stage—an accident in the first place, accepted as grace both proffers and accepts what befalls, then incorporated by Rick Cluchey in a subsequent production. And there was the other (smaller) light that happened to glow for Beckett. He delighted in it as not of his making but there for his taking:

> At the end . . . we had a fade-out and the quite unexpected and marvellous effect of recorder's red light burning up as the dark gathered, this unfortunately visible only to half the house because of the position of the machine at the edge of the table to Krapp's left. (21 November 1958)

Beckett continued to marvel at this fortuity:

> I told you about the beautiful and quite accidental effect in London of the luminous eye burning up as the machine runs on in silence and the light goes down. (4 January 1960)

For Dr. Johnson, such an effect in poetry was "a peculiar felicity, to which chance must concur with genius, which no man can hope to attain twice, and which cannot be copied but with servile imitation." True, but in dramatic performance you are at liberty to attain such an effect twice, to copy yourself—provided that you remain alert to the moment when even the greatest of effects may cease to be special or may dwindle into special effects. It is Beckett's sensitivity to these happenings, turned then to dear advantage, that does much to protect his plays against what would otherwise be his propensity to command, to check, to o'erbear them.

The theatrical notebooks, complementing them with the revelatory Beckett/Schneider letters, have much to offer to the age-old siege of contraries, the to-and-fro as to intention, the artist's intention. Beckett is characteristic in his combination of the firm and the tentative here. He wishes his actors (his director, his co-director, all who are involved) to be aware of his intentions, to pay heed to them even if in the end they cannot or should not be heeded because there are achievements that become possible only if authorial intention is overridden. You may have to override, but please be aware that this is what you are doing—and be able to give a good account of why you are having to do so. This is quite a different position from the lofty pretence that an author's intentions are both undiscoverable and irrelevant. "What matters is that you feel the spirit of the thing and the intention as you do. Give them that as best you can, even if it involves certain deviations from what I have written and said" (26 November 1963). Things come to a head with Schneider's production of *Film*. Beckett comes round to it. He never loses sight of the fact that much was lost when *Film* failed to realize so many of Beckett's intentions, but he ungrudgingly conceded that other things had been brought into being. The word "intention" and its cognates run throughout the letters in which Beckett muses deeply on Schneider's *Film*:

> After the first [screening] I was not too happy, after the second I felt it really was something. Not quite in the way intended, but as sheer beauty, power and strangeness of image.

> from having been troubled by a certain failure to communicate fully by purely visual means the basic intention, I now begin to feel that this is unimportant.

> in so doing has acquired a dimension and a validity of its own that are worth far more than any merely efficient translation of intention. (29 September 1964)

> how in some strange way it gains by its deviations from the strict intention and develops something better. (12 March 1965)

Nowhere is the question of intention more pressing than when it comes to authorizing a text. The theatrical notebooks are of supreme value not only in their riches of textual information but in the due complexity of their dealings with whether there can ever be a final or authoritative text of a play. Or (as we know all too assuredly these days) of anything, come to that. Even if we rightly eschew the word "definitive," we are still left with puzzles as to what rights we think that an author must be allowed to possess. Copyright is one of them, and in the case of JoAnne Akalaitis's famous or infamous production of *Endgame* in 1984 (Beckett sought to take out an injunction against it, but in the end settled for deploring it in the program), I was among those in the audience who believed that if Akalaitis is so damned clever, why doesn't she write a play herself? Beckett, and now the Beckett estate, seem to me well within their rights in trying to preclude gross misrepresentations of the works that he spent pains and years in creating. Yes, plays will die unless productions are granted a certain freedom. Drawing the line must mean, though, acknowledging that the lines in question are Beckett's, not yours. Why should you not have to earn the creator's respect? "But, dear Alan, do them your own way" (11 December 1981). Contrast this generosity, which rightly needed to be earned by Schneider, with Beckett's anger at the presumptuous:

> I dream sometimes of all German directors of plays with perhaps one exception united in one with his back to the wall and me shooting a bullet into his balls every five minutes till he loses his taste for improving authors. (4 January 1960)

There is always the danger of being cowed by those who are, in their dreadful phrase, "in theater." Even the editors of the notebooks are sometimes carried away, and speak as if plays were more remote on the page than they are. In his introduction now to *The Shorter Plays*, Professor Gontarski writes of Beckett's progression:

> The change is evident to anyone who has tried to read *Play, Breath, Come and Go, Ghost Trio,* . . . *but the clouds* or especially *Quad* without access to productions. On the page, without the full visual counterpart, the works are denuded, skeletal, finally unreadable—in any traditional literary sense, that is, if by unreadable we mean to suggest that their primary effect is extra-linguistic.

Now one knows what he means, and clearly there is something in this, but it remains the case that *someone* must be able to imagine a staging of the page or otherwise plays could never be realized on stage. True, a particular kind of imagination may be called for, but it is wrong to give the impression that only those "in theater" possess such an imagination, as if professionals or members of a union have been granted the monopoly. No play could ever make it to the stage unless a good many people were able to read the page and see and hear the stage. When Beckett said of Pinter's *The Birthday Party*, "I've only seen it in my skull" (15 July 1967), he may have been better than most of us at seeing plays in his skull, but he is certainly not among a caste or a cadre in being able to see plays there. We can all do it if we have the imagination and take the trouble, though none of us can do it as well as the dramatist or actor or director who is great.

I hope that I have conveyed my pleasure in and my gratitude for this series of Beckett's theatrical notebooks. *The Shorter Plays* is invaluable. Here, throughout, are things that are well worth knowing. Oh, Beckett stressing to Billie Whitelaw in *Footfalls* that the word "sequel" should be pronounced so that it suggests the homophone "seek well." Or take "His poor arm," again in *Footfalls*, a phrase that I remember puzzling me when I saw the first production of the play. Gontarski's commentary is a true help:

The 'His' is capitalized in both revised texts to suggest Christ's arm, but none of the post-production texts makes this change. The change is crucial, at least for readers, to the understanding of this line since Amy is walking along the transept of the church. That is, since churches were designed in the shape of the cross, Amy is walking along what would be the arm of the cross where Christ's arm would hang. This also reinforces the crucifixion imagery of the play. Other girls, according to the Voice of the mother, played lacrosse, for example (1. 101). The French text is more explicit on this point, 'le long du bras sauveur' (p. 13).

So far (and this is most of the way), so good. But this edition is, as all human things are, flawed. No mistranscription is ever good, but here there are a few *bad* mistranscriptions. Fortunately we are given the notebooks in facsimile, which enables us to detect the slips, but still. It must at once be granted that Beckett's handwriting often is what he called it, his "foul fist." But sometimes it is altogether clear. Three times we are given Beckett's evocation of the voices in *Play*: in the introduction to the volume, then in the editorial notes on the brown notebook, and as a transcription of the facsimile. We are given it as "Broken, breathless— exhorted." No, or even Nope. The last word is *extorted*. Perfectly clear in the facsimile (p. 186), and crucially different (not only as making much more sense), and with important filaments to moments elsewhere in Beckett, such as that in *Murphy* (chapter 9): "It meant that nothing less than a slap-up psychosis could consummate his life's strike. *Quod erat extorquendum.*" Not your usual *demonstrandum*.

I noticed several such mistranscriptions. Some of them are slight:

for Reason *read* reason (pp. 165/167);
for Thence to the end *read* Thence to end (pp. 182/184);
for Mental thugee *read* Mental thuggee (pp. 257/259);
for Something he is hiding? *read* Something he his hiding? (pp. 164/168)

—this last a mere slip by Beckett but one that should be transcribed faithfully as others are. Elsewhere a slip can damage the sense:

for If ventilator(s) the screens L & R.
read If ventilator(s) then screens L & R. (pp. 231/233).

And something is wrong on p. 297, Beckett's directions for the pacing in *Footfalls*. The editorial transcription:

involving no change in halt & steps [and?]
beyond suppression of 1st length

The "[and?]" throws up its editorial hands. (Not only does the word not look like "and," "and" is syntactically inconsequential.) I am sure that the opening words are not "involving no change in halt" but "involving no change in text," and I am all but sure that the word after "steps" is "duo": that is, the twofold relation of the words and the footfalls. Beckett has "Duo" elsewhere in these notebooks (contrasting it with Solo). So I suggest reading:

involving no change in text & steps duo
beyond suppression of 1st length

Some local objections, then. *Quod erat remonstrandum.*

In 1906, the year of Beckett's birth, two germane publications came forth. There was *The Foolish Almanack for the Year of 1906 A.D.* The title page insisted, in capitals, with one word in lowercase bold and underlined:

THERE IS NOTHING IN THE YEAR **too** GOOD TO BE IN IT;
THERE IS NOTHING PROPHESIED TOO BAD TO HAPPEN.

Under Friday 13 April (which Beckett believed to be his day of birth, and he may have been right about this Friday the Thirteenth), *The Foolish Almanack* noted: "The Theatrical Trust will probably NOT close all its theaters this year in observance of Good Friday."

Enter someone who would prove a great opener of the theater. And in the same year, 1906, George Bernard Shaw issued his collected theater-reviews from the 1890s, supplying "The Author's Apology." Its credo is magnificently the opposite of that which Beckett came to believe:

> Weariness of the theatre is the prevailing note of London criticism. Only the ablest critics believe that the theatre is really important: in my time none of them would claim for it, as I claimed for it, that it is as important as the Church was in the Middle Ages and much more important than the Church was in London in the years under review. A theatre to me is a place "where two or three are gathered together". The apostolic succession from Eschylus to myself is as serious and as continuously inspired as that younger institution, the apostolic succession of the Christian Church.
>
> When I wrote, I was well aware of what an unofficial census of Sunday worshippers presently proved: that churchgoing in London has been largely replaced by playgoing. This would be a very good thing if the theatre took itself seriously as a factory of thought, a prompter of conscience, an elucidator of social conduct, an armoury against despair and dullness, and a temple of the Ascent of Man. I took it seriously in that way . . .

I find this very stirring, in its eagerness to do some stirring. Yet for Beckett, Shaw is exactly *not* taking theater seriously in taking it in that way. "The rest is Ibsen"? The rest is Shaw, or even Pshaw. We need Beckett hugely, but not least in his bringing home how much else we need no less.

Note: *No Author Better Served: The Correspondence of Samuel Beckett & Alan Schneider*, edited by Maurice Harmon, is published by Harvard University Press (1998).

Philip Norman
Shout! The True Story of the Beatles

S hout!? (?!*) But they sang, they didn't shout, even when they sang "Twist and Shout." They weren't shouters or twisters, even if they did enjoy happily twisting things. Words, for instance. Pressed to try the *mange-tout* peas, which he'd never seen before, John Lennon finally agreed. "All right," he said, "but put them over there, not near the food."

The world—hungry in the 1960s for happy tunes, and greedy for young blood—eventually swallowed them and their music whole, sometimes distastefully. But for quite a while the world outside Liverpool, and outside pop youthfulness, had been gingerly. All right, but put them over there, not near the music.

Philip Norman's biography of the Beatles is not very near the music. Not touching the songs themselves really, he doesn't smutch them. His ear matters less than his eye and his nose: he has a very good eye for their clothes, their hair-styles, and the way they flexed their features; and he has a very good nose for substantial gossip and for the mammonist hypes. The Beatles had luck, but they worked for and at it. Luck, for instance, in that (a more desirable group happening not to be available) they got the trip to Hamburg which set things moving for a group which had recently matured into the Beatles from the Quarry Men.

Sunday Times (5 April 1981)

Mr Norman is a real Quarry Man himself. He has quarried all of rock, and left no rolling stone unturned.

The true story of the Beatles is known well enough in its outlines, from the Cavern in Liverpool ("Hi, all you Cavern-dwellers—welcome to the *best* of cellars"); via the M.B.E. (which Princess Margaret said must stand for Mr Brian Epstein), the crass Christianity-baiting ("We're more popular than Jesus now"), the last tour in 1966, and the triumph of *Sergeant Pepper* in 1967; through to the final recovered harmony (personal and professional) of *Abbey Road*.

But the fact-packed pith of *Shout!* is not in the true story of the Beatles but in the true stories, the off-guard revelations which bring the whole thing back alive again: the arrival of a live tarantula from a fan or someone; the tinned breath of the Beatles put on sale, and the card bearing the word "Breathe" which Yoko Ono handed to Lennon instead of speaking when she first met him. Ed Sullivan, whose TV show had previously been graced by Elvis Presley, had then said: "America, judge for yourselves." Since *Shout!* is being serialised in this newspaper, a reviewer may say "*Sunday Times* readers, judge for yourselves."

Yet for all the comic and artistic triumphs, the story is of great sadness. It is not just the casualties, though these are strewn everywhere: the Beatle who fell, Stu' Sutcliffe, dead at 22 of a brain tumour; the Beatle who was pushed, Pete Best, pushed out so that room might be found for Richard Starkey, alias Ringo Starr; the middle-sized middleman, Allan Williams, bilked of his 10 per cent commission in the early days, and the gigantic entrepreneur, Brian Epstein, who loved John Lennon not wisely but too well, and who lived for the Beatles, and who died (after being blackmailed as a homosexual, and anguished at the thought that the Beatles had grown beyond his man-management) of an overdose of drugs (accident? suicide? murder, even?); Cynthia Lennon, not really allowed to have any of her own devices but left to them all the same.

But the Beatles too were doomed. A nice doom if you can get it? All that money and fame and even a large true achievement with it. Yet the four parts of this book toll out their titles: Wishing, Getting, Having, Wasting. The last page of the prologue before "Wishing" mentions the inn-sign sculpture in Liverpool, "Four Lads Who Shook the World." They did too, but so did the Romans with their ambition: "For such the steady Romans shook the world." From Johnson's poem *The Vanity of Human Wishes*—or of human wishing.

Dr Johnson's great imitation of Juvenal is centuries from any true story of the Beatles. But one true story of human life is that it shows the vanity of human wishes. Off they set, these gifted strivers. (*The young enthusiast quits his ease for fame.*) When they are asked their ambitions, one says "Money etc.," another says "Money and everything." (*The dangers gather as the treasures rise . . . Increase his riches and his peace destroy.*) Drugs and drinks cease to please, and a £60-pot of caviare arrives from Fortnum & Mason for Yoko, who does not arrive for it. (*Now pall the tasteless meats and joyless wines.*) The atmosphere around these boy-Caesars, as Mr Norman calls them, becomes like that of a heated and poisonous court. (*At length his Sovereign frowns—the train of state/Mark the keen glance, and watch the sign to hate.*)

Assassination lies in wait for Lennon as it had done for an earlier kind of world-conqueror. (*His fall was destined to a barren strand,/A petty fortress, and a dubious hand.*) Could they have got together again? "If we played now anyway, we'd just be four rusty old men." (*Superfluous lags the veteran on the stage.*) Of the careers performed even by the best, it may have to be granted that *They mount, they shine, evaporate, and fall.*

When Lennon was shot, I thought of what Dr Johnson said about the death of one of the greatest performing artists: "that stroke of death, which has eclipsed the gaiety of nations, and impoverished the public stock of harmless pleasure." Boswell badgered him about this praise of David Garrick: "Why nations? Did his gaiety extend farther than his own nation?" Johnson deftly tossed in the Scots ("if we allow the Scotch to be a nation, and to have gaiety"), but Boswell pressed primly on: "Is not *harmless pleasure* very tame?" Whereupon Johnson rose nobly above the occasion:

Nay, Sir, harmless pleasure is the highest praise. Pleasure is a word of dubious import; pleasure is in general dangerous, and pernicious to virtue; to be able therefore to furnish pleasure that is harmless, pleasure pure and unalloyed, is as great a power as men can possess.

Though it sounds funny to say so, and is sad, the Beatles—whose demise eclipsed the gaiety of nations—possessed this great power.

John Sparrow
Visible Words: A Study of Inscriptions in and as Books and Works of Art

The Preface to *Visible Words* proffers that mocking modesty of which the Warden of All Souls is the master, when he is not the servant:

> The electors must, I fancy, have found themselves in difficulties in their search for a Sandars Lecturer before they decided to approach someone whose claims to be called a bibliographer were as tenuous as mine; and I was punished for the vanity that induced me to accept the honour by the difficulty that I for my part experienced in finding a subject in the field of bibliography on which I was qualified to speak.

Whether puristically bibliography or not, this sumptuous volume—graciously printed, splendidly illustrated—commands its niche: it is among other things a study, at once meticulous and ranging, of 'a remarkable and little-known extravagance of literary fashion'. Perhaps the most immediately appealing observations it makes are on the inscription in painting: Mr. Sparrow scrutinizes, for example, the inscriptions in Botticelli's *Madonna of the Magnificat*, in the two versions of Poussin's *Et in Arcadia Ego*, and in the Popean *Allegorical Scene in the Forum*, with

Essays in Criticism (April 1970)

that impassioned detection, that blend of rigour and ingenuity, which he brings to subjects other than capital punishment.

But has this anything to do with literary criticism? When in 1965 the correspondence columns of the *TLS* revealed that Hugh MacDiarmid's poem 'Perfect' consisted mostly of Glyn Jones's prose, Mr. Sparrow felt moved to contribute to the *TLS* over his own name:

> The extract (topped up with an opening line and a title, 'Perfect') acquires the unity of an independent work of art; but surely it is still not verse, and no more poetry than it was before? . . . Where such alteration is 'effective' . . . the effectiveness is, it seems to me, due to our visual awareness of the spatial relations between the symbols that convey the meaning. (This is unlike the case of conventional verse-lines, which simply afford a clue to the metre; the conventional verse-poem can be fully enjoyed by someone who hears it without seeing it.) This awareness may act upon us in various ways—take as examples (1) Mallarmé's *Coup de Dés*; (2) the calligrammes of Guillaume Apollinaire; (3) the text of the Bible as printed in verses, contrasted with a text where the verses are run together; (4) much of the stuff (by Mr. Edwin Morgan and others) printed in your 'Changing Guard' issues last summer; (5) any good (prose) epitaph or monumental inscription, which loses much (but just what?) if it is not actually *seen*.

The importance of *Visible Words* to the literary critic lies in its amplification of such questions and such instances. It provides a fresh context for thinking about shape-poems and concrete-poems, about George Herbert, Apollinaire, and Mallarmé; and it makes a contribution—unexcited but exciting—to the age-old dispute about the difference between poetry and prose.

T. S. Eliot wrote in 1958: 'I do not believe that any distinction between prose and poetry is meaningful.' But in a letter to the *TLS* on 27 September 1928 (it was exhumed during the MacDiarmid fracas), he had said: 'Verse, whatever else it may or may not be, is itself a system of *punctuation*.' The blurring of poetry into verse is unfortunate; there is no interesting puzzle as to the difference between verse and prose, since the word *verse* insists on metre: 'A succession of words arranged according to natural or recognised rules of prosody and forming a complete metrical line. . . . Metrical composition, form, or structure; language or literary work written or spoken in metre; poetry, especially with reference to metrical form. Opposed to prose.' The term 'Free Verse', which might seem to deny this, in fact establishes it, since 'Verse' has there to be explicitly qualified into an oxymoron, as in 'Free University'.

But what does it mean to speak of poetry as 'a system of punctuation'? Such a way of speaking assumes that if we set aside metre (if we set aside, in other words, those occasions when poetry is not to be distinguished from verse), the only remaining poetry/prose distinction is that in prose the lines run the breadth of the page. So that to Edwin Morgan's question about the MacDiarmid poem, 'Can prose become poetry through typographical rearrangement?', it would be retorted: 'Can prose be distinguished from poetry in any way other than through typographical arrangement?' (That it will probably become bad poetry is not to the point; in MacDiarmid's hands, the prose became such good poetry that it is lamentable that MacDiarmid has dropped the poem from his collected volume.) In prose, the line-endings are without significance, and are the creation not of the writer but of the compositor; in poetry, the line-endings are significant, and they effect their significance—not necessarily of rhythm, and whether of force or of nuance—by using their white space, by using a pause which is not necessarily a pause of punctuation and so only equivocally a pause at all.

Such a distinction is useful, and—unlike other poetry/prose distinctions—truthful. That it need not be a trivial distinction, that poetry can effect a great deal through such 'punctuation', has been most notably shown by Donald Davie. But the distinction has to concede that there remain two clouds to trouble its crystalline clarity. The writer of prose does decide his line-ending when he concludes a paragraph—and what is the sharp-edged distinction between a paragraph and a line? A line of poetry can of course be longer than the page-breadth; if it runs over, then its first line-ending is without significance, being compositorial, not compositional. So that even this distinction has to admit that paragraphs intrude into its crisp tidiness: Allen Ginsberg, David Jones, Ivy Compton-Burnett, and Samuel Beckett would all in quite different ways give the distinction pause.

But the second concession has to be the inscription, since here is a form in which the lineation is decided by the creator and yet which it would be perverse to call poetry. 'A literary form that differs both from verse and from prose as it is ordinarily composed and presented': Mr. Sparrow's words point to an important question, though it may be unfortunate that he has so totally stuck to the verse/prose, and not the poetry/prose, antithesis (despite his concluding page on Yeats's redeployment of Pater's prose).

> With prose, the length of the lines is determined only by the breadth of the page on which the text is printed. Occasionally, where there is a marked break in the sense, there will be a division between paragraphs; but otherwise the text is solid; pauses and clauses are indicated by punctuation.
>
> Verse, on the other hand, is normally printed in lines the length of which is determined by the metre; its form is designed not to please the eye but to help the ear.

But poetry—and it too, like both prose and verse, differs from the inscription—is not necessarily printed in lines the length of which is determined by the metre, nor in lines which correspond to the sense-units (though the lines often make use of a suggested pause of the sense, thus constructing a sense-unit which is subsequently withdrawn or qualified when we round the corner of the line). Nor could we say of poetry, as Mr. Sparrow says of verse, that 'its form is designed not to please the eye but to help the ear'; the subtleties of poetry's line-endings may please the eye and help the ear, but the shaping spirit of imagination is here most concerned with ripples and modulations of the sense and not simply of our senses.

Mr. Sparrow raises the most apt of questions, and his book persuades me that those of us who hold to the poetry/prose distinction as either a matter of metre or of line-ending have got to come clean about the inscription—a minor form, perhaps, but one which stubbornly untidies our binary system. Mr. Sparrow speaks of himself as touching lightly on these aesthetic questions; they could bear to be touched less lightly—though, having said that, one does well to remember the forms which the unlight can take. There is Emery E. George's recent article in *Language and Style* (Summer, 1968), on 'Calligrams in Apollinaire and in Trakl: A Psycho-Linguistic Study', with its Table 1, 'Partial Inventory of Poetic Types from Philosophical to Pictogrammatic', running—or rather limping—from 1a (Language expostulates meaning: Lucretius, *De Rerum Natura*) to 10b (Pictogram supplants vocabulary: Lorraine Ellis Harr, 'Three Haiku'). Mr. Sparrow does not dissect, but then nor does he murder, and his book is humanely relevant to a matter which cannot but turn up all the time. In such a place, for instance, as the first number of *Delos* (1968), in which D. S. Carne-Ross interviewed Robert Lowell:

> *I don't know if this is unreasonable or imperceptive, but when I opened* The New York Review *and found that your Prometheus was in prose, I was rather disappointed. I had counted on its being in verse.*

> I no longer know the difference between prose and verse. In *The Old Glory*, the first and third plays, *Endecott* and *Benito Cereno*, are in free verse—that is, there is no scansion, the lines are of varying length. And the middle play is in four-foot lines. Well, the three sound more or less the same. I remember my friend Randall Jarrell suggested to me it would have been better if *Benito* had been printed as prose—not changing a word but printing it in paragraphs rather than lines. And quite likely he was right, but it seemed to make very little difference. I happened to write it in lines, but if it had been printed as prose probably no one would have been able to tell.

Saul Steinberg
The Discovery of America

T rust the greatest comic artist of our time, Saul Steinberg, not to give a rap for political correctitude. Instead, to be happy to take the rap. *The Discovery of America*? Come now. But if anyone in this day and age is entitled to give his new book so old-world a title, it is the very graphic artist who back in 1965 created *The New World*, his brave new world that has such people in it: Steinberg, the inimitable imitator of the American ways of life and death. Endlessly inventive, Steinberg—like all true inventors—knows the difference between invention and discovery, and knows too that each needs the flying buttress of the other, if art is ever to stand high overarched. In the pictured universe of Steinberg's amazing mazes and gazings, the risks are heady, the heights are giddy, the air is bracing, the architecture has pricked with incredible pinnacles into heaven, and the view is great. Yet Steinberg, who is a comic announcer not a satiric denouncer, looks down on nothing and nobody. He climbs higher, not to look down.

Columbus, though all at sea as to just where he was, made a good landfall. Steinberg, our latterday discoverer, executes a series of landfalls, as if agreeing with the Victorian rumbler Samuel Butler that "America was too big to have been discovered all at one time. It would have been better for the graces if it had been discovered in pieces of about the size of France and Germany at a time." Steinberg himself came to America from a piece of Europe the size of Romania, namely Romania, via Italy . . .

Like everything else, America has a tragic and comic side. The sides meet where a fall takes place, or has pride of place. Tragedy began with the Fall. Comedy begins with a fall—and, since comedy isn't rebuke, pride doesn't have to come before it. Eve's apple, Newton's apple: each invokes a law, a different law of gravity. In one of his many pedestalled tributes, Steinberg pays to the very name of Newton, that great discoverer, the compliment of levity, and imagines the honored name—before our very eyes—precariously tilted, by the law of its being, and yet perforce destined never actually to shatter. Preserved in mid-air. The other great scientific discoverer, Darwin, has his name envisaged by Steinberg as crawling up, hauling itself up, letter by letter, spiritedly, from ancient waters on to dry land—and there we are, now we can see evolution spelled out, up from the ocean, and comfortably inland, in due course, sitting in an armchair. Not even having to stand erect, though well able to do so.

Thinkers about comedy have always erected the law of gravity. To the French philosopher Henri Bergson, the natural starting point—his first instance of comedy—had to be a man's falling in the street. George Meredith, who wrote a novel called *The Tragic Comedians*, saw comedy in the tragic predicament of Sisyphus, who forever rolls uphill the ball that then forever rolls down again with all the suavity of gravity. And Charles Dickens asked and answered the question why an audience takes delight in the comic world of pantomime,

> where workmen may fall from the top of a house to the bottom, or even from the bottom of a house to the top, and sustain no injury to the brain, need no hospital, leave no young children; where every one, in short, is so superior to all the accidents of life, though encountering them at every turn, that I suspect this to be the secret (though many persons may not present it to themselves) of the general enjoyment which an audience of vulnerable spectators, liable to pain and sorrow, find in this class of entertainment.

For gravity is one of those laws which no one disobeys, except, ah, in the relief and release of comedy's imagination. Gravity combines the small contingencies of daily life with the large law of things. Which is why we cock our jokey snooks, chortling when someone stumbles— Have a good trip, or See you next fall. Gravity, a law of nature, has its own eerie airy nature, for it is invisible except in its effects, an intangible presence which yet touches us all. No wonder the surrealist painters found such wonders in it. There are those marvellous—exactly marvellous—paintings by Magritte: *Universal Gravitation*, or the bowler hat suspended—not the sword of Damocles but a Damoclean bowler hat?—in *The Road to Damascus* and in *The Pilgrim*, or the hovering apple, by Newton out of Eve, in *The Postcard* and *The Idea*. Magritte may seem a far cry from Steinberg, but what Magritte had to say and to see has always been attended to by Steinberg. He once praised "a marvellous sign that could have been the envy of Magritte."

Like comedy, the discussion of comedy is a risky business, often notoriously unfunny, and when Freud bent his attention upon jokes, it was no laughing matter. To speak about Steinberg's art is to see in one's mind's eye, chasteningly, all those visionary drawings where he gives a visual embodiment to the words people utter—the smudged smutches belching from the mouth of a smutty speaker, say, or the exquisitely fluted filigree emitted by the lips of someone all-too-refined, or the public speaker who stands upon—and therefore not *by*—his words, his great many fluent words, a self-styled orator loftily based upon what has issued from his own mouth, words which have built themselves up from geometrical blocks into carven pennanted ornateness and greatness. I don't like to think what a sight these words of mine would be if Steinberg were to incarnate them visually. Or, come to that, your words, gentle reader . . .

Steinberg delights in building up disconcerting symmetries, preposterous paired plinths. There the collusive couples all are, beaming away, the amiable opposites on display, on easy terms the one with the other. Virtue well-disposed towards Vice. Art and Commerce. Science and Industry. War and Peace. Crime and Punishment. Fame and Fortune. On a plinth, S. Freud finds himself balanced by S. Claus. At the center, in the front, Uncle Tom is shaking hands with Uncle Sam. And there are our old friends Law and Order. The law of gravity, the order of levity.

All this is brought home to us by courtesy of the well-informed aid of architecture. Steinberg studied it. And gave his own characteristically unexpected twist to this. "The study of architecture is a marvelous training for anything but architecture. The frightening thought that what you draw may become a building makes for reasoned lines."

Architecture, especially on these shores, scrapes the sky. Astronauts do more than scrape it, they pierce it. And you can imagine the piercing pleasure which Steinberg must have felt back in 1966 when he was accredited by the National Aeronautics and Space Administration down at or up at Cape Canaveral. A perfect setting for this carnivalesque or canaveralesque artist. "For two days I wore a tag saying 'NASA Artist'. I had been invited to be inspired by the flight of Apollo, a scene that would have interested comic-strip artists, Delaunay or even Chagall and his flying Hasidim for the unexpectedly slow, solemn levitation of the missile. But I was much more interested in the honky-tonks around Cape Canaveral." There is a direct continuity between how well Steinberg writes (tauntingly dry, "I had been invited to be inspired. . . .") and how well he draws and paints. But then he has said, "I am a writer"—and, with a crucially different emphasis, "And when I make a drawing I'm just like a writer."

As to NASA: in the case of Steinberg's art, for National Aeronautics, read International Aeronautics, and for Space Administration, read Time and Space Administration. For such is art, and especially such is his art. His paintings and drawings are themselves missiles, aimful levities or levitations which suggest sometimes the miraculousness of scientific feats and sometimes that of religious ones. He envisages time-and-space-ships (there are some beauties in *The Discovery of America*). And he loves seeing time under the aspect of space, and vice versa, well aware that we can never conceive of the one without the other and yet that we are not in the habit of imagining time spatially or space temporally. Steinberg is just like a writer, yes, but he is alive to all the differences. Moreover he is, by the way, by way of being a philosopher.

And, as artists so often are, he is the best of art critics. Much art criticism these days is flibbertigibberish. As William Empson remarked, "The catalogue of a picture exhibition is often very intimidating; a steady iron-hard jet of absolutely total nonsense, as if under great pressure from a hose, and recalling among human utterances only the speech of Lucky in *Waiting for Godot*, is what they play upon the spectator to make sure of keeping him cowed." Steinberg, though, is not out to cow, and he writes about art with easy hard-won authority. He always shows especial acumen when the art he is contemplating involves gravitation and levitation. "Folds embalm reality and therefore deify or sublimate it. The best folds I have seen are in a portrait of Lenin. The draped chairs in it are the clouds in the apotheoses—those levitations and ascensions—in the Virgins by Raphael or Rubens." This is as politically acute (and bizarre—Lenin, the god that failed? lenitations?) as it is revelatory. Or there is the sheer wit, itself walking a tightrope for the pleasure of lovely levity, of his comments on Giotto's Saint Francis:

It is a tightrope-walking act. The rays emanating from the saint's hands sustain the angel's heavy image in the air. It is like a very solid mechanical toy. It is a miracle in which all the ingredients are visible. That is the beauty of miracles: they are normal, natural.

Or, set against the benign lucidity of Giotto, his happy light, there is the malign darkness of *The Battle of San Romano*, by Uccello, where in the corner

> every figure wears a mask. The result is an incredible tricephalous monster. It reminds me of something I saw when I was living in Santo Domingo, in 1941. One night I woke up in terror. I sensed that there was something horrible near me. I switched on the light, and saw ants, by the thousands, transporting a fat cockroach up the wall. The swarming mass was constantly changing shape—but the centerpiece and the logic of the labor gave it the sinister symmetry of the coat-of-arms.

What strikes the chill is the ants transporting a fat cockroach *up* the wall.

Steinberg's 1973 collection, *The Inspector*, listed, as though among its contents, there along with time and space, and with masks and parades, the law of gravity. The listing makes you think not only about the law of gravity but about what you might mean by *contents*. But then for Steinberg gravity is not only among the contents, it is among the forms—more, it is the element within which all of Steinberg's evocations, in their form and content, live and move and have their being. There is the man who is looking down over the precipice upon all the past years lying strewn below. There is visualized speech, and the Frozen Music which floats around—as when the name of Verdi sails in through the window, scrollingly rolling.

Or there is the warning to which Steinberg returns, the thought *Yes But*. Much of life consists of Yes But, for instance almost all conversation and art, including conversation about art. If there weren't a Yes of some sort or to some degree, we would not be able to engage with one

another. For No has a way of leaving it flatly at that. And, on the other hand, if there weren't a But, we would not be able to carry on with a conversation either—and anyway life is not designed to permit of our very often saying simply Yes. Still, the thought of Yes But is a cold one. Steinberg unsentimentally but wonderfully warms it for us. Perhaps Yes will indeed be shattered by But, a shattering thought, but Steinberg can imagine on our behalf a Yes forever suspended before a comical collision. His lines can run along Keats's lines, fixed there on the timeless Grecian Urn:

> Bold Lover, never, never canst thou kiss,
> Though winning near the goal—yet, do not grieve:
> She cannot fade, though thou hast not thy bliss,
> For ever wilt thou love, and she be fair!

A further reason for not grieving is that, caught in mid-moment, you may be protected from ever arriving at that other kiss, the kiss of death.

So, once upon a time, Steinberg showed his dear little unlikely hero, oh dear, perched on something which is a cross between a chariot and a perambulator, gliding down on his Yes towards the gigantic blockish But which bars his way. The gravity is inexorable, but so, fortunately, is the levity of the drawing. And now, years later, there is collected from

1970 in *The Discovery of America* an updated glimpse of the form which Yes But may now have to take: horizontally, not vertically, the tiny traveler is moving now. The rocketry mocks gravity, confident that it can even go through the air neither up nor down. But notice that the hopeful traveler's hat has already risen up in a puff of astonishment, comically stripped from his head. For the defying of gravity can be imagined all right, but not for long, and only with reservations. Steinberg makes comic reservations for us all. They remain blessedly comic, since after all, however obdurate the But may be which lies in wait for us all, it is scarcely likely to take the literal shape of the letters B plus U plus T.

But (again that word) there could not be the witty resilient stoical defiance of gravity, which can stand in for all the iron laws of life which close around us and which determine us, including the law of death (Philip Larkin wrote: "Most things may never happen: this one will"), if gravity were not all the time *acknowledged* by such art.

Without the ever-pressing burden of gravity, whether we are conscious of it or not (and we can be as unconscious of it as of the very air which weighs so effortlessly upon our heads), there would be no wit or humor, or courage as we wait on the guard duty of life ("For this relief, much thanks"), in these fabulous drawings. Take all those unstony Steinberg castles in the air, which are acknowledged by the very lines to be such wishful wistful imaginings, absurd hopes which we can conceive of but cannot possess, can so entertainingly *entertain* but cannot enter. From "Absurd" we are at liberty to take the ladder to "Nonsense." "Emigration" can all too easily be the act of mounting steps and ladders into air, thin air. Uncle Sam climbs a ladder into clouds but also in among skyscrapers. A leader—don't follow leaders—is prancing off to the left, off a cliff, followed by his men who have all likewise just done so—but he and they are unbelievably level still in the air, and are being levelly watched by a woman—whose hat, though, is so good as to ascend in astonishment. A ball rolls, in entire equanimity, uphill, chasing a man who feels no such equanimity. The Flat Earth is happy to explain itself. Forgetting that he is on a seesaw, a man shoots his opponent, only to precipitate himself down a precipice. For the title page of his first book,

All in Line (1945), Steinberg wrested into a profiled face a coathanger; he is no less adept at cliff-hangers. A man-statue, on a pedestal, manages to postpone, at least, his fall by clutching a branch, endearingly proffered by a cliff.

When he was asked how he works, Steinberg fell naturally to speaking of gravity.

> The nearest thing I can give you to an answer is this: in making a drawing or even starting a phrase—let's talk about starting a phrase—I have a very vague idea of what I'm going to say. During the time I say it, the conclusion and the main idea, I hope, will come in. How? By plunging into it. I'm high up on a plateau and I jump. I fall and I fall and at the last moment I reach a very comfortable branch that happens to be there. I grab it—and *voilà!* I'm safe. But I take a chance. And this is how most of the work is done.

Notice how much of the work is done there by the word *voilà!* Steinberg grabs it, as if it too were a very comfortable branch that happens to be there, even though the handy word does not belong to our branch of the language.

Hence all those wonders of his floating world. The almighty dollar, along with the Masonic pyramid and the sharp eye, can be glimpsed everywhere in Steinberg, sometimes decapitated, often levitated. "Art" can include peerers to the left, on pedestals, with the paintings being hung not from any walls but from air. In the sky there float stamps and seals, at once mysterious and formidably realistic—like the ways of bureaucracy itself, which, like God, moves in a mysterious way. (The creator of *The Passport*, 1954, is alert to all the ways in which the arts are passports.) There is all that smoke, so effortlessly superior to gravity, and there are all those balloons, including thought-bubbles. Steinberg's projects entail projectiles, and his missives are missiles. Winged women zoom down, carrying perhaps a wreath, or carrying off a man by the scruff of his jacket. Animals go on two feet, if not godlike erect, then manlike so. Motel signs pay no attention to gravity. The Statue of Liberty takes the supreme liberty of floating overhead, in its element instead of there at the junction of land and water.

And so this comic artist goes, cheeringly ignoring nothing of the sorrows and realities without which we would not feel such immense pleasure in his incredible felicities. *The Discovery of America is* a wonder, gathering as it does more than two hundred of Steinberg's wittiest works, some from years past, many of recent creation, all up to the minute and all shaped to last.

No pomposity here, in this artist, no pretension. And, for all the unremitting acknowledgement of the laws of gravity and of levity, there is none of that false gravity with which powerfully humorless people impose themselves. Steinberg, who is ever-attentive to how we carry our bodies, would agree with Sterne, the inaugurative genius of the anti-novel, who long ago in *Tristram Shandy* borrowed from a French wit the sardonic definition of the corrupt self-important form of gravity: "a mysterious carriage of the body to cover the defects of the mind." Like all true art, Steinberg's is, in its way, mysterious, but neither his mind nor heart is defective, leave alone his hand.

Stanley Kubrick
A Clockwork Orange

W hen Anthony Burgess published *A Clockwork Orange* ten years ago, he compacted much of what was in the air, especially the odd mingling of dismay and violence (those teen-age gangs) with pious euphoria about the causes and cures of crime and of deviance. Mr. Burgess's narrator hero, Alex, was pungently odious; addicted to mugging and rape, intoxicated with his own command of the language (a newly minted teen-age slang, plus poeticisms, sneers, and sadistic purring). Alex was something both better and worse than a murderer: he was murderous. Because of a brutal rape by Alex, the wife of a novelist dies; because of his lethal clubbing, an old woman dies; because of his exhibitionist ferocity, a fellow prisoner dies.

The second of these killings gets Alex jailed: word reaches him of the new Ludovico Treatment by which he may be reclaimed, and he seeks it and gets it. The treatment is to watch horrific films of violence (made by one Dr. Brodsky) while seething with a painful emetic; the "cure" is one that deprives Alex of choice, and takes him beyond freedom and dignity, and extirpates his moral existence. But the grisly bloody failure of his suicide attempt after his release does release him. Alex is himself again.

The novel was simply pleased, but it knew that aversion therapy must be denied its smug violences. And the early 1960s were, after all, the years in which a liberally wishful newspaper like the London *Observer* could regale its readers with regular accounts of how a homosexual was being "cured" by emetics and films.

"To do the ultra-violent": Alex makes no bones about it. But the film of *A Clockwork Orange* does not want him to be seen in an ultra-violent light. So it bids for sympathy. There are unobtrusive mitigations: Alex is made younger than in the book. There are obtrusive crassnesses from his jailors: when Alex pauses over the form for Reclamation Treatment, the chief guard shouts, "Don't read it, sign it"—and of course it has to be signed in triplicate. (None of that in the book.) There are sentimentalities: where in the book it was his drugs and syringes that he was shocked to find gone when he got home, in the film he has been provided instead with a pet snake, Basil, whom his parents have wantonly and hypocritically done in. Above all, Alex is the only person in the film who isn't a caricature, the only person the film is interested in; whereas in the first-person narrative of the book, Alex was the only person Alex was interested in.

One realizes that the film is a re-creation, not a carrying-over, and yet both Kubrick and Burgess are right to call upon each other in what they've recently written in defense of the film, Kubrick in *The New York Times*, February 27, 1972, and Burgess in *The Listener*, February 17. The persistent pressure of the film's Alexculpations is enough to remind one that while *A Clockwork Orange* is in Burgess's words "a novel about brainwashing," the film is not above a bit of brainwashing itself—is indeed righteously unaware that any of its own techniques or practices could for a moment be asked to subject themselves to the same scrutiny as they project. Alex is forced to gaze at the Ludovico Treatment aversion films: "But I could not shut my glazzies, and even if I tried to move my glaz-balls about I still could not get like out of the line of fire of this picture." Yet once "this picture" has become not one of Dr. Brodsky's pictures but one of Mr. Kubrick's, then two very central figures are surreptitiously permitted to move "out of the line of fire of this picture."

First, the creator of the whole fictional "horrorshow" itself. For it was crucial to Burgess's *A Clockwork Orange* that it should include a novelist who was writing a book called *A Clockwork Orange*—crucial not because of the fad for such Chinese boxes, but because this was Burgess's way of taking responsibility (as Kubrick does *not* take responsibility for Dr. Brodsky's film within his film), Burgess's way of seeing that the whole enterprise itself was accessible to its own standards of judgment. The novelist F. Alexander kept at once a curb and an eye on the book, so that other propensities than those of Dr. Brodsky were also under moral surveillance. Above all the propensity of the commanding satirist to become the person who most averts his eyes from what he shows: that "satire is a sort of glass wherein beholders do generally discover everybody's face but their own." But in the film F. Alexander (who is brutally kicked by Alex, and his wife raped before his eyes) is not at work on a book called *A Clockwork Orange*, and so the film—unlike the book—ensures that it does not have to stand in its own line of fire.

Nor, secondly and more importantly, does Alex have to. The film cossets him. For the real accusation against the film is certainly not that it is too violent, but that it is not violent enough; more specifically, that with a cunning selectivity it sets itself to minimize both Alex's violence and his delight in it. Take his murders or womanslaughters. The old woman in the novel with the cats and an ineffectual stick becomes in the film a professionally athletic virago who nearly stuns him with a heavy *objet d'art*: the killing comes after a dervishlike tussling and circling, and moreover is further protected, Alex-wise, by being grotesquely farcical—Alex rams her in the face with a huge sculpture of a penis and testicles, a pretentious art work which she has pretentiously fussed about and which when touched jerks itself spasmodically.

The film reshapes that murder to help Alex out. Similarly with the more important death of the novelist's wife. "She died, you see. She was brutally raped and beaten. The shock was very great." But the film—by then nearing its end—doesn't want Alex to have this death on our consciences, so the novelist (who is manifestly half-mad to boot) is made to mutter that the doctor said it was pneumonia she died of, during the flu epidemic, but that *he* knew, etc., etc. Or, not to worry, Alex-lovers.

Then there is the brutal killing within the prison cell, when they all beat up the homosexual newcomer:

> Anyway, seeing the old krovvy flow red in the red light, I felt the old joy like rising up in my keeshkas. . . . So they all stood around while I cracked at this prestoopnick in the near dark. I fisted him all over, dancing about with my boots on though unlaced, and then I tripped him and he went crash crash on to the floor. I gave him one real horrorshow kick on the gulliver and he went ohhhhh, then he sort of snorted off to like sleep.

No place for any of that in the film, since it would entail being more perturbed about Alex than would be convenient. No, better to show all the convicts as good-natured buffoons and to let the prison guards monopolize detestability. The film settles for a happy swap, dispensing with the killing in the cell and proffering instead officialdom's humiliating violence in shining a torch up Alex's rectum. None of that in the book.

"When the novelist puts his thumb in the scale, to pull down the balance to his own predilection, that is immorality" (D. H. Lawrence). As a novelist, Burgess controlled his itching thumb (he does after all include within himself as much of a polemicist for Original Sin and for Christian extremity as his co-religionists Graham Greene and William Golding). But the film is not content with having a thumb in the pan— it insists on thumbs down for most and thumbs up for Alex. Thumbs down for Dr. Brodsky, who is made to say that the aversion drug will cause a deathlike terror and paralysis; thumbs down for the Minister of the Interior, who bulks proportionately larger and who has what were other men's words put into his mouth, and whose asinine classy ruthlessness allows the audience to vent its largely irrelevant feelings about "politicians," thus not having to vent any hostility upon Alex; thumbs down for Alex's spurious benefactors, who turn out to be mad schemers against the bad government, and not only that but very very vengeful— the novelist and his friends torture Alex with music to drive him to suicide (the book told quite another story).

But thumbs up for the gladiatorial Alex. For it is not just the killings that are whitewashed. Take the two girls he picks up and takes back to his room. In the book, what matters to Alex—and to our sense of Alex—is that they couldn't have been more than ten years old, that he got them viciously drunk, that he gave himself a "hypo jab" so that he could the better exercise "the strange and weird desires of Alexander the Large," and that they ended up bruised and screaming. The film, which wants to practice a saintlike charity of redemption toward Alex but also to make things assuredly easy for itself, can't have any of that. So the ten-year-olds become jolly dollies; no drink, no drugs, no bruises, just the three of them having a ball. And to make doubly sure that Alex is not dislodged from anybody's affection, the whole thing is speeded up so that it twinkles away like frantic fun from a silent film. Instead of the cold brutality of Alex's "the old in-out," a warm Rowan and Martin laugh-in-out.

Conversely, Alex's fight with his friends is put into silent slow motion, draping its balletic gauzes between us and Alex. And when one of these droogs later takes his revenge on Alex by smashing him across the eyes with a milk bottle and leaving him to the approaching police, this too has become something very different from what it was in the book. For there it was not a milk bottle that Dim wielded but his chain: "and it snaked whishhhh and he chained me gentle and artistic like on the glazlids, me just closing them up in time." The difference which that makes is that the man who is there so brutally hurt is the man who had so recently exulted in Dim's prowess with that chain:

> Dim had a real horrorshow length of oozy or chain round his waist, twice wound round, and he unwound this and began to swing it beautiful in the eyes or glazzies. . . . Old Dim with his chain snaking whissssssshhhhhhhhh, so that old Dim chained him right in the glazzies, and this droog of Billyboy's went tottering off and howling his heart out.

The novel, though it has failures of judgment which sometimes let in a gloat, does not flinch from showing Alex's exultation. The movie takes out the book's first act of violence, the protracted sadistic taunting of an aged book lover and then his beating up:

> "You naughty old veck, you," I said, and then we began to filly about with him. Pete held his rookers and Georgie sort of hooked his rot wide open

for him and Dim yanked out his false zoobies, upper and lower. He threw these down on the pavement and then I treated them to the old boot-crush, though they were hard bastards like, being made of some new horrorshow plastic stuff. The old veck began to make sort of chumbling shooms—"wuf waf wof"—so Georgie let go of holding his goobers apart and just let him have one in the toothless rot with his ringy fist, and that made the old veck start moaning a lot then, then out comes the blood, my brothers, real beautiful. So all we did then was to pull his outer platties off, stripping him down to his vest and long underpants (very starry; Dim smecked his head off near), and then Pete kicks him lovely in his pot, and we let him go.

The film holds us off from Alex's blood-lust, and it lets Alex off by mostly showing us only the show of violence. The beating of the old drunk is done by four silhouetted figures with their sticks—horribly violent in some ways, of course, but held at a distance. That distance would be artistically admirable if its intention was to preclude the pornography of bloodthirstiness rather than to preclude our realizing—making real to ourselves—Alex's bloodthirstiness. Likewise the gang fight is at first the frenzied destructiveness of a Western and is then a stylized distanced drubbing; neither of these incriminates Alex as the book had honorably felt obliged to do. The first page of the book knows that Alex longs to see someone "swim in his blood," and the book never forgets what it early shows:

> Then we tripped him so he laid down flat and heavy and a bucket-load of beer-vomit came whooshing out. That was disgusting so we gave him the boot, one go each, and then it was blood, not song nor vomit, that came out of his filthy old rot. Then we went on our way.
>
> And, my brothers, it was real satisfaction to me to waltz—left two three, right two three—and carve left cheeky and right cheeky, so that like two curtains of blood seemed to pour out at the same time, one on either side of his fat filthy oily snout in the winter starlight.

The film does not let Alex shed that blood. But it isn't against bloodletting or hideous brutality, it just insists on enlisting them. So we see Alex's face spattered with blood at the police station, the wall too; and we see a very great deal of blood-streaming violence in the aversion therapy film which the emetic-laden Alex is forced to witness. What this selectivity of violence does is ensure that the aversion film outdoes anything that we have as yet been made to contemplate (Alex's horrorshows are mostly allowed to flicker past). It is not an accident, and it is culpably coercive, that the most long-drawn-out, realistic, and hideous act of brutality is that meted on Alex by his ex-companions, now policemen. Battered and all but drowned, Alex under violence is granted the mercy neither of slow motion nor of speeding up. But the film uses this mercilessness for its own specious mercy.

There is no difficulty in agreeing with Kubrick that people do get treated like that; and nobody should be treated like that. At this point the film doesn't at all gloat over the violence which it makes manifest but doesn't itself manifest. Right. But Burgess's original artistic decision was the opposite: it was to ensure that we should deeply know of but not know about what they did to Alex: "I will not go into what they did, but it was all like panting and thudding against this like background of whirring farm machines and the twittwittwittering in the bare or nagoy branches." I will not go into what they did: that was Burgess as well as Alex speaking. Kubrick does not speak, but he really goes into what they did. By doing so he ensures our sympathy for Alex, but at the price of an enfeebling circularity. "Pity the monsters," urges Robert Lowell. I am a man more sinned against than sinning, the film allows Alex to intimate.

The pain speaks for Alex, and so does the sexual humor. For Kubrick has markedly sexed things up. Not just that modern sculpture of a penis, but the prison guard's question ("Are you or have you ever been a homosexual?"), and the social worker's hand clapped hard but lovingly on Alex's genitals, and the prison chaplain's amiable eagerness to reassure Alex about masturbation, and the bare-breasted nurse and the untrousered doctor at it behind the curtains of the hospital bed. All of this may seem to be just good clean fun (though also most uninventively unfunny), but it too takes its part within that forcible reclamation of Alex which Kubrick no less than Dr. Brodsky is out to achieve.

The sexual farce is to excriminate Alex as a bit of a dog rather than one hell of a rat, and the tactic pays off—but cheaply—in the very closing moments of the film, when Alex, cured of his cure and now himself again, is listening to great music. In the film his fantasy is of a voluptuous slow-motion lovemaking, rape-ish rather than rape, all surrounded by costumed grandees applauding—amiable enough, in a way, and a bit like *Billy Liar*. The book ends with the same moment, but with an unsentimental certainty as to what kind of lust it still is that is uppermost for Alex:

> Oh, it was gorgeosity and yumyumyum. When it came to the Scherzo I could viddy myself very clear running and running on like very light and mysterious nogas, carving the whole litso [face] of the creeching world with my cutthroat critva. And there was the slow movement and the lovely last sighing movement still to come. I was cured all right.

The film raises real questions, and not just of the are-liberals-really-liberal? sort. On my left, Jean-Jacques Rousseau; on my right, Robert Ardrey—this is factitious and fatuous. When Kubrick and Burgess were stung into replying to criticism, both claimed that the accusation of gratuitous violence was gratuitous. Yet Kubrick makes too easy a disclaimer—too easy in terms of the imagination and its sources of energy, though fair enough in repudiating the charge of "fascism"—when he says that he should not be denounced as a fascist, "no more than any well-balanced commentator who read 'A Modest Proposal' would have accused Dean Swift of being a cannibal."

Agreed, but it would be Swift's imagination, not his behavior, that would be at stake, and there have always been those who found "A Modest Proposal" a great deal more equivocally disconcerting than Kubrick seems to. As Dr. Johnson said of Swift, "The greatest difficulty that occurs, in analyzing his character, is to discover by what depravity of intellect he took delight in revolving ideas, from which almost every other mind shrinks with disgust." So that to invoke Swift is apt (Alex's slang "gulliver" for head is not just Russian *golova*) but isn't a brisk accusation-stopper.

Again, when Burgess insists: "It was certainly no pleasure to me to describe acts of violence when writing the novel," there must be a counter-insistence: that on such a matter no writer's say-so can simply be accepted, since a writer mustn't be assumed to know so—the sincerity in question is of the deepest and most taxing kind. The aspiration need not be doubted:

> What my, and Kubrick's, parable tries to state is that it is preferable to have a world of violence undertaken in full awareness—violence chosen as an act of will—than a world conditioned to be good or harmless.

When so put, few but B. F. Skinner are likely to contest it. But there are still some urgent questions.

1. Isn't this alternative too blankly stark? And isn't the book better than the film just because it doesn't take instant refuge in the antithesis, but has a subtler sense of responsibilities and irresponsibilities here?

2. Isn't "the Judaeo-Christian ethic that *A Clockwork Orange* tries to express" more profoundly disconcerting than is suggested by Burgess's hospitable formulation? I think of Empson's arguments that Christianity marks itself out from the other great religions by holding on to an act of human sacrifice, and that it is a system of torture-worship. The Christian Church has always ministered to, often connived at, and sometimes practiced the fiercest and most insidious acts of brainwashing. The book in this sense takes its religion much more seriously—that is, does not think of it as somehow patently unimpeachable. "The wish to diminish free will is, I should think, the sin against the Holy Ghost" (Burgess). Those who do not believe in the Holy Ghost need not believe that there is such a thing as the sin against the Holy Ghost—no reassuring worst of sins.

3. Isn't the moral and spiritual crux here more cruelly unresolvable, a hateful siege of contraries? T. S. Eliot sought to resolve it:

> So far as we are human, what we do must be either evil or good; so far as we do evil or good, we are human; and it is better, in a paradoxical way, to do evil than to do nothing: at least, we exist. It is true to say that the

glory of man is his capacity for salvation; it is also true to say that his glory is his capacity for damnation. The worst that can be said of most of our malefactors, from statesmen to thieves, is that they are not men enough to be damned.

But Eliot's teeth are there on edge, and so are ours; those who do not share the religion of Eliot and Burgess may think that no primacy should be granted to Eliot's principle—nor to its humane counter-principle, that it is better to do nothing than to do evil.

4. Is this film worried enough about films? Each medium will have its own debasements when seduced by violence. A novel has but words, and words can gloat and collude only in certain ways. A play has people speaking words, and what Dr. Johnson deplored in the blinding of Gloucester in *King Lear* constitutes the artistic opportunity of drama, that we both intensely feel that great violence is perpetrated and intensely know that it is not: "an act too horrid to be endured in dramatic exhibition, and such as must always compel the mind to relieve its distress by incredulity." But the medium of film is an equivocal one (above all about how far people are really part of the medium), which is why it is so peculiarly fitted both to use and to abuse equivocations. *A Clockwork Orange* was a novel about the abuses of the film (its immoralities of violence and of brainwashing), and it included—as the film of *A Clockwork Orange* does not—some thinking and feeling which Kubrick should not have thought that he could merely cut:

> This time the film like jumped right away on a young devotchka who was being given the old in-out by first one malchick then another then another then another, she creeching away very gromky through the speakers and like very pathetic and tragic music going on at the same time. This was real, very real, though if you thought about it properly you couldn't imagine lewdies actually agreeing to having all this done to them in a film, and if these films were made by the Good or the State you couldn't imagine them being allowed to take these films without like interfering with what was going on. So it must have been very clever what they call cutting or editing or some such veshch. For it was very real.

The minds of this Dr. Brodsky and Dr. Branom . . . They must have been more cally and filthy then any prestoopnick in the Staja itself. Because I did not think it was possible for any veck to even think of making films of what I was forced to viddy, all tied to this chair and my glazzies made to be wide open.

The film of *A Clockwork Orange* doesn't have the moral courage that could altogether deal with that. Rather, like Kubrick's *Dr. Strangelove*, it has a central failure of courage and confidence, manifest in its need to caricature (bold in manner, timid at heart) and in its determination that nobody except Alex had better get a chance. Burgess says: "The point is that, if we are going to love mankind, we will have to love Alex as a not unrepresentative member of it." A non-Christian may be thankful that he is not under the impossibly cruel, and cruelty-causing, injunction to love mankind; both Christians and non-Christians may think that though the angels may plead, they do not special plead.

Francis Ford Coppola
The Conversation

T he skilled manipulative power of a neo-Jacobean film of blood like *The Conversation* is not the creation of any one man, even though this particular film was written, produced and directed by Francis Ford Coppola. For behind such a film there are conventions and expectations of the kind which T. S. Eliot believed to be fatally unavailable to the modern dramatist:

> What is needed is not sympathy or encouragement or appreciation— we need not assume that the best of the Athenian or the Elizabethan drama was "appreciated" by its audiences, relatively to the second- best—but a kind of unconscious co-operation. The ideal condition is that under which everything, except what only the individual genius can supply, is provided for the poet. A *framework* is provided. We do not mean "plot"; a poet may incorporate, adapt, or invent as he prefers or as occasion suggests. But a dramatic poet needs to have some *kind* of dramatic form given to him as the condition of his time, a form which in itself is neither good nor bad but which permits an artist to fashion it into a work of art. And by a "kind of dramatic form" one means almost the temper of the age (not the temper of a few intellectuals); a prepared- ness, a habit, on the part of the public, to respond in a predictable way, however crudely, to certain stimuli. A very little knowledge of Athenian

Times Literary Supplement (26 July 1974)

or Elizabethan drama acquaints us with commonplaces, as Fate in the former, or Death-and-Worms in the latter, which turn up again and again, and which we presume by their familiarity always evoked the proper response. Commonplaces they were, but capable of indefinite refinement. (*The Athenaeum*, May 14, 1920.)

Such a critical position is crucial to Eliot, as poet and critic, in that it predicates that predictable responses, even if they take the dangerous form of prejudices, are a necessary condition of dramatic achievement.

The difficulties begin when "however crudely" is set against "capable of indefinite refinement". For Elizabethan and Jacobean drama showed that it was hideously possible for there to be an increasing refinement of theatrical cunning or sensational impact, combined with an intensified crudity of moral, social and spiritual imagining. What Eliot called the case of John Webster has its affinities to the case of *The Conversation*, or of Coppola's previous neo-Jacobean grandiose guignol, *The Godfather*.

The shrewdness of *The Conversation* (a shrewdness then vitiated by heartless plangencies) is in its sensing that an audience's predictable preconceptions were the opportunity not just for springing a surprise on them but also for springing one on its hero-villain. His preconceptions, his preparedness to respond to certain stimuli, are the occupation of the film, an occupation made possible by the audience's unconscious cooperation in just such preconceptions. Unfortunately this artistic opportunity is then degraded to opportunism.

Harry Caul (finely played by Gene Hackman) is a "surveillance and security technician", or what the world of *The Duchess of Malfi* would call an intelligencer. He is hired by a very rich husband to bug the conversation of the young wife and her young man ("O but her jealous husband", *The White Devil*)—a technical triumph for Caul in that the two, who have been bugged before and are wary, meet to talk while walking round and round a crowded square. When Caul turns up to deliver the tapes, he has a tussle with the adjutant to the rich man ("the Director"); Caul, who was to give them to the Director personally, wrests them back and returns the money. And then, listening concernedly to the tapes now, he hears words that make him fearful for the young pair: are they going to get hurt? Killed? The rest of the film is Caul's fretful, ineffectual attempt to stave off disaster. Except that stave is too decisive a word. For, eviscerated both by personal malaise (morbidly private, inaccessible, and clamped) and by amoral professional non-responsibility ("I don't care what they're talking about"; "Nothing to do with me. I just turned in the tapes"), Caul cannot bring himself to prevent, or even to interfere with, the catastrophe that follows upon his eavesdropping. All he can do is—in a grimly private capacity—eavesdrop upon that catastrophe. The last twist of the knife (no, one should not give away the ending) is the belated recognition by Caul of the lethal credulity of his sentimentality. The objective hearer, the most professionally public of private eyes and ears, had subjectively misheard. The dénouement, as so often in the tragedy of blood, is what Bosola in *The Duchess of Malfi* calls a "direful misprision".

But sadly, and badly, the film demeans itself by looking upon Harry Caul with the same credulous sentimentality which infects Caul himself. We are throughout asked to give Caul the benefit of his having doubts. David Robinson, whose review in *The Times* (July 12, 1974) said lucidly everything that *The Conversation* would like to hear said about itself, was convinced of Caul's agony of conscience. But the siege of contraries—"this brilliant psychological study of a victim-villain of our times"—is always Caul shadow-wrestling with his conscience. This, too, is Jacobean. Flamineo is credited in just the same way with delicacies of perturbation that are not merely unexplained but inexplicable, and this to make the audience feel that their pity has preserved antisepsis:

> I have a strange thing in me, to the which
> I cannot give a name, without it be
> Compassion . . .
> And sometimes, when my face was full of smiles
> Have felt the maze of conscience in my breast.

The Jacobean victim-villain used to gain his muted drum-roll of troubled conscience by virtue of his "sensitive" or "poetic" language, the resonance (ringing nevertheless untrue) of his figures of speech, the verbalism which sometimes likes to deprecate verbalism (Flamineo's deathwards words, "I am in the way to study a long silence, To prate were idle . . ."). But the modern counterpart, Harry Caul, is credited—in the modern convention—with a sensitive conscience because of his silences, the fact that he verbalizes not easily but uneasily.

A hundred pressures are put upon us to make us think, and feel, better of him than he deserves. There is the plangent piano-music which accompanies him through the lonely streets, and which is forged as his signature-tune. There is the coincidental pathos of its being his cut-off age-less birthday. There is the ascription to him of a stern Catholic faith, which is credible as a matter of his being prim about taking the name of the Lord in vain but is mere bluff when it trundles him into the confessional—this deserves short shrift, for it is as much the film's as Caul's conscience which is being salved. There is his troubled dream, in which ("O I am in a mist") he hurries through swirling mist to warn his victims, and cries out about his paralysis when a boy and his nearly drowning in the bath, and cries out too the words which the film hopes we will credit to his waking self: "I'm not afraid of death, I *am* afraid of murder." There is the long arm of the plot with its helping hand, so that, if Caul mutters before he goes to sleep, "God what have I done—I'll have to destroy the tapes", the hand on that arm will have stolen the tapes by the time he awakes. And there is his face, milked for all the human kindness it can secrete—no, milked for more than even Hackman's subtle face can give. Jacobean tragedy was supremely an art of metaphor; cheating with metaphor was its easiest and worst sin. Film is supremely an art of physiognomy; cheating with faces is its easiest and worst sin.

Eliot, reviewing a performance of *The Duchess of Malfi* in 1919, said of the severed hand and the Duchess's agony:

> The "tragedy of blood" was vindicated. I mean that the horrors were vindicated; and as for the general assassination—that is merely a convention (as

much a convention as the Nuntius or the Confidante). It is a convention which even a modern audience could be brought to accept, if the modern actor understood that a violent death need not invariably be represented as an important event. The only deaths which are essential to the tragedy are those of the Duchess and Cariola; the rest are a form of Exit.

Slightly chilling, as when Eliot elsewhere spoke of Hamlet as having "occasioned the death of at least three innocent people, and two more insignificant ones". But Eliot sees how precarious are the straits for the tragedy of blood: that violent death may have to be, and somehow responsibly be, unimportant.

The Conversation goes perceptibly and perceptively further: it is not the main character, but the hero-villain, who energizes such works, and always has; there is more of Webster's genius in Bosola than in the Duchess, and more of his cunning. And since a modern Bosola—hired to bug her as he too was—would not ever need even to meet his modern Duchess, this acknowledged emphasis (upon the intelligencer's impersonalized conscience, with the violent death of his victim not necessarily represented as an important event other than in its importance to the intelligencer) is bitingly apt to the impersonal amorality of professionalized surveillance. The surveiller need *see* nothing. The figure who in Jacobean drama was the evil world's peccant creature is now, within the technology of the neo-Jacobean, the evil world's peccable bugging-machine. The long-range camera, the bugging device: these are what Marshall McLuhan happily calls extensions of man. Such extensions of man were once surreal:

> Were all Tiberius' body stuck with eyes,
> And every wall and hanging in my house
> Transparent, as this lawn I wear, or air;
> Yea, had Sejanus both his ears as long
> As to my inmost closet. . . .
>
> (Jonson's *Sejanus*)

And then *The Conversation* brutalizes it all, and instead of coming to that "moral and humanistic conclusion" which Coppola says he sought, it falls victim to the amoral professionalism which it purports to deplore. For not only is there the sentimentalizing of Caul (as skilfully pernicious as Webster's sentimentalizing of Bosola), there is also an unprincipled use of the technological media of surveillance, comparable to the Jacobean exploitations of metaphor and device. Harry Caul had photographs taken of the young pair, and he taped the conversation; he pins up one of the black-and-white photographs in front of his workbench, and he plays the tapes. But the sound of the tapes is accompanied by the filmed sight of the pair talking, so that at the crucial moment when the vital deadly words are being spoken, his eyes (our eyes) see, in living colour, the two saying those words. And not just when Caul plays the tapes, but when they later ring again and again in his ears. So that the indispensable point about preconception is fudged—that is, its misguiding credibility has to do with seeing, and not just hearing. But Caul did not film them talking. True, he did see them talking, but the very point which establishes this for us (while he is listening to the tapes, the imagined retrospect shows us Caul sitting on a bench in the square when the young pair go by) also undoes it: the one thing Caul's mind's eye would not have called up would be the frontal sight of himself on that bench.

Then there is a graver chicanery and, if it had not been that someone was recently caught bugging the reading of the Watergate tapes at the Royal Court Theatre and it made a scene, I would have been tempted to bug the two key-moments: that of Caul's listening to the tapes, and that when the words' true significance breaks hideously on him as he comes to hear them ring differently in his head. For I believe that what we are given is not the truly terrifying fact that the same words, with the same stress, can muster appallingly (lethally) different meanings, but the falsely thrilling fact that a film can muster excitements out of the rigged clash between eight words unambiguously stressed on tape and those words when they are again unambiguously but this time differently stressed. The eight words in a transcript would all have been without stress; they would have been ambiguous, but preconception could still have stifled the ambiguity. But the words on tape had their clear stress.

So Harry Caul was not deceived by his credulity (something which we shared with him, and in which we would be implicated), but by— and this is the really Watergate bit—some topmost-level hanky-panky, some tampering with the tapes. The real hero-villain or "victim-villain of our times" then becomes not Caul but Coppola—as it had once been, not Bosola, but Webster. This, unless my ears deceived me—and if they did, it would still have to be explained why the ears of the Director (whose preconceptions were very different from Caul's) deceived him, so that he apparently heard, misheard, in exactly the same way as Caul.

Best Film at the Cannes Film Festival, 1974, and one can see why. But it decided not to try to rise above being a work of artfulness. *The Times* calls it a "work of art", but it is so only in the sense in which Caul's odious competitor calls Caul's bugging of the conversation "a work of art", the sense in which Lodovico in *The White Devil* reduces plot to plotting, the play's as well as his own: "I would have our plot be ingenious."

Frederick Wiseman
Blind. Deaf. Adjustment and Work. Multi-handicapped.

B *lind. Deaf. Adjustment and Work. Multi-handicapped.* These new films by Frederick Wiseman should not reduce us to tears. True tears are not a reduction but an enlargement.

To contemplate—not only to see—the inching actuality by which the blind heroically learn those simplest needs that we take for granted; to marvel at the dexterous beauty of sign language not only in the hands but in the full-bodied quickness of the deaf; to remark the dignity with which hardwon work, transcending a "work ethic," may become—however abruptly—a spirit of faculties: you are likely to be moved to tears by these witnessings of Wiseman's.

There are tears and tears, and though the experience of the films is a groundswell of ancient compassion (*Sunt lacrimae rerum et mentem mortalia tangunt*), there are eruptions of harsher salt tears: of anger smarting at a blankness, or of exasperation wincing at an insensitivity from a parent or a teacher or a smiling public man (not that we would be likely to behave any better). There even are, though these are properly rare, tears of happiness.

Grand Street (Winter 1989)

Nothing is here for idle tears. Wiseman's art is of prophylaxis as well as of embrace, and the terms of the access that we are granted to the sufferings of others are as strict as they are privileged. The films bear witness. Witness is felt as something to be borne, not the frotting of sensibility which acutely frightened Tennyson:

> At this the tender sound of his own voice
> And sweet self-pity, or the fancy of it,
> Made his eye moist.

Neither this nor the contamination of sensibility which touches all but the most vigilant of artists, and towards which Dr. Johnson was more than stringent: astringent.

> With observations like these the prince amused himself as he returned, uttering them with a plaintive voice, yet with a look that discovered him to feel some complacence in his perspicacity, and to receive some solace of the miseries of life, from consciousness of the delicacy with which he felt and the eloquence with which he bewailed them.

Like Johnson, Wiseman has a sardonic side. It must have been with a *moue* that he dubbed this quartet of films a "mini-series." A mini-series these nights is usually less factual than factitious, whereas Wiseman's "mini-series" is an art of imaginative responsibility not only to the facts which are not of its making, but equally to its making, an art that must comprehend the ways in which it is, as well as the ways in which it is not, fiction.

Public television should be given credit where credit is due, which includes its promulgation of Wiseman's films. His quartet, on what it is to be unable to see and hear, was seen and heard on public television in private homes in June 1988. As has been well known ever since 1967 and the furor over Wiseman's first venture, *Titicut Follies* (it witnessed the State Prison for the Criminally Insane at Bridgewater, Massachusetts), Wiseman's art constitutes an invasion of privacy. But what this means is often misunderstood: the invasion is not so crucially that of the privacy of those within the institutions, as of our privacy, our understandable unlovely wish not to have publicly pressed upon us the secluded realities of institutional life.

Wiseman's quartet is not only good for television but right for it. Television, secluded, home-based, is ensconced where we adjudge our happiness and where we have the bread we win—have it, casually confident that we can cut it and can carry it without effort to our mouths, can say such words as these, can hear such words, can perform these most simple of actions. Or of signs.

> Bread. This is like a loaf of bread when you slice it. The bread. Come down with it. Yes. Turn your hand okay. Okay. Turn this one . . . put your palm forward. Okay now this one is like the knife, you're cutting it. Cutting it. Okay. That's bread.
>
> *Deaf*

That's bread. That's life. That's the staff of life, as language is, or hearing or sight. Or education. Life, the falling out of things, gave Wiseman this moment, educational and educative, but he had to know to take it.

Twenty-one such films by Wiseman, in twenty-one years, have shown his genius in apprehending institutions. Apprehension there has not only to include grasping their nature or seizing their being, but also fearing what may happen in them and to them. Cynicism towards and despair at institutions are ways of protecting ourselves against them, against not just the damage they must sometimes do but against our not being able to conceive of doing without them. Institutions have this mortifying way of being indispensable. Complacency is to be found not only among those who rest satisfied with institutions but among those who rest dissatisfied with them. Moreover, the chances are that those who know to attend to Wiseman's scenes from institutional life (*High School, Hospital, Basic Training, Juvenile Court, Welfare, Primate, The Store, Racetrack* . . .) include many for whom the more likely distortion is not the conservative one of thinking too well of institutions, whether in general or in particular, but the liberal or radical one of thinking too ill.

So when Edgar Z. Friedenberg, back in 1971, reviewed Wiseman's first five films, he saw them as constituting a challenge to America's self-estimate but no challenge at all to his own estimate. *Titicut Follies, High School,* and *Basic Training* gained Friedenberg's approval because he judged them to be duly disapproving; they corroborated his conviction, not ill-founded but obdurately previous to any seeing of any of the actual films, that "the institutions scrutinized are not merely defective but often superfluous: self-serving and self-perpetuating."

"The idea that official institutions exist to exploit more than to serve their clients is both valid and well suited to the temper of our times": but Friedenberg was too well suited by those unmisgiving words, "well suited to the temper of our times." *More than to serve*: this has just the tilt into gratified *parti pris* which, say, "quite as much as to serve" would not have. So Friedenberg was disappointed in Wiseman when Wiseman did not go singlemindedly along with the then temper of "our" times. For "the idea that official institutions exist to exploit more than to serve their clients" was Friedenberg's *idée fixe*: "When this implication is weak or absent, his films take on a different and, I think, less distinctive tone. *Hospital,* for example . . ." For Friedenberg, a Wiseman film is less distinctive if it is distinct from Friedenberg's politics.

> *Hospital,* for example, is a study of an institution physically hardly more adequate than Bridgewater: a large general hospital perpetually inundated with the victims of urban violence and decay. But the impression it conveys is not merely of squalor but of continuous, grinding, backbreaking resourcefulness under impossible conditions. Its patients are real clients, their needs are desperate, and, somehow, they are seen, however fleetingly, as human beings; and their medical emergencies, at least, are dealt with.

Far from being grateful for such human resourcefulness, and for Wiseman's so making it alive for us, Friedenberg felt gypped: "The result, however, is a film with very little irony." So much the worse for irony, one might have thought, and for its inverted complacency. But no, so much the worse for the film, for "great urban hospitals and their dedicated, overworked staffs have long been a staple of commercial TV." Yet it is one mark of an artist to raise to the level of truth the clichés that are the staple of commercial television. A cliché is a mere reflex, but then so is the assumption that a work of art is the worse for calling to mind and to heart those truths, those realities, which clichés petrify or falsify.

Friedenberg would have to be even more unhappy with these four new films, which are notably sparing with ironies, whether life's little or art's little or politics's little. There may be a larger irony in the fact that a particular political ideology finds itself vexed by the sight of "continuous, grinding, backbreaking resourcefulness under impossible conditions." But among our rights is that of being heartened at the sight of people being heartened. Anyway, Wiseman's tacit skepticism (about the glory that is capitalism, say, or about the American Way of Life, both of which are zealously promoted by interested parties in these films) is the principled opponent not only of sentimentality but of cynicism. But then what is cynicism but the thinking man's sentimentality?

Institutions resist realization, in life and in art. No book has ever raised to art, or even to first-rate second-order writing, the workings of a particular actual institution. Institutionality, a habit of mind and more, has been tellingly revealed, warned against, admired within limits. Here the work of Erving Goffman—for instance, his *Asylums*—shows how much can be realized. Yet there is no book, such as has endured with art's endurance, that has taken as its central enterprise the rendering of the daily workings of a great institution. There is no unephemeral book on a newspaper (the *New York Times* or *The Times*), or on a school (Groton or Eton), or on a hospital (Beth Israel or Bart's), or on a university (Harvard or Oxford), or on a prison (Alcatraz or Dartmoor), or on a publishing house, or a court, or a trade union—no book that has been able to transmute the daily doings of an actual institution so as to issue in the lasting witness of art.

Even Dickens (Wiseman has been recognized as possessing Dickensian gifts) was not able to make into art his passionate fact-finding journalism. *American Notes* paid tribute to the institutions of Boston, but the tribute to these actualities was paid in a coin which rang less true than did the largesse of the novelist when he apprehended such institutions (the Marshalsea prison, the work house, the school, the children's hospital) as could be fully real to him only when they were encompassed by the Dickens world of the imagined. When he wrote without the liberties of a tale peopled by his sheer creativity, Dickens felt obliged to announce his sincerity in a way that was never incumbent upon the authenticity of his great art.

> Above all, I sincerely believe that the public institutions and charities of this capital of Massachusetts are as nearly perfect, as the most considerate wisdom, benevolence, and humanity, can make them. I never in my life was more affected by the contemplation of happiness, under circumstances of privation and bereavement, than in my visits to these establishments.

It is not merely that this well-intended rebuke to England from New England did not foresee that the most considerate wisdom in Boston would one day issue in the Bridgewater of *Titicut Follies*, but that Dickens's has become a florid way of speaking, such as cannot render the contingent realities—sprawling, straitened, humdrum, cruel, grateful for small mercies—which are an institution by day and by night.

To recognize one's name on a card; to tell the time; to bake brownies; to make one's way: for those who cannot see or cannot hear or cannot do either, these are the feats of life. Dickens, like Wiseman, marvels at the education which is effected for and by the handicapped, but whereas Wiseman marvels in silence (the only sounds in his films are the ones there at the very time), Dickens perorates:

> Ye who have eyes and see not, and have ears and hear not; ye who are as the hypocrites of sad countenances, and disfigure your faces that ye may seem unto men to fast; learn healthy cheerfulness, and mild contentment, from the deaf, and dumb, and blind! Self-elected saints with gloomy brows, this sightless, earless, voiceless child may teach you lessons you will do well to follow. Let that poor hand of hers lie gently on your hearts; for there may be something in its healing touch akin to that

of the Great Master whose precepts you misconstrue, whose lessons you pervert, of whose charity and sympathy with all the world, not one among you in his daily practice knows so much as many of the worse among those fallen sinners, to whom you are liberal in nothing but the preachment of perdition!

One knows what he means, but he is liberal in his preachment. There is a terrible air of rising to the occasion, and so of reducing the deaf and dumb and blind to an occasion. Or to an instrument.

Dickens throbs. But Wiseman takes the pulse of such places and of such religious inspirations. Much of the dedicated love devoted to the handicapped, here at the Alabama Institute for the Deaf and Blind, is manifestly the fruit of Christianity. The opening of *Blind*, where the racetrack ministry honors the Lord Jesus and then the blind band makes music, is matched by the service which closes *Multi-handicapped*, where there are power and pathos in the singing of "God is here," "God's love is wonderful." God moves in a mysterious way. God loves in a mysterious way. Wiseman's quartet is a strange theodicy, one that has nothing to say for itself but which faithfully registers and unremittingly prompts.

The quartet's witness is likely to prompt some shame in those of us who, secularists, make no such sacrifices as are here made daily by those who believe in Christ's supreme sacrifice. The films' witness will prompt a contrary embarrassment too, for the quality of religious feeling may be lax and primitive and yet it nurtures such persevering loving kindness. *Blind* precedes its brief closing nighttime shots of Talladega with the dorm parent saying prayers with the blind children:

Make all God's children—
　　JASON:　Make all God's children—
Be honest and true—
　　JASON:　Be honest and true—
Amen.
　　JASON:　Amen.

At which point there is just that touch of something altogether other which surprises the rhythm of the scene and saves the poignancy from an idealized sympathy:

> I love you.
> JASON: I want you to clip my toenails.
> Clip your toenails? Let me see. Can you wait till morning for me to get the toenail clipper?
> JASON: Oh, alright.
> You want them tonight?
> JASON: Yes.
> He wants me to clip his toenails. Let me go get my clipper.

Then the darkening sky and its lights, and the end.

Jason's toenails, unignorable and unpostponable and yet from one point of view merely any child's delaying tactic, are weirdly right for incarnating the religion of the Incarnation. Jason as a matter of fact said this, and then she, the dorm parent, said that; they both come very well out of it, and so does the film, which then comes out of itself—as so many of Wiseman's films do—to traffic with the world, out to the traffic of the streets, then to the night sky and a world elsewhere.

Humphry House, who wrote so well about Dickens and the Dickens world, once defined sentimentality as the imposition of feeling as an afterthought upon literalness. One reason that Wiseman's films, though so alive with feeling, are not sentimental is that although they stimulate many an afterthought, they arrive at not one, any more than they set out from an *arrière pensée*. The feelings that matter—first, most, and last—are felt not to be ours but others', the handicapped and those who tend them; such feelings as then arise in us are therefore no infringement. And this itself depends upon the untrumped literalness, and upon that extremity of the literal which is the actual.

The world is everything which is the case. Understood. But our understanding with an artist is altered—not disqualified but differently qualified—when we are offered something that is the case because it has happened, not because it has been imagined. True, nothing is real to us until it has been imagined by us—and, in art, for us. But there remains the stubborn difference between "things and imaginings." The phrase is Beckett's, and it comes with the more authority from the supreme fiction writer of our age, a writer who is not misled, either by his fictive exuberance or by his conviction that the act of memory entails imagination, into supposing that for the artist there is then no difference between imagination and memory or between things and imaginings.

Wiseman's films, at once compassionate and dispassionate, patiently record the struggles and triumphs of memory in those people who are deprived of the primary providence of memories: seeing and hearing. The films are not only memorable, they are themselves a training in art-memory, where those who watch and listen are continually invited to return, to recover, and to commemorate, both from within their several experiences and from the communal experience of the films, retrieving perhaps something earlier in the film or something across in another of the films. The understood responsibilities are not then those attending upon imagined or fictive memories, but those of memories that are actual and factual and contractual.

Wiseman was trained as a lawyer, and he reinstates the contractual model of art in its relations to audiences. He gives undertakings, not just to the institutions but to us, and he honors all concerned. A Wiseman film operates within strict contractual constraints. These people are not actors. These pains are not imaginary. This is what happened. There is such a place.

Agreed, Wiseman has had to select from among all the records which were themselves created by his and his cameraman's selecting, and he has had to edit, and he has therefore had to exercise something akin to the novelist's or dramatist's shaping spirit of imagination. But when all these subtractions from and additions to the actual have been made, there remains an obstinately responsible contract: not to have staged, not to have impersonated, not to have fabricated.

It is therefore a pity that Wiseman proffers the term "reality fictions" for the films, since in the end this does yield to today's ruling passion for "fictions." Admittedly the alternative terms have their shortcomings: "cinéma vérité" suggests that truth is foreign to our film-making, while "documentaries" is inimical to imagination. Nevertheless, Wiseman's films are best not thought of as "reality fictions." They are more truly symmetrical than that, and they resist the lauding of invention at the expense of discovery.

In our time, fiction and fictivity have aggrandized themselves not only in art but in discourse generally. It heralded a great shift, in the first decade of this century, when there entered, with coercive convenience, the terms "nonfiction" and "nonfictional." Fiction was thereby granted a signal status, not only as hereafter differentiating all the prose we read or write, but as getting to define the alternative to itself so much in its own terms, so entirely as not being itself. There is fiction, and there is nonfiction. In the institution that is the University of Cambridge at this day, there are, first, those who are University Teaching Officers (or U.T.O.s, pronounced You-Toes, and mocked as Unidentified Teaching Objects), and there are, second, Non University Teaching Officers, N.U.T.O.s, pronounced—honestly—New Toes, as in neutered. This division by negation is brutal, impolitic and distortive. The same goes for fiction/nonfiction, where the claims of supreme fiction are too abjectly conceded. Something is then squandered, the counterclaim of fact; this, and the particular resistance that only the sense of fact can mount.

For the persistent actuality of Wiseman's films protects them against the burly condescending obligation of having to *mean*. There has never been a time in which art has been so pressed to signify, not to signify in being art, but to exude the significant, the significational. A gigantic industry of art-debriefers (to which I admit I belong) coincides with an age in which Sign, Signifier and Signified constitute the Trinity, even if, like Satan, Sin and Death, it be an infernal one. And then, the more the world and life appear meaningless, the more we want our art at least to mean most, to mean intensely. Artists become increasingly imperious as the society makes them feel impotent. Audiences come to enjoy the feeling of power which comes from cracking something. What term of art does today's critic wield? Receiving a work of art, he "decodes" it.

Beckett's Winnie in *Happy Days* is an imagined sufferer, stogged in her mound. Not the least of her mortifications is the touristic contemplation of her as if she were a work of art, understood to have the particular responsibility of works of art these days, to mean away like anything.

> Well anyway—this man Shower—or Cooker—no matter—and the woman—hand in hand—in the other hands bags—kind of big brown grips—standing there gaping at me—and at last this man Shower—or Cooker—ends in 'er anyway—stake my life on that—What's she doing? he says—What's the idea? he says—stuck up to her diddies in the bleeding ground—coarse fellow—What does it mean? he says—What's meant to mean?—and so on—lot more stuff like that—usual drivel—Do you hear me? he says—I do, she says, God help me—What do you mean, he says, God help you? And you, she says, what's the idea of you, she says, what are you meant to mean?

Wiseman's sufferers, though they are seen with imagination, are not imagined. More than ever, therefore, we owe it to them not to ask them what they are meant to mean. There is a particular liberation in these films' being at once so suggestive and so unconcerned to precipitate meaning. Happenstance has its responsibilities, antithetical ones too: to remit the craving to translate what is witnessed into something which will *mean* (how meaningless the word "meaningful" has become), and yet to let the heartfelt mind play upon what it sees and hears.

Wiseman can be trusted by us, as the institutions have trusted him not to travesty them or be snide at their expense, and even as the handicapped within these four films are shown as ever needing—and ever bringing into existence—trust in others (Wiseman among them) and in themselves. A crucial element of trust in Wiseman's art is this fidelity to the given. If the small blind boy who makes the long, arduous and poignant journey down the stairs and through the corridors, and back, to show his good work to another appreciative teacher, is called Jason, that is because, and only because, his name is indeed Jason, and not because there was once a great brave journeyer called Jason. Nothing forbids you to bring to mind the classical courage of Jason and his argosy; everything forbids you to feel required or impelled or even invited to do so, because this would be a violation of the boy Jason's rights, including the right to *be* without having to *mean*. And the right, at the end, simply to ask to have his toenails cut.

There is in *Deaf* a fluttered moment within a touching sequence of sign language (simultaneous with speaking), extraordinary in the complexity and nuance of what can be communicated, when the explaining woman is momentarily foiled—"What's the sign for *adjusting*, somebody?" This is profoundly suggestive because it is not itself any kind of deliberate adjustment, and it is humane as art, art of its particular kind, because it accepts what simply happens. A portrait accepts a physiognomy where another kind of painting need not, and art criticism is in trouble when its theoretical position propels it towards maintaining that a painting could be a very good portrait while not being to any degree a likeness.

Auden believed that poetry makes nothing happen. Wiseman's art makes happenings something. Though these four films necessarily witness more unhappiness than happiness, they themselves are full of what an earlier critical idiom called felicities, of happenings which will be happily revelatory if we will let them be. The films are anything but casual, but they are attentive to what befalls, to casualty and to the casualties of life. Without ever exploiting for symbolic purposes the cruelly literal handicaps of the blind and the deaf, the films are nevertheless the work of an artist alert to there being such dismaying things, in art and in life, as self-inflicted handicaps.

Index

Ackroyd, Peter 59–68
Adams, Henry 125
Adams, John 190
Akalaitis, JoAnne 324
Allingham, William 39
Amis, Kingsley 185, 224–5, 227, 234, 250–5, 298
Andrewes, Lancelot 265
Apollinaire, Guillaume 334
Ardrey, Robert 355
Arnold, Matthew 36, 130–1, 133, 175, 235, 261
Auden, W. H. 59, 186, 188–9, 203–4, 207, 377
Austen, Jane 225, 250

Bacon, Francis 220
Baker, Carlos 214
Balestier, Wolcott 13
Barnes, William 205, 209
Bate, Walter Jackson 98
Baudelaire, Charles 174–5, 245
Beach, Sylvia 22

Beatles, the 329–32
Beats, the 202
Beauvoir, Simone de 170
Beckett, Samuel 24, 27, 30–3, 291, 315–28, 336, 342, 374, 376
Behan, Brendan 73–8
Bell, Clive 34, 36–7, 42, 45
Bell, Vanessa 34–7, 42
Belloc, Hilaire 71
Bellow, Saul 125
Bennett, Arnold 49
Berenson, Bernard 50
Bergman, Ingrid 312
Bergson, Henri 340
Berryman, John 219, 283, 316
Betjeman, John 205–6
Bettelheim, Bruno 180
Binyon, Laurence 184
Blake, William 123, 156, 321
Blin, Roger 317
Borges, Jorge Luis 201
Boswell, James 39, 331

Bowen, Elizabeth 50
Bradley, A. C. 38
Brett, Dorothy 42
Bridges, Robert 4, 7, 10, 185
Brodsky, Michael 317
Brooke, Rupert 18–21, 53
Brooke-Rose, Christine 198
Brooks, Cleanth 158
Browning, Robert 39
Bunting, Basil 283
Burgess, Anthony 7–8, 348–58
Burke, Edmund 39
Burkhart, Charles 221, 227
Bush, Ronald 61, 66
Butler, Samuel 338–9
Byron, George Gordon, Lord 39,
    182, 204, 245–6, 255
Byron, Robert 71

Cage, John 101
Capa, Robert 311–4
Carlyle, Thomas 7, 11, 38–9, 54,
    94–5
Carne-Ross, D. S. 337
Carrington, Dora 36
Chabert, Pierre 322
Chardin, Teilhard de 170
Chaucer, Geoffrey 191, 220
Chesterton, G. K. 136–7
Chirico, Giorgio de 256
Christie, Agatha 308
Churchill, Winston 316
Clare, John 291
Clark, Kenneth 49

Clarke, Austin 239
Clough, Arthur Hugh 4, 87, 269
Cluchey, Rick 322
Coleridge, Samuel Taylor 94–5,
    156, 265, 316
Compton–Burnett, Ivy 220–8,
    336
Confucius 53
Connolly, Cyril 48–56
Conrad, Joseph 38, 205, 257–8
Cooper, Diana 71
Cooper, Gary 312
Copernicus 165
Coppola, Francis Ford 359–65
Crabbe, George 156
Cronin, Anthony 317
Cummings, E. E. 309–10

Dante 152, 284, 294–5
Darwin, Charles 339
Davidson, John 55
Davie, Donald 7, 63, 65, 182–91,
    205, 225, 242–3, 276–85, 335
Davies, W. H. 205
de la Mare, Walter 205
Delany, Paul 18–21
Devine, George 320
Dickens, Charles 76, 127, 164,
    166, 215, 236, 261, 273, 340,
    370–73
Dobrée, Bonamy 67
Donne, John 220
Dorn, Ed 183, 188
Dostoevsky, Fyodor 76

Dowden, Edward 57
Doyle, Arthur Conan 225
Dryden, John 161–3, 190, 235, 261
Dukes, Gerry 317
Duncan, Isadora 56–7
Dylan, Bob 19, 98–9, 114

Edel, Leon 11, 15, 17, 34–9
Edwards, Oliver 209
Eliot, George 232, 235
Eliot, T. S. 6, 20, 25, 30, 41, 52, 59–68, 82–3, 102–3, 112, 127, 130–1, 134, 136–7, 142, 145, 147–53, 162, 165–6, 174–7, 181, 182, 185–9, 201, 205–6, 215, 246–8, 257, 260–2, 265, 283–4, 319–20, 334, 356–7, 359–60, 362–3
Eliot, Valerie 60, 62, 65
Eliot, Vivien 60, 62, 64
Ellmann, Richard 22–33
Emerson, Ralph Waldo 23
Empson, William 83, 141, 159–67, 251, 342, 356

Feiffer, Jules 232
Fiedler, Leslie 134, 174–81
Fielding, Henry 162–7, 190
Fish, Stanley 192–200
FitzGerald, Edward 203
Ford, Ford Madox 24, 184
Franklin, Benjamin 190
Freud, Sigmund 19

Friedenberg, Edgar Z. 369–70
Frost, Robert 21, 26, 97
Fry, Roger 34, 37, 42–3, 45
Frye, Northrop 157

Garrick, David 331–2
Gay, John 293
Genet, Jean 168–73
George, Emery E. 337
Gertler, Mark 46
Gibbon, Edward 39
Gibran, Kahlil 179
Gilmore, Gary 79–90
Ginsberg, Allen 336
Giotto 342–3
Gladstone, William Ewart 11, 13
Goethe, Johann Wolfgang von 133
Goffman, Erving 93–101, 369
Golding, William 351
Goldsmith, Oliver 190
Gomme, Lionel 43
Gontarski, S. E. 315, 317–8, 325–6
Goodman, Paul 94
Grant, Duncan 34, 36, 39, 42
Graves, Robert 20, 189, 289, 291
Greene, Graham 351
Grigson, Geoffrey 59
Guérin, Eugénie de 295
Gunn, Thom 128–9, 290

Hackman, Gene 360, 362
Haley, Alex 176, 179
Hall, Radclyffe 173

Hardwick, Elizabeth 229
Hardy, Thomas 15, 18, 20–1,
    38, 50, 76, 142, 205–6
Hartman, Geoffrey 192–3, 195
Heaney, Seamus 286–99
Hemingway, Ernest 213–9, 312–3
Herbert, George 283
Herrick, Robert 220
Heston, Charlton 26
Hill, Geoffrey 137, 187, 283
Hindle, John 141
Hitler, Adolf 306
Hobsbaum, Philip 198
Hodgart, Matthew 315
Homer 284
Hone, Joseph 58
Hopkins, Gerard M. 3–10, 185,
    309
House, Humphry 235, 373
Housman, A. E. 6–7, 205–6, 226
Hughes, Ted 283, 290
Hunt, Leigh 96

Ibsen, Henrik 207, 321, 328
Isherwood, Christopher 189

James, Alice 13
James, Henry 11–7, 20, 67, 82,
    125, 182, 185, 189, 191, 205,
    244, 257, 261, 270, 295
James, Robertson 17
James, Wilkinson 12–3
Jameson, Fredric 198
Jarrell, Randall 23, 229–30, 337

Jefferson, Thomas 190
John, Augustus 41, 49
Johnson, Samuel 16, 39, 43, 80,
    155, 158, 165, 202, 209, 252,
    323, 331–2, 355–7, 367
Jolas, Eugene 23
Jones, David 336
Jones, Glyn 334
Jonson, Ben 154, 173, 251–2,
    260, 363
Joyce, James 22–33, 162–4, 197
Joyce, Stanislaus 28
Juvenal 331

Keats, John 7, 77, 96, 208, 220,
    299, 344
Kemble, Fanny 12–3
Kenner, Hugh 24, 163
Kermode, Frank 52
Keynes, John Maynard 34, 36, 39
Kipling, Rudyard 38, 206, 262
Knowlson, James 318–9
Kristol, Irving 126
Kubrick, Stanley 348–58

Laforgue, Jules 148
Lamb, Charles 220
Lamb, Henry 41–3, 45
Landor, Walter Savage 182
Larkin, Philip 201–9, 239, 267,
    290, 295, 345
Lawrence, D. H. 20, 38, 40, 43,
    46, 48, 82–3, 125, 149–50,
    175, 181, 189, 351

Leavis, F. R. 48, 51–2, 125–7, 141, 147–54, 163, 201, 278
Lee, Vernon 42
Lennon, John 329, 331
Lewis, C. S. 53, 218
Lewis, Wyndham 30, 62, 184
Lloyd, Marie 176–7
Lowell, James Russell 12
Lowell, Robert 183, 283, 299, 337, 354
Luce, Henry 314

Macaulay, Thomas Babington 198, 316
MacCarthy, Desmond 34, 39
MacDiarmid, Hugh 334–5
Magritte, Henri 340
Mailer, Norman 79–90, 127
Mallarmé, Stephane 166, 334
Malraux, André 313
Mangan, James Clarence 240–9
Mankowitz, Wolf 126
Mansour, Atallah 135
Marlowe, Christopher 218
Martin, Robert Bernard 3–10
Marvell, Andrew 160–1, 163, 165, 206
Marx, Groucho 176
Matisse, Henri 312
Matthews, T. S. 59
McCarthy, Mary 221, 224, 227
McEwan, Ian 266–75
McKuen, Rod 179

McLuhan, Marshall 90, 303–10, 363
Medawar, P. B. 170
Mellers, W. H. 215
Meredith, George 12, 38, 225, 231, 340
Merrill, James 283
Middleton, Christopher 281
Milgram, Stanley 113–123
Millay, Edna St. Vincent 142
Millett, Kate 274
Milosz, Czeslaw 281–5
Milton, John 145–6, 151, 160, 165, 193, 195, 261, 278, 280
Mitchell, Margaret 175, 179
Montague, John 248–9
Moore, Brian 234–49
Moore, George 50, 56
Moore, T. Sturge 184
Moore, Thomas 249
Morgan, Edwin 334–5
Morrell, Ottoline 40–7, 63
Morris, Jan 275
Muggeridge, Malcolm 74
Munthe, Axel 42
Murdoch, Iris 19, 220–1
Murphy, William 58
Murray, Gilbert 42
Murrow, Ed 74
Murry, J. Middleton 284

Naipaul, Shiva 263
Naipaul, V. S. 256–65
Newton, Isaac 339

Nicolson, Harold 50, 277
Norman, Philip 329–31
Norton, Charles Eliot 16, 67
Nureyev, Rudolf 192

O'Casey, Sean 77
Olson, Charles 283
One Flew over the Cuckoo's Nest
   86–7
Orage, A. R. 184
Osborne, John 75
Owen, Wilfred 21, 311

Paisley, Ian 28
Parkman, Francis 205
Parnell, John Stewart 55
Pater, Walter 336
Patmore, Coventry 54
Picasso, Pablo 312
Pinter, Harold 325
Pirandello, Luigi 34
Planet of the Apes 26
Plath, Sylvia 205
Platt, Jennifer 102–12
Podhoretz, Norman 124–9, 181
Pope, Alexander 32, 46, 155,
   158, 190
Porter, Cole 203
Pound, Ezra 24, 30, 53, 58, 62,
   183–4, 186–9, 191, 276–80,
   283, 294
Powell, Frederick York 58
Pryce–Jones, David 48–52
Prynne, J. H. 281

Quinlan, Karen 87
Quinn, John 24, 54–6

Ransom, John Crowe 141–6
Read, Herbert 67, 334
Redgrove, Peter 286
Reynolds, Joshua 39
Richards, I. A. 130, 143, 158
Richardson, Ralph 321
Richardson, Samuel 252
Rimbaud, Arthur 245
Robinson, David 361
Robinson, John 131
Robinson, Lennox 58
Rosenberg, Isaac 21
Rossetti, Christina 7
Rossetti, Dante Gabriel 69
Rousseau, Jean-Jacques 355
Rowse, A. L. 124
Ruskin, John 67–8, 270–5
Russell, Bertrand 43, 45, 60, 62

Sartre, Jean Paul 168–73
Sassoon, Siegfried 20, 41
Schmidt, Michael 188
Schneider, Alan 320–4
Scott, Walter 242–4
Sencourt, Robert 59
Seymour, Miranda 40–7
Shakespeare, William 80, 85,
   127, 142, 147, 176, 202, 215,
   228, 274, 280, 284, 299, 357
Shaw, George Bernard 318,
   327–8

Shelley, Percy Bysshe 151, 220, 260

Shirley, James 298

Sickert, Walter 42

Simon, John 181

Simpson, Alan 77

Sisson, C. H. 281, 283

Sitwell, Edith 168

Skinner, B. F. 356

Smart, Christopher 156

Smith, Adam 39

Smith, Logan Pearsall 42, 45, 50–1

Smith, Stevie 51, 206

Smollett, Tobias 220

Sontag, Susan 128

Sparrow, John 333–7

Spender, Stephen 67

Spenser, Edmund 83, 279

Spinoza, Benedict 60–1

Stead, Christina 229–33

Stein, Richard 272

Steinberg, Saul 37, 41, 98, 151, 338–47

Steiner, George 130–7, 182, 188

Stephen, James Fitzjames 17, 215

Stephen, Leslie 17

Sterne, Laurence 347

Stevens, Wallace 198, 239, 245

Stevenson, Robert Louis 13

Stokes, Adrian 277

Strachey, Lytton 34, 36–9, 40, 45

Svevo, Italo 29

Swift, Jonathan 95, 220, 252, 355

Swinburne, Algernon Charles 57, 170

Sykes, Christopher 69–72

Tate, Allen 66, 183

Tennyson, Alfred 39, 203, 207, 245, 248, 277, 285, 367

Thackeray, William Makepeace 35, 243

Thatcher, Margaret 201

Thomas, Dylan 74, 78

Thomas, Edward 21

Thomas, R. S. 234

Thrale, Hester 16

Tolkien, J. R. R. 179

Tolstoy, Leo 225

Tressell, Robert 76–7

Trilling, Diana 81–2

Trotsky, Leon 312

Turgenev, Ivan 66

Turner, J. M. W. 269

Tynan, Kenneth 320–1

Uccello 343

Valéry, Paul 166

Vico, Giambattista 26

Waldock, A. J. A. 278

Ward, Mrs Humphry 16

Watson, George 94

Waugh, Evelyn 49, 69–72

Webster, John 319, 360–65
Wellek, René 150
Wells, H. G. 16
Wharton, Edith 15–6
Whelan, Richard 311–4
White, Lynn 309
Whitelaw, Billie 318, 325
Whitman, Walt 312
Wilde, Oscar 228, 318
Williams, Raymond 209
Wilson, Edmund 217
Wimsatt, W. K.155–8
Winters, Yvor 6–7, 276, 283
Wiseman, Frederick 366–77
Wittgenstein, Ludwig 42, 95
Wodehouse, P. G. 225

Wolfe, Humbert 51
Woolf, Leonard 34, 37, 39
Woolf, Virginia 19, 34–9, 42–6,
    49–51, 60–1, 77
Woolson, Constance Fenimore
    13
Wordsworth, William 142, 146,
    245, 280, 288, 296, 315–6
Wright, Barbara 317
Wyatt, Thomas 127

Yeats, Jack B. 53
Yeats, John Butler 53–8
Yeats, W. B. 53, 55, 58, 159–60,
    166, 183, 336
Young, Thomas Daniel 141